REDEEMED
UNREDEEMABLE

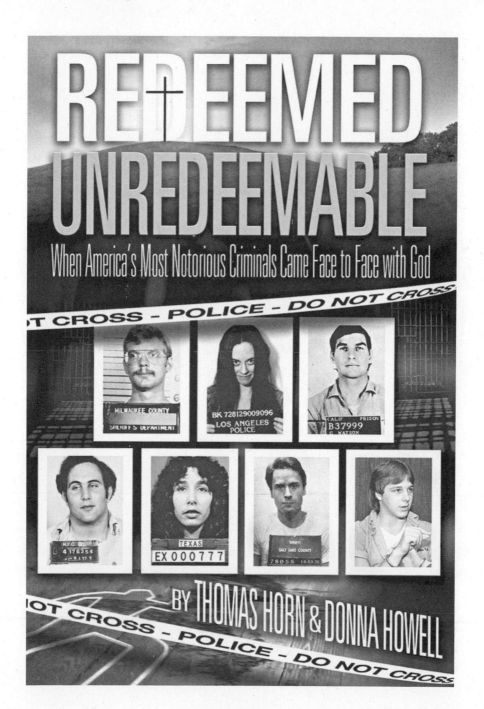

REDEEMED UNREDEEMABLE

When America's Most Notorious Criminals Came Face to Face with God

BY THOMAS HORN & DONNA HOWELL

DEFENDER

CRANE, MO

Redeemed Unredeemable:
When America's Most Notorious Criminals Came Face to Face with God

Defender
Crane, MO 65633
©2014 by Thomas Horn
A collaborative work by Thomas Horn and Donna Howell.
All rights reserved. Published 2014.
Printed in the United States of America.

ISBN 13: 978-0-9904974-2-4

A CIP catalog record of this book is available from the Library of Congress.

Cover illustration and design by Daniel Wright: www.createdwright.com.
All Scripture quotations from the King James Version; in cases of academic
comparison, those instances are noted.

To Nita, Allie, and James: Thank you for all the time you spent reviewing these materials, for your priceless feedback, and for putting the "chuga" back in the "choo choo" when a directional wall was hit.

To Angie Peters: This book required only the most dedicated and talented editor available, and you were that and more. Thank you for your editorial genius, and for making all of us at Defender Publishing sound better than we are.

To David Berkowitz and Charles Watson: As your cases have been told with hundreds of variations throughout the years, and as your names have been famously thrown around and exploited, it has taken a tremendous amount of trust in our team to agree to work with us. Thank you for your direct correspondence, cooperation, and consideration for our book, and for once again allowing your story to be told to the masses in the interest of spreading the gospel.

And finally, to Roy Ratcliff, Ron Carlson, Dr. Dorothy Otnow Lewis, Jason Freeman, Leslie Rule, and several others, whose names we will not mention here, who have provided crucial insight through their experiences with these criminals: We appreciate your willingness to provide us with a more intimate approach to these case studies. It is through your interaction and encounters with these individuals that a more profound light can be shown on their personal stories.

CONTENTS

DISCLAIMER

As you read this book, understand that the author has gone to incredible lengths to address the terrible reality of these case studies without speaking in full detail about the crime scenes or other disturbing circumstances surrounding the crimes. Please note, however, that the references cited in the endnotes are present for the purposes of sustaining journalistic integrity, and are not necessarily suggested reading material or follow-up links. Some of the study resources behind the development of this book are graphic, extremely unsettling, and should only be pursued by the reader under extreme caution.

Foreword

By Dr. Noah Hutchings, President,
Southwest Radio Ministries

As I remember, it was in the late 1970s that I received a call and two or three letters from a young, troubled man living in the New York City area. I did the best I could to help him understand and deal with some of the problems and life situations that he was burdened with. For good reason I remember this young man's name. It was David Berkowitz.

In our ministry, we deal with many such incidents and problems, so I temporarily lost my communication with this troubled soul. I later discovered that this young man I had counseled had killed several people and was sentenced to life in prison. However, I resumed my communication with David and finally convinced him that the only thing that would wash away his sin was the blood of Jesus Christ. On January 10, 2014, I received a long letter from David with the opening paragraph: "Greetings to you and everyone on staff at Southwest Radio Church. I trust you are doing well in the Lord, always being strengthened by the power of His might, and always rejoicing in our Savior Jesus Christ."

After becoming a Christian in prison, Brother Berkowitz has won many others to Christ and conducts a ministry, even behind prison walls, that reaches multitudes for the Lord.

At Southwest Radio Church, we maintain an extensive prison ministry, reaching lost souls who otherwise would never be told that Jesus Christ died for their sins and how they can be saved and become sons of God through faith in Jesus Christ.

Dr. Thomas Horn is to be commended for collaborating with author Donna Howell in the writing of this book to encourage Christians, both on a personal and church basis, to reach those in prisons with the gospel of Christ that will set them free of sin and eternal damnation, giving them the sure promise of a new life in Christ.

WHEN FORGIVENESS SEEMS IMPOSSIBLE

In February 2014, a ten-year-old girl from Springfield, Missouri (within an hour's drive from Defender Publishing), was kidnapped, raped, and murdered, allegedly by her school sports coach. In spite of several eyewitnesses at the site of the abduction and a long list of mounting evidence (including the body) found at this man's home only hours after the child was publicly taken from the street, this man is currently awaiting trial with a not-guilty plea. Immediately following the announcement of the girl's death, a candlelight vigil was held in her memory. Several staff members of Defender Publishing attended this vigil.

This book was being written at that time.

THE CANDLELIGHT VIGIL

Approximately ten thousand people marched at eight o'clock that night. The city of Springfield closed a number of high-traffic roads and coned off many popular alleyways as the crowds pushed in closer around the family in support of this young girl. Scores of those attending were wearing shirts that said, "[Victim's name] has left her footprint for the world to see." Every kind of personality, ethnicity, and community group was present and unified under one common moral law; the crowd included conservative and religious families with kids, homosexual couples, the elderly, men, women, children, gothic teens, rough and muscular motorcyclists, city officials, court officials, members of law enforcement, close family members, and friends of the victim, as well as those who had never heard of the girl prior to her murder.

As the march began, everyone lined up along the sides of the street held their candles high, respectfully allowing the victim's family to pass to the front, some straining to catch a glimpse of the young girl's mother, who led the march, others standing still with heads bowed in prayer. The victim's mother did not cry, nor did she make eye contact with anyone. In a sort of mechanical or survival mode, she simply kept her legs moving, an odd expression on her face revealing devastation edged with a contrasting refusal of defeat. The sniffles of thousands echoed off the quiet buildings along the usually bustling streets. Then, from somewhere in the back of the group, a single, brave voice rose in the silence: "This little light of mine, I'm gonna let it shine, let it shine, let it shine, let it shine…" The air was emotionally charged as an unspoken determination to remember the girl the way she was in her innocence swept over everyone present. Voices joined in the singing. Candles flickered. Grown men cried.

Slowly, the people made their way down the street. Apartments, homes, and places of business were filled with onlookers sitting or leaning out of their windows, the lights from the rooms behind them extinguished reverently, their handheld candles swaying with the song. Suddenly, bursts of wild cheering that can only be described as an uplifting excitement dominated the march from one side. As heads turned to find the source of the curious enthusiasm, handmade cardboard signs were hoisted high: "Let him hang!" "We need harsher punishments for crimes against women and children!" Amidst this group was one man who was quickly identified in the waves of whispers preceding his position in the march. It was the prosecuting attorney, a man who had been on the news earlier that day stating that the victim's legal team planned to seek the death penalty. Although the multitudes continued to sing "Let It Shine" until they reached the end of the road, spontaneous chanting of the victim's name rose and quieted in response to signs, shouted statements, or relatives of the victim who inspired a more passionate, eager, and fervent reaction from those who came in support.

Our staff, who have since agreed that one sound from our throats would have uncorked a cascade of choking sobs, marched in silence, unable to sing or chant or cheer while our tears remained concealed only by the sheer force of our will. When the crowds reached the final cross street of the march, everyone grew quiet as one girl stood and sang "Amazing Grace." The candles were raised again until the hymn was completed. Then, everyone was asked to take a moment of silence. The silence increased into around a full minute as many bowed their heads, lifting up unspoken prayers to whatever higher power they believed in.

Immediately afterward, members of the local motorcycle community offered to give rides for a small fee to raise money for the victim's family. Attention turned to the tattooed and bandana-adorned men and women, as they regarded those around them softly and soberly, revving their engines. Candles from almost ten thousand hands were then blown out, the waxy smell permeating our senses, and the smoky haze lifting into the light of the streetlamps, wordlessly announcing the end of the march.

Though there were thousands of footsteps on the ground—and shortly thereafter, the thousands of vehicles were starting all at once across the city—few voices could be heard as the masses headed to leave. It was only after our staff was a mile or so away from the event that we could take a deep breath and gather ourselves. We will never forget that night.

One of many aerial shots taken by the present news crews the night of the candlelight vigil.

FORGIVABLE?

The issue with criminals giving their hearts to the Lord post-crime and post-incarceration, at least in the minds of most, is the underlying question of whether their conversion can possibly be sincere. Ultimately, of course, that question can *only* be answered by God. Despite this, many on the outside do hear the stories of these transformations and cast their opinions immediately—without knowing, or even wanting to know, all the details.

The crowds at that candlelight vigil were angry, and to say that they had every right to be angry is the understatement of the century. Anger is a powerful force of human nature, and though it is often destructive, there are times, such as when someone is murdered, when the emotion can inspire change or action toward good. In these cases, anger is even *encouraged* by many. One might say that we should *all* be angry when the life of an innocent person is taken for such detestable and selfish gains. (Based on our conversations on the ride home, we at Defender Publishing are also *incredibly* angry at the person who did this to that little girl.) Without passionate, righteous anger against violent crime, we would have no justice system, for the very meaning of justice is rendered void by the absence of the passion that drives it.

However, God in His seat on high doesn't follow the same justice system or emotional patterns as we do. The Bible is clear that He does feel emotion, including anger, and when He walked the earth as a Man, He certainly felt human emotions. According to Scripture, He feels compassion (Psalms 135:14; Judges 2:18; Deuteronomy 32:36), grief (Genesis 6:6; Psalms 78:40; Isaiah 66:10), love (1 John 4:8; John 3:16; Jeremiah 31:3), hate (Proverbs 6:16), jealousy (Exodus 20:5; Exodus 34:14; Joshua 24:19), joy (Zephaniah 3:17; Isaiah 62:5; Jeremiah 32:41), and yes, anger (Psalms 7:11; Deuteronomy 9:22; Romans 1:18). But where God trumps our finiteness is when the balance of anger versus forgiveness comes into the equation; He has the ability to feel several emotions for every person at once as it is deemed divinely appropriate to Him. His emotions are never limited to our predetermined, fragmented, human expectations.

He does not experience "mood swings on high." He *is* emotion, and it is only by our humanness corrupting His ultimate design that we move so quickly from one emotion to another or stay longer than we should on a single emotion, never fully understanding His perfect balance of emotions (anger and love) with their corresponding or opposing actions (wrath or forgiveness).

We, as people and as victims of others' selfishness, may never find the strength to forgive some acts against humanity.

The same cannot be said of God.

Can God forgive even the sins of one as terrible as the man who murdered that little girl? What about others like Ted Bundy or David Berkowitz?

This brings us to an issue that will be addressed once, early on: It is **NOT** necessarily the opinion of this author that all of the criminals whose stories are included in this book are completely sincere and will therefore spend eternity with God; it is **NOT** necessarily the opinion of this author that these criminals are insincere and will therefore spend eternity in hell. It is only the opinion of this author that the Bible clearly says that all sins are forgivable (except for two: blasphemy of the Spirit [Matthew 12:31; Mark 3:29] and those who take the mark of the beast [Revelation 14:9]).

Survey Says? Sincere Seeking CAN Bring Forgiveness

The driving purpose of this book is to encourage readers to understand that forgiveness can and will be given to those who *are truly repentant and sincere* in their asking. To our human, finite minds, it's easy to hold to the flavor of, "Well, all sins are forgivable except *that* one…" Or, more popularly, some twist Scripture to reflect and line up with their own convictions. For example, they might state that murder is a blasphemy against God, and the Bible specifically addresses blasphemy and murder as separate sins. (It also goes without saying that, just because sin is forgivable, it isn't forgiven automatically; a sinner must honestly confess his or her sins with full accountability to the Lord and earnestly seek forgiveness through our Savior.)

Wherefore I say unto you, All manner of sin and blasphemy shall be forgiven unto men: but the blasphemy against the Holy Ghost shall not be forgiven unto men. And whosoever speaketh a word against the Son of man, it shall be forgiven him: but whosoever speaketh against the Holy Ghost, it shall not be forgiven him, neither in this world, neither in the world to come. (Matthew 12:31–32)

Notice that this verse *does not say*, "All manner of sin except heinous murder shall be forgiven…"

Flip the Switch: Conversion for the Wrong Reasons?

During the research of this book, *uncountable* feedback (blogs, articles, books, etc.) from people all over the globe concerning the general public's acceptance of a prisoner's conversion was read and studied. Although some people actually support the idea that a sinner who has committed the most atrocious sins (such as those outlined in this book) can be sincere in his or her conversion to Christ, hordes of others address the subject with a hardened skepticism—and, in many cases, hardened cynicism. This is completely understandable and absolutely expected. Questions that regularly pop up flow to the rhythm of: "How can someone who is mentally capable of ending another person's life in the most unspeakable, horrific, and disturbing ways ever be mentally capable of true sincerity to God?" Or, "If they were twisted enough to commit these crimes against God and humanity in the first place, how can they possibly untwist themselves to become a peaceful, God-fearing follower of Jesus Christ?"

As stated above, these questions can only be resolved between God and the individual. However, one popular theme in the debate is that these sinners convert: a) at the flip of a switch, and b) for the wrong reasons (boredom, fear, sociopathic attention, etc.). (Moreover, many express that the sinner, by revealing his or her "sudden" interest in religion, is accomplishing too little, too late, and unfortunately, to the victims' families, this statement seems all too true—but that logic does not apply biblically.) We will approach this more in depth throughout the book on a personal basis in each case study, but as you read and try to reach your own conclusions, it's important to keep in mind the circumstances that the sinner is living in at the time of the conversion.

The average reader of this book is going to be busy in life. This is generally a universal statement anymore. We rush here, run there, call this guy over here, email that one lady, work forty-plus hours a week, take care of kids, cook dinner, and at the end of the day, if we're lucky, we have time to chill out and read a book before doing it all again the next day. Many Christians even struggle to find time to dive into the Word or pray. When we are not in the midst of the busier seasons of life, merely because we have the freedom to do so, we fill our time with recreational activities. Prison life simply cannot be compared to our lifestyles—and this is especially true for the American prisons' higher-security divisions such as solitary confinement, death row, and special security units where the high-profile murderers such as this book is profiling are required to stay.

These people have extremely limited contact with anything outside of their cells. They are told when and what to eat, when and how to conduct personal hygiene, and when and how they can go outside their cells to stand in the sunshine…and the list goes on. The higher the level of security, the less access these inmates have to even the mundane items listed here. We, *the free*, cannot even contemplate the huge quantities of time these people have in which to reflect on their own lives, their own pasts, their own beliefs, their own convictions and guilt, and their own impending future. In addition to time comes atmosphere. The walls of the cells are daily reminders of what they've done.

In the words of David Berkowitz: "A guilty conscience hurts. There is an inner pain that is so intense, so suffocating, that all the macho role-playing, living in denial, or trying to stay busy cannot silence. Finally, a prisoner must sit in a prison cell…with his conscience whispering to him every day, 'Failure! Failure! Failure!'"[1]

So, it's easy for "the free" to look at these people who, while in their freedom, spent years and years in disobedience to God in the most horrible ways, and think that they nonchalantly flipped a switch to the ultimate universal start-over button. But when the details of their coming to Christ are studied and researched to the degree that this book required, one can see that the situation is much more complicated. Whereas a certain personality type may necessitate years of active intervention in his or her life to turn over a new leaf while free, that same personality may come to those crossroads much earlier while cut off from the distractions of everyday life. A serial killer will fill his time with distractions and recreational activities (good or bad) the same as anyone, and *stay* in the situation that perpetuates the sin. Those who have been cut off from the distractions of everyday life have *also* been cut off from the temptations they were weak to in the days when they carried out their evil deeds, which places them in the position to stop committing the crimes and actually deal with the sickness that led them to it in the first place. Lastly, the Bible does not stipulate a specific length of time one has to spend in self-reflection before he or she is eligible for redemption. The thief on the cross next to Jesus is one popular example of the truth that people can place their trust in Jesus and count on seeing Him in eternity—even if the moment of their death is just a breath away.

From those who would seek redemption or forgiveness merely out of fear of the eternal hand-slapping they've earned, to those who seek constant attention and a Christian conversion is simply the next façade, to those who convert because they are literally psychopathic or insane and can't make or understand functional decisions the same as the rest of us, certainly these are all possible scenarios. This book will state the facts on a case-by-case basis. You can be the judge. (Or, perhaps, we should leave that to God.)

THE REPORT

At the onset of the documentary *The Six Degrees of Helter Skelter*, a disclaimer is given:

> There are countless story variations and theories regarding the events surrounding the Tate/LaBianca murders, from hundreds of sources, with varying degrees of reliability.

Some theories go as far as to claim that Charles Manson had *nothing* to do with the murders at all, and that the whole thing was a massive conspiracy and a setup job.

We have tried to retell the story as accurately and as factually as possible, to the best of our knowledge, based on years of research.

Undoubtedly, some people will still find something they are unhappy with.

They always do.[2]

This disclaimer reflects much truth regarding the responses of the masses who hear the reports of serious criminals. One can't possibly know all that transpired at the scene of a crime merely by reading a few articles in a shady checkout examiner or by watching a short documentary. Yet, many will do *just that*, wondering how some other report got it all wrong, when the article *they* read was clearly the more reliable source… But we must be realistic. There are certain details in each crime story that the general population will never know with indisputable and undeniable certainty: details that only God and the criminal witnessed. Like the statement above from a documentary about the Tate/LaBianca murders involving Charles Manson and the Manson Family, no matter how much research goes into maintaining a nonbiased and factual report, there will still be other versions of the story floating around, as well as other individuals claiming to have the real truth. All one who intends to give the accounts straight can do is convey the details that the most reputable sources provide and let the evidence speak for itself. That is what the personalities behind this book have aspired to do in each of these case studies, and our extensive citations at the end of the book reflect exactly where and from whom we compiled our information on the crimes as well as on the lives of the criminals from childhood and forward. We went directly to some of America's most notorious criminals who are still living and interviewed them for ourselves. When they heard the mission behind this book, they agreed without hesitation to work with us. In cases in which the perpetrator was already deceased, we went to the psychiatrists, prison ministers, family members of victims, family members of the criminals, and even prison guards for testimony. Having said this, please note that the book you are about to experience does not read like any other true crime studies on the market. Whereas the offenses of the individuals must be addressed when necessary for the reader to fully comprehend what has transpired, the central focus of this book is upon God's grace and forgiveness, and His calling to every man—even those who have sinned in ways the average believer cannot fathom. Thus, the blood and gore of your average true crime book has been almost entirely omitted in the following pages.

Our hope is that people both inside and outside prison walls will find grace for forgiveness through the lens of this difficult investigation.

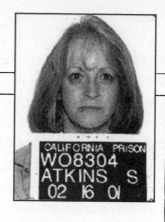

SUSAN ATKINS
(SADIE MAE GLUTZ)[3]

On August 9, 1969, just after eight o'clock in the morning, Winifred Chapman, personal maid to Hollywood actress Sharon Tate, began the day as any other. Heading through the gate at the edge of the elaborate celebrity home at 10050 Cielo Drive, she noticed a fallen telephone wire and, with uneasiness, made a mental note to check to see if the phones in the kitchen were operating properly before beginning her duties. She paid no mind, however, nor felt any alarm, upon observing the unfamiliar vehicle in the driveway, as it wasn't unusual for Tate to have guests. Making her way inside, Chapman stopped briefly at the corner of the garage to turn off the switch to the outside light; someone had evidently left it on the previous evening. Once in the kitchen, Chapman lifted the receiver to the extension phone, and her anxiety increased upon finding that the line was dead. Looking to alert the others present of her discovery, she walked into the next room.

There was no preparing her for what she would see there.

Pools of blood were splattered everywhere, all over the floor and walls, the clear evidence of intentional brutality. The door to the yard hung wide open on its hinges, revealing a bitterly chaotic and splashy trail of red to the cold body on the grass outside. Chapman's survival instinct kicked in quickly, adrenaline carrying her back out through the house the way she came in, and once again past the unknown car in the driveway. Upon closer inspection, the vehicle revealed a second body: a lifeless young driver, slash wounds in the palm of his hand and four bullets in his chest and abdomen.

Unable to cohesively articulate what she had found, Chapman fled to the houses in the surrounding neighborhood, shouting, "Murder! Death! Bodies! Blood!"[4]—still completely unaware of the three other victims, whose famous, lifeless bodies ornamented the Manson Family crime scene in and around the Bel Air home.

VICTIMS OF A POINTLESS CRIME

The murders at the Tate residence were some of the most notorious in criminal history. One cannot Google-search the episode without his or her computer screen being flooded by gruesome stab scenes and disturbing images of cruel murder, as well as textual accounts of the incident that go into more detail than most people are comfortable reading. Even merely a general overview of what took place that night has most people shaking their heads.

However, it is not the viciousness alone that rocketed this case into the media overnight and has kept it in popular news since. The victims of the heinous acts were none other than:

- Sharon Tate (aged 26), American model and rising starlet of *The Valley of the Dolls* (Film director Roman Polanski, Tate's husband, was absent from the home working on a movie in Europe; he had requested that Tate keep company with her in case she went into labor, eight and a half months pregnant at the time of the murders.)

- Stabbed in the living room (after pleading that her assailants spare the life of her unborn child, as it was later revealed)
- Jay Sebring (aged 35), famed celebrity hairstylist and founder of Sebring International Hairstyling Corporation
  - Shot, then stabbed, in living room
- Wojciech Frykowski (aged 32; known more often as "Voytek Frykowski," as spelled in the *Helter Skelter* book by Vincent Bugliosi, the prosecuting attorney during the Manson Family trials), Polish actor and writer
  - Escaped to the yard; tackled; bludgeoned by the blunt end of a gun; and stabbed on lawn
- Abigail Folger (aged 25), Folger Coffee Company fortune heiress, civil rights activist, popular socialite, and well-known charity volunteer
  - Escaped to the yard; tackled; stabbed on lawn
- Steven Parent (aged 18), young man who, although not yet famous, tested at near-genius levels in electronics and had a very bright potential future (Parent was only at the Tate residence to visit with the caretaker who lived in the guesthouse, and to attempt to sell him a Sony radio; his involvement in the killing spree was tragically circumstantial and coincidental, as he was just leaving the property when he was confronted by Charles "Tex" Watson [more about "Tex" later], a member of the Manson Family.)
  - Shot behind the wheel of his car in the driveway

America wept. The death of a pregnant actress as beautiful, talented, up-and-coming, and charismatic as Tate, and her famous company that night (along with an all-American boy in the wrong place at the wrong time), would have been a heartbreaking headline by itself. But the sheer violent nature of the crime scene during the era of flower girls, hippie love, peace signs, and harmony with the earth at the social core of our country was downright offensive and alarming. Well before the details of the Manson Family trials (including the LaBianca murders, which we will discuss later in the Charles "Tex" Watson case study) had reached full exposure, there was a unanimous verdict in the minds of the nation. America thought of this group as a circle of deranged hippies hailing from a ranch in the middle of nowhere, dropping drugs like candy, and listening to a psychotic and self-proclaimed Jesus Christ/devil-man telling them to kill people. The gavel was down. They were guilty.

As history reports, the state of California held the same opinion; the defendants were convicted with charges of murder and conspiracy of murder and sentenced with the death penalty. (Later, in 1972, the California Supreme Court abolished the death penalty for the state as a result of the *People v. Anderson* case [wherein the court ruled that capital punishment was a violation of constitutional rights[5]], automatically converting the Manson Family defendants' sentences to life in prison. Later that year, Proposition 17 amended the state constitution, once again reinstating capital punishment,[6] but by this time, the life sentences for the Manson Family were solid, which is why they were allowed to live out the remainder of their natural lives and even attend parole hearings for their potential release.)

THE MANSON FAMILY

In order to speak specifically about a single member of the Manson Family, which is the purpose of this case study, some reflection is required as to the man Susan Atkins was following and the "family" she was a part of. The Manson Family was, from the outside looking in, a rotating-welcome-door, free-love group from the '60s numbering at around twenty or thirty at any given time, twirling around in big fields of wheat in bell-bottoms, blowing soap bubbles and hugging trees, and living on a diet of lettuce and granola at the Spahn Ranch in California. Deeper down in the pocket of crazy, unseen by the public until the trials, however, they showed violence from the beginning, even amongst themselves.

Documented cases before, during, and after the murder trials show that the Manson Family was not as peaceful or innocent as they looked. Reports include various drug-related disturbances, involvement with the "Straight Satans" motorcycle gang, spiking food with drugs to silence witnesses, setting fire to vehicles, and even carrying out a string of killings known as the "retaliation murders" after Manson's guilty verdict. (To add to this are recent claims of many other potential murders at Barker Ranch and the canine digs that suggest there are human remains yet to be unearthed there.[7]) When one thinks of the Manson Family murders, it is natural to immediately remember the Tate/LaBianca cases, but Manson and members of his "family" were suspected of, linked to, and—in some cases—officially convicted of the murder or attempted murder of several other persons.

Among these, just to name a few whose names are more popularly associated with the Manson Family, were:

- Bernard "Lotsapoppa" Crowe, who threatened to kill everyone at the ranch in response to a drug-fraud conspiracy formed by Charles "Tex" Watson and was later shot in his apartment by Manson, but barely survived
- Gary Hinman, who was rumored to obtain a monetary inheritance that Manson sent his followers (among whom was Bobby Beausoleil) to garnish and, when he did not produce the money, was held against his will for two days until Manson appeared, struck him in the ear/cheek with a sword, and then ordered Beausoleil to kill him
- Ronald Hughes, Leslie Van Houten's attorney in the Tate/LaBianca trial who wouldn't allow her to testify on Manson's behalf and who disappeared during a trial recess, his body to be later found wedged between two rocks in Ventura County
- James Willett, temporarily framed by Family members in a robbery and in an attempt to keep him quiet was forced to dig his own grave, then shot and buried, and whose wife was shot and buried in the house basement where Manson Family members were living in Stockton
- US President Gerald Ford, who survived the attempted assassination by Manson disciple Lynette "Squeaky" Fromme as she was apprehended before the gun could fire

- Others, including the mysterious "Jane Doe No. 59," whose stabbed body found at an embankment is yet unknown, but has been identified by a Spahn Ranch worker as a young girl who had been present with the Family prior[8]

Upon an initially charming invitation to the Manson Family's community, many came for a passing stay at the ranch and left shortly afterward on pleasant terms with their new acquaintances, only having needed a place to "crash" for a while until they could resume their life plans. Others remained, found comfort as a member of a new family, and began seasoning their minds with drug-induced, peculiar mantras and group circles under the tutelage of Charles Manson, the Jesus Christ/devil-man, himself. Manson would begin with talk of hugs and self-sacrifice for thy fellow man and, upon establishing trust and providing excitement (and access to drugs), would then gradually introduce seemingly righteous-minded schemes of justified violence. (Note that there is some diversity in the accounts of how often, and how passionately, Manson claimed to be Christ or the devil. His direct or indirect involvement with the murders, drugs, and what kind of materials he covered in his enlightenment teachings are also debated constantly. The world will likely never have all the answers. When moments within the case studies require that we give details to paint a picture the reader can understand, we have referred to what Manson's followers' claims were when they are the only witnesses and what the lengthy court evidence documents reflect during trial when something was considered provable by the courts. We have omitted some points that seem most based on conjecture with little substantiation. In certain instances, we have cited Manson's own words directly, which you will read in the following pages. We have cited our sources throughout accordingly.)

THE TRIPLE MOTIVE: FUTILE INSANITY IN ITS PUREST FORM

If you're currently asking about the purpose of all this killing, be warned that you won't likely get an answer that completely satisfies the curiosity of anyone with normal, sane expectations. If you reflect on the consolidation of all the details of all the killing and all the strange behavior, you'll find that there simply wasn't a moment in the life of anyone closely involved with the Manson Family during this time who existed on the same plane as normal, everyday people who live normal, everyday lives. It wasn't as simple as, "They were high the night it happened and things got out of control." We are talking about multiple, deliberate, planned murders by a drugged cult whose members' idea of a motive for killing can be as simple as, "We needed money," all the way to the complicated, masterminded, villainous, and apocalyptic "Helter Skelter."

Keeping our focus on the Tate/LaBianca murders only, however—and again, not expecting these to appear rational—there were three motives: 1) "Helter Skelter"; 2) Manson's musical-career revenge; and 3) freeing Bobby. The first of these is the hardest to explain.

Motive One: "Helter Skelter"

Manson either personally believed or manipulated his followers into thinking he truly believed that the world was about to face a racial war on the heels of the black/white tension of that era. Manson endearingly named this war "Helter Skelter" after the song made famous by the Beatles (much more about Helter Skelter in the following case study). In Manson's prophecy, (again, this is according to testimonies by his Family members), anyone of a black race was going to rise up against anyone of a white race in a long-simmering retaliation of what had been historic racial persecution. During this time, the Manson Family would be safely installed in a secret, underground safe house below Death Valley until the war was over. The black race would win, entirely eliminating anyone who was not black, but, according to Manson, evidently a racist himself, the black leadership would be inherently inferior and would therefore not know how to handle the power.

This is the narcissistic point of the prophecy where Manson would rise up and "scratch [the black man's head] and…tell him to go pick the cotton and go be a good [black man],"[9] essentially now becoming the white king of the new world. Now, Manson and his Family, by this time reaching numbers near one hundred fifty thousand, would be the only ones left alive from the white race other than the Beatles (whose music and lyrics inspired much of Manson's ideas), and the black race would be again returned to slavery under his rule.

This war, Manson predicted, would begin in the summer of 1969, and the musical album that he and the Family would produce would not only make Manson and his followers popular public figures prior to the war (likely so that their emergence from Death Valley later would acclaim them as even more of a leadership people over the new world), but the lyrics to the songs on their album would also carry subliminal messages of this race tension, thereby triggering the actual war in the first place. Despite Manson's multiple efforts to gain financial backing for his apocalyptic album, it never came to fruition. (Note: There was an eventual release of his album, *LIE* [see next case study], though it was somewhat unrelated and unsatisfactory to the Helter Skelter cause. The desperation for money is the most likely motive for the aforementioned murder of supposed monetary inheritor, Gary Hinman, whom the Manson family killed without any proof that the inheritance ever existed beyond rumor.)

When the race war didn't begin as Manson had prophesied, this being the event that he had come to fulfill (claiming to be Jesus Christ[10] in the Second Coming, although he later allegedly proclaimed to be the devil[11]), he would need to trigger the event in a different way.

Naturally, the sudden and messy blood-splattering of innocent (albeit wealthy and high-profile) white people was going to be the upshot that hurled the world into the black-versus-white conflict. This is, of course, assuming that the Manson Family could effectively make it look like the murders were carried out by someone of black descent with no other motive than to retaliate against the supremacy of the white man (thus explaining the racially implicating evidence that had been left at crime scenes, cryptic political messages written in blood, etc.). (This logic has so many flaws, one doesn't even know where to begin. In a sense, the African-American race had essentially just *won* a war of a nonphysical nature in obtaining their freedom. *Certainly* a kind of oppression still existed and kept them enslaved in a different, more social way [watch the movie *Kelly Green*], but this moment in history was also a great celebration of their newfound freedom, and, to put it bluntly, it was also a time of walking on eggshells so as not to upset the apple cart they worked so hard for. Why would this motive mentality have ever applied at this time? But we digress… As promised, there is your point of reference to the first motive, sane or otherwise.)

Motive Two: Manson's Musical-Career Revenge

On more than one occasion, Manson had been chased off-property at the Tate residence while Tate and Polanski lived there, having come to find Doris Day's songwriting son, Terry Melcher, who was the previous resident of the home and who had supposedly (according to members of the Family) made promises to help further Manson's musical career.

It had started when, in the spring of 1968, Dennis Wilson (drummer and singer in the Beach Boys) picked up a couple of attractive girls who were hitchhiking. These girls were Patricia Krenwinkel and Ella Jo Bailey, members of the Manson Family. After taking them to his Sunset Boulevard home to party for a while, Wilson then left to attend an all-night music recording session. When he returned, a strange hippie was emerging from his home. After asking the man if he intended him harm, the man assured Wilson that he did not, and further greeted him by getting down and kissing his feet.

Wilson and Manson hit it off right away. Wilson liked girls—which Manson had plenty of—and Manson liked money and connections to the musical industry—which Wilson had plenty of. Within months, around twenty-five Family members were living almost full time with Wilson, costing him upwards of $100,000 (around $671,000 in today's fiscal math[12]) in living costs, including medical bills (many dental bills and, once, the treatment of a sexually transmitted disease) and the repair of destruction of personal property (including his vehicle, which was totaled). During this time, Manson had the opportunity to lay down several recordings in a professional studio on someone else's dime, which also helped him meet and greet other established names in the industry, among whom was Terry Melcher, who lived in the big, beautiful house at 10050 Cielo Drive.

Later, Melcher had relocated and the home had been inhabited by Sharon Tate. Manson had gone looking for Melcher and, when finding nobody at the residence but Tate, her photographer, and the owner of the home staying in the guesthouse out back (the owner traveled a lot and did not occupy the main house), he was strongly encouraged by the owner to leave the property and not bother the tenants.

Unable to locate Melcher directly, it has been suggested (even in court) that a strong motive of the Tate murders was an act of revenge—not only upon Melcher indirectly as an invocation of fear and a warning of what can happen when one doesn't follow up on promises made to Manson, but also upon those who would stand in his way of finding Melcher. (Melcher, of course, denied all allegations of leading Manson to believe he would be his connection to fame.)

Motive Three: Freeing Bobby

The Tate murders happened only days after Bobby Beausoleil was arrested for the murder of Gary Hinman. In testimonies given by the three girls most involved with the Tate/LaBianca murders during the trial, part of the motive for both the Tate and the LaBianca events was to create copycat crime scenes of the Hinman case in order to make it appear that Beausoleil had been wrongly taken into custody in place of the murderer (or murderers) who was still on the loose and guilty of Hinman's demise. And with that, we have come full circle, back to the night that Tate and her friends met their own.

Tate, Sebring, Frykowski, Folger, and Parent all died upon the sadistic orders of Charles Manson, and by the devoted hands of crazed youths Charles "Tex" Watson, Patricia Krenwinkel, and Susan Atkins, the latter of which this case study is focused upon.

FROM GOLD STARS IN SUNDAY SCHOOL TO A LIFE SENTENCE

Atkins' involvement in the Tate/LaBianca murders varies from story to story and from witness to witness. Depending on whom you're listening to, the tale spans from one of a sweet and innocent girl getting swept away in accomplishing what she thought were good deeds as ordered by God, all the way to one of a frenzied bloodbath by a drug-induced devil-hippie who laughed and maimed her victims as she viciously slaughtered anything in her path. According to the court, Atkins was guilty of multiple murders, which fit with several of her initial braggart claims/testimonies. However, her later retellings of the events, Watson's later retellings of the events, and the official police reports of the initial crime scenes draw much of this so-called truth under a blanket of mystery. If all the facts regarding the many varying tales of those nights were to be written out here and now, not only would the details be far too graphic to include in this book, but the information is so plentiful that this one case study would drag on for hundreds of pages. Thus, in an effort to truncate the process and keep things clean, we will include a brief bullet list of facts here and let the readers draw their own conclusion as to her involvement:

- According to many studies, drug and substance abuse can have far-ranging effects on the human mind, in some cases, even years after the abusive behavior has ceased. Many of Manson's closest followers, including Atkins, were regularly into very heavy drug use (most references are to LSD, methedrine, and marijuana).
- Manson, with the influence of the said drugs he helped put into the hands of his followers, effectively established a radical cult, the epitome of a classic brainwash case wherein, under other circumstances, followers like Atkins might be considered victims of a con man. (Some witness accounts have suggested that he was most often sober himself, sometimes pretending to take drugs but actually operating with a clear mind in order to lead or manipulate "his flock," though others say he always participated in taking drugs with the Family. In the 2004 movie remake of *Helter Skelter*

starring Jeremy Davies, Manson is depicted as waiting until nobody is looking, then secretly pocketing the drugs—only pretending to take them.)

- Atkins knew about and was involved with the plan to kill Gary Hinman, but did not directly deliver his death (the deed was done by Bobby Beausoleil; more about this later).

- After the Tate murders, Atkins was present in the car that was parked in the LaBianca driveway just before the LaBianca murders were carried out, but other than the knowledge of intent to kill, she was not involved in any way with the LaBianca case (which is why we are not discussing that at length in this case study). While the LaBianca murders were happening, Atkins, along with Linda Kasabian and Steve "Clem" Grogan, made their way to Venice Beach with the plans to murder actor Saladin Nader, but the scheme was thwarted when Kasabian intentionally knocked on the wrong apartment door.

- Atkins bragged to several people (both in court and behind bars) that she had been the one to carry out the murder of Sharon Tate, including the disturbing divulgence of tasting blood and the plans to remove Tate's unborn baby from her belly, the latter which she claimed she "did not have time"[13] to do.

- Many times both in and out of court in the days following the murders, Atkins changed her story as well as her demeanor, which erratically altered from a prim and proper lady or scared child graciously cooperating with her attorney to the giggling, singing, unrepentant court disrupter who has since been remembered most in the media.

- After a long separation from drugs, the cult, and Manson, and after a strong dose of reality hit her with a death sentence (later a life sentence) in prison, Atkins finally found one story to stick to. She stuck to it the rest of her days until death, purporting that despite the court hearings, testimonies, and sentencing: she did not actually bring an end to any human life; she did not taste blood; and she did not attempt to remove the unborn baby, nor had she ever planned to. (Tate's body showed no evidence of attempted removal of the fetus, and, despite Atkins claiming she didn't have time, there had been plenty of time and opportunity for this, especially for Atkins, whose bloody footprint on the concrete tells the story of her return into the house to increase racial/political crime-scene evidence by writing the word "PIG" on the door in blood.) Atkins relates in her book that these details were given because Manson pressured her to take full blame, denying her original statements to the grand jury, and she wanted to make it believable. Additional comments and testimonies from other Manson followers years later also reflect this as truth. As recorded by Investigation Discovery for the Discovery Channel's *Most Evil* series, previous Family member and Family recruiter Catherine "Gypsy" Share reflects Atkins' claim thus: "At the very end, [Manson] did everything he could to save his life and get the girls to take on more than they actually did, so that he wouldn't get the death penalty. He did *not* wanna go to the gas chamber." A minute later in her interview: "[The Manson girls] took it upon themselves to try to save Charlie Manson's life, and say that 'he had nothing to do with it,' uh, this, this *concocted* story."[14]

- Atkins continued to admit to holding Tate down during the attack by Watson and, upon Tate's pleading that the baby be allowed to live, Atkins told her she had no mercy for her. (When asked about this vicious comment, Atkins has always, in the original court hearings and up until her death, claimed she said this more to herself as encouragement to go through with Manson's plan than as evidence of her own lack of mercy for the victim.)

- According to Atkins' later telling of what happened that night: When Watson instructed Atkins to bind Frykowski's hands, she did so with a towel; when Watson instructed Atkins to kill Frykowski, she raised the knife above him, but did not have the nerve to bring the knife down; he easily untied the towel and managed to escape to the yard, where he was then confronted by Watson. (In her book, Atkins admits she remembers injuring his legs with a knife, but there is some question of this detail, based on the following two bullets in this list.) Afterward, when Watson instructed Atkins to kill Tate, Atkins held the knife to her, but again did not have the nerve to follow through.

- The police reports and evidence brought to court by Prosecuting Attorney Vincent Bugliosi during the trial showed that the stab wounds were caused by Watson's knife, not Atkins'. Atkins' knife was lost at the scene of the crime and later found wedged between Tate's couch cushions; the blade was clean and there was no evidence the weapon had ever been used.

- Since the trials, Watson has many times openly confirmed Atkins' version of the story, implicating himself as the actual killer.

So, what kind of person was this young girl? What was her childhood like? Certainly, she was responsible for her own actions and decisions. Nobody is attempting to dispute that here. But at only twenty-one years old at the time her life took such a serious turn, could she have even had enough life behind her to know who she was? Would she, in later years, while referring to her conversion in the true Christ, have been capable of meaning it?

Then if any man shall say unto you, Lo, here is Christ, or there; believe it not. For there shall arise false Christs, and false prophets, and shall shew great signs and wonders; insomuch that, if it were possible, they shall deceive the very elect. (Matthew 24:23–24)

This Scripture appears first and foremost in the book, *Child of Satan, Child of God*, by Susan Atkins and Bob Slosser, an "in her own words" autobiographical essay of the events up to, during, and after Atkins' involvement with the Manson Family murders. It is interesting that even the Bible offers such solid and inarguable words on the subject of whether someone can be truly deceived by a false Christ, and then follows those words with a qualifier of *who* might be deceived: *the very elect*. What does that mean, exactly?

There have been many translations and dissections of this verse, but the most popular and seemingly sound conclusion among learned theologians is this: In the same way we would "elect" a person in our modern terminology to fulfill a certain role or office (such as in government), we are choosing that person and making a certain covenant or promissory relationship with him or her. This person is "the chosen one" in and for that position. In extension, "the very elect" likely means "God's chosen people."

Beyond that, what could this verse have meant to Atkins personally? In the mind of a previous Manson follower, who are the elect, and who is the deceiver?

Let's rewind a little and take a breather from the images of the knife-wielding, giggling, crazy-eyed youths we all have in our minds from the media coverage of the original Manson murder trials and look at who Atkins was *before* the encounters with her own false Christ.

The Bible: A Child's Reward

On a Sunday morning church service in 1951, a small, shy girl outstretched a nervous hand to the man in the black robe. He shook it and proceeded to hand her a Bible with her name etched on the cover in gold letters while she stood at the front of the aisle before a full congregation of onlookers. This Bible, given to the beholder of the most gold stars received in Sunday school, was awarded to little Susan Atkins. Behind the man in the black robe stood a tall cross. As Atkins explains in her book, she doesn't know how she knew that the Man on this cross was Jesus Christ, as she had never been in the sanctuary before, but somehow she knew it was Him. With childlike innocence, she gazed up at Him and wondered why He was hanging there. This scene unfolds in her book with something familiar to many in regards to the first time we see Jesus as children. She knew He was good. She wanted to please Him, she wanted to know Him, and she wanted Him to love her, but she did not know Him and could not understand why He had to hang on a cross. Her curiosity about this Man was no different than many young children in church just barely beginning to grasp that the somber, long-haired white Man with the gentle but sad face, often depicted with blood still trickling from His wounds in His final moments before a historically violent death, was someone important to everyone…to *her*. She felt a hunger to know more about this Jesus mystery, even at such a young age.

Just weeks after this memory, the easily frightened girl watched in horror as a close friend of hers who had come to pick up kids for church suddenly screamed and dropped dead of a brain hemorrhage in her driveway. Unable to understand whether Jesus loved this man as much as He loved the children, she refused to go to church for a while.

She recalls another time when, a few years later during rolling thunder, she ran to her award Bible for comfort from the storm. By accident, she caught the back of the Bible cover on fire while looking at the pictures by candlelight. A panic ensued, she and her mother frantically attempting to extinguish the flames. When the damage was done and the book was once again still, the book of Revelation burned straight through, she hid it in her bottom drawer, certain that God could not and would not forgive her for setting His Word on fire.

As time went on, Atkins lived life recklessly (in her own words), and then repeatedly beat everyone else to the altar for prayer on Sunday mornings to repent of her sins. She also tested God: Once she offered Him the gift of a pink rose she had hidden in the backyard and, discovering that He "took" the gift in the middle of the night, came to believe that He had proved Himself to her.

On another very important occasion in her life, Atkins saw a vision in the late summer that she believed was God, Himself, reaching out to talk to her. It was an otherwise ordinary day she had spent playing hopscotch outside. Not knowing why, or even how, to explain the strength of the feeling that had come over her, she had the urge to stop what she was doing right then and look behind her. Pivoting around, she stopped dead in her tracks on the sidewalk, frozen in fear. She describes in her book what she saw: "Right before my eyes, just a few hundred yards away, was a huge burning cross. It covered half the hill—at least a hundred feet wide and a hundred feet long. I stared at it for several moments, but it was so bright it actually caused a slight pain in my eyes."[15] When she ran into the house to tell her father what she had seen—screaming that the hill was on fire and that it was the shape of a cross—and to beg him to come take a look, he told her that her eyes were playing tricks on her. Because he couldn't smell any smoke, he sent her back out to double check the frightening scene by herself while he continued to read the newspaper. The cross and flames were gone. She sat and cried, knowing what she had seen, and believing that it was God, although she didn't know why. There didn't seem to be anyone available for her to talk to about it and to help her understand what the huge burning cross may have meant, so she decided that, for the time being, she would internalize the episode. (Her father's reaction was interesting, to say the least. Burning crosses in the news in those days usually related to racial tension involving the Ku Klux Klan. Perhaps, in their area, he knew this was unlikely, or maybe little Susan was often the little girl who cried wolf. But for a man's child to rush through the door reporting a huge fire outside the house in the shape of a cross and his response to be to ignore it and continue reading the paper—that's difficult to understand.)

Early Warning Signs Ignored

The list of Atkins' interest in dangerous behavior at a very young age grew, especially after the death of her mother from cancer, to include: petty shoplifting; heavy bar drinking when she was years below the legal age; sleeping around; planning a melodramatic overdose, knowing her suicide scene would be discovered before she died, as an attempt to gain attention; running away from home until her brother hired a private detective to track her down to her seedy hotel room, where she found her drunk father begging her for a place to stay (she refused and watched her dad leave in tears); knowingly running with two prison convicts in breach of their parole and promising to marry one of them; and, of course, doing drugs.

To read of Atkins' life and feelings in her book is to read of a profound loneliness occurring in vulnerable stages of life. The decisions she made, right or wrong (and many were *very* wrong), were made alone and without support from family or friends as she slid into one temporary situation after another, practically raising herself, always leaving unful- filled and unspeakably empty. When she was eighteen, she experienced a crucial moment that reflects the kind of decision patterns she had started to adopt. She was living alone, and was old enough to start planning her adult life, yet she was very much still a child. Not knowing what to do with herself, she thought about her life and habits, pondering what she had become and asking herself some paramount questions, such as: "You've been in jail, you've deserted your family, you're an alcoholic, and you're no better than a tramp with the neighborhood men. How much lower can you get?" Feeling as if there was no point in trying, since her current decisions/behaviors weren't getting her anywhere or anything but trouble, she answered herself with, "I'll show them how low I can get."[16]

One doesn't have to tune the violin strings on this case any tighter. Whether we look at this case with pity for a little girl lost or contempt for a hardened killer, we see that Atkins had every psychological symptom one can have to reveal a young life spinning in the wake of miserable abandonment, and any psychiatrist and/or psychologist these days would agree. It's unfortunate, but not surprising, that her life quickly led her to face some very adult themes while she was still a child. Before long, she had taken to erotic dancing for money.

What many don't know is how that part of her life connected her with Anton LaVey, the founder of the Church of Satan and author of *The Satanic Bible*. Perhaps Atkins' identity is so associated with being a Manson Family killer that the contrast of her endeavors with and for the world's most famous satanic priest is evidently not as worthy of mention. Yet, when studying the course of her life and what led her to become what she was, including what happened with her faith, this experience is obvi- ously monumental, because it documents an acute point of directional change for her spiritually.

LaVey had come to see Atkins dance; her reputation as the best dancer at the club had intrigued him. After having decided that she was perfect for the part of "vampire" and "the witch in the torture scene"[17] in his upcoming topless witches' sabbath production he planned to put on at her club, she found herself uneasily participating in the theatrics, unable to go through with the performance sober. After swallowing an acid tab, she settled into the part and shocked the audience with her portrayal of life and death, pointing at them and "marking" them as her next victims. Needless to say, although perhaps not entirely beyond reach at this point, she was already, at the age of eighteen, into some very dangerous weirdness. Gary, Atkins' boyfriend at the time (no relation to Manson Family victim Gary Hinman), sensed something more than theatrics when he addressed her with his concerns later that night. When he approached her, she was still high and wired on acid, and though she was polite and pleasant, he wasn't surprised that she didn't agree with his observations of how she was changing mysteriously, spiritually. He had observed this from the first rehearsal, but the transformation was getting more extreme all the time, and the perfect execution of her character in the show was an intimidating escalation. Gary didn't like what was happening to Atkins. When she responded to his pleading with a gentle dismissal, telling him that she had not changed and didn't understand what he was referring to, he responded: "It's hard to describe. But something's happened to you. When you play your autoharp, for instance, it's creepy. There's a strange sound to it, and when you sing with it, it's like something far out, from somewhere else."[18]

Atkins goes on to describe yet again another night walking the streets alone and lonely. Gary left her. Her chapter ends with this excerpt: "The show [referring to the Anton LaVey production] was a smash hit along the strip…. But the witches' sabbath, and my total sellout to LSD, marijuana, and hashish, and to sex with virtually any attractive man, landed me in the hospital in four months. I was half dead from gonorrhea and had a complete physical breakdown."[19]

Manson and the Drug Trips

This breakdown was not heeded as a warning. Atkins moved to the Haight-Ashbury district and into a big home among a dozen hippies all living together directly next door to Janis Joplin, whose boozing, impromptu playing sessions she would listen to while she took dope and zoned out on the porch. She describes a time in her life when *finally* her insatiable hunger for drugs was satisfied. She was living a thrill—the kind you hear about in movies, including the celebrity next door and the constant adventure of the peace movement drawing the attention of the FBI to her residence. Sadly, this fixed nothing for Atkins, and she remained direly isolated from the world around her. She was now able to start counting the number of "families" (including her biological family) that she had once been a part of, only to pass through, always remaining the stranger: destination unknown.

Regarding what Atkins might have become if someone had just intervened and helped her choose another spiritual and lifestyle path early on: It doesn't pay off to stop the case study here and spend time playing the blame game and analyzing the girl who "might have been" under different psychological and developmental conditions. The details of this case study, as well as others to follow, will by default inherently and continuously ask the question regarding the intervention that could have taken place, but never happened, in the path of a person heading toward uncertainty, disorder, loneliness, and eventually destruction. What makes this (and the "Tex" Watson) case study so unique is that, unlike many others featured in this book, someone *did* intervene and "counsel" her spiritually—someone who spoke constantly of the love of Christ. Unfortunately, that person led her to believe that he was *the* Christ.

For the sake of truly understanding what Atkins faced in the days following her dancing gig at the club where she met LaVey, we are truly challenged to use our imaginations as never before. The scenes as described in the book by Atkins are so far out of this world to anyone who hasn't fully experienced the "trip" of drugs the way she and her Family had, that just short of including a word-for-word copy/paste of the first, ninth, and tenth chapters of *Child of Satan, Child of God*, there is just no adequate description for it.

While under the influence, Atkins would lie in the cross position on the floor, with arms outstretched, and calmly embrace the thought that she had to die for "these people" (her drug-dropping cohorts). She relives the accounts of feeling so "one" with those around her that when she made love with a random stranger, she was making love with herself. She saw monsters and animated skeletons and heard voices coming out of the sink.

Strengthening Atkins' testimony of these days is a statement by Leslie Van Houten (convicted murderess in the LaBianca case) in an interview with Diane Sawyer years after the murders, just after a very telling question from Sawyer to Manson:

SAWYER, TO MANSON: You had them thinking you were Jesus Christ. How did you do that?

MANSON: Just bein' myself. All men are Jesus Christ. [He makes an odd, "bet-you-didn't-know-that" facial expression at her.]
[Scene blips back to the interview between Sawyer and Van Houten.]

VAN HOUTEN: Sometimes he would reenact the crucifixion when we were on LSD, and it was…very realistic.

SAWYER: You mean, you would pretend that he was being nailed?

VAN HOUTEN: Oh yeah…yeah…and go through the whole thing, and then make the connections of Man-son, son-of-man, you know, and then the questions would begin: "Would you die for *me*?"
[Scene blips back to the interview between Sawyer and Manson.]

SAWYER, TO MANSON: Did you ask them to die for you?

MANSON: Sure, sure, sure, sure. That's basic Christian philosophy.[20]

These thoughts grew for Atkins and became more the norm for her as her mind drifted farther and farther outside the realms of reality; all the while, Manson gained more and more control over her and so many others, always entering the scene with some soft-voiced, enticing love-fest that perpetuated servanthood. (And he often assigned them names that were very different from their own. This is a commonality within brainwashing cults to further strip away one's individuality. It was in one of these moments that Atkins was given the Family name "Sadie Mae Glutz.") Atkins is not the only one who described Manson as incredibly powerful and Christ-like. Whether he was sober or also under the influence (as mentioned earlier, the witness accounts are fuzzy on this detail), when he walked into a room, men and women alike stopped and listened, waiting for the next profound revelation to grace the ears of the group that was rapidly becoming "his people."

The deeper into "oneness" that Atkins' mentality drifted, the more her sense of self or her own identity blurred away, and she "fit in." As was the popularly embraced mentality of that time, she finally found herself and her sense of belonging by completely abandoning her own identity in trade for togetherness with others. Not surprisingly, however, the more she welcomed her denial of self and identity, the more she craved attention from others for her own uniqueness and personhood. Initially, at the center of this craving was "Charlie" (Manson), who made Atkins, among so many others, feel unique, special, even magical (the belittling came later). The more attention he poured on his followers, the more they craved his interest, wanted his blessing, dropped LSD, and got high, sacrificing "selfs" and entertaining thoughts of necessary sacrifices around them for the overall good and peace of mankind. When Charlie reprimanded, heads would turn, all eyes watching and learning from the "teacher" in all his wisdom, yet there would be a continual acceptance all around from the brethren of this cult for the sheep who had gone astray, just like any family should be, so nobody ever felt left out of the "enlightened true love" that this cult spoke of. (This mentality proved later on to be the reason why, when the Family turned so radical that their earthy love mantra was an oxymoron in contrast to their growing violence, they didn't feel contradictory. It was very much the opposite. The more they "loved" from such an enlightened position away from the rest of the broken world, the more they convinced themselves, with the help of the drugs, that this love had to be protected, preserved, and passed on at any cost, evidently including the necessary evil of murder.)

But, in addition to love, Manson constantly indoctrinated life from a perspective that, although a popular state of mind in that era and often harmless for most, would eventually lead to a no-rules core for an up-and-coming slaughter dynasty. He preached that there was no time; time was an illusion, a restraint, a distraction. He made his Family get rid of all their watches and timepieces, as there was no past and no future—only *today*, only *now*. With wild, passionate eyes, he paced back and forth, telling the spiritually hungry group that they were no longer tied to any baggage or any other families or relationships, and stopping only momentarily to light another joint and pass more around for the Family. Bible verses fell out of his mouth regularly, usually out of context or twisted, supporting whatever ideas he held with an ultimate last word. He always had an answer for everything. In interviews (then and still), he speaks with confidence and authority, never having to stop and think of what he plans to say, as if he's always had the answer in his head and is waiting for someone to ask. (There is another side to this coin, however. Despite his ability to keep up with any interviewer and project himself as a learned leader, most of what he says does not make sense to the average person, and he often answers questions with other questions. His Christian theology is, when compared to most conservative Christian theologies, desperately warped.)

Manson would certainly not be the first or last in history, by any stretch of the imagination, to use Bible Scripture in twisted ways for his own attention or gain. Yet, his philosophies were delivered with just the right charismatic chemistry to inspire and charge those with ears to hear (or those with drugs to confuse) his madness and take it as gospel. To most, his speeches regarding the severance of time and past baggage were just more average, earthy, feel-good sermons delivered by your 1960s hippie-next-door. Drugs are evidently more powerful than this author had realized to have eventually inspired belief in the ridiculous Helter Skelter plan, which began to unfold rapidly after Manson had established himself as the unchallenged leader of this assembly. When he did begin to incite violent threads of thought into his followers, he covered all the bases, including the "I did nothing wrong" thoughts that they should embrace post-crime (the quote below has been dramatically shortened to remove unnecessary repetition in Manson's redundant programming style):

> Guilt. Look at guilt. What is guilt anyway? It is just something mommy and daddy put in you to control you to do what they wanted you to do…. You are your own person, and you just do what you want to do. Do what you do, and don't think about it. There is no guilt!… Guilt is all in your head. It is an illusion. It isn't real. Everything you see is an illusion, a figment of your imagination…. Get outside yourself and look back at yourself, and you will see that even you are an illusion.[21]

Ideally, for someone like Manson, who was going to become the king of the world in the apocalypse of Helter Skelter, one would need plenty of offspring within the Family, even if they weren't his, biologically speaking. When Atkins discovered she was pregnant with the baby of "New Bruce" (his given name in the Family, not to be confused with "Old Bruce," another "sheep" who had left the fold for a time to travel the world), Manson was ecstatic and celebratory, announcing that they would need a lot of children to be born among them. He followed up with his plans to raise these children to be "free," never experiencing the world around them or being forced into any expectations (including the education system).[22]

During her pregnancy and after the move to the infamous Spahn Ranch, Atkins describes a new level of spiritual peculiarity that took place within her when she and some of the other Family sisters were staying temporarily at an apartment in town. Manson had ordered Atkins and a few other girls to move away from the Family for a time, although nobody was ever sure of his motive for this, as he only said the "family" concept would never work, but gave no other reasoning. By this point, however,

Manson was allegedly beginning to show his true colors, abandoning some of the love and togetherness for power and control, and it's a theory that he ordered them to move out just to exercise this control, since they were gone such a short while. Several times, during moments of clarity or sobriety when Manson's brutality was more transparent, Atkins attempted to leave, but either stayed on or returned shortly. On one occasion she speaks of during her 1993 parole hearing, Atkins promised a man she would take care of him and his household if he would help her get away, but when she went to get her things, she says Manson led her to a back room to observe a Family sister whom he had severely beaten for threatening to leave the ranch.[23] There are *many* other accounts of this kind of control in Manson literature, to those with the interest to read further. To quote Catherine "Gypsy" Share in a different episode of the previously mentioned *Most Evil* series:

> And [Manson] looked at Clem, and he says, "Clem, would you do anything for me?" and Clem said, "Sure, you know I would." [Manson] said, "This is what I want you to do. If Gypsy tries to leave, I want you to hunt her down, find her, tie her behind a car, and drag her, don't kill her, just drag her all the way back to Spahn Ranch, slowly. Would you do that for me, brother?" And Clem grinned and said, "Sure." Then [Manson] looked at me and said, "Gypsy, are you going anywhere?" and I said, "No."[24]

During the time of Atkins' separation from Manson, Atkins had begun to nurture the same manipulation and power skills over people as she had seen in Manson, as the pages of her book tell. Slowly, she observed herself becoming more and more like him in her thoughts and actions, and she could impersonate him to others' amazement. The girls living with her during this time would follow her in the same way they would follow Manson, although Atkins had never officially been labeled as leader in his absence. As these skills increased, she began to know what the girls were thinking, just as Manson had mysteriously been able to do, and she became aware that she could control them and gain their devotion as a result. One night, during an acid trip, the comparison of herself with Manson exposed something to her in a profound way:

> It was late at night. Everyone was tripping. As I sat watching the other girls, I was aware of other persons within me.... They were alive, moving, talking, laughing. I immediately recognized them as the same beings I had sensed in Charlie. My imitation of Charlie was perfect because we had the same things inside us.[25]

Shortly after this experience, and evidently after Manson had worked out his concept of a "family," Atkins and the other girls were once again happily installed at home with the Family at the ranch. The longer these people (mostly the women) were in the presence of Manson, the more they obsessed over his attention and completed favors, waited on him, and doted on him from every angle (at one point they even hand-sewed him a vest edged with lining and tassels made with the hair from their heads[26]). The competition for Manson's blessing and attention grew extemporaneously, to the point that when his mannerisms began to grow increasingly angry, violent, or simply uncaring, the women of the Family who had been brainwashed to so much self-sacrificial thought overlooked the change and chalked it up to the burdens of leadership, continuing to follow him unconditionally.

When, at seven months pregnant, Atkins took acid (she openly acknowledges within her book that taking drugs while pregnant was incredibly selfish) and sent herself into early labor, Manson entered the room during her contractions and told her to go boil water for him so he could shave. Obediently, she did as he had asked. Shortly after the baby was born at the ranch, the umbilical cord tied off with the *G* string of a violin, Manson showed even more bipolar tendencies when he would angrily grab the baby by the feet and whirl him in circles an inch above the rocky ground, only to praise the child and dote on him immediately afterward.[27] (Atkins was the second in the Family to bear a child; the first, born of Family member Mary, was given the name "Pooh-Bear." Atkins named her son Ze Zo Ze Cee Zadfrack Glutz. He was later named, more

sensibly, "Paul" by his adoptive parents after the murders. After Atkins'
imprisonment, she never saw or heard from her son again.)

Atkins likens Manson's treatment of her in those days to playing her
like a yo-yo, praising her one minute and putting her down the next.
But while under the influence of a steady stream of LSD, she remained
convinced that he was righteous. Her desire to please him became insatiable, so much so that by the time he approached her and told her to
kill Gary Hinman for his money, she found herself considering it. When
he came to her, made her feel insignificant by telling her she belonged
in the kitchen, and then challenged her to prove herself with this dirty
deed, the immediate thought that rose up inside her was to the tune of
an adolescent "I'll show you." By this time, with the war bringing reports
of deaths and destruction, and with riot chaos daily, not to mention the
highly publicized assassinations of Martin Luther King Jr. and Robert F.
Kennedy (only years after the assassination of John F. Kennedy), essential
and necessary murder, as a lesser evil for a greater cause, was a growing
theme everywhere. Evidently, it wasn't a huge leap for Atkins to think that
Hinman might be a necessary martyr for Manson's brave and godly cause.

To Die for a Cause

Differing from some of the other senseless murders this group would
commit, Gary Hinman was actually a personal friend of the Manson
Family. When Atkins, Beausoleil, and fellow Family member Mary Brun-
ner approached his house, he welcomed them in with a smile. The story
is disturbing, not simply because it is of murder, but because of the gentleness this man showed from the moment they entered his house and
his true love for fellow man and detestation for violence, even until his
untimely end. At one moment, according to witness testimonies, during a tussle, he even managed to get his hands on the gun, which he
subserviently handed back to Beausoleil, saying that he didn't believe in
violence. When Manson showed up and slashed Hinman's face and ear
with a sword, he merely fell to the floor and cried, refusing to retaliate,
and saying naught but a reminder to Manson that he thought Manson

was his friend. Atkins, terrified to the point of shaking, cared for Hinman's wounds and fed him soup, to which he replied by calling her an angel. (Her reaction was to simply leave the room, because his kindness in the midst of such hostility disturbed her.) This went on for days; no amount of coaxing from the Manson clan would change Hinman's story that he didn't have any money. Atkins described this time as surreal and unreal. Eventually convinced that Hinman was telling the truth, his tormenters finally coerced him to sign over the papers on his vehicles, then Beausoleil saw no way out of the situation but to cover the ordeal with murder.

In the days following (Beausoleil left the Family with the intention to come back when things had cooled off), everyone was shaken, and several departed from the ranch for good, leaving only the radicals without any sounding board to play off each other's paranoia and insanity. Soon, twenty-four-hour "guards" (Family tough guys) were chosen by Manson to stand watch. Manson preached Helter Skelter like never before, imploring everyone to be prepared for anything, a kill-or-be-killed fire driving his words now. Everyone in the Family truly believed in it.

When Beausoleil was arrested for Hinman's murder, the Family was programmed thus: "He's our brother.... Our enemy has him in its territory and we have to get him out!"[28] Atkins upped her drug use to crystal speed, methedrine, and, while constantly stoned, she developed a friendship with Watson, still obeying Manson's orders and jumping on the bandwagon to free Beausoleil. When Manson told her on the evening of August 8, 1969, to grab her knife and go with Watson, she knew in her gut that the "copycat" murders to make Beausoleil look innocent were going to take place. Despite her nearly buried conscience still reaching to her with whatever warning it had left, she obeyed.

In her book, at this moment in the story, Atkins takes full responsibility for her actions, detailing the fact that, although under the extreme influence of crystal meth, she was razor sharp in her consciousness and alert to what was going to happen. With Hinman so recently on her mind, she knew that the Family was capable of true murder, and that this was not simply a child's game that would end in empty threats and somebody's front door getting egged. Manson continued to give most of the direction to Watson out of Atkins' earshot and he communicated much less directly with the girls, but she still knew what the plan was: They were to go to the house that Terry Melcher had lived in before, take all the money they could get their hands on, and then kill everyone present. The undertones that pop out from the pages in the way she describes the moments leading up to these murders speak of someone inexplicably torn between what she clearly knows is right and wrong; unendingly devoted to what she thinks is a righteous cause; and who, in the midst of everything, finds herself getting into the car with a knife and a group of uncompromising revolutionary extremists spinning out of control at breakneck speed toward a goal she didn't even understand—merely out of obedience. Yet, despite how confusing it all had been, a flash of real, untouched-by-Manson clarity hit her. As she writes in her book, this was the instant she truly grasped and understood true, pure evil, and that she, *herself*, was evil.[29]

As you well know, she followed through with the orders she had been given to participate in the Cielo Drive murders.

When the reality of the malevolence that she and the others committed that night surfaced within her, Atkins had a reaction that many who are familiar with Scripture will recognize as the final tipping point wherein something supernatural completely takes over—perhaps possession? She plopped down on her bed and felt "dead"; it wasn't like the absence of energy, but like the absence of literal life. She goes on to say: "I have no explanation for how hardened I had become in only a few hours. As I watched the TV reporters, *I even laughed* as they described the details of the horror."[30]

Insane? Misguided? Possessed? A blend of all three?

IT'S OVER

The Bible that made its way into Atkins' hands did not arrive with a flooding of fan mail. On the contrary, Atkins was a very unpopular person. She had carried out crimes against humanity in the slayings, of course, but what most people don't know is that, although the news and headlines all over the nation showed Atkins holding hands and singing down the halls with fellow Family killers Krenwinkel and Van Houten during the murder trials, it was all a front.

Raids and Final Arrest

The famously photographed raid on the Spahn Ranch on August 16, 1969 (around a week after all the killing began), resulted in little media interest at the time. The headlines may as well have said, "Big Freeloading Hippie Group Arrested Saturday in Connection with Auto Theft," which was hardly news in those parts. Those arrested were released with slightly more than a "don't do it again" warning from the judge. However, to members of the Family, who didn't know what they were being arrested for and who woke up with double barrels pointed at their foreheads by the SWAT team that *easily* got past Manson's guard monkeys, it was all over. When they were unexpectedly released, a rush of relief flowed over them as they quickly packed their bags and headed into hiding at Barker Ranch.

Barker Ranch was a great hiding place for the killers, but it also served the purpose of being a place to begin their final search for the prophesied hole in the ground. It happened to be located in Death Valley, where the whites from the blessed Family would burrow their way into the earth with foodstuff and supplies and make love, not war, until the race war was over and Manson would rise as king. Yet, one of the most important needs for the Family would still (and seemingly always) be vehicles, so despite their lower profile and better hiding spot, auto theft (and an arson charge) eventually led to a follow-up raid at the Family's new home that October. For several, this would be the last time they ever tasted freedom. Charlie was officially booked (photo and fingerprints to match) as "Manson, Charles M., aka [also known as] Jesus Christ, God."[31]

While being held, another member of the Manson Family who had not been as gung-ho for the whole war plan implicated Atkins and others in the Hinman murder. This time, it really was over. Unless Manson had some supernatural trick up his sleeve, the disciples had done their part for "Jesus" and the world would have to unravel Helter Skelter without them, as Manson and his closest followers would soon be charged with murder.

A Family Disbanded

The newly incarcerated and still-devoted, deranged Atkins found herself at the height of her confusing and energized identity crisis in the Helter Skelter apocalypse as she befriended her new cellmates. Somewhere between the need to confess her guilt and the need to brag about her role in going about "God's" work, the secrets she held about the Tate murders (still a highly publicized case of mystery in the media) were boiling within her like a raging volcano, threatening to compel her to tell all. When her cellmates continued to put forth whodunit theories while the Tate/LaBianca murders were being reported not to have a known culprit, she simply couldn't keep everything to herself any longer, and exploded into intermittent storytelling sessions, claiming to have been the killer of the actress. Her new cellmates, with their own benefit in mind, quickly came forward with this information in hopes of striking a deal for their own release. Her confessions, Atkins reflects, were the ultimate severance of any trust that her Family would ever place in her again.

During the trials, she walked the halls in song and hand-in-hand with her "sisters," smiling, clowning around, making fun of the press groups, carving x's into her forehead, shaving her head, and acting proud. Behind the scenes, however, the other girls had already disowned her and considered her a heretic. She often disrupted the court proceedings alongside Krenwinkel, Van Houten, and Manson, and was even escorted out of the courtroom on occasion. Her behavior was often of one who had carried out murder with girlish glee, and who couldn't possibly hold any remorse or comprehension of the seriousness and weight of her crimes. (It was ultimately this behavior, along with telling Tate that she had no mercy for her while Tate begged for her life, that was most likely the biggest reason for her never being approved for parole.) But when the trials were over and Atkins was stationed on death row with her Family sisters, they instantaneously dropped the act and regarded her as the tattletale she was. There were also whispers around the prison that they were planning to kill her.[32] There's no telling what Manson thought of her then.

HE CAME TO ME IN MY CELL

The Bible... A pretty one, with her named etched on the front, just like the award Bible from so long ago. It had remained untouched since the day it had arrived at her cell. That day, she had opened the cover long enough to see the prayer the caring woman had written, asking Jesus to personally reveal Himself to Atkins. Feeling that she had seen and heard too much confusion about this man named "Jesus" who was also God, Atkins tossed the book in a box in the corner, where it stayed for several years.

By now, Atkins was well aware that the man she had followed into the depths of lunacy was not the biblical Christ. And, after separation from the cult and drugs, her head was starting to clear; it had finally started to dawn on her that because the Helter Skelter prophecy was nothing more than rubbish, everything she had ever stood for and done had been in vain.

Now completely alone in her cell with her conspiring cohorts within constant earshot, Atkins reached a level of loneliness that made the rest of her life look like a homey Thanksgiving dinner feast. Society had disowned her. Her "family" had severed her from the fold. The "god" she had followed had failed her, and wanted nothing to do with her. Her sense of importance to the good of the world had blown up in her face and exposed her as nothing more than a silly kid with hallucinatory ideals of grandeur in the interest of a go-nowhere plot that had festered in the drug-altered bowels of delusion. And she had helped end lives for that goal.

She was not a soldier of Christ.

She was dead inside.

She was nothing.

Not long after these feelings had taken over her completely, a woman came with good news. Tax dollars would provide prisoners with the materials to earn a degree—this included Atkins, now serving a life sentence and no longer on death row (but still in the special security unit because she was "too famous"[33] to be held elsewhere). Having been sent ministerial tracts and letters from a small list of people who still cared about her spiritual condition over the years ("Old Bruce" from the Family days was one of them), and having the time, privacy, and mental faculties to read and understand them, Atkins' thoughts slowly began to thaw from her previously radical, faulty ideas of Christ. A small, but guarded, interest crept into her, just the tiniest light that distracted her from her guilt and pulled her away from feeling completely dead inside. It happened every time she heard or read the name "Jesus," and she grew increasingly aware of how little she knew Him outside of the messy Manson episode. She agreed to pursue a career degree, and, just as much out of boredom as curiosity at the time, she began taking classes about religion and Christianity.

One day, a visitor, an old friend from San José, came to her prison. As this man spoke about Jesus, His care, and His free offering of salvation for Atkins, the small stirring within her to know Jesus personally inflated into a need, a want. Though she haughtily resisted his testimony of what Jesus had offered her friend, she was aware of the spiritual battle raging deeply for her attention and focus.

When a letter from Old Bruce arrived challenging her to read the Bible and pray that God would help her find what she was looking for, she once again turned up her nose to the suggestion, but her resistance would not last.

Then came a dream. The beginning was confusing, but the end was perfectly clear. An entity walked gracefully through a crowd of people who instantly fell to their knees in worship. This entity was not Manson. It was not even human. It was something, *someone*, else. As this someone made his way to Atkins in her dream, the beautiful plants under his feet were unaffected by the weight of each step; they sprang back into a perfect shape behind him. She describes such picturesque surroundings. As he approached her, she saw that he was much taller and stronger than she had initially realized. Her attention was finely tuned when he regarded her directly, tapping her on the top of her head and telling her that he wanted her to think about her indifference to him.

She awoke instantly, sweaty and cold…and scared.

Later on, Atkins retrieved the Bible from its box. As she opened it again, she reread the kind woman's note, which instructed her to read Isaiah 43:25: "I, even I, am he that blotteth out thy transgressions for mine own sake and will not remember thy sin." Following the advice of Old Bruce, Atkins finally spoke to Jesus, the *real* Jesus, asking Him to reveal Himself to her personally, and then she turned the pages, soaking up every word like a sponge.

In no time, starting from Genesis 1:1, Atkins plowed through the Word, reacting to it in a way she never saw coming. She describes in her book a very strange frustration she held against the Israelites for their transgressions against God. When God delivered them from Egypt—after everything they had done, never deserving that kind of loyalty—and then they complained in the wilderness after the parting of the Red Sea event had been such an inspirational and miraculous act of grace, that was just too much. When Moses climbed Mt. Sinai to receive the ultimate list of rules to live by for the people below, just to descend and see that the Israelites had yet again forsaken their own God for a golden calf, an inanimate object, things reached a boiling point in Atkins' thinking: How could these people continuously reject the very entity that gave them creation, life, authority over the things of the earth, food, water, shelter, safe passage, and endless forgiveness and love?

The truth overwhelmed her, hitting her as hard and fast as a freight train. Suddenly it was clear: She had been just like an Israelite. She had broken every one of the Ten Commandments. She had done it alone. Nobody had committed her sins for her. She had full responsibility; there was no way around it. Manson had not forced her hand. Her own golden calf at the foot of Mt. Sinai had been carved and formed by her own sins, and she was guilty—not just guilty according to the courts, but guilty according to truth as it is written.

Days passed in her lonely cell, offering still no companion and nothing but guilt—an elevated and enlightened guilt. This feeling needled at her with newfound determination, causing more discomfort. Yet, she felt farther and farther away from what she had been the longer that she studied the ancient, blessed passages. Being reminded of Revelation 3:20, "Behold, I stand at the door, and knock: if any man hear my voice, and open the door, I will come in to him, and will sup with him, and he with me," Atkins at last yielded. She wanted forgiveness. She knew that society would never forgive her for her horrible acts against humanity, and she knew that spending the rest of her life behind bars would not take away the harm she had helped cause to those innocent victims and their relatives. Simply resigning herself to "what's done is done" and "there's nothing more I can do" would never bring her closure, as she knew it wasn't true any longer. There was one thing she always could have, and *should have*, done.

She closed her eyes and prayed that if Jesus were there, He would come in. She heard a voice, though she admits it wasn't yet literal or audible, tell her that she had to be the one to open the door. As if she had always known what to do, she closed her eyes, imagining a door, and watched herself open it in her mind's eye. White, radiant light fell in and encircled her, removing her from the black she had been standing in. A Man appeared as the source of the light, even brighter, Himself. It was Jesus.

The words in Atkins' prison cell became audible as He spoke to her. He told her that she was not dreaming, that this was really happening, that He was really here, that she was being born again at that moment, and that she was now a child of God. Then, much like the deer who panteth for water and is finally led to drink, He told her that her sins were washed away and that she was *forgiven*.[34] To some reading this book, it might be hard to comprehend, but Atkins went on to celebrate the sudden, powerful, and complete eradication of all guilty feelings within her. She felt fresh, clean, and alive. For the first time in her life, by giving her heart to the Lord and asking Jesus to come into her heart, she felt completely free. Not "Manson free." She felt completely guiltless in a way that was unrelated to anything Manson had taught her about feelings of guilt.

That night, she says, was the first night in longer than she could remember that she slept soundly, deeply, and without nightmares.

BORN AGAIN

Everybody around Atkins, including her cellmates and the prison staff, noticed the change. Anyone who attempted to rile her, to return her new attitude to the old one, was unsuccessful, and left puzzled. Atkins wanted to share her new happiness with anyone who would listen, but, sadly, nobody in that surrounding would hear her.

Signing up for the M-2 program, which sent a single visitor on regular visits to an assigned prisoner in her area, Atkins found a new sister, Stephanie, a new family member, but this time the connection was through the true Christ. Atkins openly shared with Stephanie the details of her conversion and the deep feelings of forgiveness that Christ had freely given her. In late 1974, Atkins attended the first church service she had been to in eleven years at a modest prison building just outside of her special security unit. When her presence was announced, she wasn't given the cold shoulder or attitude of judgment that she had expected. Instead, she was applauded as she stood there in the presence of her fellow inmates, tears streaming down her face. A unanimous "amen" rose from the voices in the room as she publicly thanked Jesus for allowing her to be there.

In an interview a couple of years later, in 1976, with Stan Atkinson, just after her first parole hearing and seven years into her imprisonment,

Atkins conveyed her acceptance of Christ and her peaceful reception of her life sentence:

ATKINSON: Can you understand why many people, perhaps *most* people outside, are going to feel that you don't deserve parole; that you should *never* be given parole? You are aware of that?

ATKINS: Yes.

ATKINSON: Well, so what if you spend the rest of your life in this prison?

ATKINS: Then I spend the rest of my life in this prison.

ATKINSON: Is that thought depressing to you, though?

ATKINS: No, because I know that, um… How can I put it? I'm *content*. I found that peace is not determined by my situation or my circumstance or my physical surroundings.

ATKINSON: How does it come about?

ATKINS: How does *peace* come about? *My* peace?

ATKINSON: M-hm.

ATKINS: Well I found my peace through salvation in Jesus, and just knowing that I've been forgiven by God is sufficient for me.

ATKINSON: And the fact that you know that, out there, people probably can't forgive you—

ATKINS: Yes.

ATKINSON: —has no effect on you?

ATKINS: No. Because they're not the ones that I have to face in the end, when I die. I have to face God and it's His forgiveness that determines my peace.[35]

On February 23, 1975, Atkins was baptized by immersion in front of ten witnesses by Sergeant Wright, the man who had led her mother to Christ years before.

In 1977, Atkins wrote and had published *Child of Satan, Child of God*. Her book became a number-one best seller, and every dime of the royalties went to the New Life Foundation with the intention to open a safe house for women suffering from abuse. Atkins' book ends with a sinner's prayer, available for any reader wishing to give his or her life to the Lord.[36]

Atkins went on to begin a prison ministry to reach out to young people with involvement in drugs, cults, or gangs, and she was well known throughout her life as a model prisoner who helped inmates whenever possible. She began a newsletter that grew to reach hundreds of subscribers, achieved many worthy accomplishments, and won several awards for the works that came of her ministry.[37] (See the "Interview with Charles 'Tex' Watson" section of this book for his personal observations of her later years and ministry, and the effects she had on others.)

In 1987, Atkins married James Whitehouse, a Harvard Law graduate, who stood by her from that day until the end of her life, and represented her at her 2000 and 2005 parole hearings.

On September 24, 2009, after having been denied parole for a compassionate release, Atkins passed away from brain cancer. As covered by *ABC News* on that day, Atkins was wheeled into a room by prison staff and her husband, and they read her the Twenty-third Psalm, allowing her to speak the final word of every line. (The cancer had paralyzed more than 85 percent of her body, so she was no longer physically able to read the entire passage without assistance.)[38] Susan Atkins' last word on this earth was "Amen."[39]

INTERVIEW with Jason Freeman
(Charles Manson's grandson)

In order to gain further insight on those affected by the darker events of 1969, the publishing team behind this book reached out to Charles Manson's grandson, Jason Freeman, telling him about our book. Upon hearing about our mission, he agreed to this interview. We sent him a list of questions composed by several people in our publishing group, as well as by Thomas Horn and Donna Howell.

BETWEEN DONNA HOWELL, DEFENDER PUBLISHING GROUP AND JASON FREEMAN, CHARLES MANSON'S GRANDSON AND BIOLOGICAL SON OF CHARLES MANSON JR. EMAILS BETWEEN JUNE 17–JULY 14, 2014

Although you were not a direct victim of the events that transpired in 1969, because of your lineage, you have been dealt a rougher road than many. Your biological father, Charles Manson Jr., direct son of Charles Manson, took his own life. What were things like for him, and for you?

I personally feel there were *many* victims in the Manson case. Of course there were the families who lost their loved ones through the times of the killings. The ripple effect carried long and wide. My mind cannot fathom what they have gone through personally and the national attention that was stirred up from this act of violence. The victims carried over into my life also. I lost a father (Charlie Manson, Jr.). We could have been friends, coworkers, fishing buddies, physical training partners, artists. Many things have crossed my mind. If he would have given me a chance to be his son, maybe he would have seen the love I carried and made a different choice that day. Perhaps I could have saved a life that day if he would have called me, gotten to know me as the young man I had become. He could have influenced me, or I him, to be a better person. He was a victim his whole life.

My father was, I believe, the age of twelve when *his* father, Charles Manson, committed those crimes. I can see my father being misled even up until then. That's when the downhill slide started for him as a young child. It makes more sense to me now as to why he stayed far away from me, to protect me from a distance. He now carried the name of the most notorious killer of all times. He became a victim as did the others, because of his blood relations. My uncle told me I can call him anytime I want to hear about my father. They were close. He has explained how every step of Junior's life was *very* hard as he fought his way out of many dark places throughout his days, along with battling the literal demons that were trapped in his head. There were unanswered questions and unanswered letters from my grandfather as he grew up. I asked my grandfather why he never wrote him back, expressing that Junior just wanted to know his father, also. He responded saying, "It was a crazy time and I received so many letters that I didn't know who was real." A victim, my father was, and little did I know I was going to grow into understanding I am also a victim of the choices that were made in 1969.

I was born September 2, 1976, son of Charlie Manson Jr., also known as "Jay White." My mother is Shawn Freeman. I took my mother's last name for many reasons. "Jay" is phonetic for "J," which is short for "Jr.," my grandfather tells me. My grandmother, Rosie [Rosalie], married a man named Jack White. This is how my father became "Jay White." They changed his name and moved to a new location in an attempt to protect his childhood, but sadly, it didn't work. His new name was never legalized, so on record he would remain "Charlie Manson, Jr." He, himself, could not live a normal life. He was a victim until the day I then became a victim. It was my freshman year, 1992, when he took his own life. (Or did he?! That answer will never truly be known.)

Six months or so after a few visits to Charlie Manson, Sr., his life was over. No more Charlie Manson, Jr. I, Jason Freeman, am also a victim of the events of 1969. But, I work in many ways to give my wife and kids more than I have ever had to create a better life for them.

How well did you know your natural father before his death?

I only have memories through photos and a few short letters, phone calls, and Christmas gifts. My first Nintendo as a kid came from him in the mail, along with other gifts. For some reason my family received a monthly check for around $700 from his death until I graduated. That's how we could afford my Claymont letterman's jacket I still have today. There are other memories that will always be in my heart and mind.

You and a friend have written a book, Knocking Out the Devil, *which documents your life story. The title is a play on words, considering your choice career for a time as a fighter. Can you tell us about your years as a Mixed Martial Arts (MMA) fighter using the name Charles Manson III? Were you a Christian during that time, and do you plan to return to MMA?*

We decided to write my story as my fight career came to an end, as that just seemed to be the correct timing. I ended a "pro" career at 13-6-1 [thirteen wins, six losses, one draw] with a win over Jason Riley in the first round. Weeks later, my wife and I found out we were having our third child together. No better reason to step out of the ring and save my body and mind for a career to take care of my family. As the fame of being a fighter faded, I gained back a certain focus on my family that I was unaware I had placed on the back burner while I lived a self-focused lifestyle.

It started in 1999, when I was married to a young woman and we had a daughter. When I finally came home after a tough road in prison, my wife at the time no longer wanted me around. I had landed a good job and was providing well for my family, and I had a new baby girl, yet I still ended up fighting for visitations in 2000. It was not a good time for me. I felt the atmosphere she was creating for our daughter with her new romantic relationships was unsafe for both my daughter and myself. The anger inside of me was so elevated that I didn't know what to do, so I channeled that anger into what became my career within the ring, trying to keep my mind on training hard and making a change. I started living with a good friend (thank you Kenny!) who helped my decision making processes, which aided in keeping me from repeat criminal offenses. Little did I know God had a plan. I couldn't see it at the time those fires of anger burned within me.

My career as a fighter was in full swing when I met my current wife, Audrey, in 2004. Our kids came slowly afterward. (Audrey and I have grown together through the years during struggles that cause many couples to grow apart. We are a team. A team under God. I give any of my success as a husband and father to God the Almighty and to my wife. I've had to redeem myself for my past, and she had to forgive me, which she has done.)

I achieved a lot with my career in the twelve years I competed. At one point, I came across an opportunity that may have opened some doors: tryouts for the ultimate fighter for the UFC [Ultimate Fighting Championship]. I went under the name Charles Manson III. Why, one might ask? Well, no one knew me from the next guy, and I had to be willing to step out and be noticed. There were over four hundred men there and they took maybe ten. I got cut fast, like the rest. I grappled with Jason Guida, brother of well-known fighter Clay Guida.

My MMA career had consisted of many hours per day training my body, much travel, and the forced juggling of training while running here and there and booking flights, etc. It wasn't the easiest thing I've ever done. But letting the love of the fight world go was also incredibly hard. I felt like it ripped my heart out. I stood in my gym and cried at times, asking God why this had to happen: Why twelve years for this cause, and now nothing…just like that.

The day that my eyes opened to how I had been living—putting my family behind me so they could not walk beside me—I ran into the house and sat with my family in shame. I hadn't seen it for what it was, and now that I could, I knew I had to give it up. As I walked to the cage on my final fight, I asked God, "How many more?" I didn't know that this was going to be it. It played out in that minute and a half or so: my role in life all in one short fight. Here I was, knocked down on my back (having made the wrong move), a six-foot-ten, two-hundred-seventy-five pound man on top of me, wanting this fight as much as me. I realized that this was a defining moment. For me, it was like life holding you down when you fall, right? Hard to get up sometimes; sometimes you just want to lay there, give up, let go!

Something from deep within me, or maybe a set of hands behind me, lifted me to my feet. I heard, "You may lose one day, but not today!" The Frontline Warrior that lives inside of me [see page 56] took over at that moment and I was up. I wasn't thinking, just reacting to the fight. I threw a nice combination and he ended up on his back in the same place I was just a few moments earlier. I continued to go at him until he tapped out and the referee intervened. That was one of my glory moments in my career, and I feel that it's just the same in life. We have our ups, our downs, and then our *real* lows that we refuse to ever go back to. I feel that I am a very fortunate man in many ways that God has moved in my life.

I really enjoy telling my story and I hope that it helps to inspire others, as my wife is also doing now. She has inspired me to stay in shape after my days as a fighter. I have now turned from a fighter to family man. Jaelee, my firstborn and my little girl, will always know how to find me. She has a place in my heart and always will. My home is her home. She called me last year and told me that whatever happens, she forgives me and wants to know me, and that when she is old enough to come find me, she will. I told her that I loved her, and she offered those precious words back. I feel saddened and often tormented that she is largely without a fatherly presence in her life. Yet, I cannot deny that God is fully aware of all of these circumstances, and He has a plan. I owe it all to God's grace and forgiveness and my patient wife and kids that I am who I am right now.

And one amazing thing that rose up to replace the fame and hype of my fighting career was a new stage, the *real* stage that God built under my feet along the way. Now I am involved in ministry.

How did you come to know Christ personally?

I personally came to know Christ through time and circumstances. It seemed to me that I went through trials and rough roads for the Lord to guide me back to a brighter path. It's hard for me to put an exact date on when I accepted Christ into my heart, but I remember the account.

When I was sitting in the county jail in 1999, heading to prison for selling marijuana, I had to look around me and ask myself if this was the path I was willing to travel. One inmate in the county jail was an ordained minister. He was in the cell next to mine. I spent a lot of time alone, reflecting on what was becoming of me. It wasn't my first trip to the county jail, but it was my first time going to prison. I needed answers, and needed them right then. I sat down with Mr. Washington one day, who also stayed mostly to himself. He had a Bible in his hands, and he was reading. I asked if I could join him. We sat and went through Scripture for a while. We shared some of our personal stories with each other and even joined hands in prayer at one point. I wanted to gain the understanding of the supernatural faith through the knowing of God's Word, and I wanted to discern how to apply this knowledge toward achieving a better life and behavior. Mr. Washington instructed me to start with the book of John. It was to be a good baseline of how Jesus moved across the land healing the sick and raising the dead.

I accepted Jesus Christ into my life and heart that day. It did *not* mean that my life was automatically turned around. The fight was on. I accepted Christ, and the devil came at me even harder. The way I lived before was still beside me, calling to me to remain or return. I felt a battle raging inside of me daily. I was thinking more about the future, striving to know more, to understand what I could not see. I've felt the Lord's presence around me a lot in my young adult years as I accepted Christ into my life. He is here to stay; He fought the fights I didn't know were even there, and carried me when I let Him down.

There may be times in the lives of others that mirror some of the moments I've had in mine. Sometimes I take three steps forward, make a big mistake, and take four steps back. When I spent my time locked up for over six months, I had to deal with a lot of life issues. Crack drug dealers were saying I was a "black man hater" (despite having African American friends) and I seemed to get pushed around; others thought I was arrogant. It was tough to make a real lifestyle change while locked in a cell. I was looking for peace in my heart and understanding in my mind, all the while looking over my shoulder, protectively, at those around me that would threaten my safety. I got into a few fights while locked up. (My grandfather's name never came up.) I stuck to my guns, but I tried not to carry a tough-guy attitude. Kept my head as clear as I could so I could lead a different path. The starting of one: a long road, with different options than I've ever seen before. It seemed to come off as a weakness to others. I was a certain target in those days.

After I was cleared to leave the center that I had been transferred to from prison, the road went back to the same *me*: back to the world. I had to ask the question, "Had this been a jailhouse Jesus experience for me? Or was it real?" I walked a rough path getting back out: old friends coming around, drugs everywhere, and turmoil between myself and those whose relationships were the most important to me. I knew I had to stay strong on the Word of God to see a different light, maybe a new path for us.

I joined a local church. New Life Community Church. Attending there was initially a little different of an atmosphere, but I had no basis of comparison for what a church should feel like. What I didn't realize was that it was going to be an always-changing motion of events that would lead me toward where we, my wife and kids and I, are today. We are all active in New Point Community Church. To this day, I still struggle, but not with the same issues I was faced with as a young man. These newer battles are of a spiritual nature, a fight for the ability to see more clearly and for what's ahead of me. I'm not falling down or tripping as often or in the same ways as before. Glory be to God for all that He has done. My wife, Audrey, is a one-of-a-kind lady, and she has helped me become the man I today. If it weren't for her sticking through the past ten years beside me I would not have been so focused on change. I changed to be a better husband to Audrey and father to my kids. I love you Sam, Max, and Ajay!

Since your retirement as a fighter, you have gone on to create a great ministry for youth, correct? Please tell us about this ministry.

I've always enjoyed seeing the best come out in others. It seems as if I carry a lot of infectious energy and people tend to pick up on that and take action for themselves. If I wasn't so open to bringing people in to my training circles, many of them may not have moved in a direction of their own change. This is the real stage God was lifting under me as I was pursuing my fighting career.

We as a team (me and the training centers I have always been involved with) conceived a vision of helping others. We call it "Frontline Warriors." It's a nonprofit organization.

MIND, BODY, and SPIRIT: In this world, this is what we have. We need all three to keep a proper balance through our walk. The purpose of Frontline Warriors is to give hope to the hopeless, faith to the faithless, and to have a safe, hands-on environment for young kids to be active, constructed with a youth wrestling and self-defense program. So far, we have created a list of a few school districts that we travel to each year and talk to the kids about everyday life and events they may face. We try to help them understand how the choices they make today will stay with them for life. We teach: If you're down, find a way up, don't look to someone else to fix something; make it your personal choice to get back up and move forward; don't live looking in the rearview mirror, because you will miss the present and not be able to focus on the future. I enjoy sharing my story with them from being a young kid on through my young adult years. I hope that it has inspired families to hear how a young man with all the cards stacked against him never gave up. A "never give up attitude" and "learn to get up faster" have always been sayings in my life.

I've traveled and gained understanding from my mistakes and falls. I just want to continue as a positive mentor while having my mentors above myself that hold me accountable for my steps forward.

Do you believe that your unique position as Manson's grandson has given you a platform to connect with troubled youth in a more profound way?

Working with troubled youth can have its ups and downs as you begin to see how they have lived and learn who they are. I feel that by being a professional athlete, growing up as the "bad kid," with a notorious lineage including the name Charles Manson, it's all a unique story that can break the ice and touch the bases of communication in almost anyone's life. Young to old! I really enjoy the one-on-one in groups with kids. I get to see their interest and goals, and maybe plant a seed for the future that they may not have had prior to our meeting. God has set me up to move forward as a result of my experience in life. It's been a long, rough road, but well worth the good and hard times.

As you know, this book is about the Lord's forgiveness to people who are often regarded by society as unforgivable. Your voice comes from an exceptional angle, because you were not a relative to the victims of the Manson Family, but you were, even if indirectly, wounded by what transpired. And as you were not a direct victim, you are also the voice of the general public. What would you have to say about the subject of forgiveness as it pertains to the public?

The word "forgiveness" has always been a hard word for us as humans to wrap our minds around.

According to my grandfather ("Look at what Hollywood painted, the courts got what they wanted and still make millions off of me!"), society in general will not forget, *or forgive*, the scene of 1969 still painted to this day. I've gotten to know Charles Manson personally in the past two and a half years, and all we seem to talk about is Jesus Christ, my family, and doing the right thing for my kids as they grow. We are often placed into situations that we have to forget, not so much forgive. But we must set things behind us in order to move forward. If you take the plain-as-day, open-minded view of the situation: All young kids who are very drugged up for a long period of time make very bad choices, yes! More than we will ever know of in all reality. They all *make a choice* to be influenced along the way. I can see that as well as anyone. We all have to hold our own with the choices we make. I personally think there is a spiritual point of forgiveness for us all. When we truly confess our sins and turn from our selfish ways to a new path, our past is behind us. Jesus Christ died for our sins and I'm a true believer of that. Each and every person will make the choice to know Christ or turn their head.

Making mistakes in my own life, followed by having to redeem myself, has been one of the hardest things I've ever done. From fighting in the ring to working my tail off at work. I think sticking to who I am on the inside with Jesus beside me, carrying me at times, defines what I believe in. I never give up, and I never roll over and back down from a challenge. If forgiveness was not real and the Truth of God's Word was false [and not made flesh], then I would not be married to my beautiful wife today. If I was never forgiven for the choices I've made, I'd have a lot of people that don't care for me. Everyone needs a second *and third* chance through this path of life. Redemption builds a stronger you. I'm a living example of forgiveness and redemption.

Susan Atkins of the Manson Family reportedly gave her heart to the Lord and wrote a book telling the story of how she came to Christ. Do you believe that she can be forgiven, and that she is sincere in her conversion?

As stated above, I believe in forgiveness. If Susan had the transformation *in her heart* to accept Jesus Christ as her personal savior, her past was behind her; the trials and strongholds were behind her at that point. It's not always a forgiveness from society that will change who you really are. It's the final sacrifice of Jesus' death that is needed for us to live beyond our sin. I believe that without forgiveness, we as humans would have no hope in life.

We have been in contact with Charles "Tex" Watson, the main man behind most Manson-related murders. He currently professes Christianity, and has a profound ministry operated primarily online. Do you believe that his turning to Christ was sincere? Would you have any words for him at this time?

If Mr. Watson was blessed by God to have a touching ministry that reaches out and helps change lives in this world, he must be sincere and gifted in God's grace. A man that conducted crimes that he is guilty of and sent to prison can relate to a lot of walks of life. I can see his time behind bars being challenging and overall very terrifying at the time of incarceration. We all know change comes through time and wisdom, accepting the path you're on while helping others who are facing the same fears in life. For a man that was lost in this world in the '60s, on drugs, and following a criminal path and mindset, *change* was his only way out. Accepting Jesus and repenting is the only way for the path to redeeming what he would have left as a man. I couldn't picture or imagine an entire life or the majority of life behind bars.

A note for Mr. Watson: When I was wrapped up in this world myself, it was all about me and my moves were to benefit me and the group I ran with. I can picture me being on the path you have led. No doubt in my mind. I was there just a few decades apart from you. With me personally hitting rock bottom I almost thought, *This is where I'll always be.* I had to reach to somewhere besides what was around me. There was no help or hope. I turned to reading the Bible and seeking some understanding of change. Just like you, I see. I was on the road to losing my wife and (at the time two) boys. Trouble! Always right beside me as if it were inside of me. Human nature! Yes, we as humans have a sinful nature that we only see when we are caught or land on our face time and time again. In life I have had to learn to get up faster. Life (and Satan) will hold us down if we're on that path. As we're coming off of that path to finding our new selves, Satan comes at us harder. We are no threat while we're on his side of the fence. It's when we work for the Other Guy (God) that makes him worry. As we team up together with God to recruit people for His kingdom, so do those on the other side. We're making progress, and peoples' lives are being changed; generations after us will be saved…

Let's get to work, we're behind!

In your book, you made it clear that although you had made attempt to gain contact with your grandfather, he never responded to you. That has changed now, as you mentioned in previous email exchange with us. If the opportunity were to present itself, would you make an effort to share with him the gospel of Christ?

As I mentioned prior, my grandfather and I have been in contact for about two and a half years now, once we came to a understanding of who I really was, and that I've know of him all my life. We created a friendship. Like he told me once, "I'm not a 'grandpa'; I don't know how to be your grandfather. I am me."

He personally contacted me after I released the book *Knocking Out the Devil*. He speaks about the title of the book often. "*Knocking Out the Devil*, man you must be crazy if you think you can knock out the devil. He's everywhere we turn." I have come to agree with him. The book was titled such based off of the Hollywood version of Manson and not based off of what I've learned through conversations and letters. He truly understands the gospel as outlined in the Bible and repeats it often as if he is one with where we all need to be in Christ. It's a different, less conventional gospel than what many believe, as coming from a man locked up for most of his life, having to raise himself and put his own food on the table through his childhood. My kids wouldn't make it in these conditions. They depend on my wife and me. He did it, made it through life on his own, and seems to have a different aspect on life than most. I personally would like to visit him as often as I could before he passes. No hidden agendas, just as a grandson to a grandfather. I've tried to create an image for him in the first year: my life, my family, pictures of what we do and places we go as a family, all to give him an understanding of who I am as a person. Husband and father, provider in any way a man should be.

Our journey will continue as our walk becomes closer in life. He relates our relationship as father to son. He never has had either. Now I'm here! What's next?

Is there anything else you would like to share with a reading audience while you have the platform to do so?

I used to look in the mirror for years not knowing where I was going or what I was doing in my life. I look back now and see it was all for a better tomorrow.

I would like to encourage each and every person: Reach higher than your mind can take you for your dreams, and don't stop because you fall down once or twice. It's not about whether you fall; we will all fall. It's about how you learn to get back up faster. When you can master the art of getting back up, you will start taking a different path to be successful the next time. Consider changing those you surrounded yourself with, the places you frequent, and the habits you have. I'm now spending a lot of time with my wife and three boys, training, working in the oil fields, and running a small business in my local community. I'm a personal speaker, starting the foundation of a youth-oriented nonprofit. My goals are to give back more than I ever received in my life, and help create opportunity for others. I was at one time trapped in a tornado that seemed to have no exit. Through time and a lot of praying for understanding, I am at a happier place in my life. The shadow of my family history and lineage has not and will not knock me back to where I once was as a lost young man. I have come a long way through the dirtiest parts of life in thirty-seven years and I refuse to be set back. If and when bad things come my way, my mind and heart carry a clear understanding of my path and what way I need to go.

If you fall, get back up, and if you fall again, get back up faster. Trust Jesus. He will carry you.

———

Jason Freeman now lives with his wife, Audrey, and his boys, Sam, Max, and Ajay, in Ohio. He currently works the oil fields, owns a small business, and participates in outreaches for troubled youth via the Frontline Warriors program. He maintains contact with his grandfather, Charles Manson, and hopes to see that relationship mature in the future.

CASE STUDY 2

CHARLES "TEX" WATSON[40]

It was nine o'clock in the evening on August 9, 1969. The drive from Lake Isabella to Los Angeles, California, was approximately one hundred fifty miles. Leno and Rosemary LaBianca, along with Rosemary's twenty-one-year-old daughter, Suzanne, fired up their green 1968 Thunderbird and began the drive slowly.

Rosemary's son, Frank, age fifteen, had taken a trip to stay with his friends for about a week on Lake Isabella and found himself enjoying his time so much that, when the LaBiancas had traveled that morning to pick up their son and the speedboat, they agreed he would be allowed to stay an extra night and return home the next day. After bidding Frank a good night and saying their goodbyes, they hooked up the boat and began their trek back to the busy streets of home.

Sometime early in their drive, they flicked on the radio. To their surprise and heavy dismay, broadcasts were flooding in from every station to report the death of Sharon Tate, the beautiful, pregnant actress just beginning her rising career in Hollywood. The startling mystery of a callous killer on the loose had already sparked deep, disconcerting, theoretical debate on many radio stations over who was responsible for the killing and what his or her motive may have been. The actress had been found murdered not even thirteen hours prior, and there were already theories that she and her friends had been involved in something dangerous: drugs perhaps, or was it satanism, or a sex scandal? What could Sharon Tate and her celebrity-status friends have done, and to whom, that would have caused such severe retaliation?

Rosemary was visibly disturbed. She had recently found strong evidence at her home of a break-in on more than one occasion. Her family's things had been rifled through, items had been misplaced or were missing, and the dogs had been let out by someone from the inside... Leno didn't feel that the police were actively doing anything about their complaints of an intruder, and had already, for the safety of his wife and family, priced another home in Escondido, as the intrusions—along with the rise of drugs and loose hippie culture in their neighborhood—were becoming too much to handle.[41] But, in the meantime, until they had a safer place to live, would this person, or people, come back to their home for more? Did the intruders intend Rosemary or her family any harm, or were they just after money and valuables? Having only days earlier shared her paranoia with a friend,[42] Rosemary's personal safety concerns became all the more real to her now as her thoughts were invaded by the details of a murder mystery the likes of which were so close to home and surreally, chillingly, cold-blooded.

At around one o'clock in the morning, Leno and Rosemary imparted their goodbyes to Suzanne, safely dropping her off at her Los Angeles apartment for the night. Shortly before two o'clock, they stopped at a newsstand they frequented at the corner of Hillhurst and Franklin streets. The owner, John Fokianos, saw their all-too-familiar Thunderbird pulling up with boat in tow, and automatically reached for a copy of the *Herald Examiner,* along with the daily racing form for Leno, a regular customer.

When the couple emerged from their vehicle to complete their usual transaction, Fokianos noticed that something was different. They were tired from their late-night driving and long day in the car, certainly, but that wasn't it.

Rosemary was very shaken…and it showed.

The newsstand was closing soon, and Fokianos had no other customers. Since the slower business and the late hour afforded them the opportunity, the LaBiancas stood and talked with him about the shocking news of the Tate murders. With several extra copies at the stand and nobody to sell them to, Fokianos gave the couple a free copy of the Sunday *Los Angeles Times*, which featured the story at length. Accepting the gift, the LaBiancas returned to their vehicle and drove away.

Fokianos knew that his acquaintances, and especially Rosemary, were bothered by the recent slayings. What he did *not* know was that, with the exception of the wild Manson Family disciples making their way to the LaBianca residence at that moment, he would be the last person who would ever see Leno and Rosemary LaBianca alive.[43]

VICTIMS: FROM CREEPY CRAWLS TO HOMICIDE

Before we address Charles "Tex" Watson's role in the Tate/LaBianca murders, let's visit some of the circumstances surrounding the lesser-studied LaBianca case. We learned about, and were reminded of, Manson-related slayings in the previous case study on Susan Atkins. Of course, the name "Manson" derives the instant recollection: "Yeah I've heard of him; wasn't he that guy who commissioned those hippie kids to kill that actress back in the '60s?" But not everyone is familiar with the term "creepy crawls" (an idiom the Family eventually associated with their burglaries of random, high-profile homes in the Los Angeles area). This item on the list will turn up early in the investigation of this Family's recreational activities.

It's a well-known fact that valuable items were taken during these crawls, likely for the purposes of pawning for money. But strangely, there were just as many (or more) instances of these acts occurring wherein not a single item had been stolen; the house had simply been turned upside down with fearful signs of their presence left behind as a psychological power play, and often they carried this out while the occupants of the home were sleeping at night in nearby rooms.

There is a video circulating the Internet right now that, in most cases, is purported to be an actual, videotaped occurrence of one of these crawls. (One copy of the video can be viewed here: "Manson Family Creepy Crawl," YouTube video, posted by Henrology, uploaded January 12, 2009, last accessed January 19, 2014, http://www.youtube.com/watch?v=lZ_ uMxpx-kw.) This video is *not* real footage of a legitimate creepy crawl incident by the Manson Family. It was created by an independent film producer in an attempt to secure financial backing for a potential movie about Manson.[44] Yet, as unauthentic as it may be, the film provides a very unsettling and bizarre example of *some* of the kinds of behavior that went on during these escapades. The video shows members of the Family pouring out liquids, stabbing pillows and pulling out the stuffing, embedding kitchen knives into various objects, urinating on the table, and leaving behind a bloody and skinless animal head for the unsuspecting residents to discover. (Although no reports reflected the bloody-animal head as a reality, and this insinuation seems a bit sensational compared to the typical, "my couch was upside down"-type report, their actions caused a great number of restless nights for many people, among whom were celebrities John and Michelle Phillips of the Mamas and the Papas musical group and American jazz and pop singer Jack Jones.)

The purpose behind these creepy crawls was clear from the beginning. According to witness accounts and jury testimonies, the two most often reported reasons were: 1) conditioning these reckless youths to charge into a victim's home to seek and destroy, weeding out those who had too much conviction from those who would follow Manson's orders to the fullest; and 2) to drive home the ultimate feeling of "freedom" and "no guilt," overcoming fear during moments of destruction and fear-mongering prior to escalating the deeds to delivering death. Perhaps Bugliosi (the prosecuting attorney of Manson and Family during the trials) put it best when he said: "These creepy-crawling expeditions were, I felt sure the jury would surmise, dress rehearsals for murder."[45]

Unlike the aforementioned actress and her famous friends, this new set of fatalities was not involved in any way with the movie or music industry, and there is no evidence that there had been any promises from them, real or fabricated, given to Manson to help his career, etc., nor is there evidence that they had ever met any of the Family face to face. *In addition to those listed in the Susan Atkins case study*, the seemingly random victims, as mentioned prior, were:

- Leno LaBianca (aged 44), father of three children (Corina, Anthony, and Louise), from a previous marriage, a World War II veteran, and owner and president of a chain of Los Angeles wholesale grocery businesses
  - Bound with pillowcase and lamp cord; gagged; stabbed in living room
- Rosemary LaBianca (aged 38), mother of two children (Frank and Suzanne) from a previous marriage, successful women's clothing boutique owner, and businesswoman
  - Bound with pillowcase and lamp cord; stabbed in bedroom

Before the LaBiancas' untimely end, their home reportedly had been broken into several times, with similar findings as other creepy-crawl missions in the area. Rosemary and Leno's concern regarding these discoveries led to more and more of Frank's visits with friends, as the couple began to feel that their residence was an unsafe place for their son to stay. It is unknown why they continued to occupy such an environment for as long as they did, but acquaintances have stated that the LaBiancas had already taken steps to relocate as a result of this paranoia. (Needless to say, the paranoia was a blessing, as it paved the way for Frank to be absent when his parents were murdered. Suzanne, Rosemary's daughter and the witness to most of Rosemary's terror in the car that night, had already moved out and was living in an apartment within the same neighborhood, but in a location that appeared far less wealthy. [Also please note for those interested in further research that Suzanne's name has also shown up historically under many various spellings, and she has been associated with several different last names, which we have chosen for the sake of her privacy not to list here.])

Leno's daughter, Cory (Corina), had just turned twenty-one in early April of 1969. Her mother, Alice, Leno's first wife, flew her out to be close to the family and her father to celebrate her birthday. When Leno arrived at their gathering with gifts and a card, there was a noticeable, strange apprehensiveness to his affection that was foreign to Cory and others present. Alice described it as "preoccupied and upset."[46] Cory agreed, sharing that she had also noticed it. A few days after that visit, four months to the day before he and his second wife would be murdered, Leno had written to Cory, telling her that he had enjoyed getting to see her for her special day. He then went on to give an update about the recent burglaries that he had acquired help from local law enforcement to investigate. As he related to his daughter in a letter dated April 9, 1969:

> No new burglaries, thank goodness! No new clues, either. There has been a plain clothes detective hanging around here occasionally, but I'm beginning to doubt as to whether the "culprits" will ever be caught.[47]

His letter went on to update Cory about generalities, mostly the horse races he frequented and bet on and the horses he owned. This led to the revealing of his plans to move to a new property in the interest of owning a ranch, but it becomes eerily clear in his letter that the horses were not what was really driving his need to move away:

> L.A. is getting to be a pretty scary place. There are a group of hippies that have taken over Griffith Park and two "pot parties" have been broken up by the police just next door. That's a little too close for comfort. I have a place picked out in Escondido, and as soon as I can get my affairs straightened out, we will be able to buy it and move from this house.[48]

Although it is likely that Manson (or members of his Family) had never met the LaBiancas in person, there was a small (and often overlooked) connection that might point to another of the Manson Family's motives for targeting the LaBianca residence. To keep the lengthy explanation to a minimum, let's visit a quick bullet list for the facts:

- Manson met record producer Phil Kaufman (not to be confused with actor Phil Kaufman) while in prison in 1968. (Manson has spent most of his life incarcerated, even prior to the murders.) When Kaufman heard Manson playing in the prison yard, he developed a friendship with him, with music as their bond. Kaufman would go on to say that Manson sounded like a "young Frankie Lane."[49] Kaufman at some point became a part of the Family, but "found [the] theocracy a bit overbearing," so he left them, but "remained a 'sympathetic cousin'"[50] to the Family. From the mouth of Kaufman, himself: "Charlie got a little crazy and I said, 'I gotta go.' And he said, 'You can't stay here. You're too smart.'… You can't be smart and hang out with Charlie, you know. *Charlie* does the thinking."[51] However, despite their differences, the record-producing Kaufman had allegedly made promises off and on of assisting Manson in his musical endeavors: a promise that Manson evidently did not believe was materializing fast enough. (Kaufman eventually did produce Manson's album. As mentioned earlier, it was called *LIE*, and its cover featured the photo that is most associated with Manson's "crazy eyes" [or "psychopathic stare"; see the Ted Bundy case study] in current pop culture.[52] *The album wasn't released until after the murders* and during the lengthy trials, and the gross unpopularity of Manson's name at the time resulted in a very small number of sales, so the album was largely forgotten.[53])
  - *Similar to the tension between Manson and Melcher of so-called career promises in the air, a tension developed between Manson and Kaufman.*
- In '68, during the time that Manson was waiting for Kaufman to finalize the arrangements and keep his word about a record, the two attended parties and took drugs together. Eventually, Kaufman introduced Manson to his friend, Harold True, who lived at 3267 Waverly Drive, the house directly next door to the LaBianca house. (There are photos online of parties taking place at the Harold True residence.[54] However, these would not be the same

"pot parties" that Leno mentioned had been shut down "just next door" in his letter to his daughter, like so many on the Internet claim, because the LaBiancas did not live in that house yet when the Manson/True/Kaufman parties were happening.) Manson was "dishonored" by True, himself, at one point. According to interviews with True,[55] Manson had asked to live with True at his house, and True turned him down. This would mark a moment in history wherein someone had refused further support of Manson and his drifting lifestyle. (Although it is difficult to find hard evidence, some sources say that this shame was brought in the middle of one of said drug parties, which would have disgraced Manson in front of his Family, for whom he was, by this time, the fatherly figure.)

    o   *There would have been tension between Manson and True, also.*

- For months, while the LaBianca house was vacant, Manson and his group would wander over and crash the empty house, using it as both a casual sex pad and a place to sleep.[56] Manson admitted in a more recent interview: "LaBianca's house was always an empty house. We used to use it to go there to have sex because nobody lived there. It was an empty house for a long time."[57] By the time the LaBiancas moved in, the house had become a location where Manson had left his mark during the time he was drugging next door with Kaufman and True. And, by the time the LaBiancas were murdered, True and Kaufman, like Melcher, had moved out of their party house.

    o   *Similar to how Manson might order that everyone at Melcher's old place be murdered to send a message of revenge to Melcher, he might also order that everyone at the True and Kaufman party house be murdered to intimidate them, also. Since nobody was at the True home, the house next door (the residence of the LaBiancas) that Manson previously used as an overnight crash house was the natural target in order to intimidate by association, since Manson had gone looking for Kaufman and couldn't immediately locate him.[58]*

In addition to this easily overlooked, musical-career-related motive, Manson and the Family would have been well aware that 3301 Waverly Drive was inhabited by a wealthy, "white" couple, since they had visited there for their creepy-crawl missions even after True had moved out. The LaBiancas lived in an impressive, upper-crust home, which seemed well suited for the purpose of triggering the Helter Skelter war, so that motive applies also. And lastly, as with the murders at the Tate/Polanski house, trails of evidence were planted pointing to a killer on the loose, matching those of the Tate and Hinman murders, in hopes that a blind eye would be turned for Beausoleil in the Hinman murder case. In summation: All three of the motives discussed in the previous chapter can apply here as well.

But before we spend too long literarily crucifying our quintessential false Christ and seeing the only bad guy here as the vagrant with the grandeur agenda, let's remember that, although Manson was a very twisted leader who masterminded the evils behind these tragedies, it was not *his hand* that delivered the ultimate end to Hinman, Tate, Sebring, Frykowski, Folger, Parent, or Leno and Rosemary LaBianca. For that, Manson needed followers, and one of his most devoted was Charles "Tex" Watson.

HONOR STUDENT, ATHLETE, EDITOR OF SCHOOL PAPER...MURDERER

Unlike Susan Atkins—whose personal involvement with the Tate/LaBianca files varies from one extreme to the other, thereby leaving it up to the listeners to determine how much they believe in whatever version of the story they're listening to—Watson's involvement with the murders is far easier to nail down. The story he tells regarding those nights not only lines up with evidence at the crime scene and evidence brought to court, but also with the testimonies of everyone else involved, including other Family members implicated in the crimes. As with the previous study, if we were to list all the details of what transpired during the evenings of August 9–10, 1969, the information would go on for hundreds of pages and would be too graphic to include in this book. So, here again, we will include a bullet list:

- Watson partook of mind-altering drugs with the Family on a regular basis, the extent of which could carry into and affect his mental processing for a time well beyond the nights of the murders.
- Manson's brainwashing cult, as explained earlier in this book, also included Watson. Watson would be thereafter seen as perhaps the most devoted to Manson's orders and vision.
- The telephone line severed on the Tate property, as discovered by Winifred Chapman, Tate's maid, was cut by Watson. The screen of the window that was slit and removed, providing a way into the house, was cut by Watson. (He then proceeded to let the others in through the front door.) The word "WAR," as carved on Leno LaBianca's stomach postmortem, was cut by Watson.
- Watson was the central killer in both the Tate and the LaBianca cases. Although there was certainly assistance from Atkins, Van Houten, and Krenwinkel in the events, the actual death blow to Parent, Sebring, Folger, Frykowski, and Leno LaBianca were delivered by Watson.[59] Assuming that the matching post-trial testimonies of Atkins and Watson are true, as well as evidence at the crime scene, Watson was responsible for ending Tate's life also. Specifically regarding Rosemary LaBianca: The scuffles and struggles that took place between Rosemary, Krenwinkel, and Watson do not usually allude to a concrete moment of death in the varying reports, but it is most likely that Watson's initial injuries to her, followed by further injury by Krenwinkel, delivered death to Rosemary in a joint effort. (Manson had left clear instructions with Watson to make sure that everyone involved got his or her hands dirty. Van Houten also inflicted wounds upon Rosemary's body, but she was the last to contribute, and because the evidence shows that many of Rosemary's wounds had been inflicted postmortem, it is most likely that Van Houten's personal involvement did not cause death; the victim was already deceased by the time Van Houten showed her devotion and obedience.)
- Watson deflected much of the responsibility away from himself whenever possible during the trials (including testifying that

Atkins had been the one to stab Tate), but has since recanted his innocence and claimed responsibility in the areas that lined up most accurately to the evidence and testimonies against him.

- Despite his participation as being the most violent of any of the Family, most archived news footage of the famous trials (as well as personal memories that Americans still hold in their thoughts of the circulating media during that time) do not include Watson's image. Watson had fled to Texas, his home state, before the identity of the murderers had come to the surface. He was arrested in Texas for the Tate/LaBianca murders on November 30, 1969. His attorney requested, and was granted, postponements in extradition proceedings, resulting in a lengthy absence from the others. From November of 1970 to February of 1971, Watson spent time in the Atascadus Mental Hospital (more on this later). After the judge refused a further stay of extradition (and after Watson had been deemed suitable for trial following a physical and mental regression upon his arrival to California), Watson was finally brought into the courtroom. He was found guilty for seven counts of first-degree murder and one count of conspiracy to commit murder at the closing of the trial seven months later. He was handed the death sentence, but, just like the others, it was overturned and converted to life in prison.

(Note also that Charles Watson has read this exact case study and has verified it. Although sending such tough words about him to him directly took some faith from a few of us here at Defender Publishing, it proved worth it to see that he agreed with our report of the crimes and his life, and of his story of conversion to Christ. To hear more about what Watson had to say to us directly, see the "Interview with Charles 'Tex' Watson" following this case study.)

Death by execution. The concept is most assuredly devastating, no matter who you are or what you've done, and it is a reprimand that only a unique few in our history pages have ever felt at peace with facing (and several of these were looking forward to execution for masochistic/sadistic reasons, so they wouldn't compare to one with a standard, peaceful acceptance of the death penalty).

There is a certain unexplainable finality—a shameful and appalling and disgraceful finality—that is instantly placed upon the head of someone who has done something horrific enough to deserve such a penalty from the American courts. It's unfathomable, the thoughts and feelings that would register within a person standing before God and jury, hearing the verdict spoken aloud. Nowhere to run, nowhere to hide, and nothing but a heart-stopping reality playing out as the judge's mouth opens to utter forth an order for the individual to meet with his or her Maker for the ultimate judgment. In some books and testimonies, this moment has been likened to a dramatic movie scene wherein time slows to a crawl and everything stops; wherein the temporal world that the guilty one has been living in suddenly appears for what it is in comparison to the possibility of an eternity; wherein gravity, heavier than it has ever been before, abruptly worms its way into every facet of the body, tempting muscles to give in and collapse, freeing the mind to reject this reality and escape to a happy place…

Yet, this terror is one that those sentenced to die could have avoided by choosing a different path.

"Tex" was no exception.

It's My Party, and I'll Sin if I Want To

When it comes to a promising future, a scarce few can compete with the impressive résumé held by the young Charles Watson. He was the poster child for achievement in his local area, and everyone in Copeville, Texas, was sure that Santa would have him at the top of the "Nice" list forever. Reading his childhood bragging rights, we are impressed to believe that, although certainly every human life on this planet has potential and promise before the path of destruction, some gratuitously wasteful statistics are especially shocking and unforeseen.

A child hailing from the coattails of the Great Depression, Watson had good parents, and his earliest memories reflect small-town, good-ol'-boy surroundings. Shortly after he started attending school, President Eisenhower saw to it that the Pledge of Allegiance flag salute would now hold the important words, "under God," which Watson's community embraced. The boy attended church regularly and was baptized at the age of twelve in August of 1958 at Copeville Methodist Church.

Watson's concept of God and Jesus was like that of so many others at a young age. Jesus was a blurry compilation of pale, dark-blond-haired, blue-eyed young men with sad, somber expressions and glowing rays of light peeking out from behind His perfect, wavy hair in pictures hung along the walls of Sunday school. Sometimes, the Man was pictured standing knocking on a door, waiting for someone to answer, or wearing a long, white dress with kids sitting on each knee; other times, He was bloody, miserable, nearly naked, and dying while crowds pointed and scoffed at His brutal public execution. He was a Man, yet He was the only Man who was also God. Watson did know the Man in the pictures was a good Man who died a long time ago so that everyone's sins would be forgiven and forgivable.

Church, although a pleasant place usually filled with smiling people, represented a dwelling where kids had to sit still and listen, where even away from school you were being required to learn. (Early scenes in the award-winning docudrama on Watson, *Forgiven: The Charles "Tex" Watson Story*, show a bored young boy in a church pew fidgeting with an uncomfortable necktie while others around him sang a worship song. The next words spoken by the actor/narrator, as Watson: "I didn't like church much. I liked sports."[60])

Many noteworthy titles would herald the beginning of Watson's life, including Future Farmer of America, honor student, editor of the school paper, and record-setting track star, just to name a few. His athleticism, drive, dedication, and charming smile earned him so many first-place ribbons that his mother filled an old tie box to the brim, and his was a regularly featured name in the sports section of local newspapers.[61] He had support from his community, a kind mother and father, a sports-loving brother, a sister who doted on him almost maternally, dinner on the table each night, and a job at his father's small-town store any time he needed it…his life was the epitome of an archetypal episode of *Lassie* that so many in this world wish they'd had, all the way down to the big, loyal family collie dog (…literally).

At around sixteen years old, Watson was already familiar with the fun that could be had when tossing back a few beers and cruising around with his buddies, occasionally taking a drink or two with him on his waterskiing jaunts. Not unusually, the sporty locker room talk eventually traded in the adolescent "girls are gross" mentality for a focus on the female sex much less preferred by most parents of sixteen-year-old boys. Watson wasn't entirely estranged from his family or parents, but there were certain taboo conversations that weren't allowed openly in his home or that he was never comfortable discussing. Sex, specifically, seemed "forbidden, secret, [and] dirty"[62] by the time he became more aware of the changes happening to his body. When his eyes caught the miniskirt hemline with an easy reputation in his high school, he had already begun welcoming the kicks of abandoning a moral code. He describes these moments in a way that shows a lack of self control from a very early age, writing that any guilt he felt while committing an act of sin away from the eyes of accountability only added to the thrill of the deed.

Well known and popular in his hometown for as long as he could remember, Watson had never known adventurous anonymity, and as a result, he found that a certain rejection rose within him against the stereotypical expectation he had been placed under: that "nice young man who's really going places" song-and-dance so important to *The Andy Griffith Show* generation. Every move he made, right or wrong, was the subject of discussion in the town, and thanks to his father's established store and the ever-so-harmless, small-town mentality, there was a central hub for the latest update on anything Watson. (Although Watson doesn't describe it in these words exactly as he writes about his youth in his book, *Will You Die for Me?: The Man Who Killed for Charles Manson Tells His Own Story*, you could almost say that his flings of misjudgment became a game more about how much he could get away with and less about giving into a temptation that he simply couldn't resist. That seems to be the suggested undertone, at least.)

Of course, not minding that people around him found him to be a smart, kind, talented person, the insult was buried deep in his psyche already by the age of sixteen: Nobody really knew the teenager behind the trophy. That recipe by itself could have baked into a very common case of Misunderstood Pie. The added ingredients of arrogance and self-appointed superiority simmered into something more concerning:

> My parents' world of church and God and rules wasn't what I wanted. I was a success, I could handle my life without them or that pale-faced Jesus in the church magazines.[63]

Although Watson's life did not begin tragically, little telltale signs were glaringly obvious early on of the rejection he embraced of the true God and the true Christ in his own spirit and attitude in exchange for an unfulfilling and lonely path toward regret and misery. As yet another perfect example of how material things, achievements, attention, reputation, popularity, and even sex won't bring happiness and self-worth, chapter 3 of his book ends with a flashback of his own teen thoughts, his own juvenile version of the age-old "someday-I'm-gonna-get-outta-this-town-if-it's-the-last-thing-I-do" line.

Watson pursued college immediately after graduation from high school and with a fervor to escape his hometown. It didn't take him that far away from Copeville, but it was a start. North Texas State University in Denton, Texas, provided just the right brand of mischief to whet his palate with further waywardness. The university was glad to have a student of his athletic and academic reputation, and he was glad to be away, if only by little more than an hour's drive, from the prying eyes of his childhood. Without further ado, days fell into weeks, and soon his grades were reflecting the half-hearted regard he held for a true education now that he had time and opportunity to squander it in trade for typical teenage tomfoolery. Girls were everywhere and willing to bare all. Booze flowed like milk and honey. Fashion was more mature than it had been back home, and Watson loosened his style and stance accordingly. He was *cool*. Right away, he fell in with the boys of Pi Kappa Alpha and was so well accepted that by the time everyone was scrambling to impress and showing their willingness to go through the humiliating initiation ceremonies expected in fraternity circles, all he had to do was steal a few typewriters. When he turned himself in for the crime a day or two later, his parents were devastated, and fumed with anger so fierce that "they couldn't have been any more upset if [he'd] committed murder.... A year later, when a beer bottle tossed drunkenly out of a car destroyed a boy's eye, that reputation took on a darker tone."[64] Watson had nothing to do with the incident, but the circle of friends he had taken to hanging out with resulted in the drunken episode, attaching itself to him by association.

Despite his physical distance from Copeville, word traveled fast. Already, he found himself being contacted by concerned individuals he thought he had finally received a breather from. The rules, rules, rules were closing in again, and there would be no sanctuary from them unless he increased his distance from home again. In January of 1967, he went to work for an airline company and obtained free travel tickets as a benefit, using his days away from attending class to journey beyond the oppression of his social ties, to places beyond expectation and demands—even if only for short periods of time. The first flight he took marked a moment in his life of exhilarating freedom. He recalls looking out the window and seeing the shrunken world below him so miniature and insignificant compared to him in that plane at that moment. He inflated, knowing that Copeville and Denton, all the people therein, and "all the small-town pettiness and ignorance and piety that [his] home and family represented"[65] were naught but a speck below him.

The more Watson traveled and viewed different cultures and new ways of life, the more he hungered for anything but what he'd always known. On campus, when a fellow frat boy who had moved to California returned to Denton, Texas, for a visit, this friend was a changed young man. His sideburns were longer, his clothing was draping here and there, and his manner was relaxed. Watson's interest was piqued, and he began to feel that there may actually be life outside the empty box, if he were merely brave and willing enough to venture outside of it. The trip he then took to visit this friend in Los Angeles shortly thereafter would be the one and only taste of the all-American dream that he would ever need in order to be convinced that his new life was among the long hair, the street guitarists, the love-making with no strings attached, and the mentality of embracing ultimate freedom without judgment. No longer capable of truly feeling and appreciating the genuine love that those from his past had for him, feeling only expectation and demands and suppression of self, his decision was an easy one to make.

Regardless of his parents' passionate opposition, on August 28 of 1967, Charles Watson left home, family, and friends behind him at the airport, severing all ties of subjugation as a plane lifted a young man and his dreams to the sunny, promised land.

"This Is Charlie…Charlie Manson."

Wrecking your vehicle in the psychedelic '60s was a commonplace. "Friends don't let friends smoke pot and drive" wasn't on the billboards anywhere, as the concept of the risks of driving under the influence was still in its infancy, especially in regards to marijuana, something that was already illegal to begin with. Watson, who escaped the draft as a result of a knee injury in a car accident, and who in succession lost his best childhood friend to the war and flew home for the funeral, returned to California ready for a higher dose and different brand of fun juice to escape reality. At the same time, elsewhere, Dennis Wilson was busy bringing a clumsy end to both his Ferrari and Rolls Royce, back to back. As was typical in those days and in that area, Wilson used his thumb as a backup vehicle plan, and got a ride home from Watson. Watson thought the idea of picking up a seemingly random hitchhiker and discovering that he is one of the members of the famous Beach Boys was pretty far out.

Wilson invited his driver in for a drink, and Watson accepted. This unplanned visit to Wilson's house led to a friendship between Watson and another fellow hanging out at the house named Dean Moorehouse, who was twice his age. After the initial introduction was out of the way, Moorehouse enthusiastically informed Watson that there was someone he had to meet in the next room.

"This is Charlie…Charlie Manson."[66]

Like many other testimonies of an initial meeting with Manson, the connection was immediate. Based on eye contact alone, there was a present "gentleness, an embracing kind of acceptance and love."[67]

Within hours, Manson, Moorehouse, Wilson, and Watson would all be stoned, sharing very little conversation, bonding together in what was the beginning of a deep-rooted revelation for Watson. As Watson listened to Manson drift in and out of song with his guitar, floating between spoken and sung verses regarding love, allowing yourself to love, finding and accepting love, a free love…it finally hit Watson.

He had been missing *love*.

He'd had friends and parties and romance and sex and booze and fun and adventure and even a family and community back home that truly cared about and supported him, but he'd never had the kind of self-secure love that rapidly, astoundingly, overwhelmingly made itself known as missing in his life at that moment. He was empty and unfulfilled, needing and wanting more than anything else in the world to know love. *Real* love. Love like the love this Charlie Manson was singing about. And then, as if on cue, Watson was aware that this feeling, this revealing of ultimate and uncorrupted truth within him, this revolutionary uncovering of a suddenly clear and transparent necessity that had been starved and neglected to the point of emotional emaciation, was being delivered in the soft sounds of love coming from the small, skinny guy with the guitar.

Watson felt, for the first time maybe in his life, that everything was going to work out just fine, and that the answer to all of his seeking for the next thing might finally be coming to a comforting end. At the end of a long, Lebanese hash-fest, Watson bid his new friends—Wilson, Moorehouse, and Manson—goodnight, and drove home in peace. Within months, Watson would be living with the Beach Boy in his mansion. (Moorehouse would explain over a period of months that he originally came to this part of California to track down and kill Charles Manson for seducing his daughter. Instead of killing him, he took acid with him and was now spreading the good news that the Second Coming of Jesus Christ in a reincarnated body was alive and well, and that it was only through the spiritual trip from an acid dose that people would come to accept Manson as their personal savior.)

As Watson continued to live the party life at Wilson's rock 'n' roll house, Moorehouse continued to make it his personal mission to "witness" to all others present (and at Wilson's place, the gatherings would often grow to large numbers of people staying weeks at a time) of Manson's legitimacy as Christ. Even though Watson felt a connection with this group from the beginning, the idea of Manson being a god, and the idea of completely and totally dying to "self" so that oneness might live on (as outlined and explained in the Susan Atkins case study), sounded a little off kilter. But, as Watson goes on to describe in his book for several pages, his first experience with acid, under the direction and supervision of Moorehouse, brought clarity to the yearning he had felt that day in the living room with Manson and the others. He went from: feeling that he needed something to fill a void in his life, but not knowing what that might be; to feeling like he knew what he needed, the love that Manson spoke of, but didn't know how to get it; to, eventually, feeling that he knew exactly what he wanted, exactly how to get it, but he simply wasn't ready to completely give up his individuality and deny everything he ever thought he was in exchange for a universal connection with everyone else on a single, equally identifiable plain. He had always been an individual. Good, bad, or otherwise, Watson had always been known for what he was, established as someone with his own mind and passions. If he left himself behind, truly, completely, then who would he be then? And yet, the idea that someone like him would even have to ask that question proves that he was far too interested in who *he* would *be*, and not willing to sacrifice his "self" to the enlightenment that awaited him just on the other side of self-focused ignorance.

As the internal struggle raged on and the acid drops increased, Watson pined for permanent immersion into the fulfillment and contentment that everyone around him constantly spoke of. Manson had all the answers. Manson was love. When Manson looked at someone in the way that he did, his intense eyes burning straight past the phony walls, and observed for himself all the shades of blacks and grays that crawled sinfully within them, and yet continued to love them anyway, with no strings attached and perfect acceptance, the more natural it seemed that he would be the *one* sent by God to right all the wrongs of the world. The more Watson dreamed of an everlasting rehabilitation from the empty shell that the American-establishment culture corruptively pushed upon him at birth (now even thinking his own private thoughts in Mansonese), the less important his own miniscule distinctiveness seemed in contrast to such a sick world waiting in the wings for a savior.

Perhaps he had found this savior after all.

As a long-distance phone call home to Texas would reveal, Watson accepted Manson:

> "You've always been wanting me to be religious," I had told my mother. "Well, I've met that Jesus you preach about all the time. I've met him and he's here right now with me in the desert." Charlie *was* Jesus. He was my messiah, my savior, my soul.[68]

Ready for once and for all to gift himself as a tool to the reincarnated Christ, Watson approached Manson with the keys to his truck and informed him further that everything in his possession now belonged to Manson.

After some trouble in Wilson-paradise when Moorehouse pressured some of Manson's girls to sleep with him, Watson and the others moved out. Moorehouse borrowed a personal friend's car—a friend named Terry Melcher, who was living at 10050 Cielo Drive, the ranch house that would later be rented out to Roman Polanski and Sharon Tate—to use to travel to and attend court in another part of the state for his dealings in LSD. (Watson went with Moorehouse to pick up Melcher's car. This was the first time Watson was present at the property that would eventually become his own personal crime scene.) For a few weeks, Watson traveled with Moorehouse while his case was waiting on an appeal. Eventually, Moorehouse left by himself to attend a court hearing, and he never came back to the Manson circle. Manson, who wasn't a fan of Moorehouse *or* Watson as long as Moorehouse was around to threaten the girls, quickly warmed up to Watson when Moorehouse was gone.

Right away, Manson took Watson to meet George Spahn, the owner of the Spahn Ranch that Manson and the Family had been officially calling home while they repeatedly and lengthily took residence at Wilson's mansion. As Watson had offered himself, his possessions, and his skills to Manson, Manson saw an opportunity to further impress the owner of the ranch, who had been allowing Manson and his Family to stay there in exchange for favors from the Family (among which was the use of one of Manson's main girls as housekeeper and lover). Watson had great skills in tinkering, auto mechanics included, so Manson furthered his relationship with Spahn by offering over Watson's mechanical services to any vehicles coming or going from the property. Spahn, who was completely blind, listened to the sales pitch of Watson's skills, and, when Watson spoke, picked up on the accent, immediately tagging him with the nickname that would stick with him for the rest of his life: "Tex." (This nickname would also help to distinguish him from their leader in the days to come, as "Charles Watson" and "Charles Manson" only differentiate from each other by three letters, and to some extent, as the murder cases would show, "Tex" was eventually a kind of appointed leader in the group also.)

An Empty Shell of a Man Long Gone

As time increased, so did the drugs, both in the potency of those taken and the dosage administered. Watson describes the effect of this use in detail. Whereas drugs (specifically acid, LSD) can commit a person to a peaceful, accepting state wherein the world around him or her fades into nothing but a fantasy and allows the taker to "see" into other realms and realities, other side effects include the taker being easily herded into and convinced of a reality presented to the person by a stronger personality. Manson, by far the strongest personality in the Family, had begun to share a "reality" that involved the upcoming war of races. Prolonged exposure to these mind-altering resources under Manson's teaching had many convinced that the world, or at least America, was merely an establishment to revoke your rights as a free, spiritual entity. In his common words, "There is no right, there is no wrong, there is no crime, there is no sin."[69] The only real plane of existence was one on which everyone shared an eternal oneness and bond beyond the captivity that this human world provided. True transcendence into this elevated state required an individual to see birth and death as a mere pawn in the overall game of spirituality as under "God" (Manson). Being alive, and being a life, meant nothing. Therein, to kill meant nothing. There was no sin. In many cases, it was even taught that killing actually *brought* life: the *true* life, as one on the spiritual plane. Manson's followers, Watson included, adopted this trail of thinking while under the influence and never once questioned that it may be the gospel of one man, the world as according to "Charlie," but took it as a blessing that they had been given the privilege to serve the one and only man who was also "God," the ultimate authority and creator of the earth and all the people inhabiting it. To add to their convictions came "proof" to the mind seeking it. For instance, they would look into each other's eyes or faces and see a literal reflection of their own facial features. They would predict a visitor to the ranch with drugs, and the visitor would suddenly appear. In group circles, their minds would be blown away when they all had the same thought at that same moment, and nobody was pretending; they would legitimately pass into a collective cognition and share the same cohesive thought. The longer they took drugs together, the longer they truly became "as one." (Let us not forget that, although these testimonies seem very real and miraculous, Satan is the deceiver who can imitate miracles and wonders, so the concept that these people saw miraculous things—and the fact that they experienced them while under the influence—is not at all surprising. The psychedelic '60s wasn't Satan's first rodeo.) This consciousness was shared by all in the Family (those who decided to stay on past the elevated teachings of violence, anyway), but specific to this book, Atkins also tried to witness this lesson in a letter between herself and the cellmate she bragged to about the murders (note that the spelling below is as it was in the original letter):

> In killing someone phisally you are only releasing the soul. Life has no boundris and death is only an illusion. If you can believe in the second coming of Crist… [it] is he who has come to save.[70]

Many terrible things are remembered about Manson (and for justifiable reason). However, as if this unstable hornet's-nest group needed further provocation, one of the songs Manson recorded was called "Cease to Exist," and, shortly after that recording, a song entitled "Never Learn Not to Love," with extreme similarities in rhythm, melody, chord progression, and especially lyrics, turned up on the very next album by the Beach Boys. At first, the link might seem a bit sensational, but upon listening to both songs in a row, it is obvious that the song Manson recorded was creatively the basis for a stolen song, as the odds of the number of similarities between two songs occurring by coincidence would likely be millions to one.[71] Watson doesn't know exactly the reason, but at that time, Manson once again found Melcher and his empty promises as the target for revenge, and not Wilson, their Beach Boy buddy.

Manson sent Watson to Melcher's place to ask for money. (This trip had a secondary theme, as the Family was once again trying to fund the bail/release money for Gregg Jacobsen, yet another music-industry friend busted on drug charges.) Watson's request for Melcher's money was rejected. (This was officially Watson's second time present at 10050 Cielo Drive during Melcher's lease.) This rejection would not bode well for Melcher.

What happens next in the story is a telling string of details in Watson's conscience. Watson made his way to the highway to hitchhike back to Spahn Ranch. It was November of 1968. He hadn't been alone, outside the watchful eye of some form of authority, in…he couldn't remember how long. There, sticking his thumb out to the road, he realized that it was within his human rights to be free. Free like he wanted to be free when he was first drawn into the fantasy of California. Not the spiritual "free" that the Family had embraced, but literally free, like any man willing to make his own destination his own decision. Isn't that what Manson wanted for his Family? *True* freedom, even if that freedom led to a reality possibly outside of his teachings?

Watson watched the cars go by and reflected upon the people he saw within. He was suddenly aware of an empty space inside, nagging him to question his involvement in the Family. Something seemed out of place.

Manson spoke of freedom, and Watson's interest in impulsively throwing self-sacrifice and death to "self" out the window and embracing a life of independence from accountability (Manson, or otherwise) sounded *free* to him at that moment. But how could this all be truth? Maybe somewhere in Manson's theology, true freedom would support someone living with a certain level of ego and interest in his own money, things, and adventures…but, at the moment, freedom to live with ego, if one so chose, was contradictory to embracing the true path of freedom Manson led his followers to.

In an instant, everything crashed together in a motley mix of confusion and contradiction. Watson had, within the past months, *finally* felt he had found the truth. The love, the man-god, the enlightenment, the shedding of the establishment… Now he found himself yearning for at least a false sense of self, an illusion, anything that allowed him to simply *be* in the midst of other people who, as ignorant of truth as they may have been, looked happy and content to be driving down that road that day with thoughts in their head of their own dreams and personalities. They did, at that moment, seem to differ from person to person in the same independent ways that Manson stripped from those entering into the Family.

Mechanically, Watson found himself back at the ranch, not saying a word to anyone about his recent internal questioning of Manson versus the system. He kept his lips sealed and gave himself some time to deal with the rising panic. There was no doubt in his mind that Manson loved him the way only "God" could, and that he would never lie to him, but now there was an emptiness to the man named Charles Watson. He "knew there was nothing left of [himself], and for the first time that was a frightening thought."[72]

Later that afternoon, two major events took place: 1) While at his friend's home, Manson was introduced to the *White Album* by the Beatles, which pioneered the term "Helter Skelter" (also the name of one of the songs on that album); 2) Watson called an old friend from the kitchen phone of this friend's home, and walked out the back door, leaving Manson without a word.

The Plastic World

So, there Watson was again, in the comforting arms of the establishment, indulging in "self" and daring to think his own thoughts and dream his own dreams.

Sadly, it lasted only a few months.

Everywhere he went, something reminded him of Manson's teachings. Everyone he talked to reminded him of Manson's lessons regarding the truly empty and plastic world he had fought so hard to evolve from. Sex, drugs, women, parties…even love: All of it was dry and bitter tasting when compared to the heightened sensations the Family regularly indulged in. The "oneness" was gone from his daily living. The people he had left behind in Copeville would never connect with him again. The people he would know in the future would never connect with a man who had partaken of the depth that was Manson. He couldn't go back. He couldn't go forward. He essentially had no family back home, and now he had given up *the* Family.

Slowly but surely, the reins of his consciousness drove him toward the only "truth" he had ever felt. He knew he was stuck in a limbo that would continue to torture him with possibilities of a life lived in service to the "God" at Spahn Ranch. He had fought, tooth and nail, to be a part of the world, to experience "Charles Watson" again. But he simply could not force that life to fit anymore when he had already experienced enlightenment.

(Noteworthy to this study: During this time, Watson took a couple of old friends around Los Angeles to brag about the social ties he had made during his time in California. Although nobody was home, it was during this tour to impress his friends that Watson arrived at 10050 Cielo Drive for the third time, with the intention of letting them meet Melcher, the socially impressive, successful, songwriting son of Hollywood actress, Doris Day. Watson's next arrival at this address would be his fourth, and last, and the last day on earth for five innocent people.)

Despite his earnestness to have his own identity and feed his own needs, Watson returned to the ranch, once again a shell of himself, the prodigal son welcomed back to the fold.

She's Coming Down Fast—Yes She Is

One can strongly doubt that "embarrassment" would ever cross Manson's—or his Family members'—minds, as that is an emotion that would not have fit into the "freedom" sermons. Nonetheless, when Manson spoke of the end of the world as secretly directed to him by the Beatles through their song, "Helter Skelter," because Manson and all of his Family were American, none of them knew that the song's title had been taken from an amusement park attraction, a slide from England, as it were. But regardless of the red-faced moment this detail could have offered, many other parallels were seen in that album, which Manson adopted as a commission to kill.

According to Family members' accounts in later years, this is the part of the story where Manson ups his game and begins reflecting the true vision of "God," which involves the murder of white "social piggies" who would need to die for the cause. As his sights narrowed evermore on Melcher, the new *White Album* by the Beatles trafficked many justifications of murder into the Family's one consciousness. *As taught by Manson* (not as believed by this author):

- In "Honey Pie," the Beatles called Manson from the desert to come be by their sides in England.
- In "I Will," they praised Manson's musical abilities.
- In "Piggies," an obscure song describing piggies in starched, white shirts, and including oinking pigs in the background, the Beatles pleaded with Manson to end the lives of those who contributed to the establishment. (The words "political piggy" were smeared in blood on the wall in Hinman's residence when the body was found; "PIG" was smeared on the front door of the Tate residence; and "DEATH TO PIGS" was smeared in blood on the wall in the LaBianca residence.)
- In "Revolution 1," they begged Manson to share his plan with the world.
- In "Revolution 9," they shared sounds of nonsensical chaos inter-

mittently divided by shouts of the word "rise," which was their contribution to subliminally programming the black man to rise against the white man. (The word "rise" was smeared in blood on the wall in the LaBianca residence.)

- In "Blackbird," they spoke of the black man waiting for his moment to arise.
- In "Helter Skelter," they warned Manson that the war was coming down fast, and he had to act now or never. (Although misspelled, the phrase "Healter Skelter" was smeared in blood on the refrigerator at the LaBianca residence. Many assume that the misspelling was due to the idea that some of Manson's hippie followers simply couldn't spell. Other accounts attest that the misspelling was intentional, to insinuate that it had been written by a black person, since, in Manson's opinion, black people lacked the intelligence of the white people. Neither claim can be irrefutably determined.)

And the list goes on and on to involve many other titles the Beatles supposedly wrote to confer their coded kill messages to the Family. To the reader who has a sane mind, these connections are a grasp at straws. Anyone with any extremist and radical drive can pick up any album by any musical group anywhere and find subliminal messages to point to their own convictions and agendas. Of course, some argue that a number of the links in this complicated chain were stranger and more mind-blowing than others. As just one example of several: In their song, "Sexy Sadie," they spoke of a young girl who almost perfectly described "Sadie Mae Glutz" (Atkins' Family name as given by Manson well before the existence of the *White Album*), whom the Beatles obviously had no way of knowing. Again: To the sound mind, this is coincidental and entertaining irony; to the god-man and his followers reading into everything with "oneness," this was "a sign" of something with clandestine importance between acid parties...

But whatever the reason, coincidence or fate, the Family was driven to believe that this charge as put forth by the Beatles was destiny. Manson was destiny. Manson's vision was destiny. White "piggies" would have to die for the cause.

And Watson, now back from a Family hiatus and replugged into the vision he could not escape, considered himself lucky to have been called on by "God" to free the people from their current slavery by igniting the fire of war. In his own words:

> If anyone had asked me in March of 1969 why I was going back to Manson, I would have said I had no choice. Every day I stayed away from him I felt like I was running, running away from the place I was supposed to be, running away from changes that were necessary for me. Charlie was my destiny.[73]

On the night of August 8, 1969, Watson murdered everyone at the Tate residence, and the bodies were found on the morning of August 9. It was during the Tate murder event that Watson would utter some of the most famously remembered words in American mass-murderer history: "I'm the devil, and I'm here to do the devil's business."[74] On the night of August 9, 1969, Watson murdered Leno LaBianca and initiated the murder of Rosemary LaBianca, and their bodies were found on the morning of August 10.

TO BELIEVE, OR NOT TO BELIEVE, THAT IS THE QUESTION

For a short period of weeks following the murders, in Watson's recollection, Manson grew wild with anticipation over the next victim, passing out buck knives to the Family girls and having practice sessions wherein they would learn how to properly kill piggies (the details of which are too vivid to tell here).[75] More heads would roll as long as the Family members continued to get by with it, only getting booked for small arson charges and auto theft. However, by this time, Watson's world was spinning. Once again he found himself ever pulled between two worlds, and neither of them seemed real at that moment. His head was whirling with the memories of those dark nights. He felt nothing: no joy, no remorse. He never delighted in the killing of seven innocent people. He felt no sorrow for the killing of seven innocent people or their remaining families. He was, as others from the Family would feel at some point also, wholly dead inside.

Dead and spinning, at the same time. It was a trip unlike any a drug could produce.

Soon, a phone call came through to the ranch. It was someone looking for a "Charles Watson." The concerned man on the other end of the phone only wanted to get in touch with him to see if he was alright because his mother had been trying to track him down. Watson's lie about the phone call, as delivered to the rest of the Family, was that he had called his mother and she informed him that the FBI had come to his Texas home looking for him. (The motive behind the lie was a hope that the Family would flee to the desert to look for the underground, Death Valley, white-people paradise and effectively pull himself and the rest to safety from the Spahn Ranch, a location that by now had been raided with mass arrests on more than one occasion for arson/auto theft, and he was afraid the next time would be murder charges.)

The Family fled to the desert.

Manson was different. He had reportedly beaten the women and sometimes roughed up the men in the Family when his righteous and godly seat on high required it before. (It's amazing how much control the Family members later revealed that they allowed that man to have, considering he only stood at five foot two inches and was so bone thin that Atkins, among others, described him as "almost emaciated."[76]) But now, as related in Watson's book, Manson had gone as far as to pull a knife on a young girl in the Family who tried to run away from being his "kill model" during a white-piggy-death demonstration, now forcing her to drop acid whether she liked it or not and withstand her role-play as the victim while everyone watched him pretend to drag a knife across her throat. "It was as if the Satan who Charlie sometimes claimed to be was striking out at even the Family itself."[77] Whereas several had survived the previous penalties for trying to get away from Manson, the new threat had now been manifest: If anyone was caught trying to leave, Manson would slit his or her throat.

One night, just after things had started to officially settle in the desert and the paradise-hole dig site had launched, Manson, Watson, Family member Bruce Davis, and three outsiders (who had met the Family off and on between camps) were sitting at one of Manson's campfires. Manson pulled out a knife, making the outsiders nervous, and he dramatically twisted it in the light of the fire. He asked the outsiders what they would do if he tried to murder them right there. Each of them answered (naturally...) that they would try to stop him and defend themselves. Then Manson turned to Watson. He asked Watson the same thing, in the familiar words and manner that he was used to asking all his Family:

"Would you die for me? Would you let me kill you?"
I didn't even have to think about it. "Sure Charlie, you can kill me."
I meant it. Like some mystic, so filled with the love of God that nothing is too great to ask, I was filled with Charlie.[78]

However, around this time, Manson was running out of rich party people in Hollywood from whom he could ask for money or drugs. The Family had to keep a low profile as a result of the murders, so the supplies (food, money, and drugs) were diminishing rapidly. They indulged in the mind-altering substances until the very last drop, last puff, or last snort, preferring the "trips" of the mind far more than food. And then, devastatingly, the well ran dry. As a result, Watson quickly found himself dabbling with yet another grip on that old stranger called "sobriety."

Things changed for Watson.

Things changed fast.

To begin, his identity started to pop up unexpectedly here and there as his sense of "self" once again revealed its refusal to die completely. Little questions from seemingly nowhere at all would flash into his mind, slowly but surely, the slightest evidence of a small lack of faith in his "God." The internal struggle rose up and reared its ugly head, passionately pulling back and forth: Manson's love and devotion on one end, Manson's all-too-human behavior on the other. Watson started to see

Manson feeding the little food the Family had left to the burros in the desert, placing an animal in priority over his chosen people. Instead of accepting it unconditionally as "God's" mysterious ways, Watson started to feel that something was now out of place. The more he thought about it, the more mysterious this "God" was. Watson felt that Manson had no guilt regarding the slaughtering of human lives, but he would fly off the handle in a fit of righteous rage if one of his followers killed a bug. Manson had led the people into a desert wasteland to dig for the utopian tunnel, and even after weeks of searching, they were dry, hot, and starving, with every day feeling farther and farther away from finding any leads on the prophesied chasm.

Watson was exhausted. It was too much to think about right then. Maybe if he stayed the course for the time being, Manson would come about with justification and answers and the record would be set straight again.

Days went by, and the Family became aware that they were being monitored by sheriffs and National Park rangers as they moved about. In a retaliation act, when it had been discovered that one of the roads the Family had been utilizing for travel was torn asunder by a skip loader, a merry bonfire took place in yet another act of arson, transforming the skip loader into naught but a burning mass of molten metal. Not surprisingly, the little stunt pulled a lot of attention from the local law enforcement. When officers and rangers came poking around and scouting for the culprits (whose identity was likely very transparent by now, what with the related charges the Family had), Manson drew another line in the sand. Two rangers happened to be the most persistent, and they got on his nerves. Handing Watson a double-barreled shotgun, Manson directed him to an attic in a building as some kind of crude sniper location. He was told to wait there until the two rangers got close, then kill them both. Watson accepted the mission and ascended the stairs to the attic with the gaping holes in the boards and waited.

The next morning, October 2, 1969, Watson awoke with the shotgun in his hands. He was still waiting to catch a glimpse of the two National Park rangers who had rubbed Charlie wrong and end their lives. But too many questions were presenting themselves now in his more lucid mind. In his own words:

> I looked down at the gun and knew…I was not going to use it. I was not going to kill again for Charles Manson…. I would not kill anyone. Not again.[79]

Watson threw the gun to the floor and fled the building as fast as his legs could carry him, gripped the steering wheel of his hot-wired Toyota with shaking hands, and drove like messy, brown lightning across the muddy floors of the Golar Wash.

All of a sudden, he was running from the Family, the drugs, the sex, the race war, the hole in the ground, the programming, the campfires, the murders…and he was running from Manson.

Mystery Solved

In the uncomfortable surroundings of his parents' home back in Texas, feeling at least two or three surreal worlds away from them at any moment, Watson tried to settle into a life he knew he could never live again. Somewhere in the back of his mind, he was ever aware of the possibility that at any moment there would be a knock at the door and he would be carted away, his murderous secret unveiled. For some reason, however, he wasn't concerned about that.[80] Away from Manson, his thoughts floated continuously from one extreme to another, feeling "self," feeling dead, being free, living under rules… The psychological detoxification his brain needed to think clearly required too much from him, and his careless parents were expecting too much from him also, what with all their making him meals, caring for his health, and attempting to get to know him better while the television was on. Watson was, by his own admission, incredibly selfish, and it showed. If his parents even spoke to him, he screamed back.

In the following days, Watson nervously traveled here and there, from Texas to Hawaii, to Los Angeles again, and then back to Texas, not sure what to do with himself. He almost returned to Manson at one point, but was so sure Manson would kill him or ask him to kill again, that he decided against it.

On November 30, about three and a half months after the murders, Watson entered his father's shop and met face to face with his father and his uncle. Their expressions said it all. It was over.

The day after his father, mother, and uncle dropped him off at the sheriff's office, the news of the century, that the Tate/LaBianca killer had been arrested, was the front-page headline all over the country. Within a few days, Watson's father would paint over the last name "Watson" on the sign outside the family store, a business that had taken him his whole life to build.

A Different Kind of Crazy

Watson's attorney in Texas was an old friend. He didn't even pretend to think that Watson was innocent. (Really, by this point, only a few did.) However, Watson's name had sprung into national news so hugely overnight, and so many variations of the story already existed in print and documentation all claiming to be the "true" details (not to mention that, around this time, the other Family members responsible were already starting to testify with their versions back in California), that Watson's attorney fought for his client's right to remain in Texas. The national pretrial publicity, the anger in the state of California, and the chances that the two would land a biased jury with a chosen verdict of death sentencing before trial even began, equaled Watson's stay of extradition. It would be nine months of incarceration in Texas with several legal delays before the presiding judge in California would refuse to hear of anymore unfair trial treatment, and "Tex" would be brought to California to face the same prosecution as the others.

In the meantime, what little faith Watson ever had in Charlie Manson was diminishing by leaps and bounds every day. So many secrets that Manson kept from the Family came to the surface, and his skeletons were out of the closet, whether he liked it or not. Watson hadn't known that his personal "God," the so-called Jesus Christ of the Bible, as Manson claimed, had been born not of a virgin, but, contrastingly, of a prostitute who had at one point sold him for a pitcher of beer,[81] and whose heavenly son was now nothing more than a five-foot-two, gaunt man with no more power to save the world than he had to bend open the bars of his prison cell. He was a diagnosed paranoid schizophrenic, who, self-admittedly, was now proudly "five hundred schizophrenics"[82] all rolled into one.

Watson found himself, now sober, quickly confronted with the ridiculous ease at which he threw himself at a false savior and drank from the cup of lies without restraint. On one hand, Manson's love was real! Watson had felt it and lived it and served it unconditionally, and had seen and heard things, *mysterious* things, from and around Manson that nobody could deny. On the other hand, following this "God" had resulted in draining the life out of him and turning him into a killer. Perhaps the forces that created the mystery constantly surrounding Manson weren't of heavenly origin after all.

There was nothing Watson could say or do that wasn't reported openly, and in the worst of light. Some legal advice, in an effort to help him keep his nose as clean as possible before his trial, came to him in the form of a familiar phrase.

Watson had the right to remain silent.

And he did. *Perfectly* silent.

Immediately, the walls of captivity pressed upon him night and day. Bruce Davis, another Family member in the Los Angeles County Jail cell directly above him, shouted down Helter Skelter promises and violent obscenities in an attempt to inspire "Tex" to resurface, always reminding Watson of what he had become, but "Tex" said nothing in return. Visitors from the Family came to see him with x's carved in their foreheads, and all he could do was stare at them. Television reports blared his name constantly in association with how much pain he had caused and how horrible a person he was (with almost as much news coverage as the Kennedy assassination), and no response from him would have changed a thing. Withdrawn into silence, Watson's only response to the world around him was to throw himself into the prison bars and scream like a tortured animal for some kind of release, until even that was more expression than he could take, tipping the scales with agony being the only sound he heard from his own body, and he closed his mouth again.

It was almost as if Watson had taken a monastic vow in memorial to something or someone for the purposes of internal reflection. It had not started out that way, but it was quickly turning into the inescapable side effect of a man with so much to process and nowhere to go but "in." The longer he remained without saying a word to anyone, the more he retreated into himself. But for Watson, "self" had long since departed, sacrificed for the greater and universal oneness, leaving nothing behind but a dead man wrapped in living tissue. His heart was beating, but *he* was gone.

Unbelievably, despite all the hurt he had hammered down in inconceivable, suffocating loads upon his parents, they continued to stand by him. In a way, he had killed them also. At the very least, he took away the simple lives that they'd had before and the world as they knew it in their ignorance of the person their son had the capability to be. He had brought the ultimate shame on their household and effectively muddied their name forever. Even the Methodist minister that Mrs. Elizabeth Watson had relied upon for spiritual encouragement and mentorship in her time of agony shunned her by association of her son's foul and demented reputation.[83] Yet, despite how angry in their spirit they must have been; and despite how justified they would have been to disown him, spit in his face, and declare him dead to their family; and despite how many times they must have wept in a sea of suffering as they reflected on tragically innocent memories of a little boy skinning his knee and climbing trees and catching frogs, when they came to see him in person, they spoke gently and kindly, treating their son as if he were still a human being whose mind, body, and soul had some deep-down chance of redemption.

Although Watson couldn't fathom why they regarded him with such forgiveness and hope, it reminded him of stories he'd heard as a child… stories of a Man who came and died on the cross so that others would have the chance of forgiveness. His mother and father were Christ-like, and yet, refreshingly, they were not at all Manson-like. Contrarily, they had always supported him being his own person, and hoped that he would use the talents and dreams and drive that made him who he was, his *self*, to further serve the kingdom of God. They had wanted him to serve Christ all along.

But that Man had died long ago. The evidence was in the paintings.

When Watson's mother sent a Bible to his prison cell, he wasn't surprised. With nothing but time on his hands in his impersonal and depressing living space, and an unofficial vow of silence that was turning him into a vegetable from the inside out, he had nothing better to do but to crack it open. You know...for entertainment.

He was expecting the ancient words to sound poetic and speak of a time long since washed away in the archives of history, and he was expecting the ancient rules and laws to reflect a nostalgic period of innocence when crimes were committed by hearts and minds that were inherently evil and not under the influence of acid. But he was not expecting the words in that dusty manual for old people to interest him, nor to ever bring him peace.

For the first time, he read the story of how the pale Jesus from his childhood Sunday school pictures ended up on the cross in the first place, what He stood for, what He did for the world, and how He, too, had been murdered in innocence by a group of religious radicals with their own agenda. The words started as something elegant and antique, and slowly took form as just the tiniest light in a sea of darkness, the thought he would focus on when everything else crumbled, the glue that held him together when everything in his mind tried to shut down and go completely mad.

> The stories became something more than fairy tales about men in bathrobes. It was nothing I could put words to, hardly even a feeling, far less than belief.... Perhaps the name for it was hope.[84]

Before long, Watson's physical state worsened, and he had dropped fifty-five pounds, bringing his weight from an already-lean 165 pounds to 110, standing at the athletic height of six foot, two inches. He found that screaming at the bars and shaking them violently like a madman was a release again. His name was on everyone's lips, he was trapped, and there wasn't a moment that went by under his surveillance conditions that allowed any opportunity to breathe out from under the suffocating blanket of scrutinizing supervision. The walls were closing in, and he started to believe that the prison staff was spiking his food with drugs and that his hands glowed in the dark at night.[85] Bruce Davis continued to howl messages down to him as secretly delivered from those in the Family who were still free. Manson had turned Watson completely vegetarian (as the eating of meat was a mortal sin), and he ate even less as the prison staff mixed vegetables in with the meat. He continued to read the Bible and increased his reading periods the farther into insanity his mind drifted. He wouldn't let himself eat. He wouldn't bathe. He wouldn't stop screaming from his bars and rattling his cell. He wouldn't stop throwing his meals against the wall and launching streams of his toothpaste into the walkway on the other side of the bars. And when the day came that, during a reading session, it at long last clicked with him that he had taken the lives of humans, real people with real feelings and real families, and not "piggies," the guilt that flooded every corner of his consciousness finally sent him over the edge.

Watson was sent with guards and orderlies, bound by wrists and by ankles, to a crazy bed, and was fed through a tube up his nose to keep him alive. Three court psychiatrists were brought in to examine him. Their report stated that he was bordering on terminal as a result of a deep regression into a fetal state, and that he was verifiably insane. Science practices that were the most modern at the time of the trial were presented by the psychiatrists to help show the gradual breakdown of Watson's mind into a legitimate and clinical insanity. The same judge who had already ruled on Van Houten's sanity was evidently convinced enough of the psychiatrists' professional opinion regarding Watson that he had him committed for a ninety-day observation at the Atascadero State Hospital in California. (Prosecution would eventually find a couple of hand-picked psychiatrists who would share their own professional opinions to the jury suggesting that Watson had faked the episode. The local *Californian* jury, already exhausted from hearing the bloody details from the nonrepentant, singing, and giggling Family members on trial, and, already saddened over the death of people from their own home community, would agree with the prosecution, thereby dismissing Watson's mental state as an act. This conclusion would come despite the fact that eight witnesses were called to testify, each and every one of whom provided medical and neurological evidence that Watson's state of mind fit into the "clinically insane" category. This conclusion would also come despite several medical personnel testifying to the effects of the acid and speed [commonly called the "drug of violence"] on the human mind. The judge would later state for public record that if he had tried Watson's case without a jury, he, himself, might have arrived at a different verdict and ruled in favor of Watson's insanity, as evidently the signs were that clear.[86] According to forensic psychiatrist Dr. Michael Stone from the *Most Evil* series, "Watson [was] the victim of circumstance, blinded and bullied into participating in murder by a controlling leader. Without Manson's influence, there would have been no crime."[87])

Strapped to his bed on his back and alone, without even the ability to release a scream (his body was too weak to speak at this point), only one string of words came to Watson's psyche, repeating over and over in his head and deafening the sound of all else, inside or outside of his mind. It was Psalm 23. He had been required to memorize it as a child, and now, there, he let the words play out in his thoughts until they became a prayer. "The Lord is my shepherd; I shall not want." With ninety days of no interruption besides the shuffling about by the orderlies, the tube duties of the medical staff, and an occasional assessment, Watson had plenty of time to do nothing but tell Jesus, if there *was* a Jesus, "Yea, though I walk through the valley of the shadow of death, I will fear no evil, for thou art with me." And then, one day, a presence was there with him. Even in the moments when his mind seemed to be nothing but jelly and he was farther away from being a functional person than ever before, he had never felt anything like *this*. This was not a fleeting moment when his brain tapped into some deep, psychological paranoia and revealed that he was being watched. This being was new, never felt before, real, sincere, warm, comforting, and loving to the extent that would have made Manson in his warmest moments seem a frozen wasteland. And just as sure as the being was there, it was also beckoning for Watson to come closer.

Although it was never posed aloud, an unspoken question was clearly floating between them there, somehow: *Do you believe in Me?*

Watson, by this time, had no doubt.

FORGIVEN: THE CHARLES "TEX" WATSON STORY

As soon as his ninety-day observation period was over and he was considered capable, Charles Denton Watson faced trial. On March 29, 1971, the others in the Manson Family who had participated in the Tate/LaBianca murders had been given the death sentence. Watson remained on trial behind them, and in the following October (between the dates of October

Death Row

12 and October 21 to work out all the details of sanity/sentencing), he was found guilty of seven counts of murder in the first degree and one count of conspiracy to commit murder. He, alongside Manson, was stationed in San Quentin's death row to await the death sentence by gas chamber. (As stated previously, this sentence was converted to life in prison. See the previous case study on Susan Atkins.)

For the first couple of years, Watson faced a lot of insanity rehabilitation, only offered to him via life's twists, turns, and ripples, not through an institution.

Although there were moments of weakness and moments that the distraction of rough prison life deterred him from completely focusing on this newly found Jesus without interruption, *something* happened to him in that hospital that he could never ignore. A seed of hope had been planted that he found himself always coming back to. Each and every day, slowly but surely, Watson's head began to clear and he started to find "a little more of the self that [he'd] worked so hard to destroy."[88] The closer he came to an understanding of God's forgiveness, the more he felt the pangs of guilt about the people whose lives he had truly annihilated: the victims *and* their families.

Yet, despite these changes, and these were *hugely positive* changes, his attempt at connecting with the real God and the real Jesus was strained. The Word of God spoke life and renewal into him each time he read, but something in the background was always left wanting. Something unfulfilled.

Then, one day in late 1974, while Watson was meeting with a friend in the visiting room, he overheard an enthusiastic conversation between a prison buddy of his and some girl he had never seen. Regardless of Watson's efforts to stay focused on his own guest, his attention kept snapping toward this girl's words. She spoke with such joy and life as she shared about her relationship with Jesus Christ. Jesus, this girl was saying, was everything to her, and in trade, she would give all of herself to Him. She would not merely expect Christ to be there for *her* and *her* needs, as that was a one-way relationship. She gained more excitement and satisfaction from using her talents and her dreams (and her "self" perhaps?) to be in complete service to her best Friend.

All the praying and reading of the Bible that Watson had done in the interest of getting to know the Christ who had died for even the worst, ugliest, and most monstrous of sins could not accomplish the intimacy of the relationship this girl spoke of now. Watson sensed that it was because of a commitment, but he didn't know if he would ever be ready for that, ready for more dying to his own person to focus on a higher calling.

This moment of observing the girl in the visiting room stuck with Watson just as his experience in the hospital bed had. The lasting impression that there was something more there for him to take, *and* there for him to give, affected his thoughts dramatically. During this time, Chico Holiday, a prison minister and evangelist, established a connection with Watson at the request of Watson's mother, who was still visiting her son and praying often for her his growth. Holiday sent Watson a couple of his books, which inspired Watson to start regularly attending chapel on the prison grounds. Unavoidably, word spread that the Tate/LaBianca killer was frequenting chapel, as not a single move of Watson's could be private. Nonetheless, he continued going to chapel and, as a result, heard a musical group from yet another prison ministry called Psalm 150. Their music, such a contrast to the pain, death, and war of the Helter Skelter Family music that had last affected him so deeply, left Watson with yet another moment that would tack itself to his spiritual thoughts for some time to come.

The more time he spent with his fellow brethren at the prison chapel, the more he realized that the "something" missing from his personal relationship with Jesus was something *they* all seemed to have. It would be some time before the man who killed for Manson would ever be fully capable of understanding a relationship with Christ as it was biblically meant to be.

That was when Watson met Reverend Ray Hoekstra (the prison chaplain who coauthored his biographical manuscript, *Will You Die for Me?*). Hoekstra had a rare and beautiful gift. Unlike the people within the prison yards, Hoekstra was not guarded and rough, and his understanding of God was not affected by some spotted past that rendered his theology abnormal. Unlike free people on the outside of prison walls who would find Watson's presence sickening or intimidating, this Texan minister was completely unaffected in a social setting by Watson's horrific crimes, even though he took the crimes very seriously. He loved Watson, as his big smile often showed. There was nothing perverse or conspiratorial about his friendship or love toward this mixed-up prisoner. It was simple and refreshing.

Eventually, through the intervention of those who had been placed in his path, Watson came to the understanding that although the Lord was giving him everything, he wouldn't truly be able to fully experience the real God until he gave himself and all of his talents completely over to God for His service. Manson, for all of his crazy talk, did at least get one thing right: In order to fully be intrinsically driven toward God, one has to die to self. The part that Manson theology had demonically twisted was what the true Jesus would *do with* that person once he or she had given themselves over completely. In full submission to the Lord Jesus Christ, one could be reborn into a new "self": a "self" that could reflect an individual's hopes and dreams, and the desires of one's own heart, desires that a person didn't have to feel ashamed of as a part of one's own identity.

The difference was astoundingly simple, and throughout all this time, Watson had missed it. The difference was that, when one man dies to his "self," *he becomes a new "self" in Christ*. The true identity of a person did *not* have to be erased from the pages of history in order to be of any use to a higher purpose, and God's Word was true in and of itself, even without the required use of mind-altering remedies. It was so simple, and yet no matter how many guarded moments Watson expected the truth to reveal some perverse expectation of him, this new truth continued to resonate a genuine certainty. Charles Denton Watson could be Charles Denton Watson and still give himself completely to the Lord.

On June 1, 1975, Watson raised his hand upon the invitation to dedicate himself heart, soul, body, and service to Jesus Christ. An usher at the back of the chapel came and took him by the arm and walked him to the altar. He knew in that moment that this dedication would require giving up the last nonmaterial item he wished for in this life: his freedom. Although he would patiently continue to attend parole hearings and put his best self forward in hopes that the Lord had it in His will to allow Watson to re-enter society, he knew that if the Lord so deemed his life's work to take place behind bars, it would not deter him from a commitment to the Lord's service.

On June 16, 1975, Watson was baptized in a plastic laundry cart in the chapel garden.

Within a short time, he became an "associate pastor in charge of [the chapel's] worship department, student chaplain program, yokefellow groups therapy, and [worked with] the administration"[89] in his own office at the side of the chapel.

In 1978, Hoekstra and Watson collaborated on *Will You Die for Me?: The Man Who Killed for Charles Manson Tells His Own Story*, a book that has touched "thousands of prisoners spiritually."[90] He dedicated the book to his parents, Elizabeth and Denton Watson. (Ironically, later that same year, minister Jim Jones, another cult leader attempting to radically rectify the failure of the American establishment, led 909 people of different races, including men, women, and children, into a mass suicide/

mass murder via cyanide poisoning. This event was the world's largest cult-related massacre.)

In 1979, Watson married Kristen Joan Svege, and, through conjugal visits, she conceived four children: three boys and one girl. (Later, in 2003, after twenty-four years of marriage, as a result of a state ban on conjugal visits in '96, the couple divorced. Kristen remarried. They remained friends.)

Watson "founded the original Abounding Love Ministries in 1980, and became an ordained minister in 1983."[91]

In 1986, Watson began trading letters with a young woman who was curious about his case and his Christian conversion. A year later, in 1987, this woman came to speak to Watson in the visiting room in prison and asked him to tell his story: everything from his childhood, to meeting Manson, to the murders, and beyond to his relationship with Christ. (At this point, it had been about eight years since his complete dedication to Christ.) When Watson had finished, the woman revealed her true identity: Suzanne LaBianca, daughter of Rosemary LaBianca and stepdaughter to Leno LaBianca, who personally suffered a nervous breakdown as a result of Watson's spree. Suzanne and Watson went on to form a unique friendship; further, she went on to represent him at his parole hearings with the California Board of Pardons, testifying that he was a changed man through Christ and that she had completely forgiven him. In 1990, this relationship was referred to as "an unholy alliance between survivor and crazed killer" on the popular television show, *A Current Affair.*[92] This episode played an excerpt of her appeal:

> I am the daughter of Rosemary and Leno LaBianca…. I've had much time to think about the crimes Charles [Watson] committed. They affected me as much as anyone else who loved any of the victims. It has taken time, information, knowledge, and God's love for me to come to the opinion and conclusion that I have reached…. Charles has changed, in that he is not the same individual that he was twenty-one years ago. In the past twenty-one

years, Charles' case has continually been placed before the eyes and ears of the public in a very negative way. I feel this has been unfair. I believe if this case is going to continue to be viewed by the public…they deserve to know another side of Charles' life. They should be aware that he is nothing like the news media has… excuse me.… They should be made aware that he is not rotting away in a prison cell, that he is using productively the time given to him…and that he is pressing forward to become all that God created him to be.[93]

Watson's personal testimony would also air on a 1991 episode of *The 700 Club*, wherein he would also grant a very rare interview sharing his regret, saying, "I hate what I've done. I hate having to be the person that [has] committed a crime that's so hideous. I hate that."[94] Further on in his interview, he shares tearfully about the moment that Suzanne LaBianca revealed her true identity to him in person:

And then she said, "My mother was Rosemary LaBianca," and…I just really didn't know how to take that. I said, "You're kidding," and she said, "No, I'm not kidding." And, as I sat there, I just said to myself… *I killed her mother and father!* That was, uh, really hard to take.… I think…what the experience with [Suzanne] has done is to really teach me and show me and allow me to experience the grace and the love of God. I understood before she came to forgive me that I was loved by God. I understood the love of God, and I loved God. But after she came and forgave me, I took on a whole new, uh, *love* for God, because I experienced in even a more personal way God's love working through another individual.[95]

In 1993, Cutting Edge Film International produced an award-winning docudrama on Watson's life called *Forgiven: The Charles "Tex" Watson Story*. The movie runs for slightly less than an hour and tells the story of his life and the murders in the setting of the prison visiting room with a young girl. At the end of the movie, the girl visiting with him reveals herself to be Suzanne LaBianca, to the Watson character's surprise. (The movie initially stirred a controversy, as it had been seen by some as a glorification of Watson's life, the murders included. This author has seen the film in its entirety and does not agree, on the basis that the movie steers clear entirely of blood, gore, and sensationalism, never once glorifies Watson for either his murders or his conversion to Christianity, and focuses almost completely on the forgiveness of Suzanne LaBianca.)

As the accessibility and popularity of the Internet dramatically increased in the 1990s, Watson, with the help of his friends and family outside prison walls, launched a website for Abounding Love Ministries in 1997. It is still maintained and updated today. As of the most recent report prior to the existence of the Internet website (Watson's 1983 parole hearing), Abounding Love Ministries was "in contact with thirteen hundred prison chaplains throughout the United States and Canada. [They] also [had] twenty-five hundred to three thousand people on [their] general mailing list that [they ministered] to."[96] Now that the ministry has gone primarily paperless, the website has received millions of hits worldwide[97] and releases a monthly "View" (or newsletter) with a word from Watson, as put up by the site's maintenance crew.[98]

Thanks to Amazon's recent Kindle publishing channels, Watson has been able to publish three more electronic books: *Manson's Right-Hand Man Speaks Out*,[99] *Our Identity: Spirit, Soul, and Body*,[100] and *Christianity for Fools*,[101] the first of which is free, and the second and third costing the reader ninety-nine cents.

Watson has been denied parole fourteen times between 1976 and 2011. At the time of this writing, he is being held in the Mule Creek State Prison in Ione, California, and his next parole hearing is scheduled for November of 2016.[102]

INTERVIEW with Charles "Tex" Watson

In order to gain further insight on Watson's case, the publishing team behind this book reached out to him through the mail, telling him about our book. He agreed to an exclusive interview and informed us that he would consider our project prayerfully. After his consent, we sent him a list of questions, composed by several people in our publishing group as well as Donna Howell, and the letters were sent from the desk of Thomas Horn. The following was that correspondence. Note that we have arranged the layout in a Q&A style for the reader's convenience, and that except for the omission of certain addresses, phone numbers, or names for privacy protection, all answers have been provided wholly as Watson has written them, without alteration, and all ellipses and underlining was present in the original:

**BETWEEN THOMAS HORN, DEFENDER PUBLISHING GROUP
AND CHARLES DENTON WATSON, PRISONER B37999
LETTERS BETWEEN FEBRUARY AND MAY OF 2014**

Do you have a close fellowship of believers at your prison?

Yes, we have a close fellowship of believers at services, Bible studies, Christian 12-Step groups, and prayer meetings, both in the chapel buildings and on the yard.

I rotate with two other men (elders), preaching at the Sunday service, sharing the pulpit weekly with the chaplain. I teach a week class after the Sunday service. We have a Wednesday a.m. chaplain's circle, a noon prayer meeting where we pray for the prayer requests, for the sick in-person, and for men to be saved, their families, and the world. We follow up on the requests. We see men saved, healed, and delivered from depression, guilt, and shame. Afterwards, there is a Wednesday service where younger brothers preach and teach as part of their training in ministry.

*Do you help the chaplain and would it be okay if we wrote him for a
testimony regarding your work? If you prefer we don't, that is okay.*

Yes, I've always worked closely with a chaplain for almost forty years—
saved in prison. You can email the present chaplain and call the prison
[the rest of this answer omitted for privacy protection]…

*In our upcoming book we also chronicle the arrests and salvation of
people like David Berkowitz (David is exchanging letters with us, too).
Have you ever corresponded with other such high-profile inmates who
became Christians and have had an enduring ministry? If so, please tell
me about that (i.e., how it happened and whether it is still ongoing).*

I've met several high-profile inmates who were released in the '70s–'90s
that Chaplain Ray Hoekstra of International Prison Ministries brought
into the prison, such as Murf the Surf, Clyde Thompson (I think that
name is right), he wrote *Devil at the Wheel* (Bonnie and Clyde's driver)
put out by Chaplain Ray. [Note that Bonnie and Clyde's driver was William Daniel Jones, a.k.a, "Deacon" Jones, paroled in 1941, and after the
popularity of his reputation increased due to the release of a romanticized
version of the Bonnie and Clyde story into film, he was shot in the summer of 1974. Clyde Thompson, a.k.a., "The Meanest Man in Texas," was
yet another famous prisoner for gun-related crimes who died of a heart
attack in the summer of 1979. There are several books with a similar title
to *Devil at the Wheel,* and one with this exact title was authored by Gor-
don McLean and Ken Pestana in 1974 and 1975. Pestana was incarcerated for his involvement in a brutal convenience-store murder. It could be
one or several that Watson is referring to straight from his memory here.
UPDATE: After another letter from Watson, he is sure it was the book
written by Chaplain Ray, published by International Prison Ministry in
Dallas or Los Angeles.] I write several lower-profile released inmates who
have been in the prison ministry with me, continuing strong, some in
ministry to inmates.

Please discuss what you believe are the most important aspects of your ministry now—in other words, how have you seen your ministry help people inside and outside of prison?

The most important aspects of ministry now? Love (God/Jesus loves you), grace and forgiveness, plus he that has been forgiven much, loves much; bask in His love and forgiveness. Men in prison, and those who write, say, "If God can forgive you, there is hope for me!" (See Feb. 2014, Monthly View, AboundingLove.org, plus other views with testimonies.) [Note that we have accessed this article, and it involves a letter written to Charles Watson from a college student and recovering drug addict named Jeff. Jeff wrote the following in his letter: "It was after reading your books, that God made it real to me that He could do ANYTHING; change anyone, forgive ANYONE, love anyone; that His blood had already washed my sins. It was that day that all of the guilt, those questions, those doubts were lifted from me.… God worked thru [*sic*] you to reach me; even 3,000 miles away. Your work for the Lord while incarcerated has been an inspiration, and I sincerely wish you well. I am praying for you and may you continue to be such wonderful service to our Lord. God bless you!" The rest of the article and Jeff's letter can be accessed here: http://aboundinglove.org/mv/2014/mv-002.php.]

The turn-over of men is great and because of my high profile, men always want to meet me, and there is the opportunity to minister God's love, grace, and forgiveness. This is a daily witness as men approach me and me [to] them.

There are opportunities at every turn around a 1/3-mile track (around the yard) to witness to the lost, pray for and with men both lost and believers, especially for the sick, since a lot of high-risk medical prisoners live around me. We anoint with oil and lay hands on the sick—men in wheelchairs, walkers, growths on their face, and other ailments—who need comforting, a word, or touch and prayer, which occurs often.

Please provide any special "praise reports" from people as a result of your ministry.

It's recorded in my book *Will You Die for Me?* how I ripped a drug dealer off in 1969 for $2,750.00 named Lotsapoppa, because he weighed so much. Manson ended up shooting him in the stomach when he threatened the family because of the rip-off. He testified against Manson at the Tate/Labianca murder trial. In the '80s, Lotsapoppa ended up in prison. His claim to fame was Manson's bullet still in his stomach. He ended up getting saved in prison, and ended up coming to the prison where I was housed, and came over to the chapel to see me. I had gotten word through Chaplain Ray that he had seen Lotsapoppa in another prison and had gotten saved, so when he walked into the chapel with a huge smile, I knew he had forgiven me. We sat down and shared his and my wonderful testimony of how Jesus had rescued us. The following Sunday we took communion side-by-side—Oh what a Savior!

Obviously there are those even in churches who struggle to forgive when the crime includes murder. People want severe punishment and confuse "forgiveness" with the perpetrator "getting away with it." Obviously I'm not telling you something you don't already know, but how do you deal with this earthly dilemma?

Those in church struggling with forgiveness of murders, and the like, lack the knowledge of God's love, grace, and forgiveness, otherwise they'd be rejoicing with the angels when one is saved. In my case, I didn't reap death, which I sowed, but I didn't get away with it with life in prison as the consequence. As those in the church walk in the Spirit of Grace, they will be empowered to forgive as Christ forgave (Eph. 4:32). Until then, we can't expect carnal Christians to forgive. What's impossible with man is only possibly with God. Let us be understanding! My book *Manson's Right-Hand Man Speaks Out!* addresses this subject. [Throughout this section of Watson's letter, he wrote up the sides of the notebook pages two additional notes. The first note on the left: "As a church, we must 'keep ourselves built up in the most holy faith, praying in the spirit (Jude 20, 21), keeping ourselves in the love of God.'" The second note on the right: "'Beware of bringing Conservative Politics into the Church! Rather, the Church into Conservative Politics.'"]

Do you still struggle with guilt?

I stay built up in faith righteousness as addressed in my book, *Christianity for Fools*. Faith righteousness keeps my soul above condemnation. I only struggle with guilt when I have to focus heavily on the crime, victims, and the great loss. To the contrary, we're taught by Paul to "Set our affections on things above… Think on those things that are true, honest, just, pure, lovely, and of good report…old things are passed away…and to forget those things that are behind." Healthy people heal people, but hurt people, hurt people. We can have remorse without guilt and toxic shame, which some folks call healthy guilt. Jesus came to heal us spiritually, mentally, and emotionally, so we can make good choices and walk in healing physically. This takes a continual battle against the temptation or attack of guilt and shame through faith in the finished work of the cross, and our identity in Christ, who we are, what we have, and what we can do. (See my book, *Our Identity: Spirit, Soul, and Body*.)

We know that Suzanne LaBianca has forgiven you, and has even spoken out on your behalf. How have other family members of former victims responded to your confession of faith?

Yes, other victim's family members have forgiven me, but want to remain anonymous, because others in their families don't share their beliefs; plus they see the persecution that comes with forgiveness—[Watson goes on to make a note about the name by which Suzanne LaBianca is now known, and this portion of his answer is omitted for privacy protection]…

Have old friends you knew before you were arrested ever tried to contact you?

Yes, several of my high school classmates have contacted me and presently write, especially those who are now Christians and serving the Lord.

Do you have remaining biological family? If so, do they correspond or visit you?

Yes, my biological family corresponds and visits me from time to time. They live in Texas, so they don't visit often.

You had a wife, correct?

My wife divorced me in 2003. After 24 years of marriage, with no sight of release, she wanted to move on in life. We remain friends and parents of our four children. They are successful: a marine, lawyer, nurse, and student.

From what we have been able to gather, drugs played a very large role in leading up to the events of the late 1960s. Is this correct? Are there any warnings or advice that you would give, if you could, to young people who are also seeking fulfillment in the wrong places?

Drugs led me to make a lot of bad choices. They affect the brain in such a way that causes it not to think, reason, and emote right. As a result, my actions became animalistic, which resulted in a multitude of victims—a ripple effect.

As far as advice to children [young people], "Live life for the long haul and not for instant gratification. The love that you are looking for is God's love, not man's. His love will fulfill your deepest need tenfold more than the world could ever offer." After receiving Jesus, the Holy Spirit revealed to me that His love and wisdom is "ten times better" than drugs (Daniel 1:20).

Throughout your writings, we have seen you make the statement that your story has been told with inaccuracies and misinformation, whether the teller is sincere or looking to gain attention or fame for their report.

In our case study on you, we tried to address some of these inaccuracies. If you were to be allowed to say one thing to the public on your own behalf regarding this, what would you say?

I don't feel I hearken on that often. (Please don't make a big thing out of this, no big deal, except for what I produce.) My book *Will You Die for Me?* is the most accurate book about the crimes.

We have heard you now prefer to drop the nickname "Tex." Is this because of association to the events of 1969? Or is this for another reason?

It was only "Tex" for nine months with the Manson Family. I've only been called Charles otherwise. "Tex" is associated with the old man, not my real name or the real me.

As you know, Susan Atkins (Sadie) gave her heart to the Lord while she lived. Can you give us comment on this from your own perspective? Do you believe her conversion to Christianity was sincere based on what you knew of her?

Yes, Susan Atkins [was] 100 percent authentic for Jesus, no doubts. Her testimony in prison around the girls was bright. She led hundreds to Christ and had a mighty healing ministry.

    She had a group of <u>seven</u> other women in her Prayer Band, *<u>who she led to Jesus</u>*. The girls were part of the [Symbionese] Liberation Army in the '70s. I have a photo of the seven standing in gowns around Susan. Most of them were at one time on the Most Wanted list. I don't know all their last names in the photo, but their names are: Margie, Shirley, Yolanda Melina, Emily Harris (well-known; I knew her husband in prison), Patty Hearst, Sherry, and Diane (who aren't quite as well-known).

Although many have reason to believe that Charles Manson is not a Christian and doesn't appear to be asking for Christ's forgiveness for his part in crime, if he were to ask of that tomorrow, do you believe that there is a part of him that could be sincere and therefore saved?

Only God knows CM's [Charles Manson's] heart. I can't judge if there is a part of him that can be sincere. God requires repentance from him like any other sinner, who is part of the fall of man. Let us pray that God will open his heart before long to the truth of the Gospel of Jesus Christ. That his prideful heart will be humbled to God's word, Amen.

Have you tried to witness to Charles Manson? Do you and he ever communicate? How about other members of the family inside or outside prison?

I've had no contact with CM. I ministered for thirteen years with Bruce Davis from 1980 to 1993. He was a member of the Manson Family in the '60s, came to Christ in '74, and became a Doctorate of Theology. He is a wonderful teacher and witness of the Gospel of Christ. I was once in contact with Catherine Share (Gypsy), who is also an outstanding Christian witness. That's it.

We are currently in contact with Charles Manson's grandson for our project. His biological father, Charles Manson II, took his life years ago. Have you ever come into contact with Charles Manson's grandson? If you could say anything to him now, what would it be?

No contact. I'd tell him to keep the faith. Tell his grandmother I said hello, look unto Jesus, the author and finisher of your faith—not Manson fame.

Please tell me what you would hope our book could convey on your behalf and other inmates that have been born again and are now new creatures in Christ.

God is no respecter of persons. God is Love!

CASE STUDY 3

Photo used by permission of
The Oklahoman, © 1987

SEAN SELLERS[103]

The water was cold.

Like an invigorating, electric pulsation starting at the skin and penetrating the depths of his mind, streams of liquid rejuvenation raced down his body from the showerhead above and to the drain below, bringing an alert edge to his senses. Now he was truly awake. This feeling was like nothing he had ever dreamed of or read about, even in the most enlightening of books.

It had been several years since his babysitter had taken him to the library that day, and his personal collection of resources on the world of the supernatural had grown by leaps and bounds. If it had been left to his mother, he would have never been able to study the perks of occultism, but his babysitter proved useful and educational. The library had offered a wealth of information on witchcraft, astral projection, ninjutsu, Zen, satanism…anything a young mind like his ever needed to know in order to begin a life of self indulgence and success. So much had changed since then. Now, at sixteen, he held complete literal and spiritual authority over his own life.

Turning off the shower, he didn't bother to cover his own nakedness with the black ritual underclothes on the bathroom floor as he walked back into his parents' room. The smell of gunpowder still hung in the air, dressing the darkness with a foreboding curtain of demise. He flipped the light switch, allowing the brightness to pour over the bodies of his mother and stepfather, seeing them for the first time since the blinding flash of the gun in the midst of blackness had left its imprint in his mind.

He observed their stillness.

Then he giggled...hysterically.[104]

VICTIMS OF A CULTURAL PARADIGM

The "Satanic Panic." It was an era throughout the '80s and '90s when interest in the occult, especially amid teen circles, was a nationwide phenomenon. Gone were the flower children of the '60s. The twinkling disco ball of the '70s had dulled with the dawning of the new gothic age. Kids traded in their afros and bell-bottoms for mohawks and black fishnet stockings. Dark Baphomet pentagrams shamelessly appeared on necklaces and earrings in respectful jewelry shops. Drug use landed on a much younger generation and included more powerful intoxicants than the world had ever seen. Inverted crosses and "666" became typical graffiti symbols spray painted next to gang tags on buildings. Newspaper headlines heralded a new trend in murder: ritualistic human sacrifice in the name of Satan.

There have been numerous volumes written about this cultural transition, as well as a mounting list of Internet discussion, talk-show coverage, documentaries, etc., all presenting varying reasons as to the cause of what took place during this period. Five books collectively launched a great deal of controversy: *The Satan Seller*, *Michelle Remembers*, *He Came to Set the Captives Free*, *Prepare for War*, and *Satan's Underground*. All of these titles were released just before, or at the peak of, the Satanic Panic, and they were presented as telling the true stories of survivors of the most horrific, grisly, and inhumane satanic cult and occult practices in American history. The authors of these books were welcomed into overnight fame, being treated as experts on the occult, and most obtained lucrative ministerial positions as a result of the experiences they wrote about. However, after investigations of the writers' claims, each has descended into the wrinkles of time after being exposed as presenting some of the most notoriously fraudulent "lies for Christ"[105] ever told. (John Todd was another famous fraudulent minister at the time who didn't write books about his lies regarding a nonexistent Illuminati Druid witch coven he was supposedly born into and appointed to be the high priest of. Instead of writing the tales himself, Jack Chick, who authored the renowned Christian ministerial "Chick Tracts" of the '60s through the present, published several tracts addressing Todd's warnings to the world. Although *Chick was completely innocent*, having only intended to warn the world of dangers he believed were truth as told by Todd, Chick's publications played an enormous role in the church's war on the occult during that time. Todd was later arrested and charged with rape and child molestation.) These books are only one example of lies like these, which became a trend, and soon many other insincere ministers in the Christian church would be cashing in their false claims for attention or monetary gain. Before long, this development had increased momentum, and even some who were genuine at this point, who had endured years as members of the "panic church," inadvertently perpetuated it out of habit and earnestness to lead the people, because it was the only form of leadership they had trained under. Now, the situation was to the point that a small, but ever-increasing, fraction of the Christian church was responsible for a complete misdirection of focus from "people and their closeness with the Lord" to the ongoing investigation of a covert satanic network gaining control over civilization, whether such a thing existed where they were looking or not.

Seem a bit melodramatic? It does, actually. But note that not every church was a part of this movement. Many great and strong ministries made it through this time unscathed. But for those that did not…well, what happens when an entire army has charged to the frontlines, putting all their strength against a few jumping imps, leaving their rear vulnerable to the deadly dragon creeping silently behind with the power to irreparably weaken the whole militia in one fatal, fiery breath? Satan loves a good distraction. While the Christian church was pulling its focus together to wage war against a decoy called "the satanic underground," the enemy brought a real spiritual warfare against the people in the church, attacking them from any vulnerable angle. So many pastors put their disapproving stares against those in their congregation for the way their flock members dressed or pierced their ears or tattooed their biceps or listened to music with "that devil's beat" that people became estranged from the gospel, and a rebellion arose even higher and with more zeal. And what happened when people were estranged from the gospel and feeling spiritually suffocated, losing interest in the church as a result of religious abuse, and feeling too exhausted to fight? They left their rear exposed to the dragon. When real attacks did come, sometimes now with authentic ties to the very satanic underground that the panic had assisted in establishing by this point, resulting in murder and crimes unthinkable, every fraudulent personality's "I told you this was happening; I told you so!" diatribe caught a second wind, which begat more panic and, sadly, more adherence to misdirection.

These tragic lies, of course, drove unnecessary fear into the hearts of concerned people and proceeded to fling unnecessary egg on the face of the Christian church after it was rightfully exposed. That much is a given. However, the other unfortunate side effect that is lesser recognized as a result of these famous hoaxes within religion is, both *before and after* the falsehoods were uncovered as scams, the popularity of such a war on occultism *provided something for the world to rebel against*. The more the flags of warning were enthusiastically waved by the church, whether or not the flags were legitimate, the more children and teens felt it was exciting to shock the conservative world and concerned parents around them by living on the gothic edge.

History will repeat itself. The approach and methods are different from one generation to another, but youthful, national rebellion against conservatism is a repetitious reality. In the 1960s, there was a revolutionary uprising of teens and flower children against the establishment. They didn't want to be told how long to wear their hair, whom to make love with, what kind of herbs or weeds they were allowed to put into their bodies, or what stance they should take on war and politics. Their embrace of freedom and peace—though they were more innocent looking to some than the black-donning gothics of two decades later—was their own brand of mutiny against what they viewed as oppression perpetuated by the traditional conformists—the difference being that the '60s conflict was centralized on establishment versus freedom, and the '80s conflict was centralized on God versus Satan.

Some view the Satanic Panic with a tone of cynicism, seeing it as nothing more than an unnecessary, sensationalistic, national alarm caused by a bunch of goofy ministers stirring the kettle of fear so they would have something to preach about. (And, as the list of fraud above only represents one small fraction of the religious games that occurred, with the term "religious abuse" becoming an often-spoken reality on the tails of that movement, it's no wonder many didn't take the church seriously in those days, thanks to those who rose in power as a result of fabrication or the twisting of Scripture to control their "sheep.") Others see this as a time when there was a very real and frightening satanic grip on the youth of this country. Although this author is not declaring one viewpoint over the other as personal opinion, nobody can deny that the heavily applied occult flavor of the criminal activity documented during the '80s and '90s speaks for itself. This epoch brought about an unprecedented loss of innocence. (And, although many might think that a decline in crime associated with satanism would be a natural result of the fizzling out of the Satanic Panic era, that is not necessarily the case. At the time of this writing, two of the biggest news stories in the past week covered the brutal murder of innocent people in the name of satanism. One suspect, who admitted to murdering a man who answered a Pennsylvania Craigslist ad and at least twenty-two other victims, is a soft-spoken, nineteen-year-old mother who was going on six years of activity in a satanic cult.[106] Two other suspects, sixteen- and seventeen-year-old boys from Texas, are being tried for the rape and murder of a seventeen-year-old girl whose body was discovered with an inverted cross carved on her abdomen and satanic ritual paraphernalia scattered around her.[107] Needless to say, the behavior drawn into focus during the Satanic Panic season may not be the first thing talked about in church every Sunday anymore, but it's still alive and kicking in the hearts of some troubled youth, and when red flags appear, they should be heeded.)

Among those who were more than just touched by the dark spiritual awakening during the Panic was convicted killer Sean Sellers, your *otherwise* average moody teenager. Before we visit his story, we will take a moment to reflect on those whose lives he took at point-blank range:

- Robert Bower (aged 35), Circle K convenience store clerk
  - o Shot behind the counter at his place of work
- Paul Leon "Lee" Bellofatto (aged 43), father of three children from a previous marriage, Green Beret combat veteran in Vietnam, army recruiter, truck driver, and stepfather of Sean Sellers
  - o Shot in his bed
- Vonda Bellofatto (aged 32), beautician, truck driver, and mother of Sean Sellers
  - o Shot in her bed

To the viewer of the televised news in March of 1986, seeing the heavily publicized photo of the cheerful Bellofatto couple posing next to their smiling young boy, the household that Sean Sellers had been living in seemed normal, stable, *happy* even.

It was not.

THE LATCHKEY KILLER

While not as famous a case as some of the others in this book, which equals a much longer row to hoe for the research end of things when materials are more obscure, some resources have documented Sellers' rocky developmental years and the things he faced therein. They are, not surprisingly, buried under insurmountably vast collections of the evils he committed. However, when these details are pulled to the surface and studied collectively, it is clear that from the earliest recordings of his life, Sellers suffered his own demons, as the saying goes, even before the demons were *real*. But please, before you, the reader, make any snap decisions about this sensitive case, *read to the end of this case study*. There are facts about Sellers that are so widely unreported (and when they are reported, they are instantly written off for reasons that will be discussed herein) that if we are willing to dig a little deeper, we will discover some startling truths about his life and last days in prison.

Sellers' involvement in the murders is clear: He was the one who pulled the trigger. After the three killings on two separate nights, Sellers laughed at what fools the victims had been. Like some devil-possessed, supernatural, maniacal villain in a horror movie, sixteen-year-old Sellers celebrated the deaths of three people, his own parents included, with fits of hilarity, proud of the superiority he had exercised over the common, lowly humans whose lives he had ended.

Vicious, no?

Yes.

And as the reader had likely already guessed, since Sellers' case is included in a book regarding redemption in circumstances that are more complicated than the surface headlines normally profess, he has a story of his own…a story that is rarely told. The rewind button has once again been pressed.

Holy Bedwetting Juvenile, Batman!

Sean Sellers was born on May 18, 1969, to Vonda, just sixteen years old. Vonda and Richard Sellers had married while Vonda was still only a girl of fifteen years, and by the time Sean was three years old, Vonda had divorced Richard, an unstable alcoholic. She met Paul "Lee" Bellofatto shortly thereafter, and they began a life together with occupations in truck driving, which led to a life on the road. They never stayed in one location long (by the time Sellers committed his crimes at sixteen, he would have moved thirty different times), and Sellers began "preferring isolation rather than [to] face the inevitability of leaving friends."[108] Many times, Sellers was left with extended family for long periods while his parents traveled throughout the country. Being chosen to sing "The Little Drummer Boy" in a solo for a Christmas pageant, but not being able to follow through with the song as his family had relocated before his performance,[109] was only one of many memories he would have in his adult years that reflected the effects of constant travel during his childhood.

As a toddler, Sellers had discovered a love of the ever-heroic comic book, and at five years old, he had taught himself to read by following the dialogue bubbles and pictures.[110] By the age of eight, Sellers had his first crush: Batgirl—specifically, the one from the 1960s television show. (She lived in a television; it stands to reason that she could travel with the boy from place to place, remaining a solid girl figure in his life.) Sellers frequently threw a towel around his shoulders as a cape and darted about the house with a makeshift Batman "utility belt" tied around his waist filled with whatever random items could pass in a young boy's imagination as superhero tools.[111]

Many children develop a relationship with an imaginary friend, so it was no surprise when Sellers, having never been in one place long enough to have a real companion, started to pull further into himself, befriending the familiarity and safety of his own imagination.

One day, while his mother and stepfather were traveling and he had been dropped off for another lengthy stay at a no-kids-allowed apartment complex with the next group willing to watch him for a time (in this case, it was a couple of distant relatives), Sellers lost his innocence as a result of being forced to participate in sexual acts with an older male relative.[112] (Later findings held "irrefutable proof"[113] of additional, multiple acts of forced sodomy upon young Sellers, both in and out of the family. This author established contact with Dr. Dorothy Otnow Lewis, Sellers' psychiatrist [more about her in the coming pages], and she shared some private thoughts on the subject. Out of respect to her wishes, and as a courtesy to readers who might find the details unsettling, we will not disclose more than this. Suffice it to say that profound child abuse was ever present.)

It was around this time (when Sellers was eight years old) that his imagination took a more serious turn, and the voices in his head were officially present, no longer the harmless, passing imaginary friend.

Also around this time, Sellers saw his biological father for the last time.[114] He shared one of his latest memories of their relationship with Dr. Fletcher Brothers in an interview for the documentary about his life and satanism, *Escaping Satan's Web*. Sellers said that one night when he was outside playing, his father's girlfriend told Sellers that his father loved him. He wondered why he had never heard it from his father, himself.[115]

The relationship between Sellers and his mother grew increasingly tense, despite what people on the outside could observe: Mother and son would manage to stay friends for the most part, all things considered, for a few more years, but there was no denying that the seed of rebellion was being watered now. In Sellers' words, she "[s]lapped me in the face, 'mashed my mouth'—a flat palm, straight-on blow to the lips that mashed my lips into my teeth,"[116] evidently hard enough that it would make his mouth swell. He goes on to tell of continual hitting with "wooden mixing spoons, butcher knife handles, hair brushes, [or] whatever she had in her hand"[117] anytime he showed disrespect or moved his head around too much during a haircut. According to a report on his childhood gathered by Amnesty International: "For years he displayed extremely paranoid behaviour.... [H]e would fix threads to doors and brush the knap of the rug in one direction before he would leave his bedroom, in order to see if anyone entered the room. He was subject to extreme mood swings, sometimes euphoric, other times suicidally depressed."[118] Sellers was very much a loner, and often lived the life of a latchkey kid, getting home from school and going straight to his room to be alone without spending any time engaging in pleasantries with whomever he was living with at the time. Some days early on might have been lonely, but people were hard to trust, and he learned that he liked life much better by himself.

Sometimes, he would be left with a babysitter, someone his mother trusted. On one such occasion, while Sellers was ten, the babysitter loaded him up in the car and took him to the library, like she had done several times before. While Sellers was looking at books, she went to a restricted area of the library where he wasn't allowed. When she returned, she had satanic books, an encyclopedia of witchcraft, and a few other items. They took the books to his house and flipped through the pages together; Sellers' imagination was whirling. When his mother returned home, she threatened to fire the babysitter if she ever caught her sharing those materials with her son again, but by that time, Sellers had tasted a very intriguing creativity juice. The experience would be one that he would never forget.[119]

When he was eleven years old, as the result of a cause that hasn't been documented, Sellers shattered his nose and received a concussion. It was revealed that he had cracked his skull in three places and would, from that day forward, suffer severe headaches. At the follow-up treatment, when the doctor pulled the packing out of his nose, Sellers—afraid to cry in front of his mother—gripped the arms of the exam-room chair and held his breath through excruciating pain. His tough-guy response to the situation did not go unnoticed. The doctor shared how impressed he was with the kid, as he had seen grown men cry under the same circumstances. Sellers' mother bragged to everyone for a while that her boy was tough.[120] (At the time it was not known that this head injury caused brain damage. That would not be discovered until a quantitative electroencephalogram test [QEEG] was administered in 1992.[121] Later, with little to no access to pain medications or marijuana in prison, the pain from his headaches was so ruthless and relentless "behind [his] right eye"[122] that he would lie down and beat on his forehead in an attempt to numb the pain; thoughts of suicide appealed to him as a release.)

But evidently, Sellers wasn't "tough" enough to toe the line. Reportedly, at twelve and thirteen, during a stint of time in the care of his uncle, Sellers was punished for wetting the bed. In cruel humiliation sacraments, he would be forced to walk around in diapers (or "nappies"), and if his bedwetting were to occur for two or more nights in a row, a dirty diaper would be placed on his head for an entire day. In the course of a hunting trip, Sellers would be referred to as a "wimp" if he did not show one of his uncles his willingness to "step on an animal's head and pull on its legs to kill it," or if he seemed disturbed by watching his uncle "put an axe on a wounded raccoon's head and pull on its legs until the head tore off."[123]

This weakness was one that his stepfather would reprimand him for, also, while he was around.

Whenever Sellers' parents, aunts, or uncles offered him marijuana, he turned down the offer. Finally, one day, he decided to grow up a little bit and show them he could be tough, so he took a toke with his uncle. His aunt didn't believe it at first because of how many times he had turned it down before.[124]

The voices in Sellers' head, though they often criticized him, grew more appealing to him the longer his relationship with his biological father demonstrated abandonment, the longer his relationship with his mother was a strained ticking time bomb, the longer his relationship with his stepfather and uncles continued to reveal that he was nothing more than a bedwetting sissy, and the longer his relationship with the rest of the world was...nonexistent.

Batman was still cool in a childish, nostalgic way, but Sellers was older now. It was time to trade in the comics for the Dungeons and Dragons' *Dungeon Master's Guide*.

Dungeon to Dungeon: From Board to Brain

In a documentary called *The Dungeons and Dragons Experience*, the opening line is spoken slowly and methodically by a voice that could be described as one you would hear in a fantasy film from a gentle and wise storyteller, while visually, board game pieces are being gently arranged and candles are being lit: "This game is a world, a world of weird monsters, strange peoples, and fabulous treasures. It is certainly make believe, yet it is so interesting, so challenging, so mind-unleashing, that it comes near reality. This world is not complete. It needs organizers and adventurers to order and explore it. It... needs...you."[125] By the time this sentence comes to a close and the words "It needs you" are spoken with dramatic pause and delivery, the camera blur dissipates to reveal a hand tenderly placing a small game pawn on the table: a full-color wizard (or shaman or druid) in a blue robe with what appears to be a magic scroll of sorts in one hand, and a magical staff in the other hand with the skeletal head and horns of a goat or a cow affixed to the top.

Everyone goes through seasons in life, seeking a true identity. Probably the most vulnerable age for this quest is between twelve and seventeen, when a person is not yet an adult, but too young to be a child. Is it possible that these young minds were finding an identity in this game? Is it possible that the game was so "mind-unleashing" and so "near reality" that, to a seeking, susceptible child or teen plugging his or her consciousness into a "world of weird monsters, strange peoples, and fabulous treasures," a counterfeit identity would rise from this experience?

The first edition of Dungeons and Dragons (D&D) was published in 1974 by Tactical Studies Rules Inc. (TSR). By 1979, TSR had made $2.3 million in sales, and by 1985, sales would grow to $100 million[126] (which is just under $300 million in today's fiscal math[127]). These numbers represent a lot of games sold to a lot of impressionable kiddos, right? But come on… Questions of personal identity?

Actually, the game has always popped up in this discussion, and it's not uncommon that, even years after the height of this hot-button period, it would be remembered as a plaything that would, to a degree, alter personalities. It was to *what degree* this would occur that has been the ongoing debate about the danger the game represented. Let's view a quick example.

Hollywood actor Vin Diesel wrote the introduction to a 2004 book called *Thirty Years of Adventure: A Celebration of Dungeons & Dragons*, and discussed his youthful experiences with the game on an episode of the television series *Shootout* with Peter Bart and Peter Guber:

BART: [Bart quotes Diesel's writing from the book.] "We were all drawn to the game because it allowed us to become these characters. Playing D&D was a training ground for our imaginations, and an opportunity to explore our own identities." [Bart turns to Diesel.] So obviously, gaming meant a lot to you as [you were] developing as a person.

DIESEL: Yes, it did Peter.… In the seventies growing up in New York City, or early eighties growing up in New York City, we played, very intensely, this game called Dungeons and Dragons.

And we would go and we'd buy these large canvases and treat them to make them look like, you know, old maps, aged maps, and then we'd create these worlds and we'd be in this campaign for eight months. Even while I was bouncing [referring to his work as a nightclub bouncer], which is the antithesis of Dungeons and Dragons, even while I was bouncing, if I had a night off, I was playing Dungeons and Dragons. And what would happen is, aside from the fact that it *is* a training ground for your imagination, but as you would play as a character, about two hours into it, your *voice* would change, your *body composition* would change, at any moment you could get up from the table [Diesel stands from the interview table and enthusiastically dramatizes pulling a sword from his back] and pull out a sword! And, you know. [Diesel returns to his chair.] You're more animated, as you would want to be.... [You are] able to live in this world of imagination.[128]

From a less-than-two-minute, casual clip of a Hollywood actor's memories, we received the following list of the game's characteristics: it provides the player an opportunity to explore identities; it helps a player develop as a person; it is played very intensely; some have spent as long as eight months on a single game; it is a training ground for imagination; it compels the changing of a voice and body composition (or body language); it prompts players to get up from the table to playact, or become, even temporarily, their characters; it allows players to be as animated as they would want to be; and players are able to "live in this world."

An opportunity to explore identities...

Why would Vin Diesel say that? He was not some Satanic Panic preacher at a podium, nor was he even attempting to bring fear, concern, or parental "keep an eye on your kids" focus into the conversation. In fact, it was quite the opposite. Any viewer of this clip can observe that this is a laid-back, lighthearted, nonbiased throwback about a *fun* pastime of a big, muscular, cutting-edge, famous movie guy whose only point was to discuss the *endearing* qualities of the game. If anything, his comments about discovering identities was delivered in a *positive* way, as if to suggest that the self searching that is so tied to this game was nothing more than the standard teenager's psychological process. Of course, some of this interview was said off the cuff, and it would be unrealistic to analyze the words he used in this conversation down to their literal and psychological implications. But his comment about an "opportunity to explore identities" was read from an introduction he wrote for a book—an introduction that he crafted, word by word, *with purpose and intent*, to help endorse a product. He said Dungeons and Dragons provided an "opportunity to explore identities" because, whether or not the game creators intended it to be that way, for many, that's what it was.

Diesel is an excellent example of how someone with a different set of circumstances in childhood can be far less affected by this phenomenon than others. Note, however: He never knew his biological father, his mother never really talked about him, as their relationship was evidently illegal at some point in American history due to antimiscegenation laws, and he is self-admittedly of "ambiguous ethnicity."[129] He lived in New York City, one of the roughest areas to grow up in, and he, like many others, was not above considering criminal activity. His early career in crime was cut short when he and his brother had broken into a local performance theater to vandalize it, and someone with both authority and justification to call the police and press charges acted instead within the interests and talents of the young boys and "handed them scripts and offered them parts in the upcoming show."[130] Diesel's profile as a youth, when cross-referenced with others whose names have been drawn into historical studies of the dangers of D&D, exposes a trend in the kinds of personalities this game attracted. One might wonder what alternate reality could have played out for Sean Sellers, a gifted writer, if someone had handed him a typewriter instead of a joint, or patted him on the back with a smile instead of making him prance around with a dirty diaper on his head.

In some cases, this identity phenomenon associated with D&D followed more confused individuals to the point of death, reportedly. On May 12 of 1987 (the year following Sellers' murders), the National Coalition on Television Violence publicly addressed the dangers of the game, acknowledging its link to deaths, internationally: "The controversy around…'Dungeons and Dragons,' continues to grow in the U.S.…. *Ninety deaths* have now been linked to a heavy involvement with these violence-oriented, fantasy war games. These include sixty-two murders, twenty-six suicides, and two deaths of undetermined causes."[131] Varying reports at the time (including the famous reports of Satanic Panic-era investigator Pat Pulling) presented different figures. Each study was conducted with the reporter's own ideas of what a "link to" the game would be, but no matter where you look, the reputation of D&D was constantly haunted by controversies surrounding and related to deaths in teens for more than an entire decade. In the flavor of the national rebellion of the time, the more the game was pulled into arms-flailing news by panicked parents, the more the youth with shock value at the forefront of their minds bought into the idea of the game as a lifestyle.

It's likely that, by now, some readers are thinking, *What? All this over a game?* Here, straight from Sellers, is a better explanation of how, for some, this game was much more than a game (from an interview with Dr. Fletcher Brothers in the documentary *Escaping Satan's Web*):

SELLERS: It's not a board game, you know? It's a role-playing game.…

BROTHERS: You take on the identity of a character.

SELLERS: Right, see, psychologists use role playing as therapy because it's so powerful. Role playing is where you have this character.… Now, this character on a piece of paper [sitting] before you has everything that you have, okay? It is a complete person. You know what color this person's eyes are. You know how much this person weighs. You know what color this person's hair is, how tall he is, how fast he can run.… You know what weapons he's good with. He has a past. You know what he's afraid of [and] what's happened to him in the past. This person is *absolute*. Now, a teenager who is dealing with reality and not really liking it, who is trying to get his foot in the door of life and make decisions on what's going to happen to me [note how Sellers' pronoun reference just changed from "his" to "me" and then back to "he" in the following words; more about this later], and realizing that the decisions he makes today [are] gonna affect the rest of his life, has a lot of time [spent] dealing with that reality, and that character that is in front of them is absolute. It doesn't change. It's a friend to him, and when he becomes that character, he knows exactly who he is, he knows exactly what he can do, what he can't do, and the fantasy world that he lives in has no morals, no limits, you know, no values except for his own.... He is a special person...and he can do whatever he wants to. Okay? You let a teenager loose in that world, and sometimes they don't wanna come back.[132]

To clarify some of the things that can happen during the game, Brothers interrupts Sellers at this point in the interview to ask about the legitimacy of rumors he had become familiar with. Sellers confirms that the game includes very dark role-play, including, but not limited to, murder, rape, and eternal vows offered to supernatural beings, gods, or deities. He explains that although Jesus Christ is an available deity that can be chosen as the governing Being for the characters the players develop, nobody ever chooses to make Christ that deity because, in D&D, Jesus Christ is the weakest of all divine entities, and it would be gaming suicide to choose Him. Sellers goes on to explain more of the significance of the vow a player must make to the supernatural being, and the servanthood that the player must show to his or her god of choice. Brothers responded by asking if kids playing D&D have any idea what they're dealing with.

SELLERS: No. No way.... The game also doesn't have an ending. People don't really understand that. The game can go on for *years*. People can meet every night, you know, for *years* and play this game continually. The only time the game ends is when the character dies, and if you've been playing a character for, let's say, like I was. I played it for three years, and he was tenth level. Now, this character was *my friend*. This character was *me*.... If that character gets *killed*, that devastates kids [note again here that his pronouns move from an emphasized "me" to generically "kids"; more on this later]. There have been kids who were involved with Dungeons and Dragons for four or five years, their character gets killed, they can't handle it, they blow their brains out.[133]

Right away, at this point in the study, it is necessary to debunk a popular claim associated with Sellers. Many people have casually referred to him as someone who either committed or claims to have committed horrific crimes as a direct result of D&D. This is a narrow-minded and short-sighted image perpetuated by the Satanic Panic. Too many ministers and parents found it easy to say, "Don't play Dungeons and Dragons! See where it will lead you? Look what happened to that Sean Sellers kid! That game will turn you into a killer!" Additionally, when Sellers went to trial, a significant part of his defense centered on his being a victim of D&D influence. As a result, almost thirty years after the murders, recent references to Sellers still show this imbalance.

Actually, Sellers responded to this association thus: "With the controversy over role-playing games so prevalent today many well meaning people have sought to use my past…for rebuking role-playing.… [U]sing my past as a common example of the effects of the game is either irrational or fanatical."[134] Further and elsewhere, he says, "Although I must disagree with some of Patricia's conclusions and state that D&D has not had quite the decisive role the National Coalition on Television Violence maintains, there is enough honest concern to give their declarations space."[135] ("Patricia," in the note above, was a reference to Pat Pulling. She was a huge name at the peak of the attack on D&D, a so-called investigator, and founder of BADD [Bothered About Dungeons and Dragons], an activist group dedicated to uncovering D&D's ties with occultism. Actually, many of her findings were very astute, and in a lot of cases, her studies could have had very powerful and far-reaching implications on the world of crime analysis. Sadly, though, when investigations fell upon her claims, like so many others of her time, she revealed herself willing to be swept away in the flailing panic of society, likely feeling that her research wasn't going to be taken seriously unless its intensity matched the shocking levels of her counterparts. This resulted in some, *but not all*, of her work being considered fraudulent. Her name and reputation was damaged as a result of the follow-up scrutiny, most notoriously, with one essay called "The Pulling Report." The world threw the baby out with the bathwater. Some have offered a theory that her fraud was accidental, but for the purposes of this study, that is irrelevant. That, in case any readers were wondering, is why this author did not include any of her research in this case study, even though her research on D&D is likely the most famously referenced up to date.)

So, as you can see, even though Sellers openly talks about the seriousness of the game and the idea that there is merit to the widespread rumor of the game leading to identity issues, suicide or other deaths, and the occult, on more than one occasion he has tried to set the record straight and let everyone know that he's not claiming D&D forced him to kill people. (Something to remember: For many, D&D was a game; for *some*, it was a cult.) The game *did*, however, assist in paving the way to other aspects of the occult, and eventually to satanism. For a young boy with an extreme detachment from the world, strained and abusive relationships in his family, voices in his brain-damaged head, and experimentation with his identity, this would not be a good development.

From Student to Teacher

When Sellers was thirteen, his stepfather's eighteen-year-old nephew, Steven, came to visit for awhile. Around the same time that Sellers' obsession with D&D began, Steven introduced him to ninjutsu. Sellers' stepfather almost never spent any time with Sellers, but Sellers longed for a fatherly figure, so when he saw that his stepfather thought Steven's interest in and skills as a ninja were cool, he naturally pursued it as a stepfather/son bonding attempt.[136]

Unlike the modern martial arts, wherein the purpose is self defense and often some form of inner growth or meditation as a focusing strategy, Sellers found that the study of ninjutsu in its purest form had nothing to do with any of that. Much to the contrary, ninjutsu was the study of assassination and espionage. Unlike the open and proud martial artist, kick-boxer, or karate student of the 1980s, a true ninja was one who could sneak unseen from place to place and stealthily deliver the final death blow to an enemy, the only sound ever made being that of the soft squish of a blade to a major organ or the quiet popping of a snapped neck. Whether the kill was morally permissible in some grand scheme of vigilante justice or for a darker intention, a ninja was a killer. Since Sellers' stepfather was a former Green Beret, who had taken lives without remorse or regret (in Sellers' mind) in Vietnam, there was a constant awareness in his company that someone strong enough to take a life when necessary was respectable to him. Sellers, desperately wanting to gain respect, would train for the skills to act upon that need so he would be ready if that time ever came. About the time he had mastered the discipline enough to punch out a candle flame, his studies had driven him to the central ninjutsu philosophy: Zen.

Zen Buddhism really made sense. It didn't seem to adhere to any specific doctrine, but more or less allowed karma, as a school of thought, to lead whatever was supposed to be. If two people's paths came together, met in the middle, and went their separate ways, it formed an X; if two people's paths met and one path ended, it formed a T, meaning that one goes on living and the other comes to a stop, likely dead. However death happened, whether by accident or murder, it made no difference. Karma was karma, as Sellers believed, and he adopted a thought pattern that said two paths would meet and either go on, or not. Sometimes it was a person's role to die, and other times it was a person's role to kill. There was no right or wrong; things just happened.

The young assassin-in-training fed those thoughts a meal most malicious the more miserable he became.

Sadly, ninjutsu never drew any interest from Sellers' stepfather. More or less, Sellers merely proved himself to be a silly kid. On the other hand, his uncle ridiculed him and made fun of him for wasting money on his training.[137] This didn't stop him from continuing his practices in the guilt-free assassination hobby, however.

Graduating from the ever-wise age of thirteen and heading into his fourteenth year, Sellers fell into his books with fervor. Quickly, he was starting to see how D&D connected to casting spells and becoming powerful as a Dungeon Master, which connected to ninjutsu, which connected to Zen, then karma, then occultism, then witchcraft…it was like a circle of clandestine purpose, all items agreeing with and joining the others. (Theologically speaking, there are numerous flaws in this thread of thought, but as we are telling Sellers' story here, this is frame of mind he was in. He went on in his interview with Dr. Brothers to say that all of these games of connect-the-divinity-dots really set the stage for, and prepared his mind for, the mystical satanism patterns he would later embrace.[138]) The more he tried to prove himself to the people around him, the more he was disregarded, with one exception. By now, he was a competent D&D Dungeon Master (as well as a character player) who, as the title often reflected in those days, had some level of power and control over his D&D group, and his group needed to be taught a lesson as they were getting "cocky."[139] As Zen had taught him that all battles won in the flesh were first fought in the mind, and thus, if you overcame a battle in the mind, that victory would carry over into the flesh, he devised something clever for his dungeon pals. He would search the library and find an ancient, mythological dragon, bring it to life in a D&D dungeon, and make it physically invincible, its only weakness being a riddle of the mind. He knew that his friends would attack the beast by physical means (swords, spells, etc.), and when someone's character died, maybe then the student would learn from the teacher and master the humility and wisdom needed to play *his* dungeons.

Now, his obsession wasn't just limited to looking at the pictures in these books. That was child's play. Through his growing influence and power in his group of friends, who by this point were willing to follow his role-playing plots wherever he would lead, Sellers had become the controller of others' fates. Couple that with his intense need to prove himself, his growing skills in the art of killing, and his diving ever deeper into the darker realms of the occult, and Sellers was suddenly something to be feared. Witchcraft and the dark arts were his new romance. Love was a weakling's need. Being feared was the new deal.

But then, *almost* as if in a moment of divine intervention, it was announced that his family was yet again moving to a new place, and Sellers' dive into dark practices was cut off. Unexpectedly, Sellers enjoyed his new home in Colorado. Although he continued to study his interests from before, he was far less extreme about them. For a time while he was fifteen years old, he applied himself in a very positive direction, joining the Civil Air Patrol (CAP), becoming the cadet commander of the squadron, and becoming a NEAT ranger (ranger of the National Emergency Assistance Training), graduating with outstanding merits. Now involved in leadership in a more positive way, Sellers spent his nights organizing his CAP squadron and meditating. Finally, his stepfather was not only proud, but interested. Colorado was the Promised Land and the place where he finally belonged! This was it!

A Deal with the Devil

When the announcement came that his happiness in his new setting would be short-lived because the family was once again uprooting, moving back to Oklahoma, Sellers "literally begged"[140] his mom and stepdad to let him stay in Colorado. His request was denied, and his world crumbled. He was devastated. Resentment built up within him, and all the anger he had harbored in his heart as a child boiled up and overflowed into his thoughts every moment. He was mad at his mother. He was mad at his stepfather. He was mad at God…if there was one. Why did his parents have to wait until he was in his darkest hour to bring him to a place of complete happiness, freedom, and life—just to reveal that it was all a big tease? They had left him in the care of other people off and on his entire childhood; could they not now simply let him find a place to live in Colorado? Was wanting his own life, choices, and stability too much to ask? Why were they taking that from him again?

Something inside him snapped.

If he couldn't join them, he would beat them…

Library trips, constant practice, dedicated training, meditating on ideas that consumed him…all of this became the new Sean Sellers. As he tells: "I'd been carted all around…all my life, slapped, smacked, hit, and had whatever I wanted ignored. I was mad and the idea of control-ling my life to get what I wanted was like candy to me."[141] Driven toward obtaining ultimate control over his life and over the life of anyone else who would stand in his way, Sellers rapidly harnessed every opportunity to exercise his own mind and will. Gone were submission and doubt. Arrived were confidence and power.

He met a witch. She knew Satan. It was destiny.

Sellers' interest in satanism was instant and forceful. Based on how every-one around him was living, everyone appeared to be a closet satanist anyway. Why not grip the bull by the horns and ride it into the open pit while every-one gathered around, watching and waiting for him to rebel? (One of the many great lies in satanism, in order to be a constitutionally allowed and rec-ognized religion within the US, is that God does not exist, but neither does Satan. Satan is a representation of that carnal desire that already exists within man. Since human consciousness here on earth is the only reward people can ever get, as there is no afterlife, serving self to any level of gratification is the natural and *honest* way to live. It isn't until later, when one is completely immersed in service to self, that satanism evolves into the covert operation of serving Satan as a real entity. Sellers, like many, was sucked into this lie, believing that by being honest about his service to himself, he was living the enlightened way, above the rest of the ignorant human race.)

> I looked at the way everyone around me lived and the stuff I read in the *Satanic Bible* in principle was lived out in lifestyle by Mom and Dad [his stepfather] and everyone else I knew.... We didn't go to church. We didn't talk about God. Mom and Dad cussed like the truck drivers they had been for so many years, Mom bought me a box of condoms when I was 13 and Dad told me to use them, we'd stolen stuff out of the trucks Dad drove, I'd seen Mom lie to people's faces to get a deal or sell something, my aunt and uncle and Mom and Dad smoked pot, and bought speed, so what was the point of pretending to serve God when we lived like Satanists? Satanism taught me that I should make my own rules to live by in life, and that's just what everyone I'd grown up

around did, so I got very involved in Satanism. I truly thought it was an honest way to live, and the rituals of it would enable me to control my life.[142]

I decided that what [Anton] LaVey wrote had to be true—that Satan was the force behind rebellion which led to freedom and was a way to success in a society where only the strong survive and only the ruthless attain the American dream.[143]

But Sellers' story played out much the way others' stories have when enticed by this lie. Early on in his dabbling, he decided to believe in Satan as a true ruler entity when he began to feel the forces at work, and this would give him an even higher level of power and control. The world around him was afraid of Satan. They were panicked. And he would give them something to panic about. He asked his witch friend what the first step was. A conversation ensued wherein he had to choose between white magic or black; he chose black. The witch then gave him all the tools he needed to make his dedication official.

It took a couple of days for Sellers to get up the nerve to perform the ritual incantation for devoting one's life to Satan as suggested by this witch. But, when it came about, it was dramatic and supernatural, trumping anything the little boy inside of him had ever felt. Laying his naked body down on the bed, incense and candles lit all around him, he prayed to the dark lord. He verbally renounced God, renounced Christ, and said aloud that he would only serve Satan, if Satan would serve him back.

This author has heard Sellers tell this story over and over again in many different interviews, written and verbal, and it is always told the exact same way, without deviation:

As he lay there, it felt as if he was being lifted off the bed…a floating sensation he recognized from his deeper moments in Zen meditation. A presence entered his room, and the temperature dipped low. The presence was powerful and unmistakably evil. Sellers shut his eyes tighter and tighter, while his body reacted sexually in response to being watched. The veins in his arms bulged. His heart rate increased in anticipation…and then something touched him. It wasn't a hand, but more like the lightest sensation of fingernails or cold claws being softly dragged across his skin. It was erotic and sensual, yet completely wicked. He opened his eyes and saw nothing but vision spots induced by having closed his eyes so firmly before. Hair standing on end, he was terrified and thrilled at the same time. Closing his eyes again, the caress continued until it had explored every inch of his body in some kind of twisted lovemaking ceremony between himself and the devil. Then a voice uttered the words "I love you." He opened his eyes again to see who had said them. Again, nobody was there. One final time, Sellers closed his eyes and continued to commune with Satan until the touching of his body drew to an end.[144]

This time, when he sat up in his bed, Sellers knew he would never be the same again. When he had lain down, he had been a boy. He arose a man. The old Sellers was gone, and a new man had taken his place. It was as if he was truly, literally, functionally, and comparatively a different person altogether. His heart was beating wildly, and he had found what he had been seeking. What a rush! Satanism was real, and without waiting for his biological father to say it, or for his mother or extended family to say it, Sellers was loved.

Ezurate

By this time, Sellers had begun a friendship with Richard Howard. Sellers was definitely the leader, but he, Howard, and a few others now had developed a little cult. They cast spells, prayed to Satan, performed rituals, and invited demons to inhabit their bodies. The more they participated in such things, the more powerful they felt. *Sellers had a new identity now*; he was the bad guy.

Sellers was the center of attention, and was as much loved as he was feared. He had earned respect, and he *kept* that respect by showing his willingness to strike loud and proud however he could at anyone who opposed him. Mentally, he had never been more fearless and in control. Physically, thanks to the ninjutsu, he was powerful and strong. Emotionally, he was untouchable and proud.

Academically, he soared, as usual. However, this time, he made sure that everyone knew what he stood for. If he was going to live honestly, like the satanists did, he couldn't hide his new faith. Schoolmates questioned him about his fear of the afterlife, and his quick, articulate responses that he was only living the same way as everyone else, only without the hypocrisy of the Christian label, left them puzzled. He spoke about his new beliefs openly everywhere he went, and negative responses only encouraged him to up his game and increase the shock value. Book reports in front of the class reflected his dedication to Satan, he attended classrooms with his *Satanic Bible* proudly in tow, and he talked explicitly to anyone who would listen about the demons who flew around him and entered his body, influencing his actions.

(Yes, you read that correctly: Sean Sellers was traipsing about flaunting his relationship with the most evil and malicious spiritual entity in the universe in front of the whole school, in front of the whole *world*. Readers might at this point be wondering, *Why didn't anyone do anything about this!? What were his teachers thinking, allowing him to share his dark faith in class?* And that thought would be too reasonable. To quote an earlier part of this case study: "While the Christian church was pulling its focus together to wage war against a decoy called 'the satanic underground,' the enemy brought a real spiritual warfare against the people in the church, attacking them from any vulnerable angle." Simply put: Awkward little Sean Sellers was nothing compared to the satanic network robbing the nation of its youth. How could the church take time to focus on Sellers, and why would they take some young boy's rebellion act seriously, when they had a *real* battle to fight? They had to march directly past him to the front lines of battle to save the nation's youth! Huzzah!... Circular logic, of course. Note that many online bloggers have suggested that nobody tried to help him because *so many* people were swept up in the Satanic Panic, both those with concern and those who caused it, that perhaps everyone wrote him off as one of those creepy kids running around scaring people with no real ties to any demons or dark lords. How could they have known that his claims were sincere and that he was going to end up in a courtroom for the murder of three people? Nonetheless, we digress. It is true that nobody regarded Sellers with the concern or attention that real intervention would have required, so he plowed straight ahead.)

Sellers was grateful for the voices in his head now. They had puzzled him before, but now he knew he had demons in him, and he didn't mind. He was in full control anyway; they were only there because he had invited them. No big deal.

Eventually, one demon rose above the rest and grabbed his attention. His name was Ezurate.

Ezurate was Sellers' buddy. He had a tendency to absorb the other demons and show his power by helping Sellers throughout the day. When Sellers would go to bed at night and wake up at his school the next day, having completed several classes already with absolutely *no memory of it at all*, he knew that Ezurate had taken control of his body and assisted him so he could rest… However, Ezurate was not the only alarming reality at this time:

> [B]y the time he was 15 and 16 Sean Sellers was practising satanic rituals on a daily basis. He would store vials of his blood in the refrigerator, some of which he drank at school. He would perform acts of self-mutilation, such as putting sharp objects into his scalp. He became involved with drugs, taking amphetamines in order to stay awake and carry out his rituals. When asleep he would dream of killing and mutilating people.[145]

One day, Sellers discovered that his mother wasn't happy about what he had been into. She removed some of the materials from his room, and the episode became quite an unexpectedly heartbreaking event. All three—Sellers, his mother, and his stepfather—engaged in emotionally charged interactions about the changes to his character and personality. But, the more his mother and stepdad tried to help him, the more he found himself questioning what he had become. He reflected on how often he had no tears or feelings, and something about that felt wrong, even for him. Despite his hardened state, he had only set out to make himself stronger and more in control. He didn't specifically intend to tear apart the people who may have actually loved him or whom, deep down, he also loved in return. When his stepfather told him he was no longer proud of him and that he would have to earn that pride back, a small piece of the original Sellers responded. Like the *flipping of a switch*, he cracked. When his stepfather told him that there had been Christmases and birthdays in the past when he and his mother had gone without a meal or two in order to afford gifts for their son, Sellers was able to cry. He hugged his mother and sobbed, feeling the weight of the world upon him right then. They had finally broken through to him (or was it the other way around?).

At that moment, he decided to get out of satanism. He found his occult notebook and tore it into pieces.[146]

Right away, he sought help. With every bone in his body, he wanted out. First, he looked up and got in touch with a Baptist minister who had baptized him years ago and asked how to escape from satanism. The minister said he "didn't want to get involved."

Then, since his stepfather had been raised Catholic, Sellers found a priest, but the priest used his time with Sellers to argue about Adam and Eve theology, and then advised Sellers' mother to give back all the occult property she had taken since the items belonged to the boy.

Next, Sellers attended a Bible study with some friends at school, and they quoted a lot of Scripture, but they didn't know how to help him gain freedom from satanism.

Further, Sellers called Trinity Broadcasting Network and spoke to a lady who asked him if he'd been involved with witchcraft. When he confirmed that he had his own coven, she started to pray for him. Five minutes went by and she was still praying, then ten minutes, then fifteen, then twenty… Eventually, when the counselor on the phone had been praying for over a half an hour and Sellers still hadn't spoken and didn't appear to have any answers or assistance, his mother told him *not to take his problems to other people.*[147]

So he didn't.

[W]hen I discovered I couldn't get out I had only two choices that I saw; #1 was to go to hell like all the other hypocrites who lived according to the tenets of Satanism but didn't worship Satan, or #2 worship Satan still and rule OVER those hypocrites in hell. If I was going to hell I was at least going to be a ruler. So I got back into the occult. My God, how I wish I hadn't, but I did.[148]

After rejoining his friends and resuming their rituals and practices, Sellers went on to tell a teacher at school, in one last-ditch effort, that he was in trouble, needed someone to talk to, and felt like he was losing his mind and his grip on reality. She promised to find someone to help him, but he never heard back from her about it. (Later, on Sellers' last day on earth, one of his final phone calls before he died would be with this teacher, Mrs. Noel. He remembered her affectionately and spoke of her that way in his journal. However, he had a question for her… He reminded her of that day so long ago when she had promised to find someone who could help him, and asked her why she never followed through. She told him that she had called Sellers' mother to discuss what options they had, and his mother had told her that she had everything under control and preferred the teacher not get involved.[149] In the *Escaping Satan's Web* interview, Dr. Brothers questioned Sellers further about this. If Sellers' mother had kept with the search and had continued banging on doors of churches until she found help—had Mom been willing to search outside the comfort and discretion of family—would she still be alive? Sellers answered affirmatively.[150])

Blink, Blink, Blink

The blacking-out sessions increased in frequency. Sellers was more aware of Ezurate than before, and was less startled by waking up to find himself somewhere on autopilot, not knowing how he had gotten there. He would go to bed at night and then suddenly find himself driving his truck, not knowing where he was going. People would tell him he had been places and done things that he simply didn't remember. Then came the *blinking*, which was completely different and new. One minute he was good ol' Sean, just hangin' out, and the next minute his mind would blink in and out of awareness and reality…blink, blink, blink…flick, flick, flick…and when he was brought back to the surface, he was the hardened Ezurate. It was like there were two of him, two distinctly opposite yet harmonizing personalities. He was alert and functionally aware in both phases, but what was happening between the two sides flickering and battling for dominance was a complete mystery.[151]

During one of his harder moments, back to his practice with a vengeance, Sellers wrote, in his own blood, a pact with Satan to renounce God.[152] This indicated the ultimate devotion to bring about Satan's authority, right? Or so he thought, but it still wasn't enough power. He needed more, Richard Howard needed more; they all, his coven and fellow cultists, needed more if they were going to follow through with the Elimination. Sellers explains:

> I combined all I had learned into a single philosophy. The structure of D&D and CAP, the discipline and training of Zen and Ninjutsu, and the ideals, concepts, and ritualistic practices of Satanism all combined to become what we called the Elimination. I hated the Christian community which I perceived to be hypocritical, and was determined to eliminate Christians from society.[153]

Sellers and his friends had heard of a home close by that had been damaged by fire, and was therefore abandoned. Seeking not to continue their rituals with Sellers' mother or stepfather around, the group plotted to find the house, but they didn't have an address. For the time being, they would make do. They knew that they would need more power in order to wipe out Christianity, so they would complete more rituals and await word from the underworld. Not enough demons were ever present, so more would be called upon. The group continued to pray to Satan and give themselves over to his power, but that power always fell short of what they needed, leaving their dark thirst drier than before.

Sellers/Ezurate and Howard would have to brainstorm.

Then, one day, they stumbled onto a plan. Satanism was the opposite of Christianity, and to Sellers/Ezurate, breaking the Ten Commandments would naturally be the next step in invoking ultimate control. They easily checked off nine of the Ten Commandments. Now, only one remained: "Thou shalt not murder."

Sellers/Ezurate and Howard performed a ritual, and then formally dedicated their time to Satan. They loaded into their vehicle, armed with guns. Sellers/Ezurate carried a .357 magnum revolver with hollow-point bullets. At a local Circle K convenience store, a man was working alone. This man, Robert Bower, had insulted Howard's girlfriend and had refused to sell Howard beer, so when Sellers/Ezurate and Howard saw Bower as the waste of human life described by Anton LaVey in his chapter from *The Satanic Bible*, "On the Choice of a Human Sacrifice," it was clear that Bower was the perfect target. (Here again, since human sacrifice is unconstitutional, yet satanism is a constitutional religion recognized by the United States government, the American military, and the International Revenue Service,[154] human sacrifice has to be represented in all public access reading materials to be nothing more than a curse or hex placed on someone that brings about a nonliteral death, like some kind of mystical death in the mind. However, for those willing to read between the lines and see the cover-up nonsense to mean what it really does to many satanic organizations—murder, if you will—LaVey has paved the way for this act to be carried out without guilt or remorse, chalking it up to one's sense of moral duty. As he says in writings, "When a person, by his reprehensible behavior, practically cries out to be destroyed, it is truly your moral obligation to indulge them their wish.... They are weak, insecure...and they make ideal human sacrifices."[155])

When they arrived at the store, Sellers and Ezurate battled for dominance. Ezurate wanted the man dead, but Sellers still wasn't sure. Howard meandered about and started conversations, waiting for Sellers/Ezurate to do what they had come there to do.

Eventually, when enough time had been wasted, and after Bower had come out to the car for casual conversation about a clutch pedal and then gone back in, Howard gave Sellers the signal and then went inside to distract Bower. *Ezurate* jumped from the car and headed with confidence to the entrance of the store, but blink, blink, blink, *Sellers* steered clear from the door and walked around the side of the building. He was scared, and shaking, and didn't know if he had the strength to go through with the murder. His voices called him a coward. They told him he was weak. Blink! Then he was "cold, determined, heartless, and evil."[156] *Ezurate* walked proudly and coolly back to the front of the store, opened the door, walked up to the counter, lifted the gun, and fired.

On September 8, 1985, Sean Sellers shot and killed Robert Bower.

Sellers/Ezurate and Howard returned to their vehicle. They did not steal any merchandise from the store, nor did they take any money out of the cash register, as they hurriedly left the bloody crime scene behind.

> In the car, we laughed as the evil delight of our action gripped us. We were not human. We were completely possessed by our demonic servants. We were stripped of all love, mercy, and kindness, and were consumed with hate, anger, and eroticism. We were Satanists.[157]

Bower had been such a fool! He had trusted them, casually talked and chatted with them, laughed with them and goofed around with them, came to inspect a clutch pedal with them, and had even laughed at the prospect of needing a security camera in the store when his killers had asked, because who would kill for fifty bucks? He did not catch the amused glances the two teenage boys had shared upon his revealing that.

Now, though, he was gone forever from this world, and Satan would be thrilled!

And suddenly, as if with supernatural timing, both Sellers and Howard spotted that half-burned house on the same road they had traveled hundreds of times in the past. This was the sign they had been looking for: Satan had received the sacrifice, and he was gifting them a new dark home.

Blink.

As time passed, Sellers/Ezurate, Howard, and the others in the group cleaned and fixed up what parts of the house were usable, and held numerous satanic lust and bloodletting rituals in private, away from parental eyes. Sellers invited more and more demons to enter his body as a sanc-tuary and join with Ezurate. He was going to school every day, working as a bouncer at a club called "Skully's," and performing rituals all night long. The only way to survive the demand of his time and attention was to get more stoned and take more speed, relaxing, then getting pumped, and back and forth again. It was a good thing he had Ezurate to take over when he needed a break. Conversations that his gathering had led to more plans of murder, including the idea that one day they would find and kill Howard's ex girlfriend, or that they would wait by a stop sign and shoot anyone who was idiotic enough to stop.

Blink.

Blink, blink…flick.

Mom, I Met an Angel

Entering the circle about this time was another satanist who had come to invite demons into her body also. Her name, ironically, was Angel, and that was exactly what Sellers thought she was. Sellers and Angel hit it off in a beautiful romance, and despite his inability to legitimately care about most people by this time, he fell completely and thoroughly in love with her. *Now* satanism was something even more than it had been before. It was bigger and more important. There was a maturity about his angle toward it that was refreshingly new and stable. It wasn't a child's game of "shock the world." Now a satanist was who he truly was, and even though he hadn't yet reached seventeen, he had found someone to share that with him.

But his mother wouldn't hear of it: Angel was a high-school dropout. Angel was only fifteen. Angel smoked, for goodness' sake! Mom had been exactly fifteen when she got pregnant, and that wasn't going to happen to her son and his girlfriend! Angel was a tramp! Angel was a loser!… On and on the list went, tension ever growing. Sellers' mother had nothing but insults in an ongoing attack on the only person her son had ever shown a true, grown-up, romantic connection to.[158]

Flick, flick…

Sellers' mother didn't know him, though! She didn't know or understand anything about him; why was she allowed to cast a vote, just because she had so clearly made *such* a mistake by getting pregnant with Sean at Angel's same age!

The situation reached a boiling point, and Sellers' mother told him to pack his things and get out. He felt as if a huge weight lifted from his shoulders, and he was once again giggling with glee as he and Howard packed up enough of his belongings to do exactly that. Sellers moved out that day, but was back that night when his stepfather turned up at Sellers' workplace and forcibly negotiated that he return home, confiscating the keys to Sellers' truck.

Tension mounted again. Sellers was trapped. It was suffocating. He wanted out. He wanted out. He wanted out.

Flick. Blink.

Mom didn't like Angel. Mom would hit her son over Angel. Mom "wailed on"[159] her son because of Angel.

BLINK. BLINK. BLINK…

Sellers was losing his mind, and he knew it. The more he felt Satan and his demons were taking over, the more he gave, in the hopes that he could get a grip and control his own life…or at least his own thoughts. Maybe he could kill himself. That would help. Yeah, that might be good. But then Angel…

Sellers had been awake for three solid days on speed, and even though Ezurate had been increasingly helpful in taking over for longer periods of time to give him a break, Sellers knew there would be no substitute for sleep this time.

> I couldn't get away. I couldn't move out.… [Then] blink! and everything was different. We [Sellers and his mother] argued, but I just wanted to leave, I didn't want to kill her. Then blink! and I'd be planning her death.[160]

On March 5, 1986, Sellers arrived home, performed his nightly satanic ritual, and went to bed.

On March 7, 1986, two days later, he woke up in a prison cell.[161]

IN THE SERVICE OF...

Sellers had needed a wakeup call, and he had felt that need for some time. He had wanted out of satanism and out of his parents home for so long, and now he was in a cold, concrete room with a tiny, reinforced window, profanity written on the walls, and bars on the far end. What in the world had happened? What had he done?

He raked through his thoughts, adrenaline sifting through images in his mind, rapidly lifting and lowering memories like a cerebral filtering system, skimming for clues as to what had brought him here. Nothing stood out. No matter how acutely he focused on one single item, there was nothing to see.

Suddenly, his attention was pulled to a voice coming from behind the bars at the end of the cell. Forcing his consciousness to unplug from the search, Sellers looked up and met the man's gaze, letting his words penetrate his concentration.

"Heard they got you for killin' your parents."[162]

What? No... That couldn't be real... Without a moment's hesitation, Sellers had already decided this information was false. There's simply no way that he would have ever let things get that far out of control. But then, it was true that he couldn't remember what he had done, so maybe... No way. There was just no way. Somehow, he would have to survive in here until someone arrived for him, his parents maybe, something, anyone... What in the world was going on?

Was Ezurate still there? Sellers needed a break.

Time once again swirled away into a mysterious passing, and waking up in his cell the following day, Sellers saw the same informant returning. He rose and awaited the news that it was all a big misunderstanding...but that news didn't come. The man casually greeted him with the unwelcome intel that those in the system were able to add to Sellers' list of offenses: the murder of Robert Bower, a convenience store operator.

That he remembered well.

Then, from out of a dark corner of his mind, a tiny flash dawned. He had been in the shower, the water was cold, and he could smell gunpowder… But if it were true, then what would he do now? He didn't feel anything. Nothing was real. If he had killed his parents, wouldn't he feel remorse? Wouldn't he feel *something*?

Another flash of memory came, and he remembered standing in his parents' room. He had felt relief. It had been as if the world's oppression had been removed. It was merely a feeling, one that had made him laugh out loud, hysterically, but it was at least a feeling. Maybe he was still human. But was *that* a human reaction to a crime so malevolent?

Maybe he had already officially lost his mind. Maybe in the lust for liberty and domination, he really *had been* capable of doing whatever he had to do so he could be free. But now, in a prison cell with no family, his life was completely destroyed. He was anything but free.

Satan had lied. Satan had promised freedom and control over his life and friends and…love.

Most of all, love.

But now, it was clear to him that he was no longer loved. Nor was he respected. Not by his school, not by friends, not by his parents, who were evidently now dead, not by any remaining family, and certainly not by Satan. Never by Satan. He knew that now. Nobody was on his side. What had he done?

He looked around his cell for anything he could find that would end his own life. There were no sharp objects, no pills or intoxicants, no weapons, and no rope. He looked up. He could hang himself by his pants. That's what he would do. He removed his pants and began the setup.

But then…Angel. What about her? She was just a mixed-up kid, too. He couldn't do that to her.

For her, he would wait.

Not Just Another Book

A couple of days later, a man was moved to the cell next to Sellers. He had a Book with him that Sellers had too often seen. In fact, it was a Book that he had physically destroyed and blasphemed against in every way possible, but now, he knew he was done with Satan, and there was no hope anywhere else. With no motive other than to search the pages for the next possible offering of hope or life, he began to read for answers, any answers at all. His eyes found the Psalms.

As he read about those who would walk through valleys of shadows of death, he started playing back the messages he had heard on tapes from Minister Mike Warnke that he had listened to for entertainment from the past, like a record player in his mind. They had gone hand in hand with the messages he was now putting into his thoughts. Shamefully, he had realized that he had done so much to the Bible, but he had never actually read it. How arrogant and foolish he had been to draw such life-altering conclusions about a Book he had never personally known, like he had personally known *The Satanic Bible.*

He had sat, covered in blood, at an altar to Satan to swear his allegiance, full of nothing but hate and anger toward a God whom he had never even tried to get to know! God had represented the ultimate parent, the ultimate "no" to everything he had ever wanted or needed for himself. Satan had represented the ultimate indulgence of self want and self gratification. And was this not freedom? But no, the concrete walls of his cell were proof that striving to please one's self leads to what this Bible was now saying it leads to: death. In so many ways: death. Death of a man at a convenience store; evidently, the death of his mother and father; and, now, this cell, which was its own form of death. Soon he would be brought to trial where he would be given a sentence for the absolute worst of crimes—crimes that he was now starting to suspect he had committed, the more the flashing memories surfaced.

Sellers' concept of God had been twisted and misconstrued to the point of rejecting Him without knowing the first thing about Him. How could he have been so foolish!? Now even God, Himself, didn't love him! Even that bridge had been burned because of the things he had done and the blasphemy that he and his friends had rallied against the Savior... Right? Wasn't that how it worked?

As time passed, guilt wracked Sellers to the core, and he found his spirit washed over with incomprehensible dread. Oh, how Satan had lied! Where was Satan now? Where was Ezurate? They were nowhere to be found, now that he was no longer free in the world to kill. And kill, he had absolutely done. More and more recollection slowly surfaced as he rotted away in his confinement. He was miserable, yet, based on what he was now fully believing he had done, he didn't think he was worthy enough to even feel misery.

Sellers continued to hate, now directing all of the anger he had previously held against his parents and God toward himself. However, all the while, with time on his hands and hope all but lost, save for the tiniest light that rose in his spirit every time he read, he continued to study the one Book he had so tastelessly deliberated against. And then, while still drinking in the Psalms, still reading the promises that were still bringing a ray of light to his terribly darkened soul, something hit him.

The Bible made it clear that God loved every sinner. It wasn't about whether a person was destined for hell or for heaven. The Almighty didn't, like some kind of dictator, reserve His vast affection for only those who served Him. The Lord's love extended to each and every soul on earth, regardless of what he or she had done, and regardless of where that person would be in the afterlife. Sellers' sins saddened the Father, but what saddened Him even more, according to what this Book seemed to be saying, was the idea that Sellers was eternally lost. God was not willing that any man—ANY MAN—should perish. He wanted all the world, Sellers included, to have everlasting life! How, though, could he ever be deserving of this? Satan had told him he loved him, but serving Satan had brought death. Could, perhaps, serving the Lord, whatever that meant, from his cell, bring life?

But it wasn't about Sellers. This new way of thinking wasn't simply about giving one's heart and mind over in service to the Lord in order to feel alive again or avoid hell. God was *Love*. Jesus Christ was *Love*. The Holy Spirit was *Love*. All of these three, and the three together, loved Sellers, like a daddy loves a son who has turned against him.

Like a daddy…

The presence that seeped into the walls of Sellers' prison cell at that realization was powerful, just like his experience with Satan had been before, but it was incomparable in any other way. This was a new presence, unwilling to touch him or caress him with the unholy domination that he had felt the last time he had felt something so supernatural. This being seemed to be begging to descend upon him, waiting only for his invitation.

Sellers fell to his knees and, for the very first sincere time in his life, spoke to the Lord. His prayer was that of a prodigal son coming home to beg for naught but a servant's position in the household. He didn't ask for power, richness, or glory. He prayed to be taken back, and he promised to serve—and he meant every word. When the tears came like the opening of floodgates, he didn't try to stop them. He embraced the first emotion and expression of emotion that he had felt since the night he had cried with his mother and promised to find a way out of the satanic trap he had fallen into. Prior to that, he couldn't remember the last time he had cried. He remembered that he used to walk the streets at age thirteen or fourteen and wonder what had become of his tears, and why he couldn't feel anything but anger and greed. A little boy! He had been Satan's tool when he was only a child! And now, put away behind the fortifications of manmade imprisonment, he was still only a child. He had never been anything else, and now, just like the babe he still was, he cried for hours, hungry, thirsty, lonely. He cried for his broken past and the little boy in the Batman pajamas who had run around wanting to save the world like a hero. He cried for the friends he had led astray. He cried for Robert Bower, not even knowing if that man had a wife and children who were now suffering beyond measure as a result of his warped mind. He cried for his parents who never saw it coming, who would never again grace the Thanksgiving table with their gratitude, who would never again utter words of love, pride, or affection to him or anyone else… He cried for everything, until that presence had revealed itself all around him, honoring his prayer, welcoming him, giving him peace. Something was happening inside him that he couldn't completely understand, but he knew it was even more real than that experience on his bed when he had been touched by the darkness.

Then he slept.

When Sellers finally drifted off on the chilly, hard, flimsy mattress and lumpy pillow, he slept without demons, nightmares, dark visions, dreams of murder and mutilation, or creepy presences in the room. This sleep wasn't Ezurate giving him a break. Deep, warm, inviting, and peaceful sleep at long last befell his troubled mind, and when he awoke, he was ready. Ready for whatever would come. Ready for trial, ready for life in prison, ready for death... Come what may, it was all worked out for him by Someone who understood his best interests and did not demand sacrifices of blood or family in order to be considered faithful in the completion of his works or his time on earth. Sellers simply didn't have to worry anymore. No more panic... Just peace.

Trial and Much Error

Sellers was assigned a public defender who, although he gave his all, was unsuccessful at eliciting any compassion from the jury for Sellers. Having only been allotted $750 for expert witness' fees (including travel, lodging, and food) that could have brought more psychological evidence to the jury, many details of Sellers' psychological condition were never addressed professionally during the trial. (And, compared to other cases in this book, Sellers' trial was incredibly short.) In addition, Sellers' Multiple Personality Disorder had only been recently recognized in scientific and medical communities, and was therefore not discovered until well after the trial, during the appeals process, since the research behind the diagnosis was still in its infancy. After the quick and what many now believe to be an unfair trial, Sellers was convicted of murder and sentenced with the death penalty. During his appeals, as stated earlier, his mental condition was discovered, but the natural consequences of having such a mental condition were ignored. According to the Death Penalty Institute of Oklahoma:

> The state of Oklahoma has a legal procedure that calls for post-trial consideration of newly discovered evidence under certain standards.... Sellers' case overwhelmingly met those standards. The Oklahoma Court of Criminal Appeals (OCCA) refused to consider the evidence.[163]

But what newly discovered evidence was there? What mental condition did Sellers have? To a minister, it was demon possession. To the courts, who do not recognize demonic possession as a mental condition, it was known as "Multiple Personality Disorder" (MPD), but has since been renamed in the field as "Dissociative Identity Disorder" (DID).

The symptoms of DID listed on any current medical and information website (WebMD, MayoClinic, MedicineNet, PsychCentral, PsychologyToday, ClevelandClinic, AAMFT [American Association for Marriage and Family Therapy], NAMI [National Alliance on Mental Illness], and others), to summarize, consist of having: another personality (or several personalities) that take control over a person's actions; mood swings; depression; suicidal tendencies; sleep disorders; anxiety attacks, including flashbacks, phobias, or reactions to specific stimuli; alcohol or drug abuse; compulsions and rituals; auditory and visual hallucinations (such as hearing voices); unexplainable time loss; blackouts; trances; self-inflicted injury; compulsive and impulsive behavior; delusions; headaches; and the list goes on. (Also not uncommon to patients with this disorder is to slip back and forth between identity pronouns [i.e., from "I" to "he" and back again] while talking about one's self. Recall the note in the interview with Sellers earlier.) It has been suggested on several of these websites that only a few of these symptoms alone could bring about the diagnosis of DID.

How many of these symptoms did Sellers have?

All of them.

But the disorder is specifically characterized by "the presence of two or more distinct or split identities or personality states that continually have power over the person's behavior.... As an example, someone with dissociative identity disorder may find themselves doing things they wouldn't normally do...yet they feel they are being compelled to do it. Some describe this feeling as being a passenger in their body rather than the driver. In other words, they truly believe they have no choice."[164] Sellers' case was one of the more intense cases of DID. We learn in a report by Amnesty International:

(a) [A] quantitative electroencephalogram test (QEEG) dis-
closed that Sean Sellers has brain damage as a result of a head
injury suffered as a child; (b) the QEEG dramatically changed
with each of Sean Sellers' alter states, indicating the presence of at
least three alter personalities; (c) an Evoked Potential Test (EPT),
which relies upon biological signals from the body and cannot
be falsified by the patient, confirmed the QEEG; (d) two of the
doctors, separately, spoke to two of Sean Sellers' alter personalities, named "Danny" (who demonstrated that he was left-handed,
even though Sellers is not) and "The Controller"; (e) Sean Sellers
suffered from MPD at the time of the killings; (f) one of the alter
personalities, which is unlikely to have understood the difference
between right and wrong, "must have been in executive control of
[Sellers'] person or body" at those times; (g) there was only limited
awareness of MPD in the mental health community at the time of
the trial, when tests for it had not yet been developed; (h) MPD
is a "hidden disease" which generally takes a number of years to
confirm.[165]

But of course, this is likely not something one is merely born with.
According to the most modern of psychological sciences, not known to
the world at the time of Sellers' 1986 trial, DID is found in people who
typically have faced extreme childhood trauma or repeated child abuse.
Sellers' trial did not thoroughly cover this period of his life and, instead,
focused almost entirely on the murder details. Much of what Sellers faced
as a child (and even some details that have not yet been mentioned in
this case study, as they are far too graphic) came out during psychological
evaluations well after the trial.

When evidence of his sexual-exploitation memories of abuse were later
called into question, Dr. Dorothy Otnow Lewis (Sellers' psychiatrist during
and after the trial, expert witness in the field of psychiatry in many high-
profile court cases, professor of psychiatry at New York University, and clinical professor at Yale University's Child Study Center) had this to say:

When children are subjected to early, ongoing, intolerable physical or sexual abuse, when they cannot endure it, they seem to space out. It's almost—and this is not a conscious thing, it just happens—in order to survive, they experience it as though it were happening to someone else, and they start to experience voices in their head. Sometimes very comforting voices, and sometimes almost invariably very violent, aggressive voices that try to defend them. And over time, when they are stressed, when they are further tortured, they switch into these voices and they become not just imaginary friends, but they space out, and it's as though whatever were happening happened to someone else, and they operate in a way that they have no conscious control over. And over time, this becomes a habit of mind, so that it *continues*, and it can continue even after the abuse has long ended. Now, in Sean's case, there's reason to believe that what he was experiencing continued on into his adolescence, and there is reason to believe that he committed the murders that he committed when he was in an altered state....

[H]e was sexually abused, he was sodomized by someone in the family and also by others outside the family. The evidence— the *irrefutable* evidence—that there was sexual abuse was the fact that Sean has scars on [a part of his body] to attest to this. He also has scars on [a part of his body] from self-mutilation. And this kind of self-mutilation [graphic material extracted referring to pin-sticking], and this is long before the murders, is *only* done either by flamboyantly psychotic individuals or by children who have been *hideously* abused. So there is a lot of good evidence that this has occurred.

The irony of the disorder is that it comes about in order to protect the child. Very often the child is dependent [upon] the abuser. So, he or she has one personality to deal with the abuser when the abuser is friendly and protective, and another one when the abuser is violent. But the child *does not* remember it all himself, so you have to be a detective, and you have to have a reasonably good way of relating to people before they open up and tell you some of the things that happened.[166]

Dr. Lewis goes on to describe "wildly different signatures and hand-writing"[167] on personal notebooks and school papers throughout Sellers' life, and continues to assert that Sellers' case revealed "early, ongoing, unendurable torture."[168]

But the public generally doesn't know any of this. Because the case went tight-lipped after the trial came to a close, most people will likely never remember the world that Sellers lived in versus the satanist teen gunslinger everyone thinks of now. As far as the *motive* behind the murders, well, it was certainly for Satan in trade for power, control, and freedom, and it was absolutely self-serving. As far as the *reason* for why the murders may have occurred, which is distinctly different, it was largely because a little boy had been raped, humiliated, hit, and moved all over the world, and then was unable to get help when he tried to be good, developing a very serious mental condition paired with brain damage and his immersion in games that "explore identities" as a result of all of that. Could Sellers have made the decision *not* to get into satanism, witchcraft, D&D, ninjutsu, and all the other occult-related philosophies? Absolutely, and there is no doubt about that having been the much wiser and more prudent path to take. But as far as whether he was in complete "executive" control over his body the night of the murders, there is much professional speculation. As to why he was given the death sentence despite the mounting evidence brought to trial and then to the appeals, it would take three essays crammed with legal jargon to explain, but suffice it to say that this case involved a serious game of "pass the buck" in the Oklahoma legal system. The bottom line: The judge ruled that the newfound information was not considered "newly discovered evidence" because the condition existed at the time of the trial, and someone should have said something at the time. The psychiatrists responded with proof that research of MPD (DID) had been in its infancy at the time of the trial and could not, therefore, be brought up at the time. As matters escalated and were handed over to members of other departments within the legal system, they responded that their hands were tied until some other department acted, and those other departments responded similarly. The issue was raised too late, and it was, as defense attorney Steve Presson termed it, "a horrific legal error"[169]—a case that Dr. Dorothy Otnow Lewis refers to as "bungled."[170]

WHOSE SIDE ARE YOU ON, ANYWAY?

Before we move on to the reflection of Sellers' final years, a few contributing factors regarding his reputation for sincerity should be addressed. As a result of the highly overlooked MPD/DID issues and other details regarding child abuse, and because of the "angry mob with pitchforks" syndrome occurring during the Satanic Panic, Sellers' sincerity toward Christ has been constantly called into question. Because this case study tells the story of his commitment to Christ, it seems important to touch on this.

Satanic Panic Strikes Again

When Sellers first went to prison and his case launched instant and international media coverage, the pretrial publicity had already declared a bias. People who flipped through television channels and landed on his young teenage face automatically shook their heads shamefully. Everyone who ventured outside of the comforts of his own home in the 1980s saw "evidence" of the incessant invasion of little satanist wannabes. Many mothers and fathers were a parent (or mentor) to teens who displayed alarming behavior. Sean Sellers' face represented the potential fate of so many young people. Before Sellers (and others alongside him, such as Jim Hardy, Ron Clements, and Pete Roland, the seventeen-year-old Satanic Panic murdering trio who sacrificed Steven Newberry in the woods in the late '80s) had become news, the reality of teen satanist killers at large seemed farther away. With so many ministers and parental activist groups waving flags of doom during the Panic, sometimes one couldn't turn on a television or attend church without walking away with something to lose sleep over. There were certainly very thoughtful people who wept for a young boy who had so turned against humanity, and it was these people who would have cared to know what had gone wrong in his childhood that would have turned him into what he was. But, as a matter of responsibility toward the kids in their own home or community, it was often these same people who felt they had to react harshly to the news of Sellers.

Thus, there was extreme pressure on everyone involved at the trial (judge, jury, witnesses, prosecutor, etc.) to capitalize on the evil that Sellers was, as the public was ever watching and voicing outrage. As history tells, Sellers was tried as an adult, which he wasn't. He was also sentenced as a perfectly sane person with no mental illnesses, which he wasn't; there was much proof to the contrary.

Sellers wasn't understood at the time, and, based on a lot of Internet discussion, he still isn't understood.

That's Old News

When the news of Sellers' conversion got out, the media had a heyday. From Geraldo Rivera's "Exposing Satan's Underground" special broadcast to Turner Broadcasting Network and every news station in the country, everyone was talking about this young man's relationship with God. On the one hand, secular programming attacked Sellers up one side and down the other, dubbing him as a fraud and paying him little attention other than to poke at or parody him. That would be expected even still. On the other hand, the church needed a celebrity, so many evangelists tossed his name into their sermons and televised ministries with a hearty "Amen!" every chance they could when the message that day was a tale of touching reformation or hope for the lost. But when the church decided Sellers was old news, which it eventually did, and went on to other stories, it had an unintended, adverse effect on the public's acceptance of the validity of his relationship with God. Looking at the articles about Sellers as published in the more conservative media from beginning to end, we see a chronology to his conversion that starts with "Yay! He's saved!" and moves to, "Hey, wasn't that guy saved once?" and finally to, "Oh, I dunno, he used to talk about God all the time, but then he stopped." If we follow the same chronology from beginning to end as written by Sellers in his personal writings and journals, and we happen to believe Sellers' writings, we will conclude that his faith never wavered. He just became less famous, and the instant he wasn't fighting for the chance to air his own dirty laundry to the world, preferring to be left alone by the media (and remember, Sellers was always a loner, anyway), the belief in his story fizzled with the decrease of constant exposure.

Insincerity versus Immaturity

A strong public opinion put forward by many online (and in dated historical records such as newspaper articles, etc.) about Sellers is that he was insincere, as we have mentioned. Clearly, the only one who would know that for sure is Sellers, himself. However, assuming that most readers of this book will be well into their adult years and able to understand the basic psychological differences between teenagers and someone with much more life experience, the obvious difference seems too often buried.

As an adult, when you look at two fifteen-year-olds holding hands and stroking each others' cheeks in a public place with that starry look in their eyes reserved only for Hollywood movies, swearing they will love each other forever and come what may, etc., you may not say anything, but you're likely smiling on the inside, knowing they can't possibly understand the commitment behind the feelings they're professing. You have likely felt those feelings as well at that age, and when Jenny told her friend that you had a bumpy collarbone, suddenly it was all over. Or, when Tim smiled at the head cheerleader instead of you, you suddenly found yourself backing away a little from the "'til death do us part" mentality. You've probably been there. You know these two teenagers are professing a love for each other that could easily fail at the first real relationship challenge. However, to *them*, they *are* sincere; this is honestly what they are feeling, and, although they don't understand the chemistry the way they will ten years from that moment, their feelings and emotions drive them to believe in whatever they're professing to one another. These feelings and emotions are still developing, because, unlike the passions they had a few years before, when the love of their life was a dolly or a toy train, these sensations are absolutely and beautifully new to them. It's euphoric, utopian, and magical. If you challenge them, they will likely yell something equivalent to, "I'm fifteen! I'm not a child! Don't tell me how I feel! You don't understand!"

Sellers was sixteen when he committed murder. That was when *his* childhood and chances of normal emotional development were over. In a sense, he stopped maturing by common American social standards at sixteen, because he was thereafter placed in prison with his only companions being the walls of his cell and an occasional walk around the yard with a fellow inmate who had also committed a crime terrible enough to land him on death row—far from the typical sixteen-year-old's social circle.

That said, when Sellers found God and took opportunities to publicly profess his faith, the world outside the church responded with cynical accusation of "fake" because "his tones were a little too warm and syrupy" or "his eyebrows were knitted too intensely as he spoke" (actual feedback as posted online). But was he fake? Or was he, like the fifteen-year-olds in the example above, professing the feelings he had at that time with the body language and tones that his short time in regular society had taught him were given by someone who felt passionate? Had he proclaimed his love for the Lord with a bland tone and no facial expression, people would have written him off as insincere, because he *didn't* sound more serious or syrupy. He couldn't win for losing.

It should be stated for the record that Sellers often does come across as a kid doing his best to perform an interview in front of an audience of hundreds of thousands of people he already knows are secretly wishing to drag him into the back alley and teach him a thing or three when nobody is looking. So here is a comparison to consider when judging for yourself whether he was sincere: Imagine yourself, at sixteen, having to give a speech about world peace at a high school pep rally.

You were the most unpopular kid in the school, looking out at the judgmental expressions and glaring eyes from kids who wanted to meet you out at the flagpole after last period. You spoke about world peace as best you could under the circumstances, and you *meant every word you said.* Would it be fair if later you discover that nobody ever thought you were sincere because, at sixteen, you simply didn't hold the life experience needed to execute the perfect delivery of your impassioned beliefs to a crowd that had despised you and written you off beforehand anyway?

The analyzable characteristics of someone who is insincere versus someone who is immature might be very similar. However, it is important to remember that there is a vast difference between someone who is *insincere* versus someone who is *immature.* Sellers spoke like he was a kid around the age of sixteen. This is probably because he was a kid around the age of sixteen. Lastly, many readers might be thinking, *Yeah, but sometimes you just "know," you know? Like you just get "that intuitive feeling" about someone.* Consider this: Sellers' average interview, as released to the public, was around one to five minutes long. Is that enough time to allow anyone to really learn anything about anyone's true heart?

He Partners with a Guy Like That?

Yet another name in the archives of public fury during the Satanic Panic was Bob Larson, one of several ministers at the time who instigated a huge assault against rock music and its influence on American youth. *A great deal of his research was important to the church,* as the kind of rock lyrics his ministry attacked were incredibly evil and often endorsed—with brutal language—human sacrifice, selling souls to the devil, and the spilling of a virgin's blood at a satanic altar, etc. However, when Larson, like so many at the time, was investigated, the probes raised many questions about his possible involvement in the misappropriation of ministerial funds. (This author makes no official statement on this controversy. It is only mentioned because of the effect it had on Sellers.)

Larson had endorsed and written the foreword for Sellers' book, *Web of Darkness.* When Larson's name was dragged through the mud, media vultures dove in to report that if a satanic teen killer like Sellers was sincere about God, he would have teamed up with more upstanding folks. Largely unreported is the fact that Sellers had absolutely no idea that Larson was under such public review, and that is proven by a letter he wrote to Larson asking for an explanation. Larson's response to Sellers' concerns is posted online in an article, "Bob Larson: Selling Out Sean Sellers."[171]

Devil's Child

There was a book, *Devil's Child*, written by two unauthorized individuals just after Sellers' trial, that depicted Sean Sellers in the worst of ways and likewise portrayed his family as being close, loving, and warm before he ruthlessly ended their lives. It should be noted, however, that this book has been called an outright fictionalization of many of the case details. Also, for as many people who found Sellers to be an absolutely heartless monster as a result of this work, there were just as many (from both sides of the argument) who admitted the book was not accurate at all. It served as little more than a tagalong of the fraudulent Panic pattern, and almost ended up dragging the ladies who wrote it into court for falsifying information.[172] The front matter of the book also states that the content of *Devil's Child* relates a *true story*, followed by the disclaimer naming five fictional characters. The disclaimer states, "Each of those five characters was created entirely by the authors and represents a composite of imaginary personality and physical traits and those of a number of individuals. Nothing those five characters say or do in the book should be taken to have been said or done by any specific real individual. Some conversations and situations have been re-created for dramatic effect."[173] Readers have to read the small print on this one. (As a result of this disclaimer and the extreme scrutiny this book has historically fallen under, this author has not used it as a reference and encourages anyone looking for further research on Sellers to consider it a work of fiction for entertainment purposes only.)

Interview with a Warden

As early research revealed that there were death row wardens who further questioned Sellers' sincerity, these authors attempted to establish a contact with any prison staff member who might have known Sellers at the time. We were only able to locate one, but his interview is telling. Although he is retired from his duties as a warden of death row, he is still an employee of the Oklahoma State Penitentiary, and will therefore remain unnamed. Here is a short excerpt from that conversation (conducted by Donna Howell):

HOWELL: What was Sellers like?

WARDEN: He was a pretty alright kid, actually. I think he was pretty alright.

HOWELL: Would you say he was a model prisoner?

WARDEN: Oh sure, he got along with everybody and seemed pretty happy. You know, just like anyone, he had his days, off and on, but yeah, he was a good kid. I'll tell you a little story here.

HOWELL: Oh, please do.

WARDEN: I used to drive past Sean's house and I could hear him playing heavy metal rock through his bedroom windows. It was a real rough time for him, you know?

HOWELL: Oh?

WARDEN: Yeah, yeah, a real rough time in his life. Anyway, later on, I always wanted to ask him, "Why are you playin' that stuff that sounds like devil's music?" but I never did ask. [He says no more about this.]

HOWELL: I see. You know how Sean became a believer in Christ during his incarceration?

WARDEN: Oh yeah, that was big news how he turned to God toward the end there. Actually, it wasn't really toward the end, it was much earlier than that. I'd say somewhere around the middle of his time here he really took to religion.

HOWELL: Did he ever give you any reason to believe that his conversion to Christ was insincere?

WARDEN: Well, now, I never directly approached him and asked him about that, and you know there's only one person [referring to God] that does know for sure and that's not any of us, but he seemed to really believe it, yes. I'll put it to you this way: I think he backslid during that rough time and got into some trouble and that's what brought him here.

HOWELL: He backslid? So, do you mean to suggest that he always held a belief in Christ and then he backslid from those beliefs, and his "conversion" in prison was merely a return to his spiritual roots?

WARDEN: Yeah, yeah. That's what I'm tryin' to say, yes. That's my opinion.

HOWELL: I see.

WARDEN: Yeah [long pause]. Yeah, you know, a lot of those boys on death row are first-time offenders. Isn't that something?

HOWELL: Yeah, actually I have some strained beliefs about some of those things. Our penal system doesn't really always seem consistent from case to case, you know?

WARDEN: Well, I can't say I'm for it or against it. There again, I'm workin' for the state penitentiary, you know? So, I have to leave it at that. But, yeah, Sean, that was a sad thing. He was an alright kid.

Later in the conversation, when asked if this former warden of death row had heard what other wardens had reportedly said regarding Sellers' sincerity, he answered:

Ah, well, they probably didn't know the kid. You know how it goes around here. A prisoner gets famous and suddenly everyone pops out of the woodworks with somethin' to say. I didn't know any wardens who felt that way, but it was prob'ly just someone lookin' to be that guy with the inside scoop.[174]

SET MY SPIRIT FREE THAT I MIGHT WORSHIP THEE

When the trials were over, Sellers fought the death penalty, wishing to show the world that he had much to give the kingdom of God, though he remained ready for death until the end, if that was what the Lord deemed necessary for His purposes. He poured himself into his writings, creating Christian comics, discipleship programs, and at least four full books. Despite many promises given to him by people who came to see him on death row, only one of those books would ever be published. (There are rumors of other books published by friends of Sellers, but they were likely only printed and bound at a print-on-demand-style printer, and therefore were not actually published according to industry standards.) This was the book *Web of Darkness*, and it only briefly synopsizes Sellers' own personal story in the first chapter. From close to the beginning of the book, the content goes straight into studies of the occult, giving parents of that Panic era much information about what their teens' book collections might actually mean, and how to get them help if needed. The book also speaks directly to the teen who is caught up in the occult, the lies that Satan and satanism tell to entice that individual, and how one can get out and get help. (It is surreal and sad to read Sellers' journal, "Sixty Days Before I Die,"[175] and see the hope, and then joyous celebration, that rises upon each promise that one of his acquaintances would see another of his works published. Each promise made to Sellers in his last days brought him a sense of purpose. But because none of them would ever see traditional publication, the feeling of excitement that bleeds from his last-days journal now has a contrasting sadness.)

Early in his imprisonment (around '87 or '88; when he was approaching eighteen), Sellers launched a ministry called "Radical Teens for Christ."

His book, *Web of Darkness*, concludes with a sinner's prayer and the ministry's address someone could contact for help. During Sellers' appeals and clemency hearing, letters poured in by the trainloads,[176] mostly from young teens all across the country who had bought his book or contacted him personally for his help through his ministry. So many of these kids were touched by his personal responses, likely because they were laced with understanding and Christian love instead of the judgment and scorn they had so many times received from other sources. This ministry has since been disbanded.

Around this time, Sellers saved the life of another death row inmate, one who had been relentlessly provoking him. This condemned prisoner's name was Henry Smith. A report from Amnesty International stated:

> Over a period of a few months Henry Smith had been repeatedly mocking, taunting and threatening [the life of] Sean Sellers.... One day Sean Sellers was placed on the exercise yard with four other inmates, one of whom was Henry Smith. Two of the other inmates attacked Smith with knives. Sean Sellers intervened, stepping between Smith and his attackers and calling the guards. When asked by Smith why he had helped someone who had treated him so badly, Sean Sellers replied that it was because Smith was a human being, and therefore entitled to live. They became friends.[177]

While content most days to remain in his chambers awash in his Bible studies, the music from a certain talented contemporary singer/rapper/songwriter/evangelist/actor flooded Sellers' cell with hope, love, and comfort—both on good days and on days when preparing to die wasn't as easy. This musician was Carman, whose albums, from 1980 through the present, are some of the most popular and well-remembered albums to date in the Christian world. His lyrics spoke to and encouraged Sellers in the face of deep loneliness and certain death. For the one hour per day that he was allowed to watch television, he would choose Turner Broadcasting Network, which frequently featured Carman's colorful and powerful music videos. In early 1999, just before his death, when it had been revealed that it was time to choose a second minister alongside his first, Margy Paoletti, Sellers contacted Carman and asked him to counsel him as a "pastor figure or spiritual advisor."[178] Carman, always the gentleman, agreed—and did so in person. Sellers also requested that Carman bring a light to his family, minister to them (including the Bellofattos, who showed much anger and resentment to Sellers for what he had done), and be present at the time of his execution, which Carman agreed to do. During their visits, Sellers shared his past with Carman and admitted that he had been exposed to great violence and humiliation, but that he didn't believe he had a terrible home life, and that he knew his parents truly loved him.[179] He talked about his days of being involved in satanism, his fascination with the occult, and then his dedication to Christ. He asked Carman to take his story out into the world, so that others may know that the shackles and death were real, and that it wasn't worth it, and that if they gave their hearts to Christ, they, too, would find ultimate freedom. This, also, Carman agreed to do.

At Sellers' clemency hearing, the Bellofatto family once again testified against him, laying their hurt out on the table and begging the governor to deny a stay of execution. In fact, they asked that the execution be carried out "without hesitation."[180] One of the opposing arguments came from Dianna Crawn, a juror at Sellers' trial who had assisted in establishing his sentence of the death penalty. Crawn admitted that there had been much tearful deliberation in the jury's recess room prior to sentencing. The jury had faced two options: 1) giving Sellers life with eligibility for parole, knowing that he would be up for parole in around seven to twelve years (and Crawn said they felt that he was a danger to society); or 2) sentencing him to death. ("Life without parole" was not an option until 1987, one year later.) A man in the jury room commented that the state of Oklahoma hadn't executed anyone in years and likely wasn't going to do it again anytime soon. There was a murmur of sad agreement. Crawn said of this moment: "And that's the only way I have been able to live with this."

She went on to say, "There's a definition of clemency: 'Clemency properly examines what a person has become and what he has done since conviction and sentencing,' and Sean Sellers in my opinion is the true definition of clemency. And if he's executed, his voice will be silenced forever. And so I ask you to give this young man clemency."[181]

Sellers' clemency was denied in a vote of five to zero. On February 4, 1999, at 12:17 a.m., Sean Richard Sellers was executed by lethal injection. Just before taking his last breath, he sang the lyrics from "Set My Spirit Free," a contemporary Christian song: "Set my spirit free that I might praise Thee. Set my spirit free that I might worship Thee."[182]

Margy Paoletti, Sellers' spiritual advisor next to Carman, was present at the execution. She said of this:

> The blinds opened and he popped his head up and he looked and he smiled, and the warden asked, "Do you have any last words?" And Sean said, "Yes," and he named four or five of the victim's family members and he stated: "You will hate me again in the morning. This isn't going to solve your hatred, and [then he said] don't go through life this way [and also said to] reach out to God." And then he sang and then it appeared that he went unconscious and I watched his chest and he breathed his last breath and it was very peaceful.... Then I walked out, you know, the reality of not seeing him again, that hit. And I walked down the stairs and I remember looking back and saying, "I'll never be here again, because there will never be another Sean Sellers, ever."[183]

Carman sat eight feet away from him at the execution. In the days and months after Sellers' death, Carman told Sellers' story on his live tour, in a narrative song called "The 11th Hour."

Sellers was the first person in forty years within the United States to be sentenced to death for a crime committed while under the age of seventeen. It has now been ruled that the death penalty is unconstitutional for crimes committed under the age of eighteen.

"Because he didn't die of natural causes, the state that killed him requires an autopsy. His death is recorded as a *homicide*."[184]

DAVID BERKOWITZ
(.44 CALIBER KILLER; SON OF SAM)[185]

It all started with a traffic citation issued to a vehicle parked too close to a fire hydrant in the summer of 1977. The parking ticket had been paid, and the police were able to track it to this spot.

A team of police investigators located the Ford Galaxie outside the apartment on 35 Pine Street in Yonkers, New York. A glimpse through the window revealed an assault rifle in the back seat jutting out the end of a duffel bag. It was not an illegal firearm, nor was it the .44-caliber Bulldog revolver investigators had linked to the murders, but it was a weapon nonetheless. The search warrant hadn't yet arrived, and the anticipation for the legal red tape to be cut was now overwhelming. They were feeling good about this lead.

Officers' heads turned about the area, as others kept their eyes fixed on the door of the apartment complex, ready to call out a warning to their fellow law enforcement comrades at a moment's notice. The .44 Caliber

Killer had taken the lives of too many of New York's romantic couples and pretty young women for the force to lose their suspect because of a paperwork hang-up. With no warrant in possession, the officers forced open the door of the Galaxie. Jaws clenched. Fists tightened. The air was charged with an indescribable intensity. Police stood by, adrenaline racing, as a detective extracted a letter addressed to Sergeant Dowd of the Omega task force. The penmanship was an unmistakable match to that of the Son of Sam letters.

They had him.

Quickly, the team backed away from the car and returned to their positions. The apartment building's many narrow hallways were overrun with hordes of innocent people. If opening fire were to prove necessary, it could mean the loss of life for civilians or officers. With the safety of the residents in mind, the officers had no choice but to linger outside.

The wait was agonizing. They had only the increasing intensity of exchanged glances while they steadied their beating hearts. Their guns were loaded and ready, but at this moment, the only bullets racing were those of perspiration swelling from their pores. The stakeout was a concentrated endeavor, and they all knew that if they didn't act soon, with or without the warrant, *he* would kill again. Yet, every man and woman in the crew was willing, if the events of the night required, to lose his or her life in the crossfire if it meant apprehending the Son of Sam.

Hours passed, and the tension grew.

At around ten o'clock in the evening, the door to the apartment entrance opened. A young man in his early twenties, of average height and weight, emerged. His facial features were distinctive and imposing: authoritative eyebrows, deep-set eyes, a narrow nose, and sharp lips. Not one of his composite sketches did him any justice, having resembled different men altogether, and now the reason for that was clear. The threat of his countenance could not be captured, imagined, or drawn. David Berkowitz was a creature all his own.

Nonchalantly, he headed straight for his yellow Ford, carrying a brown paper bag. When he was comfortably seated in his vehicle, a voice rang out from the quiet, commanding him to freeze.

Berkowitz calmly turned to the detective holding him at gunpoint and said, "Well, you finally got me."

The detective responded without hesitation.

"Who do I have?" he demanded.

Berkowitz made no sudden moves, nor was he afraid. He uttered a matter-of-fact, tranquil reply: "The Son of Sam."

On the seat next to Berkowitz was the .44 caliber safely tucked in the bag he had been carrying. This weapon was, in fact, the gun that had brought so much death during the reign of terror that was now ended.

Fully cooperating, Berkowitz exited his vehicle with his hands up, gave no resistance when his wrists were cuffed, and went with the officers.

Soon, the camcorders began rolling, and a never-ending line of photographers pointed their gadgets and equipment toward the callous executioner, capturing the first surreal moments in history when this assassin's true face would be shown. And what a face he gave them all to see…

All the way from his apartment to a Yonkers police station, Berkowitz grinned with a facial expression that appeared to onlookers to be smug satisfaction.

Later, when asked by baffled detectives why he had paid the parking ticket that had inadvertently led to his arrest, he answered, "Because, I am a law-abiding citizen."[186]

CASUALTIES OF THE ADOPTION OPTION

Today, the number of abortions performed within the United States is 1.21 million annually.[187] When a young girl or a woman becomes pregnant with an unwanted child or has an unplanned pregnancy as a result of promiscuous behavior or marital infidelity, it is now within her constitutional rights to hide her shame or secrets by obtaining a quick, cheap (or free) abortion.

However, in 1952—the year David Berkowitz was conceived—obtaining legal abortions as means of an escape from responsibility was not an option. It wasn't until the rulings of the *Roe v. Wade* case in 1973[188] and further liberal legal revisions in the *Planned Parenthood v. Casey* case in 1992[189] that American women and teens had such convenient access to resolving their moral dilemmas.

If a young girl in the fifties had a child "out of wedlock," she was considered by most in society as a "tramp" or "Jezebel," and the child was referred to as a "bastard." Deciding to keep the child equaled social suicide. Notable members of society spread the word that giving your body to the opposite sex under any circumstances barring traditional marriage made you a "used rag." Men didn't have babies, so they didn't have the pitter-patter of lingering, living consequences of their sexual immorality following them around should they choose to leave their lady friends behind and start afresh elsewhere. Women endured the brunt of the consequences for unsanctified acts of physical love, and the world was judgmental and cruel to them. Words weren't needed when a young, unmarried girl with a baby in tow passed an elder; the stern and critical glower expressed enough disdain. Even girls who were one's own age found it much easier to turn up their noses at their "tarnished" acquaintances than to associate with such "rubbish." It was a difficult time indeed for those who found themselves in a quandary of this nature during such a conservative period.

As a result, many families opted to send their pregnant daughters away to a boarding school (if they had the money) and let them return, visibly unscathed, with their indiscretions effectively hidden. To a woman who fell into this "rough spot" later on in life (or to a girl whose parents didn't have the money or means to send her away), the situation proved much more difficult to conceal. Any mother willing to raise the child would have to do so under the condemnation of those around her. Any mother giving up her baby for adoption was seen as one who, though "woman enough" to complete the act of physical love, wasn't "woman enough" to pony up to the consequences. Someone who had given her child up for adoption would pay for it one way or the other, and probably for years and years afterward.

But the price was not exclusively a *social* one for single moms who opted to find another home for their children. In fact, many women have written about their struggles and anxiety centering on the so-called abandonment of their child. At the time most women made the decision, they were young, weak, and scared, so they did the only thing they knew to do: give the baby a chance with someone else. Yet, often the birth mother feels that she loses more than just a child when she opts to allow someone else to raise her baby. She loses a piece of herself and, as a result, her confidence is sometimes irreparably damaged, negatively affecting her future relationships.

And what about the child? The child conceived by a single mom or "out of wedlock" in that era experienced negative effects as well: a certain, harsh punishment for simply being born. These children were also often horribly teased by their peers as not being "legitimate"; the term "illegitimate child" could often be translated "irrelevant child" by many standards of the time.

When one truly reflects on this term, it is easy to see how it came to be, considering that the word "illegitimate" is not used as an adjective to describe the person born into the situation; it is a direct reference to a child born to two people who had not established what society had deemed a "legitimate," marital relationship. However, despite how much the term originated as a reference to the relationship of the parents, being referred to as an "illegitimate child" implies an insensitive comparison to a "valid" world around them.

For example, a thesaurus offers the following words that correspond to "legitimate": "lawful," "rightful," "legal," "genuine," "justifiable," and "valid."[190] Similar are words that correspond to "bastard" (the typical label placed on most out-of-wedlock children of the '50s): "counterfeit," "fake," "imperfect," "inferior," "irregular," "mongrel," "phony," "sham," "adulterated," "misborn," "impure," and "ungenuine," just to name some.[191]

Although an adopted child has as fair a chance to thrive and succeed as anyone else, it would be accurate to suggest that an adopted child may, and often does, develop a psychological complex in this situation.

A complex, when nurtured by other factors such as social rejection and/or paranoia, can lead to "acting out" in extreme ways. This was obviously more the case in decades past, as the increasing number of births among unwed mothers (and younger teens) in recent years has launched wider acceptance of both mother and child in most circumstances. Young adopted boys or girls referred to as "bastards" at the mid of last century were sometimes reminded almost daily—by the more cruel social pressures driving the American-dream achievement—that they were little more than awkward, unwanted mistakes in a world that had no place for their kind. Thus, many adoptive parents were encouraged by the placement agencies to withhold the truth from the child as a way of avoiding this stigma: a "lie to the child to protect the child" approach, respectively. Many adopted kids would therefore spend their developmental years forming a crucial worldview around what was, at the core, *false*. This can, observably, lead to adverse effects and a certain level of psychological detachment warranting delicate management, though some statistics are clearly more extreme and severe than others.

Meet David Berkowitz, your resident adopted child, growing up in the most crime-riddled streets of New York. Berkowitz would, as the reader has gathered by this point, mature into a killer. Before we look at his developmental years, let's take a moment to remember those who were lost or injured during this string of crime in the late 1970s. (Note that all shootings in the Son of Sam case happened at point-blank range.)

- Michelle Forman (aged 14 at the time)
  - o **Survived** a knife scuffle
- Donna Lauria (aged 18)
  - o Shot while sitting in a parked vehicle; died instantly
- Jody Valenti (aged 19 at the time)
  - o Shot alongside Donna Lauria in a parked vehicle, struck by a bullet in the thigh; **survived** her injuries
- Carl Denaro (aged 25 at the time)
  - o Shot while sitting in a parked vehicle, struck by a bullet to the head; **survived** his injuries (but required the installation of a metal plate to replace a section of his skull)
- Rosemary Keenan (aged 28 at the time)
  - o Shot at alongside Carl Denaro; **survived** minor injuries
- Donna DeMasi (aged 16 at the time)
  - o Shot on the steps outside an apartment complex, struck by a bullet to the neck; **survived** her injuries

- Joanne Lomino (aged 18 at the time)
  - Shot alongside Donna DeMasi, struck by a bullet to the back; **survived** her injuries (but was rendered a paraplegic)
- Christine Freund (aged 26)
  - Shot while sitting in a parked vehicle; died within hours at the hospital
- John Diel (aged 30 at the time)
  - Shot at alongside Christine Freund; **survived** minor injuries
- Virginia Voskerichian (aged 19)
  - Shot while walking home in the evening; died instantly
- Valentina Suriani (aged 18)
  - Shot while sitting in a parked vehicle; died instantly
- Alexander Esau (aged 20)
  - Shot alongside Valentina Suriani; died within hours at the hospital
- Judy Placido (aged 17 at the time)
  - Shot while sitting in a parked vehicle; struck by bullets, but **survived** minor injuries
- Sal Lupo (aged 20 at the time)
  - Shot alongside Judy Placido; struck by bullets, but **survived** minor injuries
- Stacy Moskowitz (aged 20)
  - Shot while sitting in a parked vehicle; died within hours at the hospital
- Robert Violante (aged 20 at the time)
  - Shot alongside Stacy Moskowitz, struck by a bullet in the head; **survived** his injuries (but was completely blinded in one eye, partially blinded in the other eye, and remains visibly affected where the bullet made contact with the face)

The city had been terrorized by these murders. While some businesses in close proximity to the crime scenes closed their doors earlier in the evening, and some of the hip dance joints in the area suffered a level of decline in their patronage (as many preferred the safety of their living rooms over a night out on the dangerous town), hair salons comparatively observed an *increase* in foot traffic. Because the newspapers reported that the killer on the loose had narrowed his sights to young, pretty girls with long, brown hair, women and teen girls started wearing their hair in any style other than long and any color other than brown: they primarily got blond dye jobs and curly permanents or up-dos. Police swept the city streets more and more as time went on, knocking on the windows of occupied, parked vehicles, and instructing anyone inside to return home. Members of law enforcement went undercover, posing as romantic, intimate couples in cars throughout the city in hopes to lure the killer out from the shadows. People were scared of the hardened man with the .44-caliber revolver; every time another story hit the media, seemingly just after they had begun to return to their normal lives after the previous murders, another fatality or severe injury would shake them back into hiding.

Some time before the research on this book was compiled, these authors came into contact with a taxi driver from Brooklyn, New York, who shared that he had been present in the state during the late '70s. We recently contacted him again for comment, and the following is his enlightening narrative of the period, from a man who was no more to the Berkowitz case than a bystander (note that for privacy purposes, he will be referred to only as "Borison"; the interview was conducted by Donna Howell):

BORISON: I remember those days. It was crazy, y'know?

HOWELL: I can imagine.

BORISON: When young people, and mostly girls, were being done in, lotsa people changed jobs. I was one of them. I had been a taxi driver in Brooklyn, same as [I am] now, and the kids were runnin' all over the place lookin' for newer places to [be romantic]. I had driven home a couple girls from a disco joint. Their hair was all yellow and done up.

HOWELL: You mean they dyed their hair blond and wore it up?

BORISON: Yeah. They had both been brunettes before this, stringy hippie hair, y'know, and I told them they looked good, but I pointed out that it went against what they believed in.

HOWELL: It was against their beliefs to have blond hair worn up?

BORISON: Well, yeah, because they was kinda flower-girl types; didn't do nothing unnatural. This was weird seein' 'em all plastic like Barbie dolls or somethin'. They were some of the few who still held to the whole natural movement when the city around them was becoming some, y'know, flashy, fleshy fevers in miniskirts. They still knew how to have a good time, though.

HOWELL: I see. Continue.

BORISON: Anyway, I asked them what [was going on] about all these sudden hair changes, 'cuz I'd seen a couple other customers doin' this, and they said it was because of the .44-caliber killer. You gotta understand that I was a taxi driver, so I was listenin' to the news all day and knew probably more about what they was talkin' about than *they* did.

HOWELL: Then you would have already known why these girls had dyed their hair.

BORISON: Yeah, but strikin' up a conversation is usually part of the job.

HOWELL: Oh, of course. Okay. Yes, I have read about this in my research on the Berkowitz case. I'm familiar with the sudden trend of blond dye jobs in the area around that time. But the murders didn't happen in Brooklyn.

BORISON: Doesn't matter. The whole state was scared of this guy.

HOWELL: Well, I have also discovered that in my research. So what happened to the girls?

BORISON: Oh, nothin' happened to them. The longer the shootings went on, y'know, the fewer the customers there were 'cuz people was stayin' inside. Actually, I quit drivin' a taxi, myself, for a while.

HOWELL: Because you were afraid that the murderer was around? Or because you had fewer customers?

BORISON: Both. It started out [with] me bein' a tough guy, this whole, "I ain't afraid of no killer," nonsense, but I have to admit that I was lookin' over my shoulder all the time during drop-offs to see if anyone was standin' in the bushes with a gun. [Heck] if I was gonna get shot in the head because some young girl wanted to shoot the breeze about her cat in my taxi outside her apartment. [He laughs.]… Sometime around this point I was datin' this beautician, and she was dyin' the girls' hair, and the stories she told me, it was like conversation in the shop went from boy troubles, y'know, girly gossip and that [kind of stuff], to this serial killer. Haha! My girlfriend made some extra cash in those days, I can tell you that.… It would take me until sometime in the early eighties, I think it was, to get back into drivin' a taxi.[192]

The police called him "the .44 Caliber Killer."
He called himself "the Son of Sam."

PINOCCHIO'S GOT NO STRINGS TO HOLD HIM BACK

The murders had not been by Mrs. Peacock in the ballroom with a candlestick. It had been by Mr. Berkowitz on the streets of New York with a revolver. Nobody questions that. However, there are layers to this case that have, since its very conception, pointed to more than just Berkowitz as the guilty party. Much like Atkins, our first case study, when Berkowitz was captured and brought in for questioning as a suspect, he admitted to every shooting. This interrogation was remembered by those personally involved as one wherein Berkowitz actually enjoyed divulging deadly accurate information regarding all the crime scenes to the authorities with a prideful smile on his face. He spoke of exactly where, when, and how the murders had been committed, providing details that only the investigators and a guilty party could have known. To comb over every single report, article, press release, and detail of this case would require a much lengthier book than this truncated case study will allow, and many incredibly long books and in-depth materials on the subject have already been written. Suffice it to say that when Berkowitz readily and happily took responsibility for everything, the case was quickly closed.

What many do not know is that the case was later reopened.

Rewind.

Don't Tell the Boy…

Richard David Falco was born on June 1, 1953, to Betty Falco. On his birth paperwork, the baby's father was listed as Betty's husband, Tony Falco.

Tony was not the father.

A few days after his birth, the newborn was adopted by Pearl and Nathan Berkowitz, a modest Jewish couple. The boy's first and middle names were flipped, and he was given a new surname: "David Richard Berkowitz."

From his youngest age, Berkowitz's mother and father loved their son dearly and doted on him whenever possible. They showered him with praise and love and gave him their personal time and attention at every opportunity. His early infant days were mostly spent in the full interest of his mother, while his father worked ten hours per day, six days per week, tending to a meager hardware retail store, and these hours would continue for years. In his youth, his father sometimes took him to local sports events as a way of establishing a constant presence in the boy's life since he worked as much as he did. Other times, father and son would work on bicycles together, go to the schoolyard across from their modest apartment and play catch or, if it was hot, go out for ice cream.[193] Every time they passed the county courthouse, Mr. and Mrs. Berkowitz would repeat that it was the building where they had originally been awarded with little

David, because the judge had known that, of all the people fighting for the chance to adopt him, they had loved him so much more than any of the other prospective parents in line.[194]

Then the adoption would come back into conversation, and Berkowitz's mother and father would tell their son how his biological mother had died giving birth to him.

Berkowitz loved scary movies. He was strangely drawn to them and gained a thrill from seeing the plots build, thicken, and then play out with a climactic conclusion. But from an early age, he was living his own horror story. He would crawl into a closet or under the bed for hours on end and curl into a ball under the blankets. Then, at the next possible chance, he would watch another horror movie and repeat the process over and over, becoming so frightened that he couldn't speak. He had night terrors that took place every night and were relentless, but he could not, *would* not, stop feeding his mind with the darkest images the television and his imagination, in tandem, could produce.

When the seizures began, it "felt as if something was entering [him],"[195] and his adoptive father would have to hold him down, because he often knocked over the surrounding furniture while he was kicking and twisting like a wild animal. The troubled boy would lay awake at night, terrified that his biological father would come to kill him for being the cause of his real mother's death at childbirth. Then he'd feel the powerful tugging again to fill his mind with terror. He would watch *Rosemary's Baby*,[196] the movie wherein a woman is raped by the devil and conceives, then delivers, a healthy baby child of Satan. Berkowitz would never know exactly why this was the movie he was so often pulled toward and most spellbound by.

School wasn't easy. He was a lonely adopted child who, although he had friends, did not connect with the world around him with the same healthy social ties as other children his age. As a result of his difficulty connecting, he often preferred to be alone. Peers played a huge role in constantly reminding him that he was less than genuine. *Their* parents were "real," and his were just nice people who had taken in the sad boy who killed his mother on the birthing table. *They* were real people, and he was counterfeit. *They* had a family, and he had phony stick people

Scotch-taped together and bound by the piece of paper the judge had so kindly awarded them. Investigative journalist Jack Jones describes his childhood as a Pinocchio scenario: a young boy who felt wooden and fake, like a puppet, compared to those who endlessly teased him for being less than real because he was adopted.[197] But Berkowitz didn't have to put up with it. Kids at school got what was coming to them from the increasingly violent boy, to the point that an angry teacher once put him into a headlock and threw him out of class. Other times, he would burst into blood-curdling screams for no reason at all.

His real mother. Berkowitz constantly wondered about her. What had she looked like? How had she dressed? Would she have loved him? *Of course* she would have loved him… She would have been wonderful and strong, the epitome of passion and talent. And yet, she was no longer breathing, because he had to be born.

Berkowitz's adoptive mother loved him, too. This he was sure of, but, for reasons that were obscure even to himself, he could never truly appreciate her. When he threw things at her and insulted her in response to her outpourings of love, he became like a monster. However, a jealous rage rose within him anytime she gave anyone else or anything else her full attention. (Later, Berkowitz would tell of his mother's beloved parakeet, which he had "poisoned" out of jealousy. This was not true; the parakeet died of a sickness that rotted his beak and delivered him into a lethargic state until death [a condition known in laymen's terms as "beak rot"].[198] However, Berkowitz's lie about the bird to this psychologist after his arrest reflects of the kind of thoughts and memories associated with this yearning for her complete attention.)

Weekly visits to a psychologist for two years didn't change Berkowitz's behavior. He still craved darkness, solitude, and terror, no matter how miserable they made him. Depression was his only reality, and as lost as he had always felt, he still embraced his own demise, a brand of torment that seemed to have no origin or cure and demanded his mind.

Berkowitz's mother and father broke down and cried many times, feeling helpless and confused at their strange son's alarming behavior, but even their tears would not encourage him to respond. The fire escape outside his window was a tremendous help in getting him out of the house, and by the time he was ten years old, he was walking the streets alone, exploring the brick buildings and dark alleyways like a street rat, sniffing along the sewer lines for something of interest. This felt appropriate. Thoughts of throwing himself in front of a moving car or subway train plagued his mind, constantly needling him, tempting him, to give in to the urge to end his own life. The ground six stories below his bedroom window seemed inviting enough that he would dangerously dangle from the fire escape and imagine falling to his death. His own self-destructive and self-punishing patterns of thought were so intense that when he saw an opportunity to kill himself, his body physically trembled in anticipation of the day he would finally follow through with the act.[199] The end of his life would mean no more hurting, anger, hate, loathing, and depression—and it would mean no more having to listen to anyone else's opinion of his imitation existence or how he was merely pretending to belong to anyone for real. A real boy…

Then again, he always had his adoptive mother, and she was, in every way, precious. Oh how he wished he could appreciate that! He had his adoptive father, too, but they were only able to be so close, what with the long work hours his dad was always putting in at the store in order to bring home the bacon. Their relationship was pure and kind, but it was strained and lonely, as well. No matter how much anyone in his life tried to confirm an existence of normalcy, they maintained that his mother, his real mother, had died giving birth to him, and nothing would ever change that fact.

When he was thirteen years old, Berkowitz's Bar Mitzvah ceremony was observed. He would now be held to a higher standard of behavior and would bear accountability for his actions. As he has written in past years regarding this time, "Jews are supposed to be honest, law-abiding, and respectful of parents. I am none of these. I am a disgrace."[200]

Shortly after his coming-of-age celebration, according to documents compiled by A&E, Berkowitz shouted, "I hate you! I hate you! I hope you die!"[201] as his mother was leaving the house for dinner. She collapsed that night and never came home. Effectively, though Berkowitz saw her at the hospital while she was unconscious, that moment of lashing out in hatred would mark the last time Berkowitz saw his mother, his only living and caring mother, alive and able to communicate.[202] Nobody had known that at this point she was in the advanced stages of breast cancer, and that her body had been rapidly deteriorating with the disease. She was taken to the hospital, where she withered away in the cancer ward until her death when Berkowitz was fourteen.

For days on end, without stopping, young Berkowitz sobbed. How could he have been so selfish and foolish? How could he have said such awful things to her and why had he been so cruel? Her only offense against him had been to love him with a mother's unadulterated and unconditional affection. She had given him everything—food, warmth, shelter, and love—and he had often given her hatred and loathing in return. He had dreamed of acceptance from everyone except for her, placing her on the back burner while he strove for the world to embrace him. Not once had he truly thought that his days with the one person who had given him everything he had ever wanted from everyone else would be numbered. He had killed his first mother, and now his only remaining mama was gone forever from this world, his parting words reportedly having been that he hated her and hoped that she would die.

And then she did.

Riding his bike alone, Berkowitz visited his mother's grave often, devastatingly lonely and wishing for her to return. Her new home was in the cemetery, so, for a while, that would be a home to him, too. He recoiled farther into his own company, away from the world—especially away from girls. Dreadfully shy and afraid of rejection, Berkowitz felt his mother's headstone was now the only "person" he had to talk to. (Later in his prison journals, Berkowitz would write, "[S]he was always there for me when I got into trouble. And after all this time, I've never stopped missing her. She seems to have been on my mind every moment of each day for the thirty-four years she has been gone.… Thinking about my own mother on this day, as I do every day, I can say that I still miss her tremendously."[203])

The more time he spent at the cemetery, the more rapt he became with others who had been laid to rest there. He was intrigued, particularly by those whose tombstones and epitaphs revealed very young girls' deaths. He wondered if they had been pretty…

His father tried often to break through to him and connect with him, but his efforts always proved to be in vain. Berkowitz sadly reflected:

> My dad used to cry and plead with me to come and talk with him, and he [would say], "I don't even know you, you're my son, and you're like a stranger." That's just the way I was. I don't know why! It was just these blocks that were up, where I didn't wanna share nothing that was on my mind, nothing that was on my heart. I was a closed book, and that was that.[204]

> I put my father through hell.… I remember the times I saw him break down and cry when I was cruel to him, and how he struggled trying to care for me when my mother got cancer.… Today I have a lot of guilt about how I mistreated him, and I know he deserved better than me for a son.[205]

Mechanically, Berkowitz walked through the mundane steps of each day, the darkness that had befriended him seeing him through more horror movies and fascination with, and addiction to, terror. Eventually, he carried himself to his inevitable high school graduation, since his father had dutifully pushed him to his educational end.

The summer after he graduated, his father remarried. Berkowitz did not bond with the woman and his new stepsister, and a great strain grew at home. The new Mrs. Berkowitz wasn't like the previous one, and there wasn't going to be any changing that. Luckily, Berkowitz wouldn't have to even try. Shortly after his father and stepmother had tied the knot, the increase in New York crime (and reportedly an armed robbery of his hardware store[206]) encouraged the newlyweds to relocate to Florida, leaving Berkowitz to enjoy his apartment alone. (Note that Berkowitz, around thirty years later, would refer to his stepmother as "a wonderful widow" his father had met and lived the rest of his days with, and he said that they were blessed by the Lord.[207])

Barely eighteen, Berkowitz enlisted in the US Army to start a new life. He just knew that after enlisting, he would die a horrible, but celebrated, death, be heralded as a hero in his home town, and be buried a decorated man. Instead, however, the service found it within its best interests to ship Berkowitz to Korea, where he received the Sharpshooter Marksmanship Badge with an M16 rifle. Although he had dabbled with alcohol use as an adolescent, this is when his substance abuse began. According to one documentary: "He went off into the service, spent a year in Korea, spent a year in no uncertain terms of just getting intoxicated on drugs every single day."[208] (Note: Army service is often considered a "red flag" in murder investigations, depending on the circumstances, because of the effectiveness military training can have on one's ability to take another person's life [an enemy target] by matters of instinct, and not the lust for blood. Later, when Berkowitz's name landed on the list of those under investigation for the New York murders, one of the many reasons his name became a more imminent focus of the investigation team was his service and notable marksman experience.)

Berkowitz had been lonely for a female friend for quite some time, but had never been able to work up the nerve to open up to a girl long enough to gain her romantic attention. Finally, in Korea, as a soldier of the United States, there were girls everywhere who were willing to shower him with attention—for a small fee. He wanted a girlfriend, someone to hold, but found, instead, degradation.

Depressed and disappointed in his anticlimactic involvement in the now-obligatory and seemingly useless role in the military, Berkowitz floated from place to place, following orders and being one face among many others equally or more skilled than he in combat training. The army-hero idea had been nothing more than an empty, romantic pipe dream, and he was not going to die a hero. In a letter to his father around this time, he wrote about his remorse for "'being a burden and amounting to nothing in society.' He wrote that he was sorry he turned out the way he did: 'stupid, hateful, ugly, destructive.' Berkowitz begged his father to pretend he never had a son, to forget that he even existed."[209]

In 1973, now twenty years old, Berkowitz was transferred to Fort Knox, Kentucky, an area with strong ties to the Baptist doctrine. All around him, people were enjoying the family life, sharing hugs and fellowship in a close-knit, family-oriented culture, so much so that he was willing to abandon his Jewish upbringing to convert to being a Southern Baptist. He attended church for a while, and was even baptized into the Christian faith, but many reports of this portion of his life suggest that this new religious interest was born out of a deep yearning for a family like those in the Baptist church community. Nothing could curb his desire for a real family, one that did not have to be explained, justified, or proven with laws and papers. Nonetheless, the preaching from his church's particular pulpit did little more than remind him that he was a bad person on the inside and that nothing more awaited his afterlife but hell. His nickname for himself became *die schmutz*, Yiddish for "the dirty one."[210] He soon stopped attending the Baptist church.

In 1974, Berkowitz's service obligations ended, and he left the army to return to the solitary confinement of his apartment in New York City, where the interest he had held his whole life for the occult and witchcraft rose to a more dramatic level. *The Satanic Bible* by Anton LaVey drew him into new philosophies, and the more he read of the freedom, power, and family available for anyone willing to apply himself, the clearer it became that, by trying to be a decent person, all he had ever brought about was a sad attempt at forcibly wedging himself into a life he was never born to lead. He joined a satanic cult and started down the deceptive road that so many before him had traveled. On the onset of his journey into satanism, the rituals and incantations seemed harmless and entertaining, just like in the movies he frequently watched. (More information about who led him into this and how he became mixed up with this life will follow a bit later. In addition, read Berkowitz's personal comments of this time in his life in the exclusive interview that follows the close of this case study.)

With more time on his hands after landing a job as a security cop with IBI Security at the docks of Manhattan, he dedicated himself to learning his biological lineage, if for no other reason than to track down the woman he had "killed" as a baby and perhaps stumble across others he could earnestly call his own through his relationship to her.

It was then that he uncovered the truth.

Truly Illegitimate

Berkowitz was around the age of twenty-one or twenty-two when he finally landed a big break in the search for his roots. According to journalist Jack Jones:

> He had gone to one of these "freedom of [information] adoption movement" meetings and told them the story of how his mother had died giving birth to him, and he had a father out there somewhere, and people [were] laughing at him. He said, you know, "What are you laughing about? This is a tragedy!" you know. "My mother died!" They said, "Man, that's what they tell all of us."[211]

He left the meeting and called his father in Florida. His father confirmed that Berkowitz had been lied to all his life, and went on to explain that the parties involved in the private adoption arrangement agreed that the truth never be fully divulged, likely because the truth would not have been pleasant for the little boy to hear.

The truth: His mother was alive.

One can only imagine the emotions that hit him at that moment. He had been loved all his life by the most generous and giving people anyone could ever dream to handpick. He had loved them in return, though he had always struggled to show them that love the way he should have. A burdening pressure had always been present because of deep-rooted anxiety over so many storms of the heart and mind, often related somehow to his concept that he was the reason a good woman had died. Agony had built upon anguish since childhood, and he found that over the years, he had been slowly but surely drinking from a cup of psychological poison, fearing the world, then wanting the world; feeding his fear, then starving it out; watching *Rosemary's Baby* and thinking about devil children, then curling under blankets in the closet; preferring his own company on the streets and in cemeteries, then longing for company other than his own… Confusion, uncertainty, chaos, disorder, turmoil… All these were his closest friends. Be what they were, harmful and all-consuming, they were at least familiar.

And now, suddenly, new feelings washed over him: relief, excitement, happiness. He hadn't been the devil child after all. Nobody had ever died as a result of his existence!

He had it all figured out: He would go to his real mother. Maybe she would explain that the law hadn't allowed her to contact him all this time. Maybe she would wrap her strong, maternal arms around him and profess her never-ending love for her long-lost son. Maybe she would weep with him and finally tell him the reasons she had been coerced into giving him up in the first place. Maybe she would tell the tragic tale of evil people who had torn him from her loving embrace.

Maybe they could be a family.

Then he struck gold. His birth mother, found through obsessive search, was Betty Falco of Coney Island.

Upon meeting her and sharing a joyous reunion, Berkowitz came to the knowledge that he had not been given away for noble reasons at all. Much to the contrary, he understood from her story that he had been a casualty of a marital affair. Tony Falco was not his real father anymore than Santa Claus had been. His biological daddy was a real-estate agent who had been cheating on his wife for years with Betty Falco. Tony had left Berkowitz's mother and her little girl for another woman, but he had remained legally married to Betty, and she had run into the first pair of arms that would speak little nothings into her ear. Betty Falco went on to explain that when she had discovered her pregnancy, the immoral duo agreed to do the dishonorable thing for the sake of their public reputations. Berkowitz's biological father couldn't have his real-estate business affected by the news of his infidelity and an illegitimate child, so he had refused to support the child, monetarily or otherwise. Betty was ashamed of herself and had her own reputation to think about, the societal pressures upon a woman so given to her own desires to the point of bearing another married man's child more disgraceful than she could bear. The decision was easily made, and Betty gave birth to a boy she had already known she would never keep. To save face, she had listed Tony Falco as the father.

During their meeting, Betty "apologized profusely for abandoning her 'Little Ritchie.'"[212]

Berkowitz had always wanted to see his beautiful, strong mother and learn who he was and where he had come from. Meeting her had dispelled everything. Seeing the woman who had given him away, no matter what that would do to him, in trade for keeping her nose clean didn't settle well. Additionally, the idea that she had kept his natural sister, *but not him*, was a world-crumbling devastation. His newfound relief over the discovery that he had not caused his natural mother's death quickly heated into a boiling rage.

There he was again, like a little Pinocchio, a little wooden boy, a mere replica of the youths who had so vindictively taunted him, ping-ponging around by life's strings like a marionette, made to dance, made to frolic, a smile painted on his face for all the world to ignore while he performed in the shadows of the *legitimate* showstoppers…and all of it fake.

(Note: This author does not pass any judgment upon this woman or this man for their past indiscretions. The flavor of this narrative reflects Berkowitz's point of view during the more extreme moments of this dark time in his life, as gathered from numerous interviews, articles, reports, documentaries, and other biographical sources. Berkowitz today refers to his birth mother as a "good woman" [see the interview following this case study]. It is also worth noting that when Berkowitz read this case study, he had the following to say: "My [birth] mom [who was Jewish] was a loving and kindhearted woman, abandoned years earlier by her former husband, and even by some of her family, because she married a Gentile and married out of her faith and against the advice of her parents, who were very strict and religious. Sadly they disowned her. This then thrust my [birth] mother into a life of loneliness and desperation. When she eventually met Joe, my birth father, she clung to him for dear life.… [She] also did her very best to raise her daughter, my half-sister, and maintain a home under difficult circumstances."[213])

Fires, Knives, and Burgers

Berkowitz located his half sister. He didn't blame her for her part in why she had been kept and adored by Betty and he hadn't, as she had likely never been given an opportunity to do anything different. He did envy her, however, and her beautiful family.

By the time the following Thanksgiving season rolled around, Berkowitz had become, for a while, a regular visitor at his half sister's home. His nieces welcomed him and ran to his arms every time he came around, calling him "Uncle Richie." Yet, just like all other families he had witnessed, being around them merely reminded him of his yearning for a family of his own, and of his unremitting seclusion.

On the inside, a monster was awakening. From somewhere deep, a desire to kill began to grow. His dark philosophies and relationship with his personal demons took on a more serious edge than the mere entertainment he had derived from the practice before. He was a hated man, and hatred was what he wanted to give back to the world. He began setting fires about the New York City, burning heaps of rubbish, abandoned buildings, and anything else he could find that he deemed suitable for destruction, and he kept a log of every fire he set in his journal. (According to the documentary, *David Berkowitz: The Son of Sam*, the number of fires he set about the urban area would climb to 1,488 before his capture.[214])

Mysteriously, one day, he informed his half sister that he would never harm her or her family, and then he stopped coming to visit.

Around this time, he sent his adoptive father another letter. Though Berkowitz likely did not know this or intend this, the letter appeared to be a last and final call for help:

> It's cold and gloomy here in New York, but that's okay because the weather fits my mood—gloomy. Dad, the world is getting dark now. I can feel it more and more. The people, they are developing a hatred for me. You wouldn't believe how much some people hate me. Many of them want to kill me. I don't even know these people, but still they hate me. Most of them are young. I walk down the street and they spit and kick at me. The girls call me ugly and they bother me the most. The guys just laugh. Anyhow, things will soon change for the better.[215]

(When Berkowitz read our case study, he shed some additional insight about this time in his life: "Just want to make a comment on the letter I'd written to my father. This, to me, clearly shows how sick and paranoid I was getting. I do not recall the circumstances in which I penned the letter, but obviously I was losing it.... [C]learly I was coming under the control of lying spirits and demonic influences."[216])

Berkowitz continued with his occult-related practices and began to fantasize about death at every turn. He felt his grip on sanity departing with a resilient finality he didn't know how to contest. He chanted the various names of Lucifer repeatedly, appealing to forces he had only recently thoroughly welcomed into his home, his thoughts, and, eventually, his body. He now saw himself as a vessel to control: nothing but a puppet, just another Pinocchio, but this time, on the frontlines. If he was going to be puppeteered by something or someone external, at the very least, he would reserve the right to choose who would do it and how it would come about. He had always wanted a family, and now, in his cult surroundings, he not only had one, but he had one of his choosing. But, everything was so dark...so constantly dark. Any original personality Berkowitz had left was draining from him and another, newer man was replacing the weakling within.

Fires begat fires begat prayers to Lucifer, and Berkowitz was hungry for more. There wasn't a logical explanation for his carnal need to destroy. An insatiable, incurable requirement to dominate impeded upon his consciousness continually.

> Eventually I crossed that invisible line of no return. After years of mental torment, behavioral problems, deep inner struggles, and my own rebellious ways, I became the criminal that, at the time seemed to be my destiny. I now see it as the horrible nightmare it was, and I would do anything if I could undo everything that happened.... Many...suffered at my hand, and will continue to suffer for a lifetime. I am so sorry for that.[217]

On Christmas Eve, 1975, Berkowitz obtained a hunting knife and left his apartment on a hunt for blood. (In a statement to psychiatrists later, he would state that the demons in his head had begged him for blood, and that killing his first victim with a knife had only been in an agreeable attempt to quiet them. However, as we will discuss later in the study, he would follow these claims with a slightly different tale.) When Berkowitz found his victim outside a shopping center out in the dark streets of the city, he emerged from the shadows and attacked. A knife scuffle ensued, and the girl, Michelle Forman, ran away to some nearby apartments, screaming. He retreated from the scene. She would live, but for now, his hunger for blood, his hunger to please the demons, was satisfied. (Forman was hospitalized for her injuries.)

After the attack and attempt on a young girl's life, Berkowitz happily sauntered off to a restaurant, indulging in a burger with a side of fries.

The .44 Caliber Killer

The New Year came and went without incident. After moving in January of 1976 to a new home in New Rochelle (southeastern New York), for a time, Berkowitz kept to himself when he wasn't setting fires to someone's car or garbage can. He held his job with IBI Security for a time, protecting the docks from danger. At night, he struggled to sleep while his landlord's howling dogs made incessant noise. Their cries inspired the rest of the dogs in his neighborhood to howl back. The ruckus made him scream for silence, but the silence never came. He would often take walks on the beach in his spare time; sometimes, he would park at the beach and remain there for the silence, stealing some shuteye in his Ford Galaxie away from the noisy chaos of the city. Eventually, the loneliness and dogs' howling drove him to move to a residence in the neighboring area of Yonkers.

Despite his seemingly peaceful hiatus from the obsessive thoughts of murder, inside Berkowitz's head, a war for dominance rose again and fumed. The girl he had attacked with the knife was no doubt fine by now, and he was not a suspect of anything. He had gotten away with his assault with a deadly weapon, and nobody was any the wiser. It wasn't surprising that he was still invisible, but this time, invisibility made him powerful and more of a threat to the people—especially to the women, who had hated him and punished him so.

Not long after his most recent move, his new apartment produced another problem. Dogs again. Specifically, a solitary black Labrador retriever named Harvey, who barked and barked and barked without rest from his owner's yard just below Berkowitz's apartment. Harvey didn't belong to the landlord, so nothing could be done about it from that angle. The ceaseless and alarming sound was inescapable and intolerable, but Berkowitz wasn't planning to relocate this time—and it wasn't just because of his lease. If it came to it, he would kill the dog; he was done adjusting his life around the uncontrollable whims of a canine.

Thoughts of murder, canine and human alike, consumed every waking minute of every day. He waited in silence like a predator, processing reality and fantasy simultaneously as they unfolded around him, floating, drifting, and leading the double life of a man who, by day, held down a job and made his way in the world, and by night, roamed the streets thinking about victims and blood.

When Berkowitz flew out to visit his adoptive father in Florida, his father showed much concern about his son's behavior. After he had caught Berkowitz staring at his reflection in the mirror and pounding his hands against his head, he pleaded with his son to seek psychological counseling again like he had when he was a child. Berkowitz refused, saying ominously that it was "too late."[218]

Back in Yonkers, all over the walls of his apartment, Berkowitz scribbled occult symbols in permanent ink. In an attempt to get to the demons that some sources say he believed were hiding behind it, he busted a large hole in his wall. Next to this was an arrow pointing into the hole, where Berkowitz wrote:

Hi My Name is MR WiLLiams And I Live in this hole I have SeveRaL Children Who I'm Turning Into Killers. WAIT TiL they grow up[219]

Again, the dogs made him scream. Again, the air seemed to cry out for blood and the freedom from evil women in the world. Again, Berkowitz suppressed the longing to act out in pure destruction, committing only petty arson when what he wanted now, more than anything, was to carry out the perfect crime.

April rolled by…

The dog.

May…

The dog.

It was as if the dog demanded blood! (See later notes in this study for how facts surrounding Berkowitz's relationship with this dog have been greatly misconstrued.) Berkowitz had taken all he could stand from the world, and he was going down. He had long since lost his mind and couldn't take it any longer. Still just a shell of a person, his life was molded perfectly into a frenzied decoupage of horror movie screams, vomit, and darkness, like a broken traffic light frantically blinking back and forth from one ungraspable, anarchic moment to the next. Disorder and mayhem flooded his psyche and the universe was spinning out of control. He wanted to leave his mark on the world that had begged for him to lash out and hand it the bitter taste of what it had coming. And, like Anton LaVey had said in *The Satanic Bible*, in the chapter regarding the choosing of a human sacrifice, when one shows by his or her actions that he or she is begging to be destroyed, it is a moral and obligatory duty to help out with that…

He would later divulge:

I was not in my right mind…I was living in utter torment, under strong satanic influences and powerful delusions. All my thoughts were twisted and illogical. The good became the bad and the bad became good…. Yes, I knew right from wrong…. But I was in such a weakened state of mind that there was nothing left in me to offer resistance. I was at a point where I did not care anymore. My feelings were gone, my emotions had died, and so I went along with the forces that had been reaching out to me for so long.

It was as if an evil hand from the unseen realm was engineering everything that happened. There were so many ways that the bad things seemed to supernaturally fall into place. I was totally sold out to the belief that this was my calling in life.[220]

June…

Berkowitz had decided he was going to kill, and that his victim would have to be a woman—maybe many women, because of what women had done to him, humiliating him, rejecting him. Knives were a problem, though. They brought him too close to the victim.

He traveled to Houston, Texas, to visit a friend he had stayed in touch with since his years in the service. A story quickly fell out of his mouth about how he would need protection on the long journey back to New York. His army buddy kindly and innocently obliged Berkowitz by helping him purchase a Charter Arms .44-caliber Bulldog revolver[221] in his own name, then he bid his friend goodbye.

This gun would soon become one of the most famous weapons in American history.

On July 29, 1976, at a little after one o'clock in the morning, while parked in a vehicle and visiting with her friend in the Bronx (the northernmost borough of New York) after a night at the disco, Donna Lauria was shot and killed; Jody Valenti was shot in the leg and survived. The perpetrator was described as a male around five feet nine inches, and about one hundred sixty pounds, with short, black hair in a modern style. Neighbors reported seeing a yellow compact car they had not seen before driving in circles around the block.[222]

Berkowitz read later the same day that one of the girls had died.

Spree

Having now tasted murder, Berkowitz would be unstoppable. He hadn't known at the time of the first kill that he would become recognized as one of the world's most notorious serial killers, but he did know that he would kill again. Like the madman that he was, he prowled the streets of

New York at night looking for anyone vulnerable enough to permanently remove from his city. Strangely, he began to cross-fantasize about *saving* lives, too. He would imagine rushing into a building and saving everyone—women, men, and children—from life-threatening conditions. He kept an emergency pouch with him at all times in the hopes of assisting anyone he might find in trouble as he crept quietly around the streets of New York in his Ford looking for victims.[223]

On October 23, 1976, in Queens (the easternmost borough of New York), the windows of a parked car imploded on Rosemary Keenan and Carl Denaro, the first of many couples whose romantic date would end differently than they had planned. Keenan had minor injuries from broken glass, and Denaro survived his injury as well, but had to have a metal plate installed in his head. No bystanders saw the attacker or noticed any unfamiliar vehicles; thus, no descriptions were given to offer any clues about the identity of the perpetrator.

On November 27, 1976, just after midnight, Donna DeMasi and Joanne Lomino were shot while walking home from the theaters in Queens. DeMasi took a bullet to the neck and survived; Lomino was shot in the back and survived, but the injury caused her to become a paraplegic. DeMasi, Lomino, and a neighbor responding to the girls' screams all provided clear descriptions of a man with long, blond hair.[224] The bullets fired were so deformed by the impacts that they could not be positively linked to the other shootings, but the police confirmed that they had been fired by a .44-caliber weapon.

On January 29, 1977, Berkowitz kindly offered his assistance to a group of teenagers who had managed to get their car stuck in a snow bank. Waving goodbye and wishing them great tidings of joy, he drove away.[225] Hours later, just after midnight on January 30, Christine Freund was parked in a vehicle in Queens with her fiancé, John Diel. Shots were fired into the car, striking Freund. Diel started the vehicle and tore away from the scene, looking for help, and eventually ended up at the hospital, where Freund died hours later. Diel did not see the attacker, and no description was given. Police compared the string of killings and confirmed a possible connection between them,[226] as each incident had involved young girls with long, brown hair, and each bullet had been fired by a .44-caliber weapon. An official release of the composite sketches of both the short-black-haired and the long-blond-haired shooters were released to the public. Sergeant Richard Conlon of the New York Police Department (NYPD) gave an official statement that the force was searching for *multiple suspects.*[227]

On March 8, 1977, Virginia Voskerichian, a student at Columbia University in Upper Manhattan, was walking home from an evening class at around 7:30, when she was shot and killed instantly, the bullets traveling through the textbooks she held up in self-defense. Nobody witnessed the shooting directly, but multiple bystanders reported seeing a clean-shaven, short, chubby teenager around the age of sixteen fleeing from the scene. One witness said that after the youth realized he had been seen, he suspiciously covered his face with his watch cap and said, "Oh, Jesus!" as he ran past.[228] (Note that some sources say the youth did not respond.[229]) Others in the area also reported spotting this same young man loitering nearby about an hour prior to the shooting.[230] Like in the other shootings, the victims had been brunettes, and bullets had been fired from a .44-caliber weapon. Unlike the other shootings, however, which involved primarily couples, groups, parked cars, and extremely early hours such as midnight and one o'clock in the morning, this girl was walking, alone, in the early evening. The media put out the word that the police were claiming the suspect was a chubby teenager.[231]

Two days later, a press conference was held after a ballistics report confirmed that the bullets from the first murder involving Lauria matched those used in the most recent shooting of Voskerichian, and that the police were now sure the weapon was an unusual Charter Arms .44 Bulldog revolver. Later the same day, it was made known that a task force involving more than three hundred police staff had been formed and would be led by Deputy Inspector Timothy J. Dowd. The Omega task force created earlier would be investigating nothing but the .44-caliber shootings. It was then announced that the chubby teenager who had suspiciously fled the scene had been confirmed to be a witness only; the suspect attention should now be placed solely upon a man fitting Berkowitz's description.

As the media exploded with hundreds of versions of the case details, some accurate, many sensational, Mayor Abraham Beame contributed astronomical funds to the investigation from every possible source.

About this time, Sam Carr, owner of the black Labrador named Harvey, was contacted through the mail anonymously by a concerned citizen who spoke of taking legal action against Carr if he did not quiet his dog, as it was impeding upon the letter-writer's time with his wife, their love-making, and their rest together.[232] (This letter had been sent by Berkowitz, and the details of his fabrication stood as another reflection of his loneliness.)

On April 17, 1977, around three o'clock in the early morning, Valentina Suriani and Alexander Esau had stopped on the way home from a movie and were visiting in a parked vehicle in the Bronx. Both were shot twice. Suriani was killed instantly, and Esau died within hours of being taken to the hospital. A description of the killer was unavailable. Police confirmed the bullets matched those used in the previous shootings, and reasserted that the chubby teenager was still considered only a witness. A quick once-over of the crime scene unveiled the first letter penned by the killer and left ten feet from the bodies on the street,[233] featuring a collection of nonsensical ramblings. The words, formed with both capital and lowercase letters and bizarre punctuation, spoke of a "Father Sam" and his vicious abuses toward the author of the letter, his requirements for murder, and his command that the author of the letter continue to kill as he had been programmed to do. An early portion of the letter states that it was written by someone called the "Son of Sam." The letter ended with the famous taunt (misspellings intact):

I SAY GOODBYE AND GOODNTGHT.

POLICE: LET ME HAUNT YOU WITH THESE WORDS:

I'LL BE BACK!

I'LL BE BACK!

TO BE INTERRPRETED AS—BANG, BANG, BANG, BANK, BANG—UGH!!

—YOURS IN MURDER

M.R. MONSTER.[234]

Investigators quickly released psychological profiles to the experts, and before the killer was even captured, he was already diagnosed as a neurotic, paranoid schizophrenic who likely believed himself to be demon possessed.[235] Forensic tests on every registered .44-caliber Bulldog revolver in the area, as well as interviews with every owner, showed no connections to the Son of Sam killings.

Carr, Berkowitz's neighbor with the loud dog, was contacted a second time with a letter postmarked April 20 from the same anonymous citizen who was angered about Harvey's barking. This letter said:

My life is destroyed now. I have nothing to lose anymore. I can see that there shall be no peace in my life, or my families [sic] life until I end yours. You wicked evil man. Child of the devil. I curse you and your family forever. I pray to God that he takes your whole family off the face of the earth. People like you should not be allowed to live on this planet.[236]

On April 27, the Labrador was shot, but survived.[237]

On May 30, 1977, another letter surfaced, this time addressed to news columnist Jimmy Breslin of *The Daily News*. The letter featured more unintelligible ramblings, encouraging the columnist to speak on his behalf to the police and tell them to keep up the search. Only a couple of other details about "Father Sam" were mentioned, and they had no ties to anything within the investigation that the police could find.

In part, the letter said:

NOT KNOWING WHAT THE FUTURE HOLDS I SHALL
SAY FAREWELL AND I WILL SEE YOU AT THE NEXT
JOB. OR SHOULD I SAY YOU WILL SEE MY HANDI-
WORK AT THE NEXT JOB?

It also provided a list of names that the police should investigate ("THE
DUKE OF DEATH," "THE WICKED KING WICKER," "THE
TWENTY TWO DISCIPLES OF HELL," and "JOHN 'WHEAT-
IES'—RAPIST AND SUFFOCATOR OF YOUNG GIRLS") and
went on to promise that the killer would buy everyone involved in the
investigation a pair of new shoes if he could drum up the money.[238] This
time, the writing appeared in all capital letters and did not involve the
same crude misspellings and punctuation as the first.

Not only did the release of this letter cause the media to explode, but
the people of New York did as well. Thousands of calls rang the precinct's
phones, because everyone in the state had his or her own ideas of what the
names in the Son of Sam letter meant. All tips from the public panned out
to be baseless, wasting time and tax dollars and leading investigators into
confused manhunts all over New York City—while beauty supply shops
struggled to keep hair dyes and wigs in stock.

On June 26, 1977, around three o'clock in the morning, Sal Lupo and
Judy Placido were sitting in a parked vehicle in Queens outside a popular
disco when bullets tore through the car, striking both of them. Each survived with superficial injuries. Neither Lupo nor Placido saw the attacker,
but reports came in from people in the neighborhood that a dark-haired
man had been seen sprinting from the scene *as well as* a blond-haired man
with a mustache driving away from the neighborhood in a Chevy Nova-
style car with the headlights turned off.[239]

On July 31, 1977, Stacy Moskowitz and Robert Violante, at half past
two o'clock in the morning, were sitting in a parked vehicle in Gravesand
Bay on a date, under the Verrazano Bridge, across from Staten Island in
Brooklyn, watching the ships on the water. Bullets rang from outside the
vehicle, striking them both. Moskowitz (who had styled her hair short,
blond, and curly) died within hours at the hospital. Violante survived, but

was blinded in one eye, was partially blinded in the other, and sustained lasting facial disfigurement. Neither victim could provide a description of the attacker, although Violante did remember seeing a "hippie" with stringy brown hair covering his forehead hanging around the nearby park a while before the shooting.[240] By this time, it seemed that everyone in New York was on alert, keeping eyes peeled and ears open for the sight of runaway vehicles or the sound of gunshots. Lovers tended to do their "parking" in less-secluded areas. As a result, people were already surrounding the scene of this increasingly careless killer's latest crime. Consequentially, this murder had the largest number of eyewitnesses.

- One individual, with the help of a bright moon and fully lit streetlamps, clearly saw a man with medium- to light-brown hair (that appeared to be a wig), about five foot nine inches, and probably between twenty-five and thirty years old.[241]
- One woman saw the same man, whom she described as wearing a "cheap wig" as well. She had written down what she could remember—the last four digits—of his license plate number: 4-GUR, or possibly 4-GVR. (Another witness claimed to have seen the first three numbers: 463.)[242] The woman watched as the suspicious man ran from the scene and drove off in a "small, light-colored" compact car (Berkowitz's large, boxy-shaped Ford Galaxie had the license plate number 561-XLB).
- Two witnesses reported a small Volkswagen with its headlights off fleeing the scene, but another woman looking out her apartment window saw a man she later identified as Berkowitz casually walking away after the shooting. This man was wearing a jacket, unlike the suspect observed by other witnesses who said the shooter was wearing a long-sleeve shirt rolled up to the elbows.[243]
- At the same time the man later identified as Berkowitz was walking away from the shooting, another man driving through the area almost collided with a yellow Volkswagen Beetle, headlights off, speeding frantically away from the scene. The door of the vehicle was evidently damaged; the driver had to hold the door shut as he

drove. (Berkowitz's car did not have any damaged doors, nor was it a Volkswagen.) The driver of the VW was described as a man between twenty and thirty, with long, brown, stringy hair, and a five-o'clock shadow. The witness driving through the area followed the Beetle for several minutes, angry about the careless way the man was operating the vehicle. He was not able to write down a license plate number, but he thought the plates were from the state of New Jersey. (Berkowitz had never lived in New Jersey.)[244]

- Immediately following the Moscowitz/Violante shootings, police set up roadblocks in the surrounding area to question everyone passing through about what they may have seen. So many people reported having seen a Volkswagen Beetle with no headlights that the police agreed that it was owned by the person responsible for the murders.[245]

The Parking Ticket

As more and more dots in the case were connected, the picture being formed appeared to be one of multiple people, because of consistently differentiating eyewitness testimonies and dramatically diverse composite sketches. The one thing that seemed to keep nagging at the police from all angles was the little Volkswagen Beetle with its headlights off. There were more than nine hundred of the popular VWs registered in New York and New Jersey, so the police began tracking down and questioning the owners of each and every one.[246]

However, the search for the Beetle ended abruptly when a few final details of the most recent shooting came in unexpectedly.

At around 2:30 in the morning on July 31, 1977, just a few minutes before Moskowitz and Violante were shot, a woman had been out walking her dog, Snowball.[247] She had observed a traffic cop citing a long, four-door, yellow vehicle with boxy edges that had been parked too close to a fire hydrant. When the cop had gone, a man, looking agitated, emerged from the shadows near the vehicle and pulled the ticket from the windshield.[248]

About four days later, the woman brought this information to the police. An exploration into traffic records revealed that the owner of a yellow 1970 Ford Galaxie, license plate 561-XLB, had been ticketed at the time and location the woman had described. According to her testimony,[249] the man had pulled the ticket from his windshield and then leaned on the open door of his vehicle, defiantly watching the policeman ticket a few other cars in the row. She took a long look at the man who had received the ticket and his vehicle. When the police officer returned to his patrol car and drove away, the man who had been ticketed left the scene and followed the police—in a direction opposite that of the shooting that occurred immediately after.

Later that day, back in Yonkers, the ticketed vehicle's owner, David Berkowitz, quickly paid the fine (with check number 154 in the amount of thirty-five dollars made out to "Parking Violations Bureau N.Y.C." and cashed on August 4 by the city of New York[250]), and went on with his life. However, since the citation had been issued so close in time and proximity to the Moskowitz murder, the NYPD had a strong interest in asking Berkowitz, as a potential witness, if he had seen anyone that night while he was in the area. Maybe this Berkowitz fellow had seen the driver of the Beetle also.

After some deliberation, the NYPD investigators called the Yonkers Police Department (YPD) for assistance in locating a potential witness named David Berkowitz for an interview since he was not answering his phone as promptly as they would have liked. When the YPD received this call, the first operator transferred the call to a second operator ("Operator 82"), whose real name was Wheat Carr—Sam Carr's daughter, who would refer to Harvey during this phone call as "my dog," even though Sam was the dog's true owner. (Note that Wheat Carr is not to be confused with her older brother John Carr, whose nickname was "Wheaties" [important later in this case study].)

A conversation between NYPD Detective James Justus and YPD Operator 82 (Wheat Carr) exposed how Berkowitz's name had been recently drawn into suspicion by the YPD for a few cross-referencing crimes mentioned in the demented "Son of Sam" letters, as well as the similarities of those letters to the letters sent to Sam Carr. The transcript from that conversation was not released to the public until 1987, ten years after the arrest of David Berkowitz. An excerpt (between "JJ" and "82") reveals:

> **JJ:** I'm trying to contact a party that lives up in Yonkers who is possibly a witness to the crime down here. That's a Mr. David Berkowitz.
>
> **82:** Oh no… oh no…
>
> **JJ:** Do you know him?
>
> **82:** …This is the guy that I think is responsible.…
>
> **JJ:** He got a summons down here that night [of the Moskowitz murder], right in the vicinity…
>
> **82:** Oh my God…he…he…you know, because we [Wheat and Sam Carr] have seen him and he fits the description [of the perpetrator]. This is why my father went down there with his whole file of copies of letters we have received from him.… My dog was shot with a .44-caliber bullet.

As the shocking conversation continued, covering more information, there was a very telling moment when Justus was placed on hold and started speaking to people in his office:

> **JJ:** I have something beautiful here. I wanted to talk to this guy about a summons…lives up in Yonkers. I was talking to [YPD] to get a notification made and she [Operator 82] says, "Oh, not him, he shot my dog with a .44 about a month ago. He's crazy! He's sending threatening letters to the deputy sheriff's office."[251]

The evidence was stacking up rapidly. In addition to this enlightening phone call that quickly placed Berkowitz at the top of the list as a suspect instead of a witness, the YPD went on to inform the NYPD that they had received reports of other harassing letters to a number of people in the area; they had also received a tip from an employee of IBI security calling Berkowitz a "nut job"[252] "who once in a while would smile a Mona Lisa kind of smile."[253] The NYPD took a second look at the statements that had been given by Sam Carr a short time prior. They matched what his daughter, Wheat Carr, Operator 82, had told Detective Justus. Sam Carr had recently reported, "I have a lunatic who lives near me, he shot my dog, and his name is David Berkowitz."[254]

They had their lucky break: a man who had been seen near the crime, who had written other letters in the area that had caused concern, who had used a .44-caliber firearm against a neighbor's dog, whose crimes drew suspicion in the Son of Sam letters, and whose previous coworkers found the his mental functionality and social behavior questionable.

On August 10, 1977, police surrounded Berkowitz's apartment. When he was approached by a detective and told to freeze, he said, "Well, you finally got me."

"Who do I have?" the detective asked.

His answer was given plainly: "The Son of Sam."

The next morning, August 11, David Berkowitz confessed everything in great detail, and let everyone know he intended to plead guilty to everything.

Below is the mug shot from that arrest.

SATANISTS AND TALKING DOGS

Author and journalist Maury Terry had already begun digging into the more overlooked details of the Berkowitz case even before the "Son of Sam" had been caught. Terry's work has uncovered an astronomical number of items on the docket that many resources don't mention (even though the facts are well founded) pointing to the idea that Berkowitz did not act alone.

If one were to look at the reasons Terry's research may not be accepted by some minority groups, two main arguments surface most often:

1) Once Berkowitz admitted to all of the crimes and the legal system had its guilty boy behind bars (someone to blame and direct their anger toward), the world embraced a closed case; there weren't any picketers demanding that more of their tax dollars be spent on further investigation that could lighten Berkowitz's responsibility.

2) Terry's books were released during the Satanic Panic era and often pointed to a huge, satanic underground network wherein several famous murder cases were linked as having the same mastermind, and by that time, almost any book released with those types of claims were under scrutiny before anyone had even read them—despite whether they were truthful. (Readers can refer to the Sean Sellers case study for more information about the Satanic Panic era.)

However, let us keep in mind that although some of Terry's research might have pointed to some fairly extreme theories, we shouldn't dismiss it altogether in regards to the Son of Sam case; part of the information he compiled may, indeed, have been factual. Many reputable sources have given Terry's work much attention, one of which is well-known author and journalist, John Hockenberry.

Hockenberry, a four-time Emmy Award winner for his excellence in upstanding and truthful televised journalism and three-time Peabody Award winner for his meritorious public service in radio and television, knows well enough not to put his reputation on the line with petty hearsay just to get a story. When he observed the additional details of the

Berkowitz case put forward by Terry, he partnered with NBC News to get to the bottom line. In a special called "Inside Evil," he and reporter Stone Phillips address the missing links in the chain.

To begin with, many members of the original crew of investigators working on the case in New York also doubted that Berkowitz was the only one present at the shootings. That yellow Volkswagen Beetle, the one that couldn't possibly be confused with the size and shape of Berkowitz's Ford Galaxie, didn't just go away when Berkowitz claimed responsibility. According to Jimmy Breslin, *The Daily News* journalist who personally received one of the Son of Sam letters, "Everybody was looking for a yellow Volkswagen. 'That was the car! He was in that! Get the yellow Volkswagen!'"[255] Then, as Phillips reports, when Berkowitz admitted to the crimes, "the contradictory sketches, the elusive yellow Volkswagen, and its driver, all that went away."[256]

Berkowitz has always admitted that he was present at all the shootings, so it is no wonder that his physical description was offered so many different times. He says, "I was there at all of them and in the scouting. I'm responsible for my involvement in those things, and I'm definitely guilty."[257] However, he may not have been the one to pull the trigger each time, and therefore might not be guilty of as many murders as he was eventually convicted of. In an exclusive interview in 1993 on the popular television show, *Inside Edition*, Berkowitz claimed that he was only the gunman for the murders of Lauria, Esau, and Suriani,[258] which represent only two of the eight shootings. The rest of the shootings, he said, can be attributed to those who were involved in his satanic cult.

Ritualistic murder was only one of the disturbing activities the cult dabbled in. James Rothstein, investigator of a vice unit in Manhattan, told NBC News that cult-related crime in that area had been occurring for many years before Berkowitz ever owned the .44-caliber gun (and the crime had included pedophilia and the production of child pornography, although there is no evidence that Berkowitz was ever involved in that specific activity).[259] The locations of these reported deeds were the same woodsy parks Berkowitz frequented during his days as a practicing satanist.

The NYPD has never completely nailed down a motive for the Son of Sam killings, though many were ruled out by default (none of the victims had been raped or toyed with, they were targeted without any social ties to the attacker, and nothing was left behind at the crime scenes that pointed to any connection whatsoever). However, satanism, though not taken very seriously by the courts in 1977, would, by today's standards, be a perfectly viable motive in a case like this. Therefore, it stands to reason that with all the evidence of there being more than one person behind the murders, and with more modern testimonies by Berkowitz, the idea that fellow satanists assisted in the murders and were sometimes personally guilty for murders that Berkowitz bragged he had committed is also viable. In the "Inside Evil" special:

> Terry took us back to the scene of the Moskowitz/Violante shooting.… Remember, in one of the cars was eye-witness, Tommy Zaino [who had a close proximity to the shooter, under a street lamp that illuminated the perpetrator very well].… [He recalls a] description that would not suggest the pudgy, dark-curly-haired David Berkowitz, a description that Zaino could still recall, years later. [Zaino speaks:] "He had like, um, straight, strurry [we believe he meant "stringy"] hair, it was long, all outta shape, and it was like a light brown hair, light blond."[260]

In another report, Zaino had said, "I didn't believe it was him then, and I don't believe it was him now."[261]

The special report goes on to talk about the varying composite sketches, a couple of which few have ever seen, and it presents more information regarding the elusive Volkswagen Beetle. When questioned about who these other shooters had been, Berkowitz named a couple of people who had also been indirectly referenced in the original Son of Sam letters, and he illustrated on a chalkboard the getaway paths he and the others had allegedly agreed to take. Had the NYPD not dismissed much of the content of the Son of Sam letters as the lunatic ravings of a psychotic killer, they may have been able to spot some of the obvious cult associates Berkowitz had identified.

The reference to "John 'Wheaties'" was probably the easiest associate to identify. John Carr was the brother of Operator 82, Wheat Carr, and the son of Sam Carr, who was the owner of Harvey the Labrador. John's nickname among his comrades was "Wheaties." Sam's other son, John's brother, was named Michael Carr. Berkowitz implicated both John and Michael in the shootings. Interestingly, the composite sketches that do *not* look anything like Berkowitz, have an alarming likeness to the Carr brothers. Both are now deceased: John Carr died in a shooting that was written off as a suicide in 1978, but police came to believe it was a murder (and likely ritualistic, as "666" was carved in his hand).[262] Michael Carr died in an "unusual"[263] automobile accident on a highway in Manhattan.[264]

Berkowitz shared that the others involved in the shootings (and that number possibly reaches twenty-two, referring to the "Twenty Two Disciples of Hell" mentioned in the Son of Sam letter) were still free, and were therefore a threat to his personal family. He refused to name anyone else.

Strengthening these claims is John Santucci, the then district attorney of Queens, who said, "I believe that David Berkowitz did not act alone, that, in fact, others did cooperate, aid, and abet him in the commission of these crimes…in fact, it has crossed my mind that his .44-caliber pistol was passed around among a number of people."[265]

When NBC News contacted the Yonkers Police Department, its spokesmen refrained from comment. However, when NBC sent an official "freedom of information" request, the YPD responded with a letter. (The special report shows this letter on screen.)

The letter confirms that an investigation was started in 1996 [reopening the Son of Sam case] and has not been closed to this day…. Dateline contacted three parents of Son of Sam victims. While they remain bitter about the man locked away for killing their loved ones, all three told us they think Berkowitz probably did not act alone. [Victim Carl Denaro speaks:] "There's no way that David Berkowitz did all the shootings…I personally think it was a cult.…I am convinced, and no one can unconvince me that more than one person was involved."[266]

Though the special report ends with a dig against Berkowitz for not being more verbal about other suspects who might be out there, the reporter allowed him one last chance to speak to the public:

It was a time of foolishness for me, a time of spiritual darkness, a time of a lot of confusion…I made a lot of bad choices, I made a lot of bad mistakes, and I'm truly sorry for the lives that were destroyed. I'd like to say that I'm very, very sorry.[267]

The *Inside Edition* report called the similarity between some of the composite sketches and the Carr brothers "indisputable," and involved an exclusive interview with the woman who spotted Berkowitz removing the parking ticket from his vehicle within seconds of the shooting, which happened nearby, but not close enough that Berkowitz could have traveled there on foot.[268] This report goes on to offer proof to the angle that Berkowitz was friends with the Carr family as far back as a social party he attended in 1975, and that it was his friendship with Michael Carr that led him to involvement in a satanic cult in the Bronx—more specifically, the infamous and long-established cult of Untermyer Park in Yonkers. Berkowitz quickly began to make his presence in his new "family" known by purchasing and reading the satanic and occult materials that others recommended and by welcoming opportunities to chant with fellow members the various names of Lucifer and his demons. When the cruel animal sacrifices and dangerous drug dealing began, he was seasoned enough in the dark arts that he didn't balk. He admits that certain demonic personalities (Lucifer, Molech, and other deities) wanted fire sacrifices, which led to his interest in the chronic and numerous spot fires he started around the city, because those entities had to "create an atmosphere that would be conducive to [Satan's] coming upon the world's scene."[269]

When the cult's activities turned to murder, Berkowitz, according to *Inside Edition*, was merely the fall guy, a responsibility he happily took upon himself. Berkowitz's testimony in this *Inside Edition* interview and Terry's research reveal that there were other accomplices assisting the shooter at each of the crime scenes. When asked about the duties of these accomplices, Berkowitz named a short list of tasks involving scouting, get-away driving, and being armed and ready at any moment to join in the gunfight (assuming the shooter opened fire on someone who was also armed, most likely).[270] Later in the interview, while responding to why he had instantly accepted the blame for all the killings, including those he had allegedly only witnessed, he answered: "I was told... 'If any of you betray this group—you know we're all brothers and sisters now—if you betray this group...you have to understand that we're gonna get your family...there are no Judas Iscariots here. You know what happened to Judas, don't you?'"[271]

Additionally, Terry tells of a letter found in Berkowitz's apartment that had been written prior to the arrest, issuing a warning to the police of this cult, the people involved, and their plans to see to the murder of one hundred young people in the city; this letter had been impounded by the New York police, where it continues to be withheld from public knowledge. Terry goes on to explain that many others (besides the Carr brothers) who were affiliated with this cult and the Berkowitz case have met violent deaths.[272]

Father Sam

When Berkowitz came forward with his confessions immediately after his capture, he made claims that would launch his case into a nationally, historically, irretrievably famous status.

A talking dog, he said... That was what made him kill.

Sam Carr, as discussed prior, did not quiet his howling animal when he had received threats through the mail requesting that he do so. When he ignored the warnings of legal action, he had no way of knowing that a paranoid schizophrenic man in an apartment above his house would hear the incessant wailing of the dog and be provoked to the levels of violence that eventually stained all of New York. Berkowitz had been on his last sane thread for a long time, well before Harvey was the antagonist. Yet, when Berkowitz decided to tell the whole world that it had been an ancient demon demanding blood to soak the overpopulated streets of the urban cities using the dog's wailing as a mouthpiece for evil, it was a decision he made while perfectly sane…but was this a lie?

As Berkowitz later stated, "'The Blood-Thirsty Demons' was just a concocted story invented by me in my own mind to condone what I was doing."[273] This newer confession was given in 1979 at a press conference he had called from Attica prison. He went on to admit that he had never heard demonic voices coming from the dog, he had never been insane, and he wanted nothing more than to simply be left to live out his days in prison.[274] (Later, Berkowitz would write in his journals and his online reflections that, in fact, demonic activity did play a leading role in his motives. This author reached out to him for some clarification as to the reason for this later claim, and he answered with priceless insight. See the interview with Berkowitz following this case study.)

This is where many choose to close the lid on the subject, at ease that the world is not filled with people who will take life-altering advice from an English-speaking canine. But, according to Berkowitz's current personal friend (this author's personal friend as well), Noah Hutchings, although "Berkowitz…admitted to an FBI investigator, Robert Ressler, that he made up the 'Son of Sam' story to make the police (and courts) think that he was insane…whether this was a case of demon possession or mental illness, they both could be related."[275] This is because paranoid schizophrenics, often diagnosed only after chronic symptoms of self-destruction have been detected (whether before or after murdering innocent lives), can hear voices from alternate sources at certain times and not others. If Berkowitz admits that this was all a big lie, then it's safe to assume that the information from the horse's mouth is good enough, right? Maybe regarding the dog, sure. Yet, it's clear from later interviews with Berkowitz and from several of his prison pamphlet printings and journal entries that the name "Sam" was not referring to his neighbor, or his dog, as so many sources have suggested. In fact, "Sam" was used as a shortened version of the name *Samhain* (pronounced *sah-win* or *sow-win*, technically, although it's often spoken, *sah-ween*).

The name *Samhain*, with Gaelic origins, refers to a celebration of the end of the harvest season and the beginning of the "darker" seasons, such as winter. In North America, we don't say "Happy Samhain Festival!" Instead, we say "Happy Halloween!" More than just a big candy party on October 31 celebrating the coming of the first of November, however, *Samhain* can refer to many concepts associated with its original context: The festival, also known as "All Hallow's Eve," "All Saints Day," or "All Souls Day," additionally refers to a haze between the physical and spiritual realm, representing just a few hours when spirits emerge into the natural world as we see it. (This is the reason kids dress up as evil entities on Halloween in order to "blend in" and be safe from the spirits. Originally, the trick-or-treaters went door to door, asking for offerings of treats in trade for their prayers for the dead. There are thousands of twists in and deviations from this short explanation of the origin of Halloween and trick-or-treating, but we will not visit the topic at length here.)

Samhain has, through the years, become an entity in pop culture. There are characters in movies, books, video games, etc., with this name, suggesting that it is no longer seen by all as the name of a festival or party, but that it has evolved into an actual entity or spirit.[276] Theology may argue these facts until the end of time, but to a person listing the various names of Lucifer, developing a personal relationship with the beast, and being willing to, in his or her schizophrenic mind, embrace new given names or nicknames of Satan or his demons, it stands to reason that *Samhain* would be one of them.

Berkowitz, after having told the truth about his claims of a talking dog, went on in many instances to refer to one entity he and/or his cult circle referred to as "Samhain." Berkowitz pronounced the name *sam-hane*, maybe because he and his fellow cult members believed that the entity introduced himself to them with a more Americanized pronunciation of the name, or because "Son of Sam" had an easier and more infectious ring to it for a serial killer than the "Son of Sah" or "Son of Sow." More simply, it could be because the spelling of the abbreviated name simply *is* "Sam," and the first mention of this murderer's identifier was delivered in writing, not in spoken words; by the time the world picked up on the title, it was "Sam," regardless of what Berkowitz initially intended. Whether he knew it at the time he coined his own moniker or it was an idea that developed later, when Berkowitz gave his story of insanity to the police (the story he later recanted), there was a fuzzy line around the identity of the "Father Sam" individual he had named.

Clearly, based on common sense and Berkowitz's admissions later, "Sam" had very little ties to his neighbor or the Labrador. The name did, however, have momentous ties to an entity that Berkowitz and his fellow cult members were speaking directly to. So, was Sam the voice of a Labrador? No. Was Sam a real entity to Berkowitz as spoken through a Labrador? Possibly. That depends on your willingness to believe that either: a) Berkowitz and his cult fellows had tapped into a real, two-way communication with the dark forces of the underworld; or b) Berkowitz was not in his right mind at the time, which he has *many* times admitted, and had two-way communications with voices as a result of a mental condition with which he was later diagnosed. Was Berkowitz insane at the time of the murders? The world may never know if the courts would have made that conclusion, since there was never a trial and, in 1978, he pleaded "guilty" instead of "innocent for reasons of insanity." Was he tormented? This seems obvious.

In a letter from Berkowitz to Thomas Horn:

[T]he reality is that I was, at the time, making actual contact with demonic entities.... I know from experience that there exists evil spirits, and they do seek to gain control of people. Such a thing is, sadly, often the brunt of jokes, "Oh the devil made him do it."... And while the devil cannot "make" someone do something they don't want to do, he can break that individual's resistance down to a point where they could no longer withstand the pushing of demons. Only someone who has experienced such things could understand this. The average person, obviously, cannot.

All told, it is my opinion today, even though I spent years in denial, that I was truly "out of my mind" when the crimes were happening. I may have known right from wrong. But my thinking was twisted. While not legally "insane," I wasn't sane, either.

Also…when one is under a strong demonic delusion of some kind, and may at times be thinking or acting irrationally, if he was being seen or observed by a psychologist, no doubt he would appear to the psychologist to be delusional, paranoid, schizophrenic (maybe), or suffering from some kind of mental malady. Hence, the tragic inability for such "experts" and professionals to discern the true cause for this individuals behavior and misconstrue everything. I believe this was true in my case.[277]

It is also sad to see, nowadays, Christians [going to] psychologists and other "mental health" experts for answers, when we of all people have the Word of God at our disposal. Where is the "discerning of spirits" and the gift of "knowledge"? Where is the God-given, Holy Spirit-given ability for the church to "judge all things" and to recognize, at least to a good degree, the workings of satanic entities who seek to bring harm and oppress the human race? Why the constant seeking after worldly, inexact, often conflicting Freudian-based psychologists?

This baffles me. We appear no different than worldly counselors and "experts" who grope in the darkness for answers and continually contradict one another.[278]

Another form of torment began in Berkowitz's conscience even before his capture. Recently, this author reached out to Noah Hutchings of Southwest Radio Church to inquire of his dealings with Berkowitz. This is an excerpt of Hutchings' email response, dated March 15, 2014:

Yes, David B did contact me by phone [in the late '70s], but I am not sure now about the exact date. I also answered several of his letters. As I remember, he seemed confused but was trying to understand why certain things were happening in his life and the world in general. I assume that was at the time he was killing people in New York.

One day, one of the secretaries [here] asked me if I knew who I had been writing to, this "David" somebody. When I told her no, she replied that he was the "Son of Sam" who had been killing a lot of people. Then, the District Attorney of Queens called me and asked for David's letters for possible use at his trial. I informed him that these were personal letters and he would have to use legal means to get them. The next day, an officer came to the office with a court order, and I gave him the letters, of course. I suppose they were used at David's trial or at least considered. [Hutchings, at the time of this email, had probably forgotten that Berkowitz never had a trial.]

I have continued to write to David since he has been in prison, and I like to think that I had some influence in his accepting the Lord Jesus Christ as his personal savior. *This was the beginning of our prison ministry that now reaches prisoners from California to Maine.* I received a letter this past month from a prisoner who said he had used our calendar for prisoners to win eighteen souls to Jesus Christ.... [A woman] here at the office...supervises the prison ministry and answers hundreds of letters every week from prisoners.[279]

This testimony points to the fact that well before Berkowitz was incarcerated, and likely during his killing spree, he found himself in a position to question his actions like a technically "insane" person would not do (and it also shows how Hutchings' dealings with Berkowitz led to the start of a prison ministry that has led many to Christ).

Either way, insane or otherwise, in more recent interviews, when questioned about these topics, Berkowitz tends to want to move beyond talking at length about those dark times. His interest in leaving the past behind is consistent, since he has now found a new freedom. Let's visit those circumstances now.

SON OF HOPE

Despite his behavior and insane claims regarding the voice of a demon coming through a dog, the courts found Berkowitz mentally capable to stand trial. However, because he immediately pleaded guilty to the charges, he was never placed on trial for murder, and his case went straight to sentencing. During his visits to court for the sentencing hearings, Berkowitz disrupted proceedings several times (with antics including an attempt to leap through the glass of a seventh-story window) and had to be subdued.

Around this time, famously, he began chanting an offensive phrase about Stacy Moskowitz, the young girl who died in the last and final Son of Sam shooting. When he learned that Neysa Moskowitz, Stacy's mother, wanted revenge upon her daughter's killer, he taunted her, saying in a sing-song tone, "Stacy was a [expletive]," over and over. (The word we have extracted here, likely offensive to many readers, could easily translate to "tramp" or "harlot.") The stunt caused instant uproar. As security officers seized Berkowitz and attempted to take him from the courtroom, he fought against them, shouting, "That's right! I'd kill her again! I'd kill them all again!" Moskowitz stood and shook her fists at Berkowitz in anger, shouting retaliatory obscenities and referring to him, ironically, as "Son of a [female dog]!"[280] Berkowitz was tranquilized with Thorazine,[281] and the sentencing was unexpectedly and abruptly ended and rescheduled for a later date.

On June 12, 1978, Berkowitz was sentenced to twenty-five years to life for each murder, a total of six life sentences. His incarceration began at the Attica prison (just after a brief stay at Clinton Correctional Facility in Clinton County). In the early days of serving his sentence, minister and prison chaplain Don Dickerman wrote a letter to Berkowitz, sharing with him the love of the Lord. Jesus Christ, as Dickerman said, still dearly loved Berkowitz and wanted him to be saved. Berkowitz wrote back immediately to let the minister know that, upon his release from prison, should that day come, he would seek Dickerman out, and kill him.[282]

The Beginning of Hell

Alone in his cell, Berkowitz began to feel the oppressive weight of what he had done. It wasn't from remorse for the lives he took; it was merely a suffocation of solitude that led to self-hatred. In a letter, he wrote that he was a "cursed person, *beyond hope.*"[283] Thoughts of suicide plagued his mind as he withered away from his celebrity status in a lonely, forlorn room. His books on the occult were all gone, his dark "family" members were still free on the outside, and, now that he had silence away from the rejection, judgment, fake families, and barking dogs, he found silence a forsaken reality. Isolation was a familiar feeling, but on the outside, his isolation had driven him to execute power. Inside the hellish walls of Attica, the isolation was its own form of death.

Berkowitz had always been horribly teased, dismissed, and humiliated by the world, and thus had never been a part of it to begin with, but now he found himself locked away from the human race and from the potential of ever having any family of his own, the family he had always secretly fantasized about celebrating. The Thanksgiving tables of his future would be surrounded by fellow criminals, never by his own lover or offspring. Yes, the world had deserted him, but he had deserted the world, and had forever given up his right to the happiness he had always pined for.

Now, he had nobody to blame but himself.

Soon after his imprisonment, another inmate made a dramatic attempt at Berkowitz's life, lunging at his throat with a prison-made razor blade. (The injury is still visible in a grisly scar along his neck.) This was proof that even behind bars he was vulnerable. He was hated, he hated himself, and a presence was always nearby, reminding him of the sinister promises he had made to the shadowy beings at the park with his cult family years before. Forced to face the truth—and only that: no more insanity, no more talk of trials or sentencing, no more killing or wishing for normalcy—Berkowitz slowly became far more meditative. Before long, he became far more meditative about what he had done and why he had done it, and those unanswered questions fell like bricks against his already compromised sanity.

Attica was a nightmare, and it was a nightmare he deserved. To the media, for the next fourteen years, he would remain silent.

Then Berkowitz was transferred from Attica to the Sullivan Correctional Facility in Fallsburg, where he would meet someone who had his interest in mind. A fellow inmate made another dramatic impact on Berkowitz's life, but this time, it was without the intent to kill.

A Bible, a small pocket Bible, in 1987—ten years after Berkowitz had been carted away from the public to rot behind friendless walls—was placed in the hands of a hated, hopeless man.

The Beginning of Hope

It was winter…and it was freezing. Out in the prison yard, an inmate named Rick approached Berkowitz and informed him that "Jesus loved [him] and *had a plan for [his] life*."[284] Berkowitz laughed in the man's face, telling him that, after all he had done on the streets of New York and elsewhere, he was far too evil and the man was wasting his time. But, before he turned to leave, his heart somehow strangely softened toward the man. There had been something about the fellow inmate—a sincerity, a glow that couldn't be described…[285]

The two men quickly became friends, despite Rick's convictions about this "Jesus" personality. Days grew into weeks, and the pair met every day in the yard or in the workout room, establishing trust—a rare quality behind bars. Every time they came together, Berkowitz's new friend would share the gospel of Jesus Christ, telling Berkowitz that this Christ was always there, on standby, waiting for His children to accept His love and forgiveness. Although Berkowitz was not convinced of his friend's beliefs, he respected him and continued to listen to what he had to say. Before long, Berkowitz noticed a change in his own attitude, and it was then that Rick gave him a pocket edition of the New Testament.

So many times in his past, Berkowitz would have tossed the Book to the wayside and ignored (or threatened to kill, as he had with Dickerman) those who had anything to say about the Book, but this time, he took the little volume and opened it. Though he had seen a Bible many times, he had never before read one. Like so many others thirsty for living water, when his eyes fell on the Psalms, he admitted they were some of the "most beautiful words" he had ever read.[286]

Day after day, alone and contemplative, Berkowitz read page after page, drinking in the poetry of the authors, mostly finding himself drawn to King David, a man who had more in common with Berkowitz than a first name. That ancient king had suffered much, and, like Berkowitz, was not a spotless creature when it came to upright and appropriate relationships with women. His life had been filled with immense pain, and when King David's heart ached, he had cried out to God. Berkowitz, even in his most grieving hours, had only ever cried into his pillow.

Then, one night, as he was burning the midnight oil with the profound expressions of the Psalms penetrating his soul, he read Psalm 34. The sixth verse jumped off the page like the living word that it was:

> *This poor man cried, and the Lord heard him, and saved him out of all his troubles.*

Berkowitz broke.

He made his way to the light switch, flipped it off, and returned to his seat, his cell bathed in stillness and darkness, and his tears flowing like rivers from his eyes. Falling to his knees, he wept anxiously, bitterly… wonderfully. Everything hit him at once: the happiness he had always wanted, the happiness he had never truly felt, the guilt of his crimes, the pain he had caused others, the lives that would forever be altered because of his actions, the blackness where his heart should have been, the vile monster he had become…

And the Man who died on the cross to deliver him from all of it.

Right then and there, it was just Berkowitz and God. For once, Berkowitz had nobody to answer to on this earth for anything. He had only the Lord, with all of His forgiveness, grace, and divine understanding, to bring truth to his burdened and weary spirit. Berkowitz decided, both for the man he was and the Pinocchio boy he had been, to turn from every evil thought and throw himself into the service of the Lord. Rick was right: Even Berkowitz's life, despite all he had done, had a purpose.

In 1987, Berkowitz was radically saved.

The Reflection of a Real Boy

As Berkowitz's spiritual hunger grew and he sought to hear more from this Good Word, he turned to the pages of Scripture, including the Old Testament, where he found something else: A poetic spiritual justice for all mankind, good men and bad men alike, was spoken of in the book of Micah.[287]

> Who is a God like unto thee, that pardoneth iniquity, and passeth by the transgression of the remnant of his heritage? he retaineth not his anger for ever, because he delighteth in mercy. He will turn again, he will have compassion upon us; he will subdue our iniquities; and thou wilt cast all their sins into the depths of the sea. Thou wilt perform the truth to Jacob, and the mercy to Abraham, which thou hast sworn unto our fathers from the days of old. (Micah 7:18–20)

God had been there the whole time, the Bible said. And even Berkowitz, the satanic killer, knew that there had been no hiding his terrible transgressions from the Lord. Yet, the Bible didn't say that the God of all people ("God like unto thee") would only pardon crime and wickedness ("iniquity") for people who were otherwise *mostly* good; its boundless pardons applied to all mankind. It also said that the Lord would pass by the offenses ("transgressions") committed by one who held on to the leftover residues and remains ("remnants") of his inheritable birthright ("heritage"); God, according to this Holy Script, didn't forever bear a grudge against the sinner for the sin, because He *delighted in mercy*. The Lord would return, and He would have compassion upon people, bring defeat over their past, and cast their terrible, horrible, evil, shameless, hideous, and ghastly wrong-doings into the sea!

It was becoming clear that there was no end to the grace of God.

Berkowitz's illegitimate birthright had worn him like a stain upon the land and had so deeply rooted the resentment in his heart against his fellow man that no one could have stood in his way of retaliation. The remnants of his past were so powerfully manifest that when it had come time for his transgressions, he had met them head-on with a gun. Then, when his lifeline became nothing more than a slow, sad heartbeat thumping against the tainted glass of human tissue decomposing in a concrete-block wasteland called prison, his retaliatory acts as the underdog in a corner proved to be, at best, a child's tantrum. He had given everything, including his life, future, and possible family, to a child's fit of temper. People had *died* so he could earn his dark trophies of accomplishment and revenge, and in the end, it was *he* who had been the fool. He had earned nothing but a slow, agonizing death behind bars far away from both those he would ever love enough to find true happiness, and away from those he would ever hate enough to extract retribution upon. He had been lost. So completely lost. Everything had all been for nothing.

And now, this Book he held in his hands talked of a God who would not only allow him to be eternally and mercifully pardoned from the otherwise unforgivable acts he had carried out against the innocent, but delight—*delight!*—in bestowing him with unearned mercy...

Even still, God was a Father, a *Parent*, as much as anything else. Berkowitz had loved his earthly father, and would burn up the rest of his life wishing that he had spent more time sharing with him and opening up to the man, and words could not express the heartache that he would always hold for the lack of affection he had shown toward his earthly mother. Yet, these people were exactly that: earthly. They were finite: the best parents a young boy could have wished for, and yet they were of this world, assigned to him by a court judge who knew they would love him with the greatest love that any *human* can possess toward another *human*.

It didn't take more than common sense to know and believe that the Almighty God above was more than human, more than finite, more than a parent. He was the highest Father. Closer to mankind than even biological mothers and fathers could ever be, and more understanding of how Berkowitz felt and hurt than anyone, including Berkowitz, himself. Why hadn't he seen that? He had spent so much time obsessively wishing, wanting, searching, and yearning to have something, *someone*, to call his own, *really* his own—and that Father and Family had always been a prayer away from a little boy who had, from the beginning, been real to his ultimate Parent in heaven.

Berkowitz had a Family.

The Body of Christ Behind Bars

By early 1988, Berkowitz had already begun to involve himself in every outlet of good deeds a prison could possibly provide. Within a short time, he became a leader within the prison chapel, serving as the chaplain's clerk, and began an outreach ministry working with special-needs prisoners (those with physical, emotional, and psychological needs). He became the only man incarcerated at Sullivan Correctional Facility, a maximum-security prison, with the security clearance to enter the Special Needs Unit to pray with, read the Bible with, and minister to the inmates there. (He is still active in this endeavor.) Early on in his service to the Lord, he changed his moniker from "Son of Sam" to "Son of Hope." In a letter he shared with us personally: "[T]he term 'Son of Sam' came into my mind by a demon. I also believe, and I state this [for the record] now, that it was the Lord Jesus who spoke to my mind, and said, 'David, you are now the Son of Hope.'"[288]

In 1993, Berkowitz broke his media silence, coming forward with new details of his murder case involving other cult members in the shootings. Although he has still not named every associate of the original circle for safety reasons, his allegations were well supported by many, as discussed previously. The case was officially reopened. As media surged with this story, Berkowitz had many opportunities to share the love and mercy of Christ on high-profile, public, secular television shows and news programs. He did so, without hesitation.

In 1997, he met with Scott Ross of *The 700 Club* for a televised interview in which he told his story to millions nationwide. Here is an excerpt from that interview regarding Berkowitz's testimony and the sincerity of Christ:

ROSS: Now there are those who are the skeptics.

BERKOWITZ: Yeah.

ROSS: They say, "Okay, jailhouse conversion. Foxhole religion."… One woman I talked to out on the streets said, "Yeah, God, yeah, but he's crazy." Now you've got to deal with people who don't believe this and are very, very skeptical. So, how do you deal with it?

BERKOWITZ: I know what Jesus Christ has done in my life. And I can understand that people in prison, out of prison, can be skeptical. But I have put my faith in Jesus Christ. He has done so much for me. I believe in Him, and no matter what people say, I'm going to continue to serve Him. I serve the Lord, ministering to the men in here, uh, doing Bible studies with the guys, I go into the chapel, I'm a chaplain's clerk now, and I preach the gospel even overseas through correspondents and testimony tracks, and so forth. So, I know I'm living for Jesus, and no matter what man may say, I belong to Him. I've been purchased by Jesus Christ with His blood.

ROSS: I lived in upstate New York the time these crimes were taking place. On one occasion, my wife and I prayed for you. And prayed, and said, "God, the man is demonized, and we take authority over the demons." Now this was prayer, and I was a pastor of a church, and we prayed. And now you're saying here, telling us, that this had actually happened in your life.... That these demons had been brought under control. That you're now serving Jesus Christ.

BERKOWITZ: That's right. That's right. The Lord delivered me. The Lord set me free. I cried out to the Lord, and one night in my prison cell God spoke to my heart. And He set me free.[289]

Ross responded with an ironic observation: *God had brought Berkowitz to prison to set him free.*

(Berkowitz is grateful that Ross recognized the forces he feels were truly at work, and felt led to pray for him. When he reached this moment in our case study, he stopped to jot down the following enthusiastic note: "Yes! I'm glad someone in the body of Christ recognized this truth. That I was a demonized person, that the whole Son of Sam case was a demon-organized event, and that the works of darkness can be overcome by the word of the Lord, and by the Christian who recognizes and uses his God-given authority over all evil entities. Amen!"[290])

In 1998, Heinz Fussle Productions invited both Berkowitz and former drug dealer Steve Hill to appear in a documentary about forgiveness and repentance called *Son of Sam/Son of Hope*.[291] Because the film was produced by a Christian group, it presents one of the lengthier testimonies of Berkowitz's turn to Christ.

In 1999, Berkowitz was invited to share his story, including his incredible testimony, on *Larry King Live*, again, in front of millions of viewers.[292] The show was so popular that it was given an encore airing.

In January of 2000, Bill Myers, writer and director of Christian short films, produced a movie called *The Choice Is Yours*.[293] The short film addressed concerns regarding the nation's youth and their wrong choices during their teen years. Berkowitz was invited to be the featured guest on the film to talk about the wrong choices he had made at a young age and through his teens into adulthood. His transparent and informative presentation included offering details about some of the painful memories of the murders, in order to bring strength and attention to the issue of troubled youth.

The response from the angry public to news of Berkowitz's conversion to Christ was overwhelming, especially when his initial parole hearing became news. However, the irate citizens would be surprised by Berkowitz's response to the invitation for his potentially obtaining freedom. On March 25, 2002, Berkowitz wrote New York Governor George Pataki, explaining why he did *not* want to be considered for parole. On July 9, 2002, after having completely skipped the first scheduled parole hearing a month earlier, Berkowitz faced the parole board members as a courtesy when they arrived a second time. Politely, he explained that he did not believe he would ever be, *in his own opinion*, eligible for parole. He believed that his crimes against humanity had been too substantial to ever justify reintegration into society. The victims who had been murdered pointlessly in cold blood, their families, and the state of New York (along with all those nationwide who had been affected by Berkowitz's acts) would never appreciate the news that he had been set free to roam the earth. He would grant them this. Others in his position, and especially those who had found God while incarcerated, had found encouragement in showing their faith by accepting their punishment on earth. In response to Berkowitz's argument, the parole board agreed that his crimes were heinous enough that he would not yet be released, but they did make a note in his file regarding dramatic improvements in his behavior and character.

Two years later, in 2004, Berkowitz attended his second parole hearing. Again, he explained to the parole board members that, due to the gravity of his crimes and the public outrage he had caused, he was politely requesting that the board deny his parole—despite the pouring-in of letters he had received from Christians nationwide asking him to consider his ministerial opportunities on the outside and what God might be able to do with his freedom. Again, the parole board, without Berkowitz providing evidence on his own behalf that he was a good candidate for returning to society, had little choice but to agree that the model prisoner with excellent behavioral reports was too dangerous to be approved for parole.

Around this time, Berkowitz and a man named Hugo Harmatz met under less-than-ideal terms in court. Harmatz, a New Jersey attorney, had represented Berkowitz in a previous case to stop the *National Enquirer* from publishing personal letters between Berkowitz and another individual that the tabloid magazine had obtained. During a consultation meeting about the *Enquirer* case, Berkowitz had given his private letters (and several pictures) to Harmatz for safekeeping. Harmatz, for reasons this author could not find (although it's rumored he wanted to make money), rushed to a self-publisher with the letters and released a textbook-sized, hardcover book called *Dear David: Letters to Inmate #78-A-1976 (David Berkowitz)*. The book's contents included all the memorabilia Berkowitz had entrusted to Harmatz.

This resulted in a court case between Berkowitz, a man with essentially very few rights, and Harmatz, a man with full constitutional rights and a law degree. The parties settled out of court on October 25 of the following year (2006), and Harmatz agreed to donate a portion of the profits to the shooting victims' families. The book has since been taken out of print. (For research purposes, this author obtained a used copy of this oversized exploitation of Berkowitz's privacy. After reading hundreds of the letters published in the book, it is obvious that Berkowitz has had an enormously positive effect on an uncountable number of people. Many letters came from people thanking Berkowitz for his life-altering advice. One came from a young girl who, because of her correspondence with Berkowitz, had decided against murdering an ex boyfriend. Another letter, from the father of a Columbine, Colorado, shooting victim, thanked Berkowitz for his work with troubled teens, and told Berkowitz that their letters had been essential in his coping with the loss of his daughter. Other prisoners, including juveniles, wrote Berkowitz to express gratitude for his advice on life issues and how to survive behind bars. Parents of troubled teens wrote him to let him know they had found hope from his story. College students informed Berkowitz that he had given them insight that had helped them turn their essays or documentary projects into a story of the gospel instead of a story of cold-blooded murder. And the list goes on. It is interesting to note that Berkowitz would take a man to court for publishing a book that would otherwise shine such a brilliantly virtuous light on himself.)

In 2006, Berkowitz decided again not to attend his parole hearing. He wrote his lawyer, stating, "I humbly ask you to please cease and desist from any and all further efforts to seek to obtain parole for me."[294] (The law mandates that Berkowitz be given a hearing every two years. His hearings in 2006, 2008, 2010, and 2012 produced similar results as the first two. As of this writing, the results of his 2014 parole hearing prompted the following headline: "Son of Sam Serial Killer Skips Parole Hearing Because He Believes 'Jesus Has Forgiven Him and Set Him Free.'"[295] Note that in one of the letters sent to this author from Berkowitz, he writes, "Actually, while it is true that I have been forgiven by the Lord, this was not why I did not attend my last hearing." He goes on to say that there were a few theological discrepancies in this, and other, articles regarding his involvement [or lack thereof] with a group called "Jews for Jesus." He explains that he has "never abandoned Judaism" in the way that the media has reported, and then states, "I am simply a Jew who believes that Jesus…is my Savior and Messiah and Lord. In other words, I am simply a Jew who believes in Jesus, just like there are Gentiles who believe in Jesus. Minor stuff, really. But it shows how misinformed people are."[296])

Also in 2006, Berkowitz released his book, *Son of Hope: The Prison Journals of David Berkowitz*. After a two-page synopsis of his life and the dark forces at work in him leading to his eventual imprisonment and the surrender of his life to the Lord, the book's only remaining content features diary entries he had written from his cell. The entries cover little to nothing about the murders or his past (except for his remorse toward the victims' families, which is mentioned frequently) and focus mostly on Berkowitz's relationship with Christ, his fellow non-Christian inmates whom he prays for, and his Christian brothers behind bars. Despite numerous media attacks claiming that Berkowitz released the book to make money for himself (some reports, such as one issued by Nancy Grace of CNN, say he intended to make "millions"[297]), the contract between Berkowitz and his publisher had, from the beginning, stipulated that all monies made from sales would go directly to the families of the victims.[298] This agreement had been established well before the uninformed reporters and talk show hosts said otherwise. (The irony is that, although Berkowitz has stated on several occasions that he wouldn't have intended to make money to begin with, legally he couldn't have if he'd wanted to, which makes the sensational reports even more imprudent. When the Son of Sam was captured, a new executive law for the state of New York was passed, called the "Son of Sam" law, which stated that no monies could be earned by any prisoner as a result of his or her crimes; several other states have adopted the same law. Many incorrectly theorize that this law originated because Berkowitz originally asked media outlets for money in exchange for his story. However, the law was passed in 1977, immediately after his capture, while he was in court. He would have therefore been silenced from wheeling and dealing with the media at the time, so this theory that Berkowitz was communicating with the media about his story to make a dime at the victims' expense falls flat. Straight from the New York State Office of Victim's Services (OVS) website: "Section 632-a of the Executive Law, also known as New York's 'Son of Sam' Law, was enacted in 1977 in response to *numerous media offers of payment to David Berkowitz* [they offered, he was not asking], notoriously known as the 'Son of Sam,' for his 'story.' The law was intended to divert any such payments to the victims of Berkowitz and the victims of any other criminal who received 'profits from a crime.'"[299])

On September 26, 2006, Neysa Moskowitz, the mother of shooting victim Stacy Moskowitz, passed away. Prior to her death, her relationship with Berkowitz had dramatically changed. Even after the extraordinary explosion of rage during Berkowitz's sentencing, when he had taunted Mrs. Moskowitz with his obscene sing-song chanting about her deceased daughter being the equivalent to a hussy, Moskowitz had miraculously forgiven the repenting convict. He had long since written public apologies for his crimes online (because he wasn't legally allowed to contact the victims' families directly). Moskowitz (and her husband, while he lived) had extensively researched the case and eventually concluded that Berkowitz was a changed man. Moskowitz had previously said, "I hope he lives a long time with this in his heart. And I hope he never has a minute's peace. Never. Never."[300] Yet, in a more recent interview filmed by

Maury Terry for personal viewing by Berkowitz, himself, she said: "You are not the same person I saw sixteen years ago. You talk differently, you act differently, and your mannerisms are, well, you're not the same person."[301] Shortly before her death, Moskowitz wrote Berkowitz, expressing her forgiveness of all of his sins against her. (Note that there were a few ripples caused in this relationship when a media producer offered to pay Moskowitz for the right to film her first in-person meeting with Berkowitz since the sentencing. Moskowitz asked Berkowitz to go along with this plan, and Berkowitz politely refused to participate in a filmed reunion. Her reaction to Berkowitz's caution was not ideal.[302] However, according to members of her family, Moskowitz went to her grave with forgiveness in her heart toward him.[303])

Years after Berkowitz's threat to kill Don Dickerson (the prison chaplain who wrote to Berkowitz of God's love shortly after his capture), the two became friends. They were seen praying together and embracing in many news clips and documentaries on Berkowitz.

Today, Berkowitz continues to counsel troubled inmates, work as a clerk for the chaplain, and write fervent, Christ-centered essays regarding keeping the faith and repenting of sins. His writings are published in free pamphlets and on Christian websites. His "Official Website of David Berkowitz" receives a lot of constant attention, and is maintained by a church group on his behalf. He is a model prisoner, having held a spotless record since his conversion in the late '80s—except for one misbehavior written up on November 11 of 2004, regarding the breaking of a contraband rule (rule "113.15—Unauthorized Exchange"). The "contraband" seized was a Gideon pocket Bible Berkowitz had given an inmate. (He had assumed that the rule did not apply to a miniature Bible, and that his role as a prison counselor allowed him to give away Bibles as part of his daily responsibilities.) Berkowitz was fined five dollars for the infraction.[304]

As of this writing, Berkowitz never intends to seek parole. He has written that prison is a lonely and depressing place, and his aging body yearns for the comforts of home that freedom would give him, but he finds strength each day as a direct result of his deliberate faith in his Father. He reflects: "While none of us wants to be here, and in spite of our prison sentences and present confinement, we realize that God actually used our forced confinement in prison to save our lives. Because the Lord loved us even when we were in rebellion toward Him, He had to use extreme measures to save fools from their own folly. And He definitely saved a fool like me!"[305]

Below is a photo from May of 2014.

The lives that were taken during that terrifying summer in New York, and the family members who remain, have never left Berkowitz's memory. A journal entry called "1975–77" in *Son of Hope: The Prison Journals of David Berkowitz* ends with his prayer for them: "Lord, I ask you to continue to bring healing into the lives of those I have hurt in the past. Touch them with your love and help them to cope with the pain, loss, and grief that never seem to go away. Thank you, Father God. In Jesus' name, amen."[306]

INTERVIEW with David Berkowitz

("Son of Sam")

In order to gain further insight on Berkowitz's case, the publishing team behind this book reached out to him through the mail, telling him about our book. He agreed to an exclusive interview. We sent him a list of questions, asked by several people in our publishing group as well as Donna Howell, and the letters were sent from the desk of Thomas Horn. The following is just a part of those correspondences. Note that we have arranged the layout in a Q&A style for the reader's convenience, and that except for the omission of a certain name for privacy protection, all answers have been provided wholly as Berkowitz has written them, without alteration; underlining was present in the original.

**BETWEEN THOMAS HORN, DEFENDER PUBLISHING GROUP
AND DAVID RICHARD BERKOWITZ, PRISONER 78-A-1976
LETTERS BETWEEN FEBRUARY AND AUGUST OF 2014**

We would like to ask you about our mutual friend, Noah Hutchings. We recall, years ago, one of the Southwest Radio Ministries publications (The Gospel Truth) running a story at the time of your arrest. In the article, Hutchings had said he was corresponding with a "David" from New York who had questions about life, and only later did he learn those letters had come from you. Do you recall this, and if so, can you give details about why and what you were writing to Noah back then? It seems you were already seeking God—or at least the Holy Spirit was convicting you.

I am vague on how I first learned about the Southwest Radio Church [SWRC]. I assume someone sent me some of their literature. Probably a Christian who simply wanted to witness to me and share the gospel.

I think someone had heard me mention demonic possession and my using the *Satanic Bible*, and some of the SWRC's material may have been discussing this. So in desperation I wrote to Pastor Hutchings and this is how our correspondence began. This is all I could recall.

If Pastor Hutchings is still in possession of my initial letters they should shed light on why I first reached out to SWRC.

When the district attorney asked Noah to turn over your letters, at first he refused, then when a court order was delivered to the ministry, he was forced to surrender them. Did those letters ever come up in court?

The letters sent to Pastor Hutchings never came up in court because I <u>never</u> went to trial. I ended up pleading guilty to all charges and received multiple life sentences, later made into one life sentence with no guarantee of parole.

Do you have a close fellowship of believers at Sullivan?

I have a very close fellowship with believers here at Sullivan Correctional Facility. I have shared a lot about my experiences with the brethren in my journal book, and in my online journal writings as featured on the website, Ariseandshine.org.

My former chaplain, who retired in 2010 and has never been replaced, assigned me as the congregation's "Worship Leader," an assignment I did a number of years, and still do when asked to. I have taught the Bible studies and am often asked to open our worship services and Bible studies with a prayer. I also give exhortations [encouraging words or sermons] during Sunday services, most of the time, plus at other chapel events as well.

Do you continue to help the chaplain at Sullivan, and would it be okay if we wrote him for a testimony regarding your work? If you prefer we don't, that is okay.

You are more than welcome to do this if you could locate my former chaplain. As stated, the former protestant chaplain, who's known me for the approximately fourteen years he was here, retired in December of 2010. No one has been hired to replace him. His name is [name omitted]. He retired after twenty-five years of service as an employee of New York State, and I've no idea where he is now. You could probably locate him, maybe on Facebook? Just guessing.

In our book we also chronicle the arrests and salvation of people like Charles "Tex" Watson. (Charles is exchanging letters with us as well.) Have you ever corresponded with other such high-profile inmates who became Christians and have had an enduring ministry? If so, please tell us about that.

As for corresponding with other inmates, I am not allowed to do this because in New York State it is against the rules for inmates to correspond with anyone else who is incarcerated. This includes with prisoners who are out of state.

Other states have their own rules concerning correspondence, however, where such a thing is allowed—but not in New York. And concerning Charles Watson, throughout the years I have heard many good and God-honoring comments about Brother Charles and his testimony. He and I have never corresponded, of course.

You wrote the book Son of Hope *that is a compilation of your prison journals. Have you ever thought of writing a book that tells your life story? Also, how has* Son of Hope *been received by churches, Christians, and secular media?*

As for the *Son of Hope* journal book, it was never originally my desire to put together a book—this one being a compilation of my journals entries. I am, however, a prolific writer and I best express myself through words. But over time a handful of close friends began to suggest having my writings in book format. The rest is history. The Lord opened a door and I went through it by faith. I receive absolutely no payment or royalties from the sale of the *Son of Hope Volume 1* journal book.

Overall the book only has a small circulation. The publisher has all but disappeared and I never hear from him anymore. Although the publisher did a good job putting it together, the book is virtually unknown.

Please discuss what you believe are the most important aspects of your ministry now. How have you seen it help people inside and outside prison?

To tell a story of someone I have helped, I am enclosing with my answers several copies of recent articles from the *Woman's Christian Temperance Union Journal*. You may also wish to contact the publisher of my testimony. The "Son of Hope" tract was published by Moments with the Book of Bedford, Pennsylvania. See the back of the tract—which I am enclosing with this paperwork—for their contact information. Feel free to call Mr. Don Johnson of Moments with the Book [this author has obtained permission from Mr. Johnson to publish his name] for his comments on how the tract has been used, how many have been distributed, etc. I don't even know this information. But I believe you will be pleasantly surprised at the extent of the tract's outreach. It was first published in 1999 in both English and Spanish.

[This author has read the aforementioned *Woman's Christian Temperance Union Journal* article. It tells the story of how Berkowitz has discovered a strong link between adolescent alcohol consumption and the corresponding probability of later crime. He ministered to his fellow prisoners about this connection, and his observations were published in this journal as a warning to others. This author also contacted Mr. Don Johnson at Moments with the Book for a comment about the "Son of Hope" tract's distribution and response. When asked how many copies have been printed, Johnson said, "Just shy of a million; 960,000 at this time." He went on to give us insight on the public's reaction, saying, "There have been a lot of responses. This tract has been a blessing to many. People have requested additional copies. Mr. Berkowitz's story is a remarkable testimony of what God can do."]

There are those even in churches who struggle to forgive when the crime includes murder. People want severe punishment and confuse "forgiveness" with the perpetrator "getting away with it." Obviously, I'm not telling you something you don't already know, but how do you deal with this earthly dilemma?

I have always stated both during interviews with ministries such as Focus on the Family, or in my writings, that forgiveness does not mean escaping the consequences of one's sins. Forgiveness from God is a gift, as God delights in showing mercy (Micah 7:18–20). But in no way does one necessarily escape the consequences. I have often said that forgiveness is not a get-out-of-jail-free pass. But, as we know, the Lord gives the Christian who is incarcerated the grace and inner strength from the Holy Spirit to continue to live out his or her life as a believer even while behind bars.

Yes, many church folks have difficulty in the area of forgiving a criminal offender, and this is understandable. In the flesh and with human understanding, it is a hard thing, especially if the crime committed was a heinous one. But this is where trusting in the Lord and living by His Word come into play. It is only by the inner guidance and strength of the Holy Spirit that such a level of forgiveness can be achieved.

I could write volumes on this. And while I again stress that forgiving an offender is no easy matter, Christians need to look at a handful of biblical examples of those who deliberately took lives, but were forgiven by the Lord, and were used mightily by Him.

There was Moses, King David, and especially the Apostle Paul. By Paul's own admissions in various Scriptures, he took the lives of both men and women—fellow Jews who believed in Jesus as their Savior and Messiah. He persecuted them and beat many of them, compelling some to blaspheme. Paul was a murderer. But look [at] what God did. The Lord made Paul into a mighty minister. And Paul suffered for his belief, too.

Do you still struggle with guilt?

On occasion, yes. Sometimes such guilt is overwhelming. My sorrow of my past crimes is beyond words to describe. But then I recall the precious promises of the Lord, that I am a new creation in Christ, and "old things" are passed away (2 Corinthians 5:17). While Colossians 3:1–4 says that my life has been "hid" with Christ.

I often tell fellow believers that we need to see others with the eyes of Christ and with the mind of Christ. God does not look at us as sinners, but as winners. And it is through Christ and Christ alone that we have the "victory" over the world, the flesh, and the devil.

How have family members of former victims responded to your confession of faith (we know that you received Stacy Moskowitz's mother's forgiveness)?

For the most part the victims of my crimes and their families have not forgiven me, and while I hope that one day they will, I do not expect them to. As far as I know, none of them are professing Christians. But I continue to pray for each to be saved and to come to faith in Christ.

I did, however, by the grace of God, make peace with the mother of one of the victims, Mrs. Neysa Moskowitz. Mrs. Moskowitz and I, back around 2000, began to correspond and I was even able with her permission to speak with her over the telephone. It was a productive time for forgiveness and healing, at least to a degree.

Unfortunately, Mrs. Moskowitz died from cancer a handful of years ago. I still have the handful of personal letters she sent me, too.

Have old friends you knew before you were arrested ever tried to contact you?

As far as I could tell, no "old friends" have tried to contact me. I'm referring to good friends I had when I was growing up. However, there were a couple of "bad" friends whom I knew from my Satan-worshipping days who did try to reconnect with me. I sent their correspondence to an investigative journalist and made him aware of such. He is very familiar with the "Son of Sam" case.

Do you have biological family? If so, do they correspond or visit you?

I do have a biological family whom I love and miss very much. Today, however, I am estranged from them. My half-sister stayed in touch with me during the first few years after my arrest, but I burned the bridges, so to speak. The same with my birth mother, Betty. My birth mother passed away in the mid 1980s, I believe. But by this time she and I had lost contact. My mother was a good woman, and so was my adoptive mother, Pearl. Today, my only family is my fellow Christians.

Do you have a girlfriend or wife?

Do I have a wife? No. A girlfriend? I wish to keep this private to avoid media problems and intrusions. You know, I'm sure, how terribly destructive the secular press and media can be.

We understand that Stacy Moskowitz's mother, Neysa Moskowitz, forgave you before her death, and your connection with her was a result of a mutual friend in Georgia, correct? Have you been able to establish connections with any other family members of victims?

Yes, it was my friend from Georgia, a Christian couple whom I am still in regular contact with, who were instrumental in helping me to connect with Mrs. Moskowitz. My friends visited with Mrs. Moskowitz, too, down in Florida where Mrs. Moskowitz lived until the time of her passing. They remained in regular contact with her as well. This was the grace of God at work. But, as stated [before], I have no connections with any other victims or their families. According to prison rules in New York, inmates are not allowed to attempt to contact the victims of their crimes.

In my case, regarding Mrs. Moskowitz, she first sent a letter to me, but without a return address. Thus, it took some "behind the scenes" work to connect with her. But, as I said, this was all the Lord's doing.

Throughout your journals, we have seen you several times make the statement that your story is constantly being told with inaccuracies and misinformation, whether the teller is sincere or is looking to gain attention or fame for the report. In our chapter on you, we address some of these inaccuracies. If you were allowed to say one thing to the public on your own behalf regarding this, what would you say?

Concerning the misinformation that's out there with regard to the so-called Son of Sam case, I wish to say that it was a terrible tragedy and I regret more than words could ever express about the loss of lives and the pain that has been inflicted upon many innocent lives. I believe that, at the time, I was under extreme emotional and mental distress, as well as under deep and very dark spiritual bondage. And while I accept responsibility for the crimes, I know I was under a degree of demonic control. I know firsthand what it was to be oppressed and possessed by demons. I have many times tried to explain this to various individuals (police officers and FBI agents, psychologists, lawyers, and to the public in general), but I was for the most part written off as a "nutcase" and a psycho.

Perhaps one day the door will open for me to discuss in greater detail, and from the vantage point of the present, all the different elements which led up to the Son of Sam shootings.

In a press conference in February of 1979, it is reported that you retracted your statement of demonic possession, saying "'The Blood-Thirsty Demons' was just a concocted story invented by me in my own mind to condone what I was doing." However, during your exclusive interview with Maury Terry for Inside Edition several years later, you stated that the press never really got this correct, that there was a demon called Samhain. *Would you mind elaborating on this?*

With regard to the confusion about denying my story of "Blood-Thirsty Demons," I was in desperate straits. So many inmates as well as the media were—at the time—teasing and harassing me about the story of the "dog" and that of demons, that out of desperation and disgust and always being thought of as a crazed madman, I wanted to show people that I was a human being, that I was a rational person, even though there was a time I was irrational. I thought that by publicly denying the truth, it would all go away. It was classic "magical thinking," and it did not work except to create more overall confusion. As I have stated many times and continue to do so, when I was in my devil-worshipping days, I believed in my twisted and possessed mind that I was a soldier for Satan and for the Druidic demon, Samhain, the deity who demanded human sacrifice. Again, I regret this. I was a lost, confused, and tormented young man. I'm not making excuses, but this is what I had foolishly believed at the time.

[When Berkowitz sent his response and reflections to our case study, dated August 19, 2014, he elaborated on this answer. He shared that during his time in Attica, he was a high-profile inmate who received a great deal of unwanted attention from "bullies and tormenters." He carried a knife with him often around the time when another inmate had ambushed him and made an attempt on his life in 1979. Between the incessant hassling, the yelling *from both inmates and guards,* the dog-barking noises they would throw at him, and the lingering threat of his environment, he "had to struggle to keep going and not sink into despair." He described this time in his life as "pure torture," and went on to say: "And in desperation, I one day declared that everything had been a hoax. It was my way—once again with my magical thinking—that by uttering these words and making some kind of official announcement, all this would go away. It did not. It only created more confusion. In time, thankfully, all that teasing and harassment stopped. I was slowly earning respect amongst my peers and the staff. It took a handful of fights, confinement in 'The Box' for ninety days for fighting with staff, and a host of other 'Stand Your Ground' actions for me to finally be left alone. Yet I know today this was the Lord, working behind the scenes, watching over me because there would be a day I would come to Him with a heart of repentance and faith."]

From what we have been able to gather, there is some evidence that satanism played a role leading up to the events of the late 1970s. It is also alleged there were others either acting with you or in parallel to your activity. Is this correct?

Yes, I was involved in satanism and often went to Untermyer Park in North Yonkers to engage in demon worship. Shortly after my arrest, John and Michael Carr, the actual sons of Sam Carr, a neighbor, both died under mysterious circumstances. John Carr died first, by either suicide or possibly homicide in North Dakota. Michael, a devout scientologist as well as satanist, died in a mysterious car crash on the West Side Highway in Manhattan. And had it not been for the mercy of God, I, too, would have died violently, when, in 1979, another inmate snuck [up behind] me and sliced open my throat, narrowly missing my carotid artery. This was in Attica Prison. Had he been successful, I would've died right around the time the Carr brothers did.

Are there warnings or advice that you would give, if you could, to young people who are also seeking fulfillment in the wrong places, such as the occult?

Never get involved in the occult. Satan is a liar and a deceiver. He will promise you whatever you want, but it will come with a price. The most precious thing a person has is his soul. This is what Satan wants most of all.

David, please tell us what you hope our book can convey on your behalf and on behalf of other inmates who have been born again and are now new creatures in Christ.

What I hope your book will convey is that God is able and more than willing to forgive even the worst of criminal offenders. I always use myself as an example of the Lord's great mercy and grace. That if He can forgive me—and He has—then He is willing to forgive any man or woman who is willing to repent of their sin, and place their faith totally upon the Lord Jesus Christ, and upon His finished work on the cross of Calvary.

In addition, that God keeps many of His treasures in jails and prisons all across the land. That there are sincere men and women who are truly doing their best to serve the Lord while confined, many like myself knowing we may never be released, save for death or the rapture, whichever comes first.

God bless you.

KARLA FAYE TUCKER
(THE PICKAXE KILLER)[307]

The people of the courtroom were more than just shocked and bothered; they were bordering on traumatized. The longer that appalling confession tape played on, the longer the ladies and gentlemen of the jury were convinced that the defendant several feet away from them, Karla Faye Tucker—that attractive, petite, curly-headed brunette with the feminine, puffy-sleeved dress and plastic, prison-issued, white, religious cross[308] around her neck—needed the death penalty.

The witnesses could testify, saying *whatever* they were going to say about the case, for or against her, but the utterly animalistic bloodbath this young woman was being tried for had its own voice. The photographs of two bloody bodies—a nude man hanging half off a mattress on the floor, surrounded by his own blood, and a woman in a night shirt with a pickaxe buried seven inches deep into her chest and heart—were repeatedly shown, to the disgust of everyone present.

The case had broken wide open when a man who was close, *very* close, to the defendant had secretly come forward with information about and incriminating stories of Tucker and her co-op killer boyfriend, Daniel (Danny) Garrett, and their loudmouthed, post-kill, bragging antics over the past several weeks. When Tucker's friend had told all, investigators knew the case was sensitive enough and held too many suspects in the druggie/biker circle to focus so acutely on these two individuals without irrefutable evidence. The informant friend was outfitted with a monitored transmitter wire taped to his chest and a recording reel in his boot, and was sent into the lion's den to poke the drugged beasts.

Nobody could have hired a man better for the job than this one. Because of his unique relationship with the killers and his wife's equally unique relationship with them, he had been able to walk into their home, give a shallow greeting to the biker-crowd visitors on Tucker's couch, casually grab a beer, head to the back bedroom, and fill a few minutes with small talk before initiating the conversation that would put Tucker and Garrett away forever.

"I been wondering. Did y'all go over there with it in mind to kill them people?"[309] The tape echoed in the quietness of the courtroom. Another voice, one of three in the recording, was that of Garrett.

"It was a freak thing… It happened."[310]

As Tucker can be heard in the background shaking her addiction out of a pill bottle, she explains with mumbling, drug-laced incoherence that they had used a pickaxe merely because it was simply there.[311]

The man with the wire reminds her of a particularly disturbing detail she had shared with him just after she and Garrett had committed their crimes. He asks her if it is indeed true that, while she was bringing the pickaxe down on the man she loathed, she did achieve multiple erotic gratifications, *physical* gratifications, as she had previously claimed…

Her answer to this question had done her in as to whether she was guilty of murder. And now, to an exhausted jury at the end of an emotionally taxing trial, the prosecution lifted the tape recorder into view, his finger hovering on the "play" button one last time for his final summation…to repeat Tucker's answer to that delicate inquisition just once more before the eyes and ears of those the state had appointed to sit in the seat of her judgment.

"Does Karla Faye Tucker deserve the death penalty?" he asked the jury. "I'll let her answer that question for herself."

He hit "play," allowing Tucker's stoned and stupefied Texan rasp to play out in one of history's finest ironies:

"Well, hell yes."[312]

PROSTITUTION: A MONSTER OF A DIFFERENT COLOR

Charlize Theron is an incredible talent. Her gripping portrayal in the crime drama *Monster* (the tale of a lesbian, man-shooting, prostitute serial killer based on the true story of murderess Aileen Wuornos, who was executed in 2002) had an intense effect on the nation in 2003. People still talk about Theron's transformation from curvy, blond bombshell of Hollywood to freckled, rough-skinned, foul-mouthed, oddly dressed social reject with bleached-out eyebrows and cigarette-stained teeth. And the transformation wasn't just the result of perfect application of special-effects cosmetics from the makeup department. Actress Theron mastered the curious body language and animated eye and neck movements, and she even nailed that strange, frumpy half frown, accurately displaying the awkwardness that characterized the real Wuornos.

When the Wuornos character in the movie tried to clean up her act, get off the streets, and get a job, and was met only with further dismissal and rejection from society because of her hardened appearance and spotted background checks, the audience members found themselves connecting to Wuornos as a person with feelings and, at some point, as a woman with a conscience. When she was brutally beaten and raped by a man who had been depicted as one who had every intention to kill her, or at least leave her to bleed to death in the woods, the audience felt anger toward the man and pity for the woman, who had killed her first victim in self-defense. When Wuornos' character shortly thereafter returned to hustling to make money for her female lover (the only person who had ever showed her kindness) and found herself justifying the murder of some of the more forceful men she had lured into the woods after barely escaping her own bloody death, the audience understood why she had snapped and taken out her resentment on men who rubbed her the same way as the one who almost killed her. When the end of the movie drew near and Wuornos' character was facing trial and a potential death sentence as a cold-blooded serial killer of seven men, the audience saw her as a sad victim of a hard life, a life that had trained her up in the ways of a violent prostitute, and when she was older, she had not departed from it.

This was just a movie, and some, though certainly not all, feel the film wasn't accurate. If we review a fact sheet on the real Aileen Wuornos, we see the following list:[313]

- Her mother was sixteen when she had Wuornos, just after having filed for divorce from a clinically schizophrenic man who, by the time of Wuornos' birth, was incarcerated and was later convicted for harmful sex crimes against children.
- Wuornos never met her father; she was three years old when she and her older brother were legally adopted by their grandparents as a backup plan when her natural mother abandoned them.
- Her alcoholic grandfather, according to Wuornos, would make her take her clothes off, then he would beat her and "sexually assault"[314] her.
- By the time she was nine years old, Wuornos was trading sex for drugs and food, and was committing incest with her brother when unsupervised.
- At age thirteen, just after her father hung himself in prison, Wuornos became pregnant via rape by her grandfather's friend; the baby was born in a "home for unwed mothers"[315] and given up for adoption.
- At age fifteen, Wuornos was thrown out of the house and started living on the streets, becoming a prostitute to survive.
- The teenager went on to marry a man twenty years her senior; he was the president of a yacht club, who later placed a restraining order against her for assaulting him with his own walking stick.

This marriage lasted only nine weeks before annulment a few days after she was arrested for assault at a local bar for hurling a cue ball toward the bartender's head.

- Between the summers of 1982 and '83, Wuornos served time in prison for the armed robbery of a convenience store.

And the list goes on, detailing incidents involving fraud, violence, disturbance of the peace, and life-altering tomfoolery that always leads to moral depravity and desensitization of conscience. Wuornos claimed her first murder had been in self-defense, and there was evidence to support that claim from several angles, not the least of which being that her first victim had been a convicted rapist prior to his encounter with Wuornos. She stuck to that story until only days before her death, when she "came clean"[316] to a documentary filmmaker, stating that it had all been a big lie. However, many sources (including some personalities behind the making of the movie *Monster*[317]) hold to the theory that she offered the eleventh-hour confession in order to keep her execution date set. In the end, she admitted several times that she carried hatred against humanity so deeply that she just wanted to be executed and get it over with. In one of her final interviews, Wuornos said of herself, emphatically, "This is the last time I'm gonna say it. You have to kill Aileen Wuornos, cuz she'll kill—*again*."[318] By the time of her death, she had many times proclaimed that she was a believer in God and Jesus, and her last words on the day of her execution even mentioned going to be with Jesus. (Yet, she also talked about coming back on June 6 on a mother ship like they did in the *Independence Day* movie, and nobody really knows what she meant. It was for odd and seemingly irrational moments like these that Wuornos ultimately was not considered for featured focus in this book, since her story of conversion drew more questions than answers. This author and others behind the production of this book consider Wuornos' story a sorrowful one, and hope that she is now and forever resting in peace with the Lord.)

As this is not a case study on Aileen Wuornos, we will stop her story here, but there is a palpable lesson that can be learned from her and from the epic, Academy Award-winning and Golden Globe-winning performance Charlize Theron gave depicting her hard life and murder spree.

When people hear the news reports of a killer, their first compassionate thoughts usually go out to the victims and their families, as they view mug shots of the murderer with contempt. As this author has read so many times during the research for this book, many reactions escalate to the equivalent of, "The death penalty by lethal injection is not inhumane enough for this waste of life! He (or she) should be dragged out and shot! Boy, if I'd have been there, I would have (fill in the blank with a violent act)," and so on. These are very understandable reactions; nobody is trying to argue away those natural feelings—*especially on behalf of those who have lost loved ones in similar circumstances.*

But, when an audience is drawn to the personal experience and understanding of the killer, such as his or her story is expressed with Charlize-Theron levels of brilliance, suddenly hearts soften and people move to the edges of their seats munching their popcorn and almost *hoping* that the rapist in that terrible, graphic scene will be stopped by any means of force before he can kill the character they now find themselves connected to. They nod with sad resignation and some level of sympathetic acceptance when the abused woman who captures the bleeding hearts within American theaters turns to violence or murder.

(Even if some readers of this book do not agree with this sentiment, many crowds emerged from theaters with this report on their lips, going as far as to say they were actually rooting for Wuornos' character and had pity on her during the scene of her sentencing. Google the public's reception of this movie and its effects on viewers to see some of these reviews. Also along this thread of thought, there is a struggle between censure and acceptance in the hearts of American viewers of *many* current entertainment trends that follow this theme. Take, for instance, the immense popularity of television shows *Breaking Bad* and *Dexter*. In the former, drug dealers/manufacturers Walter White and Jesse Pinkman are each responsible for *multiple* cold-blooded murders, for the worst of selfish reasons. Yet, because he has cancer, White feels an urgency to financially provide for his precious family any way he can before his death. The young and likable Pinkman is lonely and inexperienced, and finds himself caught up in the drug circle with no way out. By the time the show's tension reaches the point that White or Pinkman commits murder, the audience may not think their actions are morally right, but viewers still, *despite themselves*, root for the bad guys as the victims of a terrible situation. In the latter program, Dexter Morgan, a blood-splatter pattern analyst for the Miami police, secretly hunts down and delivers vigilante justice to perpetrators who have somehow dodged the legal system. [Essentially, Morgan is a serial killer who brutally kills serial killers.] Yet, because of the perception that he is offing bad people who otherwise would have continued to hurt or kill other victims, once again, audiences across the states root for him… It is odd that human nature tends to place judgment before understanding when it comes to real people who fall into destructive behavioral patterns that lead to murder, but they place interest and understanding before judgment when it comes to the fictitious life of a spellbinding television character. But, we digress…)

Because of Theron and the movie *Monster*, a whole nation adopted a kinder collection of concepts for the inexcusable behavior of a woman who killed seven men, with six of those murders being carried out in cold blood (assuming the first was actually self-defense). (Please note that this movie is very graphic, and this author does not recommend it personally for any reason barring viewing for research purposes.)

Yet, what also can be said of prostitution, and what that may lead a woman to do?

As the subject matter is by nature troubling, we won't visit the topic in detail, but a little bit of research would reveal that sex for money is not only unfulfilling and degrading, it is also extremely dangerous and life-threatening. Prostitution not only presents the obvious risk of contracting sexually transmitted diseases, of course, but it also places participants in a jeopardizing reality of constant violence that often leads to cruel and unusual death. (Statistically, the death rates related to prostitution are higher in foreign countries than in America, but the risks are still very real here.)

Prostitutes are also potential victims of another kind of danger: emotional death. Most often, women who sell their bodies in exchange for physical pleasure rob themselves of the joys of genuine love and affection. Without it, understandably, their worldviews become warped. They find themselves between a concentrated and extreme need at all times for any- thing that's real love, be it a sweeping romance or simple family stability, and yet their surroundings consistently point out that this utopian ideal does not exist. Their vision for a better life is clouded by sexually trans- mitted diseases, heroin needles, seedy hotels, unfulfilling parties, and bar brawls. The occasional compliment that temporarily strengthens their self esteem loses its benefit when it is revealed that, once again, the kind words spoken were only empty forms of flattery to get them into bed. Many prostitutes depend on superficial, flirtatious, or ostentatious attention to bring a little sunshine to their dark lives, or to provide a sense of belonging. Not surprisingly, prolonged exposure to this kind of "sunshine" ultimately burns deep. Unable to recognize legitimate concern or affection when it's offered, opportunities to connect with others in an authentic way can be missed, leading to more emptiness in place of an ever-decreasing hope. This standard of living can draw hopeless people farther and farther away from having faith in humanity. And, of course, a side effect of this can be their inability to *value* humanity or individuals as much as they once did, to the point that the worth of others' lives pales over time.

Essentially, though typically consensual, prostitution is almost never a chosen career or position taken by anyone who feels she has a choice. Often it seems to be the last or only way to survive. We can't even count the number of testimonies along the lines of, "My daughter was starving, so what else could I do?" or "I had nowhere to live, and the streets were cold." This obviously doesn't even include the motive of drug supply for those who are addicted to a substance abuse. Sometimes, the cause is even harder to swallow when children are sold or trafficked into prostitution at a young age, forced to participate, and then continue the practice even when they are older because it's the only life they know.

Situations like these are heartbreaking, and many prostitutes find themselves trapped in that pattern of behavior for the duration of their earthly lives. Their resulting reputation and criminal activity drives them farther into the inescapable state of affairs, as fewer windows of opportunity exist for those with such a sordid past.

However, very few who have found themselves in this snare can say that they did so for the same reason as Karla Faye Tucker. Her story is inimitable.

Before we get into the details, however, let's take a moment to remember the victims who fell in the wake of her habitually unhealthy decisions:

- Jerry Lynn Dean (aged 27), Yeoman 3 (YN3) in the US Coast Guard and installer of cable television
  - Bludgeoned with a hammer by Daniel Garrett (Tucker's boyfriend at the time of the murders), then dealt deadly blows by pickaxe by Tucker and Garrett
- Deborah Thornton (aged 32), wife, mother, and sister
  - Dealt deadly blows by pickaxe (more information on who/why in the following pages)

It is incredibly unlikely that Tucker would have sought to kill anybody that night if she had been by herself in Jerry Lynn Dean's house, as the purpose behind the sneaky visit had never been murder until her boyfriend initiated an attack that would go beyond the point of no return. But when she *did* put her mind to kill, she massacred.

And her motive?… Well, things "just happened"…

Was that all?

TRAIN UP A CHILD IN THE WAY SHE SHOULD KILL

Culprits (those examined in this book and others not featured herein) have "motives" for their murderous acts, all of which seem surreally insane to the rest of us, when compared to alternate paths the killer could have taken to rectify their pressured, ready-to-snap situations. But "motives" are, as we discussed in the Sean Sellers' case study, different than "reasons." Many have said that killers are not born, they're "raised," "programmed," or, more popularly, "made." The situation or person who "raises," "programs," or "makes" a killer obviously differs on a case-by-case basis. But for Karla Faye Tucker, complications in her childhood abound. If only we could devote hundreds of pages to focus exclusively on her...but then, that's already been done.

Author Beverly Lowry was becoming obsessed with death and the stories of murderers when she lost her son in the early 1980s in a hit-and-run. Nobody has ever been brought forward as the guilty party, and her son fell into the archives of history as a victim of a careless act by one who lacked the integrity, decency, and/or bravery to admit to the crime. Lowry was devastated. As a writer, she was accustomed to looking at topics of interest with a fixated infatuation to translate into a better read. When her estranged and troubled son had not come home that night, Lowry was at first angry at him: Not showing up was the kind of stunt he was always pulling. But, when she received news that he had been walking home after his automobile broke down, had been hit by a car, and found almost dead (he died within hours at the hospital), she was angry at herself. Her journalistic method of mourning his death and letting him go was to immerse herself in stories and reports of death all around her.

One day, Lowry stumbled upon a newspaper article about a woman named Karla Faye Tucker who had brutally murdered two people in the middle of the night with a pickaxe. The story covered Tucker's conversion to Christianity. Lowry found that odd. How could someone capable of such brutality be human enough to call herself religious? It was a new concept for her. Against her own better judgment and the advice of those who knew and cared about her, and without even the slightest inkling of understanding as to what drove her to this decision, she scheduled a personal visit with Tucker.

Nothing during that time in Lowry's life made much sense, and she would go to her grave years later never having completely grasped what had sparked an insatiable desire to let go of her son via a method of therapy as unconventional as going to meet a death-row killer. Her contact with Tucker, however, showed her that sometimes the average person (such as herself) has more in common with the convicts than she would have ever guessed.

Lowry and Tucker formed a friendship that changed history.

To date, Lowry's research into Tucker's case and her articles and book stand to be the most authoritative and exhaustive documentation any-where regarding Tucker's childhood. And, as with Wournos, when a motion picture about Tucker was made—starring high-profile actresses Diane Keaton (as Lowry) and Jennifer Jason Leigh (as Tucker)—the world took a second look at Tucker…four years after her execution.

(Note: To avoid last-name confusion in this study: Carolyn and Larry Tucker [Karla Faye's mom and dad] will be referred to simply as "Carolyn" and "Larry"; Kathi and Kari Tucker [Karla Faye Tucker's sisters] will be referred to simply as "Kathi" and "Kari"; Shawn [Karla Faye Tucker's best friend, whose name is "Shawn Dean" during certain points in the timeline of this case] will be referred to simply as "Shawn"; and Douglas Garrett [Daniel Garrett's brother] will be referred to simply as "Douglas.")

Two Daisies and a Weed

From her earliest memories, Tucker had known there was something dif-ferent about her. The rest of her family could have been viewed as the quintessential, all-American, cereal-box ad of happiness. Her older sisters, Kathi and Kari, were blond, fair-skinned, voluptuous, and "perfect." She, on the other hand, was tan, bow-legged, and scrawny, with curly, dark tresses. The two older girls had the likeness of graceful flower-pickers in pastel paintings, and Tucker resembled the black sheep in a darker paint-ing, standing alone in a shadowy forest of grays and dark blues. Kathi and Kari were daisies, and she was a weed. (One report says Tucker "had always felt like the ugly duckling between two blond-haired, blue-eyed, fair-skinned siblings."[319]) Yet, she simply had too much of her mother's traits to question that her birth had been biological.

The beginning of Tucker's life was happy enough, with a mother and father, Carolyn and Larry, who loved their girls and appeared to love each other. Carolyn taught them to cook and clean and be cheerful homemakers as soon as they could walk, and she spent time with them, playing board games and getting to know their individual personalities. When the Tuckers bought a house near Brazoria, Texas (when Tucker was seven or eight years old), the family traveled there for frequent getaways. Tucker's father taught her how to drive a truck and a boat while she was still small enough that she could barely reach the pedals and see over the dashboard, and she would drive with her sisters down to the water in her two-piece swimsuit and curly, dark brown mane to play in the water, fish, or water ski. Her mother told her many times that she had "rare qualities."[320] Tucker cherished her memories of these days her whole life, as they would end very early on, replaced almost overnight with a season of turmoil within the home, when it became clear that "Mother and Father" were not meant to be. They split up for a while, and when they got back together, they never demonstrated a true sense of harmony.

Immediately after the happiness deteriorated, Tucker saw her older sisters (also harboring the stress and anger of the parents' relational strain) smoking. They weren't smoking cigarettes, but something more *fun*, something more *dangerous*. Something they called "dope." Tucker thought she would try it, too, and when Carolyn found out, her response was surprising: "If you're going to smoke, little lady, you're going to do it right."[321] Her mom left the room momentarily and came back with paper. She made her youngest daughter roll one joint after another, giving her pointers until she had learned to roll them perfectly. It was like Carolyn had undergone an overnight change from Suzie Homemaker momma to a buddy, a pal, an older, bad-influence friend who would not only join in her daughter's mischief, but who would educate her in it as well.

None of the girls could have known that Carolyn had always carried wild oats in her back pocket while questions of morality were stewing inside her, but this tension in the home was the missing ingredient needed to make the pot boil over. One night, Tucker and her sisters went to the theater with their father. When they returned home, their mother and all her things were gone. "Devastated" would hardly describe how the girls had felt at this discovery. Carolyn had left her stamp, however, and now eight-going-on-nine-year-old Karla had Mama's go-ahead to engage in substance abuse.

With Carolyn no longer in the household to speak for herself, Larry felt free to begin calling her names. (We can't list these names here, as they are offensive, but they are equivalent to names like "hussy" and other words that can also mean "female dog.")

According to a report on the subject from the Crime Library:

Mr. and Mrs. Tucker had an on-again, off-again marriage, literally. They divorced and remarried several times, trying to make a go of it, but each time they would regress. Each time it was because of infidelity. The three daughters felt the sting of the breakups, only to rejoice at the reunions, only to be torn asunder again when the parents' union did so. When Karla Faye was ten, the final dissolution took place. It was messy.[322]

According to Tucker, herself:

If you can imagine seeing a movie about the parents divorcing and fighting over the children in the worst kind of way and then the father getting them and separating the mother from children and children crying and hanging on to Mother at the courthouse while they are being taken away, then you get the picture of how I remember it.[323]

It was when she was ten years old, in the midst of the divorce and her mother's final split from the family, that Tucker learned she had not legitimately been born of both parents.[324] A nagging little voice that reminded her constantly of the two daisies she would never compare to rose up with an announcement at the worst of times. Mama was gone, Dad wasn't really Dad, sisters were legitimate…and Tucker was a weed that had sprouted in the middle of the happy daisy garden to rob them of their sunshine—a bony, prickly reminder of her mother's infidelity.

Isolation and detachment set in.

Mama Knows Best

When the divorce was finalized, custody of the girls was awarded to Larry, likely because the courts saw him as the more stable parent.[325] That might have been the case at the time of a custody battle, but, hard as he tried, he couldn't gain control of the girls from day one. When Tucker had barely graduated into her double digits, at ten years of age, her sister's boyfriend buzzed up to their door on a motorcycle looking to find Kari. Since Kari wasn't around, the young punk invited Tucker to come with him instead, promising her a new substance that would blow her mind in hopes to get her strung out and sleep with her. However, the heroin made Tucker sick, so the boy's plans were thwarted. By the time Tucker recovered from the illness, she had tasted enough of the mind-blowing that she would never stop wanting more. By the next year, at age eleven, she was addicted to heroin,[326] as well as to the feeling the needle produced upon entering the skin (she had become a "needle-freak," as they say in the drug world). (From this moment until her future incarceration, Tucker would be a serious drug addict, taking anything she could get her hands on in any way that it could be ingested, and for any price.)

Tucker went wherever her sisters went and hung out with whomever her sisters befriended, including a group of bikers the girls were flattered to be allowed to follow around like admiring street puppies. During wild and crazy drug parties that often morphed into open celebrations of sensuality and multiple-partner intercourse, Tucker would stare "wide-eyed" and "take notes" about the "birds and the bees."[327]

As the awkward, tween-age year of twelve dawned, Tucker attempted her first sexual experience at a house Kari had run away to, but the escapade ended in utter humiliation. A crowd was there, and, because she was a virgin, the boy had difficulty completing the act. He made a public spectacle of her, shouting sarcastic obscenities about her body. Everyone at the house got a big kick out of the moment, except Tucker, who was red-faced over the ordeal. She couldn't wait to become sexually active, just to show them all she could have fun like the rest of them. When that day came, she was a maniac from the start, proving her womanhood anywhere and with anyone she could.[328]

Around this time, Tucker started to see her mother again off and on. Carolyn, who was working somewhat of a "bad cop" position at a local law enforcement establishment, had the inside scoop and was able to warn people in advance of impending busts. When she learned that Tucker and her friend, Debi, had gotten their hands on a hundred Valium pills, she called to warn the girls to dispose of them because someone at the station had found out. Instead of throwing away the drugs, Tucker and Debi took more than thirty pills each and were wasted for several days.[329]

Between the ages of eleven and thirteen, Tucker watched her sisters grow to the ages at which the courts would allow them to choose which parent they would live with. Kathy and Kari moved in with Carolyn, the *fun* one. In the meantime, Tucker grew closer to Larry, but because he was working many hours at the docks to pay the bills, he could never keep up with her constant hunger for self-destruction. Her repeated offenses at school, getting her kicked out several times, were just the tip of the iceberg. Her intensifying need to show violence whenever challenged was overwhelming as well, and fistfights became the norm. After Larry came home one day to find Tucker sitting on a toilet, stoned, he knocked her into the bathtub.[330] Shortly after that, Larry gave up the effort to help his daughter, figuring that he was failing and thinking that perhaps the girl's mother could do better.[331] Soon after, when Tucker was completely naked and strung out on a bed in Larry's home, Carolyn came to the house to collect her for good. From then on, Tucker and Carolyn would "share drugs like lipstick."[332]

Drugs were not the only thing they would share.

Now living with her mother, having no responsibilities, she was free to lie around the house with six other women (Carolyn, her two sisters, Tucker's long-time best friend Shawn, and two other acquaintances) and absorb drugs on a constant basis. Occasionally, she traveled with the All-man Brothers Band, whose members had shown some interest in her when they had seen her dancing at one of their concerts. The boys in the band had soon been willing to adopt her as a road buddy; shortly after that, she became the exclusive sex partner of a head roadie. Later, at least once, she was a bed partner of lead singer/songwriter Gregg Allman, himself.[333] (Many reports also include the Marshall Tucker Band and the Eagles in the list of bands Tucker and others from her circle traveled with.)

At fourteen, and barely so, Tucker met a stranger while hitchhiking. The man offered her forty dollars in exchange for letting him see her chest. She obliged. It was the first time she had ever exchanged any aspect of her own sexuality for money. When she got home, she told everyone, including Carolyn, about the incident. Her mother took a portion of the money, stipulating that if Tucker was willing to trade her body for money, she could now help pay living expenses.[334]

So, at fourteen, Tucker became a prostitute.

Carolyn, who was now the owner of a successful prostitution business, passed her clientele (her "johns"[335]) to her daughter, Kari. When Kari was finished with them, she passed them on to Tucker. (Once, according to Tucker's friend Debi, one of these johns was willing to pay the hefty price of two hundred fifty dollars for Debi, who had been at Carolyn's house watching cartoons. Carolyn had forwarded the offer to Debi, the thirteen-year-old-virgin watching cartoons, who quickly declined out of fear.[336]) In a vulgar episode of bisexual goings-on, a group of men and one woman took young Tucker and a bottle of honey into a back room to show her what she was missing and attempted, together, to help her achieve physical climax. The older woman who had pitched in on the event was Carolyn's best friend, Adele. Around this time, Adele's boyfriend, a rough man usually wearing army fatigues, would also "help" Tucker, giving her lessons in oral copulation, which she welcomed. He also offered his casual assistance in the martial arts, which, for Tucker, was likely more fight training than she needed for the uses she would give it.[337]

(Just before her eventual execution, Tucker wrote to Governor George W. Bush, asking for a stay of execution. In that letter, one note she made was the following: "At fourteen [my mother] took me to a place where there was all men and wanted to 'school me' in the art of being a call girl. I wanted to please my mother so much, I wanted her to be proud of me.

So instead of saying no I just tried to do what she asked.… Her friends took me at fourteen and 'schooled me' in the art of adult sex…and with their warped and perverted sense of street values taught me that this was the thing to do to be respected and sought out in the 'world we lived in.'"[338] Around this time, Tucker had a hysterectomy for medical reasons. She was glad she no longer had to worry about pregnancy with the kind of "job" she held.)

But it wasn't always just Tucker's mother who was the bad influence. Tucker was the reason her mother developed a dangerous addiction to heroin. Carolyn previously had been afraid to try heroin, knowing she would love it and have one more addiction to put on her list of terrible habits. Yet, when her youngest daughter, Tucker, the weed among the daisies, couldn't kick her own heroin practices to the curb, Carolyn eventually gave in to the temptation and set out to find a vein. Tucker had come home that day to find her mother on the couch, poking at her arm. She asked for help finding a vein. Tucker refused. Her mother continued to jab at her arm, figuring that, with or without help, she was going to accomplish the task.

Tucker had once watched a man in this exact position die at a drug gathering. Fumbling at his arm with intent to shoot heroin, he had hit an artery. Tucker described the result graphically, saying "his arm blew up."[339] When he had instantly died in front of everyone, the party had quickly ended and everyone fled. Unable to get this image out of her head as she watched her mother, Tucker reluctantly made her way to the couch and helped her mom locate the right spot. (Tucker's mother now had a new hobby, and Tucker would live with regret over the part she had played in it for the rest of her life.)

The never-ending, bordello-and-drugs lifestyle and increasing physical hostility against anyone who looked at her funny embedded themselves into Tucker's way of thinking. She was, by this point, a force to be reckoned with should someone try to cross her, but she always had her mother. Carolyn, unlike the others in her immediate family, was of the same blood, made from the same cloth. They understood each other.

Tucker *idolized* her mother, and loved her even more.[340]

A Picture of Pure Motive

Tucker's mother had fought and won the battle against hepatitis she had contracted from her lifestyle of drugs and needles—twice. But her third battle, she would lose.

It was a sudden and tragic loss, and the physical deterioration of Carolyn's body before her final hours haunted Tucker forever.

While Carolyn was still in the hospital for treatment of her disease, Tucker, age twenty, helped out as much as she could, sometimes staying overnight in the care facility, and other times going home in the evenings to her then husband, Steve Griffith. (His and Tucker's marriage had been impulsive and short-lived, and has very little to do with this case study, because it had very little to do with who Karla Faye Tucker was and would become.) One night, Tucker and her sister, Kari, helped Carolyn to the bathroom. She had requested their assistance, saying she wanted to smoke her last cigarette while she sat on the stool. The tone of finality in Carolyn's request greatly bothered Tucker, but what bothered her much more was the blood that began seeping out of her mom's mouth[341] as they walked her and her medical equipment to the next room. Tucker started to panic, but her sister gave her a warning glance, so she kept her intense feelings of horror to herself.

That night, Tucker went home and slept. In a dream, as she was standing by her mother's hospital bedside, Carolyn took a ring from her finger, a ring that had been a birthday gift from Tucker, and told Tucker, warmly, to have it. Tucker took the ring just as affectionately and slipped it on her own hand. At that moment in the dream, her mother died. Tucker awoke from the dream to the sound of a ringing phone: a call summoning her to the hospital. Tucker hurried there to discover that her mother had just passed on. After Tucker fell to her knees and wept bitterly for a long while, her grandmother approached her with Carolyn's birthday ring, telling her that, in her mother's last moments, she had said she wanted Karla to have it.[342]

This was a loss that Tucker, still just twenty, was in no way ready for. The reality that she would face a lifetime without belonging, a lifetime of anxiety and drug-induced madness, and a lifetime of picking fights that grew more serious and fatal with each passing moment landed on her with a weight that no pills or needles could relieve, now that the one person in her life she truly felt at home with was departed. And what had Tucker done to save or help her? Besides teaching her mother the arm-poking methods that likely propelled her toward her disease-riddled death, Tucker had nothing good to say about her own role in Carolyn's gloomy and distressing last years on earth. Carolyn was gone from this world forever, and she had left nothing behind but a now-defunct brothel and memories of needles and smoke.

And a picture.

She had left a picture.

The photo had been snapped before Carolyn's body had been eaten alive by the disease that killed her, and it was Tucker's most prized possession. If she could never look at her mother's attractive face again, never share another joint or a "john" and laugh about it later, never again sit at the table with her, surrounded by multicolored and cheap cosmetics dealing a game of cards around an ashtray, then she would hold fast to this last remaining and treasured memory.

Tucker and her friend Shawn had been friends for longer than Tucker could remember. Shawn had fallen in love—or so she thought—with a man named Jerry Lynn Dean.

With her mother dead, Tucker was looking to explode about anything or anyone that irritated her. The first day she met Dean, he had parked his motorcycle on her living room rug, and it had dripped oil all over the floor. She had marched through her house looking for the party responsible, and found her very own bed occupied by the lovebirds Shawn and Dean. Tucker threw Dean out of her home, making it clear she didn't like the man. A little time passed, and she came home a second time to find oil drops on her rug from Dean's motorcycle parked in the living room. Once again, she found the man and her best friend making love in her own bed. The repeat offense stirred a rage within her, and this time when she threw Dean out, she made herself *very* clear. She explained that whereas Shawn was a beloved friend and welcome anytime, Dean was not welcome. Period. Her home was the only safe haven she had from the free love of shared beds and messy living rooms. His presence would not be tolerated.

Shawn married Dean, and they lived happily ever…briefly.

Tucker had a new man: Daniel Garrett.

THE PICKAXE KILLER

Tucker had moved in with her sister Kari temporarily, leaving her photo collections (among which was the snapshot of her mother) with Shawn for safekeeping while Shawn was married to, and living with, Dean. Shawn's friendship had become even dearer to her since the passing of her mother, and Tucker trusted Shawn like a sister. (Kari, around this time, had formed a relationship with Douglas Garrett, Daniel Garrett's brother.)

Tucker was still occasionally traveling with rock bands, and on the next road trip to New Orleans, she brought Shawn along. Despite the fact that the women were separated the entire time—Shawn was with the roadie van in one city and Tucker was with the band members in another—Dean was jealous of his wife's partying with other men and quickly became convinced that her actions were a direct result of Tucker's forceful persuasion. Feeling that retaliation was in order for this and for having made him and his oily riding rig unwelcome, Dean ruthlessly slashed up Tucker's photos with a butcher knife…including the precious picture of her mother.

An Eye for an Eye

Tucker had always been a ticking time bomb on any given day, and for any reason: She was a hothead, a fireball, a self-destructive rabble-rouser. The death of her mother intensified this ever-increasing deterioration of integrity like a virus, catching and spreading through her moral convictions corrosively, killing off honor and principles and leaving nothing but depravity and festering thoughts of radical aggression. Dean's choice to annihilate her personal property—and with it being such a precious thing he had taken from her forever—had brought a raging flame dangerously close to her shortening fuse. It was only a matter of time before she exploded on someone, and her crosshairs were fixed upon the man with the oily motorcycle.

When Shawn came to Tucker's house to pick up something she had left behind, Tucker once again…*once again*…told her friend that *she* was welcome anytime, as long as Dean was nowhere around. It was revealed at that moment that Dean was right outside.

The fuse was lit.

Tucker tore through her front door toward Dean and, without allowing him to remove his eyeglasses, punched him in the face with so much force that he spent the next several hours in the emergency room undergoing the removal of embedded glass from his eye. (Just after this incident, Dean called his sister, Peggy Kurtz, who said, "He told me, 'Man, I've never met a woman like her before. You say anything cross to her and she'll just hit you.' His glasses were broken. Karla had hit him. I told him, 'Jerry, stay away from her. If a woman is that violent, you don't need to be around her.' That was the first time I heard her name."[343] When Kurtz received the phone call letting her know that her brother had been murdered, she passed out.)

This would be the beginning of a dangerous and violent game, Tucker's already-lit fuse creeping ever closer to the imminent explosion.

Tucker and her boyfriend, Daniel Garrett, were living together with several others. Their drug use was always increasing, and that meant more opportunity for bad drug deals to go down. Rumors abounded that one of the bad deals had involved Dean.[344] Shawn, by this time no longer emotionally honeymooning with the jealous and demanding husband she had been back and forth with since they had taken their vows, helped Tucker, sister Kari, and Garrett get back at Dean by providing them with his bank cards. With disguises on, so as not to be recognized later by the ATM camera, they withdrew every last dollar he had (reportedly about $460). Dean didn't appreciate the stunt, and he especially didn't appreciate that his wife had been involved.

This time, when Shawn left Dean, it was for good. She took her things from their home, including the most recent gifts that he had given her—a busted nose and bloodied-up lip—and moved in with Tucker's clan. Tucker couldn't take it anymore. Something had to be done about this Dean guy. Her tough talk, as well as her drug doses, got heavier and heavier. She always intermingled with the most hardened personalities who not only put up with, but encouraged, tough-guy talk. It was nothing new that a masculine, burly, strong, tattooed drug addict wearing black leathers on the highway during the day and purchasing prostitutes to shoot up heroin with him at night—the kind of company Tucker kept—would talk "big talk" back to Tucker, whether he was capable of carrying out his threats or not. That was old news, worthy of little attention. When conversation around the drug circles ensued that Tucker had said she might "off" the guy, nobody took the remarks seriously. Besides, compared to Dean, she was tiny. Tucker, however, was an anomaly that very few people understood. Everyone knew she was a feisty little thing, ready to pop at the slightest provocation, but, as the victims of her closed fist would say, she could hit harder than any man—and nobody ever saw it coming.

Perhaps that is why Dean reportedly heeded her warnings more than the others, and felt the need to act first. According to Shawn, who still had some contact with Dean and members of his rough group, Dean had put out a contract on Tucker for three hundred dollars. The job wasn't for her murder, but for what he figured would be worse: He wanted her to be flare-gunned to the face, forcing her to live with scars and disfigurement for the rest of her life. Shawn said Dean kept the flare gun he intended for the hit man to use on the top of his television.[345]

The fuse sparked ever closer. Dean had crossed a line, and whether she would exact revenge was no longer debatable. He had beaten up Tucker's best friend, hired someone to flare-gun Tucker's face, and had taken her most sacred material possession: the photo of her mother.

A plan simmered. It needed to happen for Dean to know his place. Since he couldn't be taught in any other language, Tucker would take his most sacred material possession. Eye for an eye. Tooth for a tooth.

Reconnaissance

Kari's birthday party in early June lasted three days and involved a never-ending, free-for-all, conveyor belt of drugs—*all kinds of drugs*. "Whisky, beer, and tequila were the drinks of choice, often in combination with illicit drugs such as marijuana, cocaine, and methamphetamines, and illegal use of prescription drugs such as valium, dilaudids, and mandrex."[346] Forensic pathologist Janis Amatuzio said of this combination: "[Tucker] had so many drugs in her, almost a dozen... She had uppers and downers. This is an enormous number of drugs." Explaining the "altered state" that Tucker was in, Dr. Amatuzio went on to say, "This cocktail would certainly have put her out of her mind."[347]

When the extended party was finally fizzling to an exhausted close, the hosts of the party, Tucker, Douglas Garrett, Daniel Garrett (who had slipped away from the party for a short shift at the bar where he worked), Kari, and a few others, had not slept for the full three days, having kept themselves awake with wild activities and stimulants. Most of the conversation during the lengthy party had been associated with the recent split between Shawn and her allegedly abusive husband.

Tucker picked up Garrett from his workplace at around two o'clock in the morning. When Garrett slipped into the vehicle, he shared an idea with Tucker, and her response was wildly positive. The two were tired, cranky, riled up, and drugged out of their minds on a cocktail of mind alteration (including speed, the "drug of violence") when they formed their plan.

Garrett considered himself to be the one with the most experience of the three—himself, Tucker, and a man named James Leibrant—who would participate in the act of revenge. Tucker's manner was too abrasive compared to the more silent demeanor of Garrett; they might get caught if they followed Tucker's lead. Leibrant wasn't the leader of anything; he was more along for the ride, and would help Garrett keep watch and take notes regarding the layout of Dean's residence. (Leibrant would later testify that he was "overamped" and "to the point of 'Yeah, okay.'"[348]) As

Garrett was the chief voice behind the mission and the one with the most self-proclaimed tactical know-how from his days in the military, Tucker and Leibrant followed his lead. (Note that Garrett frequently boasted of the military expertise he had gained in 'Nam. Sometimes, he and Tucker would get drugged up, dress in dark clothing, and run through ditches, scramble over fences with weapons, and spy on people at random for something to do. They hadn't hurt anybody during these escapades, but they could have if the opportunity had come up. So Tucker was, by this point, used to following Garrett.)

The plan was simple: The three of them would put on black clothing and drive to Dean's house. Leibrant would come along in case there was any rough stuff, while Garrett and Tucker would scope out the area, see what lights were on in the windows at such an hour, locate the doors, and get a feel for the general layout of Dean's apartment. If circumstances worked out right, they would carry out the full plan that night, but the ultimate scheme, the final intention, would need to be done carefully, in order for them to get away with it.

They were going to steal Dean's Harley-Davidson motorcycle.

A Simple Plan

Get in. Get the bike. Get out.

That was all there was to it.

As the three burglars were heading out from Tucker's house, where they had gone to change their clothes, they stopped long enough to get Shawn's blessing. She said Dean deserved to have his bike stolen, so they bid her goodbye, got into the car, and left. Tucker had a set of keys to Dean's place, so entry wouldn't be a problem.

When the three arrived at Dean's, Liebrant stood watch outside. Tucker and Garrett crept inside, where they were instantly greeted by the rugged smells of gasoline, oils, and leather. As the flashlight's beam lit up the darkness, they saw that pieces of Dean's Harley were strewn here and there. That was convenient. Perhaps this night *would* be the night the complete plot of motorcycle thievery would play out. Dean had made their job easy by disassembling the bike. All they would have to do now is carry out the parts.

They set to work.

In all of their inebriated planning, they hadn't considered what to do if they were caught in the act. They had simply intended to grab the bike and go. So, when Dean, who was asleep in his bedroom, woke up, demanding to know who was in his home, panic struck the duo. Tucker ran to the back bedroom, saw Dean on his makeshift mattress-bed on the floor, and without exactly knowing why (the moment was fuzzy), she climbed on top of him. As soon as Dean recognized her, he tried to calm her down and negotiate. Garrett appeared in the room with what has been documented as a ball-peen hammer. He aggressively separated Tucker and Dean and began violently waling on the helpless man. Although Dean's protests ended abruptly, Garrett continued the merciless beating. Then, without a word, without showing remorse or recognition of what he had done, Garrett went back to loading up the motorcycle parts.

The Silencing

Due to the graphic nature of the scene that follows and the effort to keep this book clean, this author has no choice but to jerk the reader out of the narrative here, as a comprehensive continuation would not only be unsettling to some readers, it would reignite the more sensational details of these two victims' last moments alive, and we wish to leave that kettle unstirred for the sake of their memory and their remaining families.

However, what happened next absolutely must be told in order for one to understand the *whys* behind Tucker's decision to go ballistic and therefore understand the rest of her story (otherwise the detail would not be mentioned at all), but we will visit it as quickly as possible and move on.

When Garrett had left the room after the bludgeoning, Dean started to emit a gut-wrenching, gurgling sound, a phenomenon that sometimes happens in specific cases of head trauma. Tucker, who was still in the bedroom with Dean, heard this noise and knew immediately that he was barely alive but likely wouldn't survive long enough for anyone with rescue knowledge to reach him. Tucker had only signed up for a mission of theft. Even though she, when talking tough with her buddies, had made more serious threats in moments of self-inflation and braggartism, she, Garrett, and Liebrant have testified multiple times they never intended to murder. Garrett, for crazy reasons of his own, had reacted to the situation dramatically, escalating the crime from theft to battery or even attempted murder. And, when Tucker had been alone with Dean in that dark room and he started to utter that chilling, inhuman sound—that noise that told her that this human was truly and thoroughly suffering in agony, that fluid-filled and bubbly grinding that seemed to crawl venomously through the air and pop like mellow firecrackers proudly heralding a man's pain—she reacted for crazy reasons of her own as well.

Dean's pickaxe, which he used to break up the ground during his various installation jobs, had been right next to his bed. Tucker had to make the sound stop. This is what she repeatedly testified later on. What exact thoughts going through her mind or emotions going through her system right then is anyone's guess. Even she, herself, couldn't remember any thought or feeling during those intense moments other than a *make it stop, make it stop, make it stop* sensation. She grabbed the pickaxe off the floor and tried to bring silence to the room.

The sound continued. So did she.

After a number of strikes, Garrett entered the room and once again took over. He grabbed the pickaxe from Tucker and used it to deliver a final, fatal blow to Dean's chest. The sound stopped. Garrett again went back to loading motorcycle parts. Tucker impulsively turned on the light. Once it shone on the scene, Tucker saw a shaking movement under a pile of blankets next to the wall. *Another person had been in the room and had witnessed the whole massacre!* This second person was a woman: Deborah Thornton. The subsequent happenings have been told in two ways (the account gets a little foggy here because, with all the drugs in their system, the scene was a blur, and it's likely they wouldn't have wanted to remember such things even if they could have during trial):

1) When she saw the woman, Tucker went crazy with the pickaxe and

could not be stopped. In some versions of the event, this is despite the intervention of Garrett—and in addition to a smile she gave to Liebrant over her shoulder as he saw her through the doorway.

2) Tucker reacted to seeing the woman by swinging the pickaxe, barely grazing Thornton's shoulder. The woman struggled and almost bested Tucker. Garrett appeared and began attacking Thornton until he delivered the final blow.

(There is also an account floating around in some circles that states Tucker saw Thornton before she attacked Dean and instructed Thornton to put the blanket over her head prior to the rest of the violence, but this is the least believed and hardest to prove, which is why we are not giving it specific focus here. Note that in all versions, when Liebrant broke from his watchman duties outside and observed what was happening at the house, he fled, wanting nothing to do with murder. He did return later to help move the remaining stolen goods. He kept quiet about the murders until the trio was arrested. Also, by all accounts, Deborah Thornton begged for Tucker and Garrett to spare her life until the pain of the injuries became so excruciating that she begged them to kill her.)

Which version is the truth? More evidence suggests that the second version—as told by Tucker[349] the exact same way several times on witness stands, in interviews, and in conversations related later by personal jailhouse friends—is the most likely story. Homicide Detective J. C. Mosier, one of the leaders in the investigation, also believes that Garrett was all but solely responsible for Thornton's death.[350] The evidence relates to several issues:

- Tucker's small physical frame, which some believe makes her an unlikely perpetrator because of the large size and heavy weight of the weapon
- The varying depths between injuries inflicted on the blows Tucker admits to delivering versus the ones she denies having caused
- Injuries of Tucker's arms the previous year, which had affected her strength and thus her ability to handle an overhand/overhead weapon

- The consistency among Tucker's storytelling versus that of the others, whose accounts of what happened have been called into question far more often than hers

Yet, without any other witnesses, nobody really knows exactly who delivered what injury at what moment and why. This is why this case is strongly tied to phrases like, "It just happened," every time motive is considered. We know the facts about Karla Faye Tucker's life, the rapidly building tension between her and Dean, and the remarkable story of her life post-incarceration (which we will address soon). But, other than the note regarding Tucker's reaction to the sound she heard, the whodunit-and-why theories are still out on this one.

Well, at least that's true concerning the literal events of that evening. However, as far as the reasons Tucker was eventually caught up in something that spiraled so far out of control and landed her on death row, some have said that she had been trained up in the ways of a violent, ticking-time-bomb, drug-laced, prostitute lifestyle, and when she was older, she did not depart from it. ("Train up a child in the way he should go: and when he is old, he will not depart from it" [Proverbs 22:6].)

This we know for sure: On June 13, 1983, Karla Faye Tucker and Daniel Garrett brutally silenced Jerry Lynn Dean and Deborah Thornton.

CHANGE

For weeks following the grisly pickaxe scene, police investigators had many suspects. Everyone who knew everyone else in that circle could have been angry with Dean at some point. Crimes of passion, revenge, drug-related skirmishes, and even cocky showmanship, a glorified muscle flex with a bloody side effect, were all motives in the kinds of people that Dean knew. And, because Thornton had been scheduled to testify at an upcoming Internal Revenue Service hearing as the only person with information that could lead to an arrest, there were suspects on her side also—even though she had only met Dean earlier that day at a party before going home with him. Nobody was talking, and yet everybody was talking. There were lots of false leads, and many biker-crowd groupies offered the names of people they wanted to turn in for something.

But Karla Faye Tucker and Daniel Garrett, now dubbed in the media as the "Pickaxe Killers," had big mouths. They had come back to the house, dropped drugs, and spewed the truth to two people they *thought* they could trust. In the following weeks, the subject of the murders would come up often, and each telling of their part in it became more macho than the last. Then Tucker proclaimed that she had experienced physical and erotic gratification during the kill.

On July 20, 1983, some five to six weeks after the motorcycle-theft-gone-bad, the most unlikely duo came forward with inside information about who had killed Dean and Thornton. The informants were Tucker's sister, Kari, and Kari's boyfriend, Douglas Garrett—the brother of Daniel Garrett. It was a romantic Tucker/Garrett couple betraying a romantic Tucker/Garrett couple. A brother and a sister outing a brother and a sister. Despite all their other illegal dealings, Kari and Douglas wanted nothing to do with murder, including keeping their siblings' dirty little secret. (Kari and Douglas were married by the time Tucker's trial began.)

After being instructed by the detectives on how to effectively get a confession (by allowing the guilty parties to do most of the talking), Douglas wore a wire and nonchalantly strode into Tucker's house. A couple of blocks away, officers sat in an unmarked van, listening to the sounds coming over the transmitter. Douglas grabbed a beer from the fridge, headed to the back bedroom, and made small talk for a few minutes before initiating a conversation that would put Tucker and Garrett away forever.

"I been wondering. Did y'all go over there with it in mind to kill them people?"...

"It was a freak thing... It happened...."

With the complete confession on record, including the incriminating admission that Tucker's pickaxe rampage gifted her with an erotic climax, the police had their guy...and their girl. Tucker and Garrett were arrested immediately.

Elsewhere in Houston, a man named Ron Carlson wanted Tucker and Garrett to pay for what they had done to his sister, Deborah Thornton. He wanted revenge, and he wanted to deal a hand of justice in the same suit that had been dealt his innocent sister. As he told one reporter, he "wanted to take that same pickaxe and leave it buried in Karla's chest just like it was left in [his] sister's chest." He "wanted to get even." He "wanted to kill her."[351] Thornton had been much more than a sister to Carlson. She had been like a mother, too…

Puppets

Unlike other names featured in this work, it didn't take years, or even months, for Tucker to begin questioning who and what she was. In fact, before she even attended her own trial, there was evidence of divine intervention in her life, evidence that many people to this day consider irrefutable. While charged with a murder and awaiting trial at a correctional facility in Harris County, Tucker was faced with some new realities.

Sobriety.

It was a bitter thing. It was a sweet thing. And it was a *new* thing.

Tucker now had nothing to lose. She had already lost her mother and may as well have lost one of her sisters, what with Kari—her own blood—having turned her in to the police. Garrett couldn't visit her and whisper sweet, dirty nothings into her ear. Tucker couldn't turn tricks behind the walls of a women's prison. Her days of tough talk and punching faces were only a memory now that her surroundings presented her with people who had no reason to be impressed by her tales of ruffian leadership and intimidation; they were all there for their own rough reasons, so weaving tales of being the bad girl would only be met with shrugs of indifference. The only claims to an identity she had ever known was a laughable redundancy in a place like this, filled with women who were locked up for crimes that made Tucker's bragging rights irrelevant in comparison.

She needed a joint.

She needed a needle.

Reality had never been easy to take, even when she had enjoyed the ability to slip into alternate and escaping realities under the influence.

This was hell.

Weeks into her stay, there was a sudden buzz around the prison yard. Tucker's fellow strangers headed out with excitement. She followed, both out of curiosity and because she had little else to do. When she emerged, she saw something that she never expected to see in this setting.

Puppets. Was this a joke?

Childish music came from behind a squat barrier as little cloth people with yarn hair, manipulated by the hands of an adult ministerial group, popped into view with enthusiasm and simple dialogue. Tucker looked around her at the other women. It was an anomaly: These were full grown women, and *all of them* had every reason—with all of their toughness and sordid, knife-wielding, erotic-dancing, drug-dealing pasts—to think this was literally the stupidest thing they'd ever seen. Yet, nobody was acting like the puppet show was stupid. In fact, there was joy and happiness and, despite herself, she, too, was curious.

Laughter…here? Inmates were singing. They were enjoying. They were living. There was *life*. And all of this from an inappropriate showcase of immaturity and doll-people. It was absolutely absurd!

And yet, it was also absolutely *innocent*—a vocabulary word that Tucker had all but forgotten—and a sensation she wasn't sure she had ever experienced. If nothing else, even though it seemed illogical and out of place, this innocent production was, at least, a taste of *something* on prison grounds that wasn't another story of disparaging, insufferable loneliness leading a woman to believe there was nothing else. Now, at twenty-three years old, Tucker was in prison awaiting trial for capital murder, having assisted in the deaths of two people in the privacy of a bedroom, trembling with the physical and psychological need for illegal substances to flow through her veins and release her back into the familiar void of cohesion, dreaming for just one filthy and lucrative moment in a hotel room with her military boyfriend or some john, and…watching a puppet show.

She took a seat.

A pretty woman soon made herself known at the front of the outdoor congregation and began to speak.[352] She didn't look like the rest of them. There was a lightness to her: freedom, happiness, hope. Tucker focused on the woman and found herself surprisingly intrigued by her tale. She spoke about being a topless dancer, a drug dealer, and an addict who had been shooting heroin since she was twelve—in Houston, the same area that Tucker had grown up in. In the 1970s, this woman had been incarcerated, facing a minimal term of five years in prison and a potential term of life. How had she come so close to the same fate as Tucker and pulled herself from the grip of destruction? Nobody could begin that lifestyle so young and still make anything of herself... Why was this woman different? How had it come to this positive outcome for her? And yet, Tucker wasn't dreaming or high. This was *real*.

The speaker attributed her graceful ending to a higher power. Jesus Christ, whose name Tucker had heard before, was the Man who had brought the woman out of the darkness and turmoil of never-ending hunger and desolation. This, she said, had been her escape from a fate similar to that of those in attendance, but there was no questioning that her life prior to that escape had been similar to, or just like, that of those in attendance.

Tucker had only left her cell in the first place to follow the others and see what the excitement was about. The puppet show had grabbed her attention...and this woman was keeping it.

On and on the sermon went, from the mount of a puppet show stage to the congregation of prostitutes and druggies. When the speaker's message reached a close, the inmates scattered, some gathering around to talk with her. Tucker waited for the crowd around the minister to disperse, and then she approached.

"You really did that?" Tucker asked. "You started shootin' [drugs] when you were that young?"

The minister told her that, yes, she had.

"I started when I was ten," Tucker said.[353]

In a later interview with a Dutch film company for a documentary, *The Power of Forgiveness: The Story of Karla Faye Tucker*, the minister, who had been traveling with Teen Challenge Ministries, explained:

I mean, you just can't hardly imagine, you know, her life that she lived, you know. Her mother was a prostitute and drove her around, introduced her to drugs and prostitution, and, you know, of course she never saw any hope in that....

She came up to me at the end of the service, and this was the only time I'd ever seen her with an emptiness, you know, just so pale, and no life in her....

[I]t really made her start thinking then. She took a Bible. In fact, she thought she was stealing one, because she didn't know they were free [she laughs], but she took one anyway, that's the important thing. And she went back to her cell and began to read.[354]

And when Karla Faye Tucker started reading the Bible, she couldn't stop. Tears flowed from her eyes. Guilt welled up, torturing her spirit for what she had done. There was no going back: no un-killing Dean, no bringing back a woman who had merely been in the wrong place on the wrong night.

Now, there was a Book that spoke of love everlasting, a Man who had allowed Himself to be brutally killed in order to preserve any one person for eternity regardless of what he or she had done, and a Father who knew exactly how to father His children. He would never lead her into drugs, prostitution, crime, disease, loneliness, or death. He would give only companionship, success, and love, as well as fruits of any labor she put forth from that day on. All she had to do to qualify for such a free gift was to lift her heroin-needle-scarred arms upward and accept Him.

Yet, that was *not* the only thing she needed to do, was it? A true acceptance, in her opinion, meant a change of one's self, and she knew that regardless of whether anyone on this earth ever understood or accepted her turning to Christ, this was something she had to do for her own reasons. She had to confess her sins to the Lord and to the world.

I don't know that I felt forgiven [by God] at that point, but I do know I felt love. I knew that no matter what I had done I was loved, just like that, just like I was. That's when the whole weight of what I did fell on me. I realized for the first time that I had brutally murdered two people and there were people out there hurting because of me. Yet God was saying, "I love you." It was supernatural. I don't really know how to explain it. At that moment, He reached down inside of me and ripped out that violence at the very roots and poured Himself in.

I knew then that I had to tell the truth about everything. Before I knew the Lord, I didn't care what anybody else felt or thought.... When the Lord came into my life and changed me, I realized I couldn't count the cost of my own life. I had to tell the truth about everything.

I was not fearful of what man could do to me.... After that night in the Harris County Jail I was set free. God is so real. He is awesome.[355]

Tucker had spent weeks blaming anyone and anything but herself for her actions, and whereas it was true that she had felt controlled by a drug-induced state that made her feel like someone else on the night of the murders, the decision to take the drugs in the first place had always been her own, and she had been well aware of the dangers those decisions could lead to. She had also been well aware of the animosity among the members of the group she led and Dean before she had first stuck her arm. Nothing she said, felt, thought, or justified would remove any of the responsibility now. She knew there was no way, spiritually, mentally, or emotionally, to go on with lies or blame games on her lips.

She was *guilty* of murder.

The Trial of Life, Death, and Thereafter

[A]nd the spirit of the Lord touched her, and she cried out to God that night in her cell. You know, she gave her life to him, and he saved her, just like he saved me, and all the other Christians I know.
—Teen Challenge minister and puppet show operator, 1999[356]

Tucker's trial lasted only a couple of weeks. It didn't take long to sort out who was guilty; by the time her trial began, Tucker had already decided that no matter what it meant for her sentencing here on earth, and despite all advice from her lawyers, she had nothing to offer anyone ever again in this life but the truth. The hard, incriminating truth.

She gave the same story repeatedly in her and Garrett's trials, and to many, *many* interviewers. Not one detail ever deviated from one telling to another. According to Tucker and the conclusions/suspicions of psychiatric professionals on her case and for years following, her sick claims of sexual climax during the horrendous pickaxe crime had been nothing more than tough talk for an audience used to her outlandish boasting. (Additionally, a detail from Liebrant's testimony suggesting that Tucker had turned and smiled in between blows to Dean was explicitly denied more than once by Tucker. Liebrant was the only one present besides Tucker and Garrett the night of the murders, so his testimony was initially highly regarded by prosecutors. However, once the case was in the bag, even the *prosecuting attorney* admitted that Liebrant was "not a credible witness."[357] There were several reasons for this conclusion, including the fact that Liebrant "didn't...mention a smile the night [he] made [his] statement, yet now [it was] a thing [he would] never forget" when he took the stand.[358] When questioned about the sudden change in the story, he responded by shuffling his feet.[359])

Just before receiving her sentencing, Tucker said "she [did] not deserve mercy for what she [had] done and that she [didn't] know what could be done to her that would be bad enough to make up for it,"[360] "testifying during the punishment phase of her trial that even being pickaxed herself would be insufficient to atone for her crime."[361]

At that time, the world—and the jury—agreed. Tucker was sentenced to death by lethal injection.

But for Tucker, the trial had been over before she ever set foot in a courtroom. The trial had been her life, and that part of it was over. With its death came another life to be lived behind a sign that read "Death Row," an opportunity that would land on her lips in praises all day every day until that life also came to a peaceful closing. Then, and only then, would life *eternal* begin.

From this day until her last, Tucker would refer to "Death Row" as

"Life Row," because, she said, "the Life of the Lord is here!"[362] The state assigned her an inmate number: 777. Lucky jackpot slots. The Lord's number.[363]

"According to Rusty Hardin, a former Harris County prosecutor, 'By the time I met her, you had a person who was extremely remorseful. The proof of her change came as I was preparing the murder case against Danny Garrett [in 1984].'"[364] He was not the only one who would observe her change.

SEVENTY TIMES SEVEN

Forgiveness is not based on how we feel, because if it was we would never forgive.—Karla Faye Tucker[365]

The Public

When Tucker initially received the death sentence, she became very quiet toward the media. She felt that there was enough publicity about her already, and that she would never be fully able to let go of the hurt she had caused the families of her victims, so she chose for a spell to remain silent behind bars. She didn't want to force the victims' families to have to relive the hurt each time her name appeared in the papers. Eventually, having never known what kind of publicity it would cause, she did step forward to publicly acknowledge Jesus Christ to the news on screen. When she did, her announcement sparked a huge and overnight fame for her case. Although some rose up to demand her death, their demands often had less to do with her original crime and more to do with opposing the masses of people who defended her. Most of those who were in opposition to her stated that she shouldn't be given special consideration because she was a pretty Christian girl. Yet Tucker truly seemed to be the people's choice.

Reformation for Tucker went largely unquestioned. Almost everyone—including much of the secular media—saw the young woman on death row with a smile on her face and a testimony on her lips and believed in her story of change. But it wasn't just her story. There was something else about her, something about her countenance that touched people's lives and convinced them her conversion was genuine. When one watches interviews with her to this day, she doesn't come across as a prisoner with a set date of execution looming. Her attitude is not a memorized set of words. Her smile doesn't seem practiced. Her joy doesn't appear phony or forcibly perky. Until the day she died, she radiated a kind of internal peace, acceptance, and tranquility that even some on the outside, in their freedom, envy. It's no wonder that so many members of the public became her supporters, rushing to the nearest picket line to protest her execution, making strongly worded phone calls on her behalf, or writing passionate letters begging anyone with authority in Texas to commute her sentence to life in prison. Support for her commutation flooded in with incomparable and unprecedented demand not just from a concerned public, but from such notable people as Pat Robertson of *The 700 Club* and "Pope John Paul II, Italian Prime Minister Romano Prodi, U.N. expert on summary and arbitrary executions Waly Bacre Ndiaye, [and] the World Council of Churches,"[366] as well as members of uncountable foreign media outlets that devotedly reported on her case. The level of demand to see her spared by those who believed she was a new creation was so profuse and zealous that it culminated in a highly televised refusal of George W. Bush (governor of Texas at the time) to commute her sentence. The world had tuned in to see, and complain, about Governor Bush's decision. Why did the state need to go through with the execution? The world had already expressed its majority opinion. The girl had said she wouldn't hurt anyone ever again, and the world believed it. The world had forgiven her!

But these were people on the outside, people who were unaffected. These were individuals, organizations, and groups that held a steadfast opinion about the woman she appeared to be so many years after her involvement in the slaying of two innocent people who weren't given a comfortable amount of time in self-reflection to ponder their standing with their Maker. She had assisted in taking that away from them. And, what about the victims' families? What did they have to say about all this?

Ron Carlson

In 1999, Ron Carlson, victim Deborah Thornton's little brother, came forward to the public with an inspiring story. His sister, whom he called Debbie, had been his sister, yes, but she had also been a stand-in mother to him. Their lives had been hard from birth. And, when their mother died during Carlson's fifth year, leaving behind two children whose father participated in a lifestyle that perpetuated less-than-desirable parenting skills, Thornton provided everything she could in her mother's absence: she put food on the table, corrected Carlson's behavior, made sure they had clothes to wear, helped Carlson with his schoolwork, and provided him with precious companionship. Growing up with that kind of bond made her death catastrophic. The nature of her death had been unbearable for Carlson; his world had exploded when he had received the news of her violent passing. In his heart, Carlson held nothing but hatred for and a desire for vengeance against Garrett and Tucker, who had caused his unnecessary and heartbreaking loss. At one point, Carlson said of this misery, "If I would have had a chance I would have killed them myself. I read the transcripts and looked at the evidence, including all of the photographs of the crime scene. I saw the dead bodies lying on the mattress, so I am well aware of what happened that night."[367]

And his grieving would be given no break.

A year after his sister's murder, he suffered another loss, when his father was also murdered in a sordid case unrelated to his sister's killing. His father had been shot in the foyer of his own home during a crime of squalid revenge. Carlson's grief and boundless anger was renewed.

He turned to his usual drugs for comfort. But then, one day, his drug dealer, who had managed to obtain something unusual, came to him and casually returned an item that had belonged to his father. It was a Bible.

Carlson's dramatic testimony would be much like Tucker's, in that it did not take years or even months for him to conclude that he needed divine interference from Someone whose understanding of and grace toward his situation was more infinite and authoritative than his own. As he later shared in an interview: "I came to a point in my life, where I knew I had to do something with the hatred.... All I wanted to do was destroy things and kill people. I was being just as bad as the ones that [had] destroyed my family."[368] After one crucial night, he would never be the same:

> Now this was weird! You know, here you are, drug addict, boozer, your whole family's dead, and what are you doin'? You're sittin' there smokin' doobies [and] readin' the Word of God! Well, I'm cruisin' along, goin' through the Bible, and I get to the part where they kill Jesus.... I got down on my knees, and I closed my eyes, and I folded my hands together like this [he demonstrates], and I just said, "Lord...I just want you to come into my life, and...I just want you to be my Lord and savior, and just make me the kind of believer that you want me to be." That was basically [he chokes up, wipes tears, then continues]—That was basically what I prayed that night.[369]

In the days following that experience, Carlson came to another conclusion while reading the sacred passages of the Lord's Prayer. The verse, "And forgive us our sins; for we also forgive every one that is indebted to us" (Luke 11:4a), could easily be translated in Carlson's circumstances to say that we will be forgiven for our sins against God as we also have forgiven those who have committed otherwise unforgiveable crimes against us. He felt convicted about his hatred toward the people who had taken away his family, and knew that if he was going to be the believer that God wanted him to be, as he had prayed, then he would have to extinguish this internal cauldron of hate.

Carlson cried out to the Lord, saying that there was no way he could possibly obey *this* command. Not *this* one. Perhaps anything else, but he couldn't do *this*. And he heard back from the Lord, who told him that he was right. Alone, Carlson could never forgive; it was only *through the Lord* that he would ever be capable of doing so. Alone, humans act like humans. It is only through the intervention of Christ's power and favor that a finite man can rise above his own understanding and into a transcendent implementation of the Bible's holy advising.

Carlson and Tucker had something in common, whether his human mind could fathom it yet or not.

The day he went to visit Tucker on death row, she did not know who he was. When she asked whom she had the privilege of speaking to, he wasted no time in delivering the shocking blow of his identity; he told her that he was Deborah Thornton's little brother. He equally wasted no time in delivering Tucker the reassurance that the Lord had given him the strength to pass on to her. Through Tucker's pressing tears, Carlson told his sister's murderer that he held no grudge; he had already forgiven her. When the guards saw Tucker crying and headed over to remove her from the upsetting situation, she told them she was alright. When the guards had backed away again, Carlson reiterated his purpose for the visit.

He did not hold a grudge. He had already forgiven her.

At that moment, Carlson felt the same lifting sensation that so many have spoken about, a weight that controls and holds people down. It elevated off of his weary shoulders, and he was free.

After that meeting, Carlson and Tucker became close friends. Very close. Carlson continued to visit Tucker, initially to see if her relationship with the Lord was sincere, and later to be near her as a brother in Christ.

In a final and amazing statement in Carlson's testimony, filmed after Tucker's execution, he says, "I miss 'em. I miss 'em both. I miss my sister because of what she taught me, and I miss Karla because she helped me [in] my walk with Jesus. Karla was an inspiration to my faith."[370] He cried openly as he spoke.

Carlson, the man who wanted to embed a pickaxe in Tucker's heart, went on to become an advocate for her life, fervently supporting a sentence commutation until the day she was executed—the day he believes she went to be with Jesus.

Peggy Kurtz

In 2000, Linda Strom, a prison chaplain and spiritual advisor who was extremely close to Tucker, wrote a book called *Karla Faye Tucker SET FREE: Life and Faith on Death Row*. In it, Strom describes another inspir-

ing tale. Peggy Kurtz, Jerry Lynn Dean's sister, passed out on the day
she heard about the murders, and doesn't clearly remember how she got
home. As she spoke with Strom, she shared openly about her brother in
the troublesome days following *her own* powerful conversion to Christ.
As this author has contacted Strom and obtained permission for lengthy
quotation from her book, we will let this woman's testimony speak for
itself:

"Jerry was my buddy. He was eleven years younger than I was. He
had lived with my husband and me in Sugarland, Texas, when he
got out of the Coast Guard. We went to the movies and out to eat
together. We had such good times.

"My dad wanted him to come back to Alabama because Mom
had a stroke, but Jerry knew that opportunity lay in Houston. He
had a really good job with a security company, they were talking
about putting in a computer room, and—"

Peggy stopped, crying harder. Bowing her head, she prayed, "I
am healed, I am healed....[371]"

"I saw Jerry again in January 1983.... I said, 'Jerry, your life
is in a turmoil and you need Jesus. You'll never know until you
receive Him what healing, what peace He brings.'

"He replied, 'You know, Peggy girl, there's something different about you. I was going to tell you and Fred on the way to
Alabama that I have noticed a real change in you.'

"'Jerry, you can have that change.'

"He said, 'Well, I'm not ready yet. But I'm going to think
about it.'...[372]

"I called him in March.... I tried to witness to him more—
you just never know what God's doing in a person's heart. If I
could have known that this was the last time we'd talk, I'd have
talked more about Christ.

"Father's Day was coming up and I hadn't heard from him.
I called his work and they told me he had been killed. I said, 'I
think you've got the wrong person.' Nobody's ever prepared. I

thought maybe he had been killed in a car accident or on the job. They said, 'No, he was murdered.'… I passed out. My supervisor called our pastor. He came over and helped me. Somehow I got home that day.

"But then everything started: newspapers, TV, radio. My parents had to come from Alabama. I've never, never seen two people as devastated as they were. Mama broke down at the funeral home; it was all Dad could do to stand. I guess what hurts more than anything else is what that type of death does to a family. It comes in and rips you apart.

"Week after week went by. With all the news media and everybody talking about the murder, I had nightmares almost every night. I'd see the walls covered in blood and I didn't know how to get out. I'd wake up screaming.

"I knew that if I heard one more thing about this murder I was going to go through the roof.… I asked God to relieve me from this ball and chain. Wednesday night, July 18, 1983, I went to church. The minute I walked in, Pastor John said, 'Peggy, come down front, we want to pray for you.' As people gathered around me he instructed, 'Just lift up your hands, put all your anger, all your bitterness, all the bad dreams in them. Then give everything up to the Lord.'

"I was so ready. I couldn't work; I couldn't sleep; I couldn't eat. I couldn't escape it. It was constantly on my mind. I was literally filling my mind with the Word of God. I was eating it for breakfast. I was eating it for supper. I knew the answer was in the Word, but I couldn't figure out how to apply it.

"So as my church family stood with me, I prayed, 'God, make a way for me. I forgive whoever did this. I don't want to go backward in my walk, I want to go forward. You said to forgive. Your Word says I'm supposed to cast everything on You. You've helped other people; help me.'

"There is power in a praying church. Karla and Danny were apprehended that night, thirty-five days after Jerry's murder.…

Peggy gulped back fresh tears. "I loved that boy. I loved him so much. Sunday morning as I sat in church, I realized there was a battle going on in my mind. I wondered what brought Karla to the point of taking another person's life. What hatred and bitterness must have been in her—Jerry could have been me, he could have been anybody that got in her way at that time. Every time I saw something on TV, it triggered a memory of what took place.

"I didn't want to be consumed by hate. So, I told the Lord that now that I had a face to put to the crime, I still chose to forgive, and that if He made it possible, I'd tell Karla....

"A man at our church was in prison ministry and several months later told me about the reports of Karla's conversion. He said that if I wanted to talk to her, he would arrange it....

"When the phone rang, I tried not to think of anything but God. I said, 'Karla, I forgive you. I told the Lord that if He made it possible, I'd tell you I forgive you.'"[373]

Kurtz went on to share more of the pains that the constant media reminders caused in her daily life and walk with God. Although, by the time of Strom's writing, the pain that Garrett and Tucker had caused had never left Kurtz, she, also, acknowledged the change in Tucker and believed it was sincere. She went on to say:

"My decision to forgive became my anchor, something I came back to time after time. Jesus said we're to forgive seventy times seven. Sometimes we need to do that with the same person. I hated the circumstances that took Jerry out of my life, but he is in the hands of the Lord. I didn't lose him. I know where he is. Karla became like a little sister to me."

Peggy had begun to gather her things, preparing to leave. But then she sank back in the booth. She whispered, "You know what I miss most? Karla's prayers. I know she prayed for me. How I miss them."[374]

In a conversation between Strom and Tucker in one of their many meetings on "Life Row" prior to execution, Tucker admitted that she believed her conversion to Christ had much to do with Kurtz's intercession. She shared the following with Strom and several others in a prayerful and reflective Bible study group setting:

> Forgiveness is so powerful. It reminds me of what happened in my life because of Peggy Kurtz.... Back when I committed my crime, and no one knew who did it, she went to church. When she walked in, her whole congregation began to pray for the salvation of the person who killed her brother. Yes! I know the angels in heaven were shouting praises to the Lord as He smiled and knew right then that another lost soul would be won to Him. She prayed for that person—me—from day one. Those prayers are what moved God's hand in my life. I know that just as sure as I am sitting here.
>
> Right after I got the death penalty and was still just a babe in my spiritual diapers, I got a note from her saying she forgave me and loved me, and Jesus forgave me and loves me. She asked if I would call her so we could talk. After about a week or two I finally called. It was awesome. That conversation grounded me in my love for Christ. I knew then that I would never turn from the Lord. I knew He would always be my life.[375]

LIFE ON "LIFE ROW"

While Tucker lived out her final days on death row in Gatesville, Texas, people who knew her saw and reported that she lived what she believed: She demonstrated peace in the face of certain death; she showed love for her fellow death-row "sisters"; she exuded joy in spite of all sadness; she gave glory to God for His acceptance of her despite criticism from the outside world; she showed friendliness to all those around her, including hardened prison staff; and she carried out spotless behavior in a place where women had every earthly reason to sew any last-minute wild oats before they headed to the fatal gurney. (Through all the research this author has done on Tucker's life, there doesn't seem to be even one statement from anyone who knew her in person that reports a different behavioral pattern.)

Tucker made it a habit to fill everyone's day with happiness. She was constantly knitting and crocheting clothing articles, afghans, dolls, and other crafts. When Frances Newton (another inmate on Texas' death row, who was executed in 2005) arrived on death row in late 1988, having never met the other women held there, Tucker had arranged with a friend to decorate Newton's bed with gifts to make her feel welcome. When Christmas came and all the women were opening their gifts (Tucker had made dolls for each woman, designing them to look just like their owners), Newton, who was a very dark African American with short, braided hair, was surprised to see that Tucker accepted her well enough to make the black girl on death row a black doll that celebrated exactly who she was in the midst of all the white women.[376]

In addition to the many people who came forward with stories of Tucker's joy, the bounce in her step, her contagiously positive personality, the beautiful and almost dance-like sign language that she graced the prison chapel with during worship, and all the little crafts and trinkets she fashioned for people (including "Parole Pals," a doll that was made by the inmates and put to good purpose through the prison staff; Tucker's special friend Beverly Lowry received one of these), Tucker "had also already earned the respect of prison guards who credited her with helping prevent the suicide of two other inmates."[377] Her name comes up constantly in stories from people who were hurting and struggling with issues that nobody else, except a condemned woman on death row with an infectious and optimistic attitude, would understand. According to the research, her life touched many people in very permanent ways.

One man who saw, and believed, Tucker's devotion to Christ was Dana Brown, a prison minister who frequented the women's chapels to pray with the inmates and to help spread hope. Because he was constantly surrounded by women—women who had no men around and nothing

to lose by flirting—he made it a practice of keeping himself at a respectable distance from them. However, when he met and spoke with Tucker,
he was as taken by her as anyone else. He fell in love with her soon after
they met, but kept his feelings to himself for quite some time. Through
letters and occasional visits, he eventually shared his feelings with her, and
was surprised to learn that she had always reciprocated his secret love.
Neither one had any idea what could or should come from the relationship, and both prayed that the Lord would either swell or temper the
flame between them according to His will. Eventually, after their feelings
grew, rather than diminished, they were forced to address the question of
whether their relationship should be taken to the next level. If her execution were to be carried out, despite all that the powerful leaders and voices
in the nation were doing to see her sentence commuted to life (and, many
hoped, to secure her freedom after that), then Brown would be forced to
stand back and watch the love of his life die. He didn't let this prospect
deter him. He believed that the Lord had told him directly, "If you'll walk
through the circumstances, I'll deliver Karla into your arms."[378] They both
felt their love was based on mutual excitement for the Lord and didn't
feel that they needed to live together, or even physically touch, in order to
enjoy the relationship they believed God had put together. So, in August
of 1994,[379] Brown proposed. The two were married on June 24, 1995,
with the service held in two locations, miles apart, at precisely the same
time by proxy; each had to state the marriage vows to a stand-in spouse.
Immediately after the ceremony, Brown traveled in a vehicle decorated
with a "Just Married" sign to death row to visit his new bride. They celebrated their marriage through visiting-room Plexiglas. Brown and Tucker
both received some support for their relationship, but they also lost a few
friends and ministerial connections as a result of their decision to marry—
the union of a prison minister and a death-row inmate a forbidden idea,
for some. This hurt them both, but they didn't let it dampen their happiness. Tucker had given away her body to many people who had asked for
it throughout her young life, but nobody had ever asked for just her heart
or her mind—so it was her heart and mind that she followed into that
proxy wedding ceremony.

Brown, who later shared his thoughts on the matter, said: "People think I'm crazy.... That's fine. Karla and I touch in ways most people can never understand."[380] He was so convinced that the Lord would deliver Tucker into his arms in a literal sense that he bought a condominium for them to live in upon her freedom.[381]

Tucker's dates with death were postponed several times as a result of appeals, stays of execution, and new evidentiary hearings. Many wanted a retrial for Tucker based on her being under the influence of drugs at the time of the incident, and also based on much evidence that indicated the crime had not been premeditated. Many attempted interventions included one on January 17, 1998, called the "Save Karla" rally, wherein a letter was read by a fellow inmate who revealed that Tucker was "responsible for many of our [the death row inmates'] conversions [to Christ]—and the positive changes in our lives."[382] Chaplain Linda Strom's husband, Dallas, promised to blow a shofar (a ram's horn, blown to announce either war or worship; Dallas would have meant it as worship) upon Tucker's pardon, a gift that everyone wanted to see bestowed on Tucker in her final days.

Yet, despite the outrage and efforts of so many who opposed Tucker's death, the state held to the original sentencing. This decision has, many times throughout history, been viewed more as a political stance than as a personal judgment against Tucker. If the state had allowed a commutation, there would be those who saw it as showing pity toward a female who was young, claiming Christianity, and physically beautiful, rather than pity on a woman who had done something wrong and was truly sorry. What kind of example would that set? Tucker's execution would be carried out.

Just before the scheduled execution, Tucker was interviewed again in a recording that was broadcast all over the nation. The question on everyone's mind was whether she was fighting for her life. She said she was not. She answered that those who follow Christ are not in any eternal way affected by an earthly death, and that it was only the case for Christ that she was now fighting for. If the Lord willed for her to be finished in this life, then she was ready for death. Based on the justice system of this world, she deserved death; she knew this. She had heard the angry words of some of the people whose lives she had destroyed and affected, and she said she understood those who spoke out against her in their pain, and would not seek to minimize their rightful feelings. There was nothing she could do to change the past or undo her crimes, so if her death would bring the victims' family members and loved ones closure and peace, she was ready to take that step, and she wished them harmony.[383] Regarding those who might not believe she deserved divine redemption, she understood where they were coming from and regarded their thoughts and opinions with grace and acceptance. She ended her statement with, "But who *does* deserve forgiveness?"[384]

Tucker herself had made several attempts to achieve commutation from death to a life sentence, but everyone who knew her knew very well that her main reasoning behind these actions were for those who wanted, *needed*, her to stick around. In her book, Strom said, "I knew Karla wasn't fighting to save her life. The primary reason she was going through the commutation process was for countless other lives."[385] Tucker shared the following words:

> God is doing something so big we can't even begin to know what it is. It is for His glory. I remember when Gideon was facing a vast multitude. God said, "Cut your army down to three hundred because when you go out there, I want people to know it's Me who wins the battle." In my life or in my death I want that, too. We don't know what He is going to do. I think one of the reasons He doesn't show us is because He only gives us grace for today. He will give us grace to do what we need to do. He is moving in a lot of lives out there. He knows whether He is going to reach more lives through this happening or through stopping it. That's okay, isn't it? That's what we want.[386]

At the execution, there were two viewing rooms: one for the family of the victims, and one for the family of Tucker. When all of those in attendance had filed in and taken their places on their rightful side, Ron Carlson was standing in the viewing room reserved for those who were a part of Tucker's family: He was there as a friend of Tucker, not as her victim. Dana Brown stood next to Carlson. Beverly Lowry wasn't related to Tucker, so she had to remain outside the execution building, but she was there, as close as she was allowed to be. As per Tucker's personal and passionate request, Linda Strom was with a few others in her prison ministry circle in Gatesville's death row, offering comfort and prayer to Tucker's prison sisters. At exactly six o'clock, the scheduled beginning of Tucker's execution, Strom and the others joined the inmates in singing "The Battle Hymn of the Republic."

Tucker's last words were:

> I would like to say to all of you—the Thornton family and Jerry Dean's family—that I am so sorry. I hope God will give you peace with this. (She looked at her husband.) Baby, I love you. (She looked at Ronald Carlson.) Ron, give Peggy a hug for me. (She looked at all present, weeping and smiling.) Everybody has been so good to me. I love all of you very much. I am going to be face to face with Jesus now.... [T]hank all of you so much. You have been so good to me. I love all of you very much. I will see you all when you get there. I will wait for you.[387]

On February 3, 1998, Karla Faye Tucker was executed by lethal injection. She was the first woman in 135 years to be executed in the state of Texas, and only the second woman in all of the United States to be executed since the reinstatement of the death penalty in America in 1976.

Tucker's executioner, Fred Allen, had seen and carried out one hundred and twenty executions prior to this one. He was pro capital punishment. After the death of Karla Faye Tucker and his having observed the person behind the prison clothes before she died, "he suffered an emotional breakdown. He resigned his job, giving up his pension, and changed his position on the death penalty."[388] Others affected by Tucker's situation showed gentle actions that were just as unusual for their positions. For example, Strom shares of a communal moment between all at the prison during and after the execution: "I was deeply touched by the guards' kindness," she said. "A gray-uniformed officer placed a hand on the shoulder of a weeping inmate. Another sat down in a pew beside one of the women and spoke a word of hope."[389] She also said she saw "several guards wiping tears from their eyes."[390]

Because she had been visiting Tucker's prison sisters on death row, Strom had not yet received the word regarding the exact minute of Tucker's death. The scheduled time to begin the procedure had been six o'clock at a Huntsville facility (a completely separate location from the Gatesville facility), and that was all she knew. As Strom and a friend were driving past the prison chapel that night at 6:45, they looked out the windows thoughtfully, strangely, looking for a "sign" that Tucker had, in fact, been taken home to be with the Lord. In Strom's account:

> Suddenly the emergency lights in the chapel came on, lighting up the entire altar area. The cross was illuminated as I'd never seen it before. (No one was ever able to explain why this happened, since the electricity in the prison was still functioning.) Then [back inside] I heard the phone ring in the chaplain's office. A moment later Andy [the chaplain] came to the altar where I was standing. Slowly he announced, "At 6:45 P.M. Karla Faye Tucker went home to be with her Lord and Savior, Jesus Christ."[391]

At this same time, Dallas Strom went tearfully to his hearth at home, retrieved his shofar, and blew a commemorative call to worship.

As Strom visited Tucker's grave in the emotional days following the execution, she thought of a verse that conveyed a profound truth. John 12:24: "Verily, verily, I say unto you, Except a corn of wheat fall into the ground and die, it abideth alone: but if it die, it bringeth forth much fruit." She was reminded that sometimes people have to die in order to bring about their greatest usefulness in the kingdom of God.

INTERVIEW with Ron Carlson

In order to gain further insight on Tucker's case, the publishing team behind this book reached out to Ron Carlson, telling him about the project. Upon hearing about our mission, he immediately and graciously agreed to be interviewed. We sent him a list of questions, asked by several people in our publishing group as well as Donna Howell.

BETWEEN DONNA HOWELL, DEFENDER PUBLISHING GROUP AND RON CARLSON, YOUNGER BROTHER OF DEBORAH THORNTON, VICTIM OF KARLA FAYE TUCKER AND DANIEL GARRETT EMAILS BETWEEN JUNE 17–28, 2014

The story of how you came to forgive Karla Faye Tucker after the murder of your sister (and maternal figure of your life) is a powerful one. Did you also come to forgive Daniel (Danny) Garrett? Had you ever gone to see him also? If so, what transpired?

Yes, I did forgive Daniel Ryan Garrett also, as well as Elbert Smiley Homan, the man who murdered my natural father, William Gerald List. I did not have the same opportunity to visit with Mr. Garrett as I did with Karla and Elbert. Mr. Garrett died from liver problems while awaiting execution in prison in 1991. I did write a letter to him explaining that I did, indeed, forgive him for the death of my sister. (Danny was the one who left that pickaxe in my sister's heart.) I wrote to him saying "I forgive you," and I shared some Scripture verses that explained my thought patterns and how they were based on the teachings of Christ as well as other things within God's Word. I did not hear back from Danny. About six months later, I received a warm but brief letter from his lawyer. He stated that Danny did not know how to respond to my letter, but that he appreciated that there were people in this world that could process things this way, it gave him hope, he felt comfort throughout all that had happened, and that I probably would have heard back from Danny at some point in time, but that he had passed on.

The lawyer ended the letter by personally thanking me for doing what I did, and that he thought that my actions and my beliefs brought a sense of peace to Mr. Garrett. From what I understand, Danny died not very long after he conveyed this to his lawyer. I wish I could have met the man, but evidently God did not open that doorway for me.

When you first went to see Karla, you knew before you saw her that you were there to forgive her, but you likely had no idea that the two of you would become such close friends, correct? How did that come about?

When I went to see Karla, my intentions were to simply forgive her and then go my separate way. She was the first of many that I would contact the way I did. You might say that she was the testing of the waters so to speak. I had no experience in this, and I was walking in faith, trusting that God would help me work through all of this. I recall how the meeting took place. I had been on the phone that day and I was talking to Willis Ash. Mr. Ash was a former employee of my natural father, William List. Mac (Mr. Ash) said to me over the phone, "You know that she is in town today, don't you?" I told him that I did, and he said, "Well, you ought to go over there and give her a piece of your mind." Mac had no idea where I was in my walk with Jesus, and frankly neither did I. All of this was so new to me.

I went downtown to the Harris County Jail. Karla Faye Tucker was in town for an evidentiary hearing. Normally, you would have to be on a visiting list in order to see someone in prison, but if that individual is in the "county lockup," you can simply go to the jail and request to see them. So I did just that. I went to the jail and made my way to the twelfth floor. I filled out a slip of paper and gave them my driver's license. Next thing I know, I see Karla Faye Tucker walking up to a glass. I then walked over to the glass and picked up a phone that we could talk on. She spoke defensively in response to my sudden visit, asking who I was. I responded "I am the brother of Deborah." She said the same thing again, but her tone of voice changed dramatically. She spoke softly and with hesitation. "Who…are you?" I again replied by saying "I am the brother of Deborah."

At that point she began to cry. In the midst of her tears, I said, "Karla, for whatever comes out of this; I just want you to know that I forgive you and that I don't hold anything against you." At that point, I felt like a great weight had been lifted off of my shoulders. All that hatred and anger that I had stored up over all those years was taken away from me. I felt a sense of calmness and peace. About that time, the guards saw what was going on. They were preparing to pull us both out of there. But Karla waved them off and said, "Everything's alright, leave us alone." After she regained her composure we talked briefly. She asked me for my address and phone number. She wanted to know if she could call as she had phone privileges there at the county jail. I gave her both my phone number and my address (for the home I still live in to this day). That action is taboo in most prison ministry settings. Warnings are very plain to not give out pertinent and revealing personal information. But all of *that* comes from man, and I believed this was a GOD thing.

We spent the next ten minutes or so of the fifteen-minute visit trying to learn about each other. We both promised to keep in touch by writing letters and calling when we could. Both of us held true to those promises.

This took place in late '91 or early '92. I can't recall exactly. As I look back now, I initially doubted Karla's sincerity, as well as her so-called "Christian faith." However, as I, myself, was only just becoming a new believer, I did not understand the power of God. I have only an inkling of that understanding today. From that day on until February 3, 1998, I kept in touch with Karla Faye.

What did you feel the moment that you told Karla that you forgave her, when you heard yourself utter those words aloud?

As I stated previously, I felt like a great weight had been lifted off of my shoulders. The pain, the hatred, and the anger went away. I actually felt compassion for Karla Faye Tucker. I realized that she was no different from me. She was not that "monster" that the media, politicians, lawyers, and pro-death penalty people portray. Rather, she was a human being who simply made a mistake. If you look at it from a Christian viewpoint, I saw a sinner. God's Word instructs us to hate the sin but love the sinner. One might say that my actions and reactions are Scripture-based and follow what the Word of God says. All I know is that I simply surrendered to God when I got saved. I asked Him to take the pain and the hate away. It was only when I forgave that God answered that prayer.

Was the nature of your relationship with Karla ever romantic?

Funny you should ask that. Karla Faye Tucker was a "VERY" attractive young lady. She did apply makeup very well and appeared to be a very beautiful person both physically and spiritually. However, I did NOT at any time have any type of romantic or sexual thoughts or acts throughout all of the time I knew Karla Faye.

We know that your story of forgiveness toward Karla has inspired many, but not everyone in your immediate circle supported your decision to forgive. What was the reaction of those individuals, and have they come to accept this since?

Well, each individual has handled it differently. Some have yet to accept this. Others accepted it, but did not agree with me. Some claimed they accepted it, but in the end you could see that their words were hollow and untrue as shown by their actions over time. One of my cousins who was close to me for a long time no longer communicates with me. However, her mother (my aunt) still does and respects me for what I did. She never said one way or the other how she felt about it, but I think she understands. She, too, is a Christian. My nephew doesn't understand. He won't speak to me, and refuses to have any sort of relationship with his uncle. Most of the family has accepted me now, but there are exceptions to that. Time has a way of healing things, and God has a way of working on people, too.

Almost all of my friends tell me I did the right thing and that they respect me. Many have told me that they could not have forgiven in this way, that I must have been so strong to forgive. Frankly, I am a weak individual. However, I gather my strength and courage from God Almighty. He is the source of my faith, courage, and inspiration.

At the time of Karla's execution, the state of Texas would not allow anyone into the viewing rooms other than family of the victims, family of Karla, and an extremely small list of others on official business. You were allowed to be present at the time because you were the brother of the victim, Deborah Thornton. When it was time to file in, you chose to stand in the viewing room alongside those who were present for Karla. Why did you make this decision?

The last time I saw Karla was in January of 1998. We both felt that her execution was imminent. We had agreed previously that if she was ever executed, I would be there standing for the Lord. The last thing Karla said to me as they led her off in chains just before I exited the building—I heard her call out, "Ron, I love you!" I responded by saying, "I love you too Karla!" I still carry that love of her today.

On February 3, 1998, at 6:45 p.m. Central Standard Time, I witnessed the execution of Karla Faye Tucker. I stood in the room reserved for Karla's friends and family. I was there in that room as per "her request." The prison system could not deny her request, so I was granted the opportunity to be in that room rather than the "victims' family room" where my former brother-in-law Richard Thornton was alongside my nephew (and only child of Deborah) and Richard's daughter Katy. In doing so, I became the "first known victim" to actually witness an execution in the friends and family room of the inmate.

I actually thought that God wanted me there to comfort and reassure Karla as a forgiving Christian. In the end, it worked out that both Karla and I ministered to one another. Karla Faye was an inspiration to my faith, just as I was an inspiration to hers.

I had hoped and prayed for "closure." That is a term that a lot of people use. But it didn't happen. All it accomplished was that a whole new set of victims was created: Dana Brown, who was Karla Faye Tucker's husband; Kary Weeks, who is Karla Faye's sister; and her grandmother and the rest of the family.

On February 6, I attended Karla's funeral in a closed setting where she is buried. Her grandfather walked up to me, introduced himself to me and said the words: "Thank you for being here and for everything that you have done. You are the only person in all of this that has made any sense to me."

We have heard that Karla passed on very peacefully, and with a song on her lips. Do you remember what song she was singing or humming at that moment?

One local television reporter stated that she hummed. What he heard was the sound of her lungs exhaling all of the air because of how the lethal injection works. All of that was explained to the witnesses before the execution took place. I believe she was praying, and this is what she seems to have said, "Father, into your hand I commend my spirit." That is exactly what Jesus said the day He was crucified. But Karla strived to be Christ like in every way. It would not surprise me one bit for her to utter that with her dying breath. I watched her die that night with tears streaming from my eyes, just as they are now. She died with a smile on her face looking straight up to heaven. She never closed her eyes. I believe she went straight into the hands of Almighty God and is there in heaven now, holding hands with my sister Deborah and praising God every time I tell this story.

Like I have said over and over, this is a God thing. There is no way around it. This is not normal. It has to come from God Almighty!

The position that you have been in is a delicate one, and it is unusual to forgive someone who has hurt you so personally as to take the life of your sister. Holding on to the anger inside against someone that has devastated you can destroy you from the inside out. This is according to your own testimony, and nobody knows this better than you, a man who lost both his sister and his father to murderous acts only a year apart. Many more remain traumatized by the hurt that others have caused against them and their loved ones. What advice might you pass on to another who is in the midst of this pain and holding on to this hurt?

You have to search your own heart, try to form a bridge between yourself and God, and simply trust and obey Him. If you lean on your own understanding, it becomes very difficult to do this sort of thing. I am not saying it was easy to forgive in the way that I have. As a matter of fact, it was the hardest thing I have ever done. But I do know that if you truly mean it, and you are willing to give it to God and lay it down at the cross, He will take it from you just as His Word says.

Christ, Himself, said we are to lose our life, and to pick up our cross and follow Him. The old must pass away so the new can come in. Unless you are willing to submit to God and allow Him to lead you through all of this, the pain and the hurt will continue. I dealt with it for eight years of my life. It almost killed me. It was not until I asked God to take over and gave it to Him that He gave me the courage to walk in faith and forgive those that have hurt me. When I forgave them, they were no longer the monsters who destroyed my family, but rather sinners, like me. I am a sinner; I want to be saved by Christ through His blood that was shed at Calvary for the remission of our sin.

The Lord's Prayer plainly says "Forgive us our trespasses AS we FORGIVE those WHO trespass against us." If I want to be forgiven, I NEED to forgive. I don't know about you, but I need to be forgiven, too. I have sinned and fallen short just like everyone else in this world. I am simply a sinner saved by grace. Simply trust in Him and allow Him to do His magic in your life as He did in mine.

If God can do this sort of thing in my life, imagine what He can do in yours.

What advice might you pass on to another like Karla out there who might be reading this book—someone who feels remorse for what he or she has done, and feels that God's forgiveness is so far away? Will the Lord forgive anyone who is sincerely seeking, no matter what he or she has done?

God is not a one-sided individual. We are His creation. He wants His creation to live life to the fullest, no matter what. We are all sinners; therefore, none of us are any better or worse than another. We are all the same in God's eyes. Black, white, yellow, brown, purple, etc. It doesn't matter. We are all God's children. All have sinned except for one, and He walked on water.

And all of us will do things that are wrong. Some of us get caught and end up in prison. Others are luckier, and get to live outside those prison walls. But we are all still sinners.

God knew that Adam and Eve would do what they did in the garden. He made it so their sin would be passed down through the generations to each and every one of us. We can't help but be a sinner and be imperfect as long as we live in these fleshly shells called "bodies." But through Christ we can be redeemed.

Man may not see it that way, but God will.

Who else in your life has been touched by your encounters with Karla? Has your relationship with her opened doors for you to minister to others?

From what I have learned by the amount of books, magazines and also one particular DVD that I am aware of, I would venture to say that my encounters with Karla Faye and the other's has been heard around the world. I have been told more than once by different individuals that the

DVD, *The Power of Forgiveness: The Story of Karla Faye Tucker*, is being used around the world and happens to be one of the best materials available on the subject of forgiveness. I have personally observed how the viewing of this documentary in a prison setting has opened men and women's eyes to the power of forgiveness and a relationship with God Almighty. I know that all of this glory comes from and belongs to Him.

Many doors have opened before me. Some of them I did not walk through, of which I now regret, for now they are closed. But God is not finished with me, nor is He finished with this work by any means. It will not end until Christ returns.

I want the world to know what I have learned. I really believe that forgiveness is the key. That if you can forgive, you can truly LOVE one another. Jesus was once asked which was the greatest commandment. He said, "Love the Lord God with all your heart, soul, and your mind and then to love your neighbor as yourself." He then said, "If you do all of that, then you have fulfilled all of the law and the commandments."

Is there anything else you would like to share with a reading audience while you have the platform to do so?

Simply take the time to read the Bible, especially the first four books of the New Testament and Ecclesiastes. The book of Psalms is comforting to the soul.

Don't trust in what "man" teaches you about God. Rather, allow the Spirit of the Lord to enter into your life and let Him teach you about what the Word of God really means. This is what changed me. For years people told me, "You need Jesus in your life." I lived thirty-five years before I got down on my knees and asked Christ to be my "Lord and Savior." Think about what God has done in my life. If God can do this sort of thing in my life, imagine what He can do in yours!

Finally, the last thing I can say is this: All of us make up the "Body of Christ." Jesus taught that we should reach out to those who are sick, in prison, and so forth. By doing that, we are improving the "body." We can either help or hurt, and those are personal decisions that each one of us will be held accountable for on Judgment Day. It is important to understand what the blood of Christ did for us all when He was crucified. It is truly "walking in faith." I give "thanks" to almighty God for all of this, for without Him, none of this would be possible. He is truly my source of strength and the author of my faith.

———

Ron Carlson grew up in the Gahanna, Ohio, area with his sister, Deborah (Debbie). Although a former successful machinist, he is now disabled. Around 1990, he asked the Lord to come into his life, and has been a new creature in Christ ever since. He now lives with his wife, also named Debbie, in the state of Texas.

TED BUNDY [392]

Ann Rule, a crime journalist and part-time volunteer for the Seattle Crisis Clinic hotline, was waiting for her fellow crisis-hotline operator to arrive at his desk next to hers. The two made a fantastic team, and she didn't think she could have handpicked a more suitable man to work with at this tiresome and weary job. She liked him. Everyone did.

His reputation was that of an upright man who would listen, watch, and respond to those in need around him. When a thief snatched a purse from a woman and took off with it, he had chased him down, seeing that the purse and all its contents were returned to the woman. For this, he had received a commendation from the Seattle Police Department. [393] When a three-year-old girl whom nobody else was watching began to drown in a lake on the north end of Seattle, he had jumped in and saved her like a hero. [394] When he had moved in with an older couple, one of whom was ill, he paid his rent faithfully and asked for nothing in return as he cared for both of them, kept up the house maintenance and repairs, did their chores, and tended their garden.[395] And of course, when it came to his lady friend, he always remembered special occasions, sending flowers to both her and her daughter from a previous marriage—a little girl he was just as devoted to as any biological father could hope to be.[396] People were always grateful and impressed by his character, but they were no longer surprised when he set another distinguished, yet humble, example for all others around him to live by.

That was just Ted.

Ted Bundy.

The perfect citizen.

Arriving for his shift at the desk next to Ann Rule's, he got straight to his duties, lifting the receiver from the ringing telephone and listening to the distraught voices on the other end. His voice was calm, gentle, encouraging, and never rushed. Those answering the hotline never knew when what initially seemed like a nonemergency phone call—older women wishing to remember the good old days of Seattle city, people who were sick and miserable, or regretful men and women who had once again had too much to drink—could turn into a suicide or violence call. The phone counselors had to expect the unexpected, be ready for anything, care about every person who called in, and hold an elevated level of patience and tenderness despite what could sometimes be extreme panic.

When an occasional suicide call did come in, Ann Rule and Ted Bundy had developed wordless ways of communicating with each other to flag the emergency. Thus, while the one stayed on the line with the caller, who was often showing signs of an overdose, the other would get in touch with emergency personnel. Even with the most modern technology in 1971, it took about an hour to trace a call. The minutes Rule and Bundy spent waiting for help to reach the caller were intense, charged with a sense of panic until they heard the audible evidence of the break-in on the other end. That was when a paramedic would retrieve the phone from the caller's hand and let Rule and Bundy know the person still had a heartbeat and was being taken to an emergency room. Thanks to Bundy and his kindness, warmth, and understanding for callers in distress, many lives were saved.

Rule considered herself lucky to have a friend with such a moral core as Bundy.[397] They would be friends for years to come...

Four years later, after the brutal and bloody murders and disappearances of many young and beautiful college girls in Washington, Rule took a second and third glance at the composite sketch of a suspect on the wall of the police station. The man was dangerous and roaming free, prowling for innocent blood like a vulture diving down to take living prey. The wanted man had reportedly been knocking out young girls with a blow to the head and then shoving them into the trunk or the passenger's side of his Volkswagen Bug.

As Rule studied the drawing tacked to the bulletin board, she couldn't ignore its likeness to her gentleman friend and covolunteer She reviewed the facts: The killer called himself "Ted," which was probably a fake name. He drove a car, which, to her knowledge, Bundy did not have. Certainly, this crazed lunatic who was reported to have a British accent could not be the up-and-coming, southern-drawl psychology/law student and governor's assistant Ted that Rule knew. No doubt about that. The very thought of that dramatic and outlandish comparison was the most ridiculous Dr. Jekyll-Mr. Hyde assumption anyone could make of pure-hearted Bundy.

But, as a crime journalist, her brain was always connecting the dots and ruling out the obvious only by official means. So, she reluctantly placed a call—just to put her mind at ease.

When Seattle Homicide Detective Dick Reed picked up on the other end, Rule explained that the reason behind her call was pretty much nothing, but she wanted to know if Reed could run a check through the Department of Motor Vehicles to see if her friend owned a car.

"His name is Ted Bundy. B-u-n-d-y."[398]

She waited patiently for a response.

Then it came.

"Theodore Robert Bundy. 4123 12th Avenue N.E. Would you believe a 1968 bronze Volkswagen Bug?"[399]

Mr. Hyde was no longer far-fetched.

VICTIMS OF THE STRANGE CASE OF DR. JEKYLL AND MR. HYDE

In each of us there are two natures. If this primitive duality of man—good and evil—can be housed in separate identities, life will be relieved of all that is unbearable. It is the curse of mankind that these polar twins should be constantly struggling.
—Dr. Jekyll, from the opening scene of *Jekyll & Hyde: The Musical*[400]

In 1886, Robert Louis Stevenson wrote a novel, *The Strange Case of Dr. Jekyll and Mr. Hyde*. The tale that piqued the interest of readers worldwide for well over a century to come was of a scientist who wishes to separate good from evil within the heart of man via scientific dabbling, with the intention to eventually rid the world of all immorality. The scientist, Dr. Jekyll, a kind and gentle man, uses himself as the guinea pig on which the experiments will be performed. As the experiments go awry, from within Jekyll rises an unexpected evil that, over time, emerges as a separate identity: Edward Hyde. This personality commits every act of wickedness imaginable, marauding, raping, pillaging, murdering, and terrorizing the residents of London. Jekyll remains unaware in the beginning that the crimes committed are by his own alternate personality while he is in his altered state. Eventually, as Jekyll begins to run out of the ingredients for the potions and tonics, evil completely dominates good, and Jekyll surrenders to becoming Hyde permanently.

Now, in 2014, more than one hundred and twenty years later, the tale is still popular, being told more often than many world classics. It has been adapted into at least eleven stage plays and musicals, thirty-two films, two radio theatricals, six television shows and/or series, five famous songs and/or albums, and twenty-three spoofs/parodies—plus, it has been mentioned in other works of fiction at least fifteen times.[401]

Success of this magnitude speaks of more than just a public interest in a good story. There is a *reason* so many people stop what they are doing in their crazy-busy lives and pause for a while in front of the television or stage to experience yet another rendition of the classic saga.

In the case of Jekyll and Hyde, the beast lurking within is a scientific anomaly, of sorts, as the quote on the previous page suggests, "housed" in a separate identity. Dr. Jekyll, an otherwise good and pure-hearted man who likely had no such murderous evil on the inside to begin with, loses "executive control" over his body and his mind, only to regain it later, not knowing what events took place while he had temporarily blacked out (much like a chemically induced version of the Dissociative Identity Disorder [DID] discussed in the Sean Sellers case study).

Today, Dr. Jekyll would likely land himself a diagnosis of clinically insane or DID (depending on the details of the case, his childhood, and the psychology experts' consideration for the intentional chemical tampering that led to the induction of said other personality), and the killer would be considered dangerous, but to the courts and the public, he probably would not be found guilty of his wrongs, assuming he had a good attorney with "innocent by reason of insanity" in mind for his defense.

But, obviously, this story did not actually happen. Dr. Jekyll was not a real man, and yet there is an underlying psychological fascination that continues to follow him around with such attention that it is as if he *were* real. Why is that? Is there something about the story that leads us to tune into it over and over again, hoping that *this* time the scientist will break new ground and ride off into the sunset with the girl (in some renditions)? Or, does the fascination have more to do with the fact that every person who has ever lived (except for Christ, Himself) has both good and evil within, and the two natures are always fighting for dominance? Does this plot intrigue because it points to the fact that each of us has something in common with Dr. Jekyll, therefore we understand his plight simply because we're human? Could it be that people are lured to the story by the concept that these two contradictory sides could effectively be separated, allowing the bad nature to indulge without consequence during the night and the good nature to engage in kind deeds and earn its warm fuzzies during the day?

These thoughts sound preposterous when simplified to this degree, but, if we're all being honest, we have probably all felt this way at one point or another. The desire to sin without consequence, though varying from one individual to the next and from one extreme category of sin to the next, exists within us all. The battle of good versus evil rages in *every* person, and temptation can be anything: lust, greed, vanity, gluttony, laziness, rage, envy, pride, etc. They are all sin, and they are all "deadly."[402] If we didn't, in our humanity, feel the desire to do something bad, temptation wouldn't exist.

To struggle is to be human.

This is our Jekyll versus Hyde.

This was Ted Bundy.

As discussed previously regarding serial killer Aileen Wournos and "Pickaxe Killer" Karla Faye Tucker, when a visual adaptation of a murderer's story is brought before public scrutiny from the *cutthroat's perspective*, the acceptance of one's evil acts is delivered far differently to an audience of entertainment than to an audience of that day's cold, journalistic, news-channel headlines. Clearly, the Jekyll and Hyde story is not in every way an adaptation of Bundy's life, and this comparison should not be taken to suggest that. But, the Jekyll/Hyde story has often been used as a basis of comparison to people much like him, people who lead two dramatically "separate" lives.

When Bundy was Jekyll, he was *very* Jekyll. Everyone loved that man and had the highest expectations of what he could accomplish. As far as most people knew, until his sudden and unexpected arrest, he had been on his way to becoming the next president! He was the ideal student, classmate, citizen, babysitter, caregiver, and guy next door.

Yet when Bundy was Hyde, he was *very* Hyde. He plotted out his steps carefully, snatched the victims away—sometimes in a crowd in the middle of a sunny day at the park by luring them away and other times by grabbing them in a dark alley at night—and killed them without ever feeling shame.

Ted Bundy came as close to being a literal personification of Jekyll and Hyde as anyone ever has been, but Bundy was *real*. His Hyde took pleasure in unleashing his rage and lust, just like the classic character, but there is *one crucial difference*: Jekyll invited the beast haphazardly, having only set out to improve the nature of mankind. His effort simply spiraled desperately out of control. Dr. Jekyll never had full control over himself in order to fix what he'd done or discontinue the evil as a result of chemistry (and in some adaptations, alchemy). *Bundy invited the beast knowingly.* He fully intended to feed his Hyde, completely aware of what this other personality within him was capable of doing. Bundy could have gotten help or stopped his evil…but he chose not to. That brings to mind what the apostle Paul had to say about the inner conflict caused by his own, competing natures:

> For we know that the law is spiritual: but I am carnal, sold under sin. For that which I do I allow not: for what I would, that I do I not; but what I hate, that do I. If then I do that which I would not, I consent unto the law that it is good. Now then it is no more I that do it, but sin that dwelleth in me. (Romans 7:14–17, KJV)

For academic comparison, let us look at this same verse, quoted from the KJV above, and here as translated in the New Living Translation:

> The law is good, then. The trouble is not with the law but within me, because I am sold into slavery, with sin as my master. I don't understand myself at all, for I really want to do what is right, but I don't do it. Instead, I do the very thing I hate. I know perfectly well that what I am doing is wrong, and my bad conscience shows that I agree that the law is good. But I can't help myself, because it is sin inside me that makes me do these evil things. (Romans 7:14–17, NLT)

Our actions always involve making choices, and unbelievable strength is often required to make the right ones. Bundy is a famous example of a person who shows a great lack of willpower associated with a lust for blood that normal people can't even comprehend. And, just like the character from the classic tale, Bundy had everyone fooled, with a kind and gentle man appearing on the outside as an exoskeleton covering the wicked demons within. The theme of his story, other than serial murder, is the unbelievable tale of a man living two lives that produce opposite fruits that cannot in any conceivable way originate from the same person. Likewise, Bundy's good fruit could never occupy the same space as his bad fruit, and everyone who knew him (and many who didn't) said as much, which was why it seemed impossible for Bundy to be guilty of the terrible crimes the investigators said he had done.

But he *was* guilty. He very much was.

The Deathbed Conversion of Jekyll

To this author's knowledge, there hasn't yet been an adaptation of the Jekyll/Hyde story that relates a conversion to Christ. However, almost every modern version features a moment at the end when the true Dr. Jekyll steps away from the beast's control for one final moment, unveiling himself long enough to leave those he loves with a memory of the man who sought their forgiveness and deliverance from his own evil. Although this is a secularized portrayal of redemption, the idea of a spiritual and literal escape from one's oppressive and dominant internal tyrant is clear. And in Jekyll's case, his "I'm so sorry, I never meant to turn into this, I love you all, forgive me" moment is celebrated.

Can people—whether serving an animal they awakened in themselves because they were swept away by something bigger than themselves, *or* they chose to selfishly feed the animal, no matter the cost to those around them—be saved in the final hour?

Not only was the thief on the cross next to Jesus forgiven in his final hour, but his conversion has been *celebrated* as an illustration of how God extends grace. It is not seen as a shameful, last-minute, cash-in story like the explanation so many have tried to peg onto more modern examples of deathbed conversions.

Karen Edmisten, author of *Deathbed Conversions: Finding Faith at the Finish Line*, dove into this question, addressing the unfairness of the concept, and transparently revealing the thoughts many of us seem to have at one point or another. To quote from the profound first chapter of her book:

Deathbed conversions sound suspiciously like loopholes, like unfair, unaccounted for, last-minute ducks inside the pearly gates....

The thought of a deathbed conversion inspires a host of reactions, usually strong ones. Some people relish the idea of last-minute U-turns. They're heartened by these conversion stories or know someone who knew someone who experienced finish-line contrition. They love to hear about others' spiritual treks, and sigh with satisfaction that lost sheep have been found. After all, an honest-to-goodness deathbed conversion offers everything good storytelling demands: drama, pathos and sin, despair, chaos, confusion, love, enlightenment, and, finally, redemption.

On the other hand, there is the Smirk-and-Snort Contingent. Such skeptics don't believe that genuine conversion occurs late in life. They don't believe people can authentically change, or they suspect duplicitous, mercenary motives. Some chafe at the unfairness factor. Why should the rest of us kill ourselves being "good" all our lives when those lifelong slackers get a final-hour free ticket into heaven? Who let them cut in line anyway?

Living one's entire life without God, though, is hardly a free ticket. A true deathbed convert doesn't rub his hands together at the final hour, snickering, "Hey, I pulled a fast one on the Big Guy!" Rather, he sees the tragedy of a wasted lifetime, the pain of his prolonged denial, and the foolishness of his stubborn *Non Serviam*. The only glee is the relief and gratitude that God's mercy is offered and poured out to us until the final and bitter end [whether or not we think we have earned it or deserve it].

Because we can never know what is happening in another person's heart and mind, we don't have an inkling who is quietly seeking God, or how long they may have been doing so.... We can't see for certain when or how someone has begun inching toward Him. We can size up a person's outward actions: we know what is objectively sinful or intrinsically evil. But there's a reason that the Church never definitively answers the question, "Who is in hell?" While the Church does, through the process of canonization, highlight examples of holiness for the faithful to emulate, [it] never makes a pronouncement about who has been damned. That's because we can't know the state of another person's soul....

Oscar Wilde...said, "One's real life is so often the life that one does not lead." Real life—our interior, mental, emotional, and spiritual processes—is at the heart of conversion.[403]

The end of Bundy's life generated a huge public reaction, and not for his proclamations of Christian convictions, which from the masses received little more than a scoff and a smirk. In his final days, Bundy spent so much of his time trying to figure out how to prolong his life and delay the execution by electric chair by claiming his innocence that very little documentation exists of his conversion story. That was never the central focus of the media's attention.

The event that sent overnight and worldwide attention to this sinner's claims of having entered into the body of Christ was when Dr. James Dobson (acclaimed founder of Focus on the Family Ministries and author of a great number of best-selling books in the Christian market) agreed to jump on a plane with a camera crew and grant Bundy's request to give a final interview just hours before his date with "Old Sparky" (Florida's electric chair). The purpose of this interview, according to Bundy (who ignored hundreds of requests from other members of the media for a final interview), was not to give a Christian testimony of a changed man, but to, before the world, finally admit that he was guilty of the crimes for which he had been convicted (since he had been claiming innocence until that day) to try to take full responsibility for the murders and issue a profound warning to the country...

Did Dr. Jekyll unveil himself from beneath the beast's control for one final moment?

The Hyde Side

What you are about to read is not the compelling story of a man who made some mistakes, lived the rest of his life trying to right his wrongs, and brought the beauty of a dynamic ministry out of the ashes of a prison cell. You are not about to read the story of a criminal who found forgiveness from those whose lives he damaged. There is no stage in this case study upon which any reasonable person would want to defend the bad guy as one who had been given little other chance in this world but to become a cold-blooded killer. On the contrary, in the end, this man was alone, unforgiven by the world, having become one of the most hated serial killers in history. He died as he lived: lonely, scared, tragic, and grasping. He rejected most interventions that might have contributed to his life taking a morally upright turn, he embraced and fed a polluted and defiled appetite, and then he spent the rest of his life trying to duck out of the punishment he earned. He fooled people with many different masks, took advantage of people in the worst of ways, and, when it was time to head to the electric chair as the consequence of having conducted such madness, he went like a child to the paddle: fighting against the guards and having to be physically dragged to the straps.

Bundy was, by no exaggeration, incredibly foul and corrupt in the later days that he walked free. To say anything other than the truth where that is concerned would show nothing less than bias or imbalance in a work like this. He was a living, breathing, unbelievable, nightmarish monstrosity.

Some of the details of his murders are too disturbing to be included here; we will hit the surface-level facts about his crimes and skip the graphic particulars.

When his Hyde side emerged, by Bundy's invitation, to plunder the streets, he did so in at least six states. He took the lives of many defenseless and innocent females, most of whom were college students. These women were, in the years before their deaths, prom queens, cheerleaders, musicians, vocalists, artists, karate students, and public service volunteers. Almost all were brunettes who wore their hair long and parted in the middle. Most were slender, athletic, and absolutely, breathtakingly beautiful at the time of their deaths. They were girls with happiness and joy, heartache and troubles. They laughed and cried. They had families. They had been young women (several were underage) who were taken at the peak of their education with nothing but pure, untapped potential ahead.

They lived and loved and thrived—and those who hadn't yet wouldn't be given the chance to.

Bundy killed them all.

In an exclusive interview with Ann Rule's daughter, Leslie Rule, our publishing team asked about those delicate days when she and her mother were watching young girls disappear around them. At the time, Leslie wore her hair the same as those who fell prey to Bundy, and she was pretty enough to turn heads, which put her in the same class as the ideal victim. She gave us the following insight:

> Few teenagers think about their safety, and I was no exception. I was just like the thousands of other girls walking around with long hair parted in the middle. That was the style then, and at least 90 percent of girls wore their hair that way in the 1970s.
>
> I was no more a target than any other female. I've always had a strong sixth sense, and if I got a feeling I shouldn't walk down a particular street, I wouldn't. I have felt that just a few times in my life, and I always pay attention to it.[404]

Unfortunately, many other girls did not. Usually, Bundy's victims' deaths were caused by head trauma, and some, *but not all*, of the victims were found at the crime scene with physical evidence of a lust-driven motive. A small number of the women were found right away (usually in their beds), most of them were not found until long after the murders, and some of them were never found at all.

To this day, nobody knows the final body count, and some believe Bundy started murdering even before his earliest confirmed case. He's not around to talk facts anymore, so all we can do in this case study is document the memory of those who have been confirmed as victims of Bundy's disgracefully contemptible and despicable crimes:

- Karen Sparks (often referred to as "Joni Lenz"; aged 18 at the time); **survived**
- Lynda Ann Healy (aged 21)

- Donna Gail Manson (aged 19)
- Susan Elaine Rancourt (aged 18)
- Roberta Kathleen Parks (aged 22)
- Brenda Carol Ball (aged 22)
- Georgann (often spelled "Georgeann") Hawkins (aged 18)
- Janice Ann Ott (aged 23)
- Denise Marie Naslund (aged 19)
- Nancy Wilcox (aged 16)
- Melissa Anne Smith (aged 17)
- Laura Ann Aime (aged 17)
- Carol DaRonch (aged 18 at the time); **survived**
- Debra Kent (aged 17)
- Caryn Campbell (aged 23)
- Julie Cunningham (aged 26)
- Denise Oliverson (aged 25)
- Lynette Culver (aged 12)
- Susan Curtis (aged 15)
- Margaret Bowman (aged 21)
- Lisa Levy (aged 20)
- Karen Chandler (aged 21 at the time); **survived**
- Kathy Kleiner (aged 21 at the time); **survived**
- Cheryl Thomas (aged 21 at the time); **survived**
- Kimberly Diane Leach (aged 12)

Man or monster?
He was both.

THE BEAST WITHIN THE BOY

From the onset of his life, Bundy would face certain deception. Lies followed him around his whole childhood. His very identity was a mystery kept from him until he sought out the shocking truth after forming suspicions of his own. This would prove an unsettling development in his more sensitive days to come. From birth, a strain would be ever-pressing.

On November 24, 1946, he was born in a home for unwed mothers. For the first several months of his life, he had no home, and was passed around the facility, receiving institutional care, but having no opportunity for developing closeness with a consistent, affectionate mother figure. According to Rule, "The nurturing, cuddling and the bonding, so necessary to an infant's well-being, was put on hold."[405] When he was brought to his first home as Theodore Robert Cowell, he was immediately exposed to an aggressively controlling, loud, and explosive, dictatorial household.

A Perfectly "Normal" Childhood

Samuel Cowell, the man young Bundy would call his father in his earliest years, was a very unstable man—tense, unpredictable, touchy, hotheaded, short-tempered, and addicted to pornography, a large collection of which he kept in the greenhouse. He "was known to be an extremely violent and frightening individual…a man with a maniacal temper who read pornography, [and] who tossed his daughters down the stairs if they slept too late."[406] He was also "known to sadistically spin cats by their tails,"[407] and was referred to as "a tyrannical bully and a bigot who hated blacks, Italians, Catholics, and Jews, [who] beat his wife and the family dog."[408]

Eleanor Cowell, the woman Bundy would call his mother, was chronically affected by severe bouts of "psychotic depression"[409] and panic attacks, and she even sought to treat this unrelenting disorder with electroshock therapy.[410] (She also suffered from agoraphobia, the intense fear of open spaces.[411])

In his toddler years, Bundy came to know these people as his parents. But something told him they weren't his real mother and father, and there was always a mystery that bothered him, even in his earliest of years, that solidified itself intensely within him as a deficiency, a need of belonging. His older sister, Louise, was very kind and treated him with love and affection, befriending him in the less-than-stable atmosphere, but, despite her friendship, what he adopted in his psyche as the "norm" was anything but normal.

Life continued, and Bundy turned two, then three…and before his fourth birthday, he was showing extremely concerning signs in his behavior, alerting those around him that he "was not a well adjusted child."[412] A famously documented event covers the day that his fifteen-year-old aunt was taking a nap and awoke to see her nephew smiling at her while she slept. Every knife from the kitchen cutlery drawer had been arranged in a circle around her body on the bed, blades turned in toward her. She had not been injured, but waking to find knives all around her and a motionless, silent toddler grinning was enough to cause her heart to pound.[413] (This happened several times.[414])

Sister Louise stepped in and removed herself and Bundy from the harmful home situation, taking him to the courthouse and legally changing his last name to "Nelson"[415] just before relocating to Tacoma, Washington, near her uncle, Jack. Bundy was devastated by the move, but since he was only a toddler, he was unable to understand or question why he was being taken away from Sam, his father figure.[416]

Louise Cowell and her little brother, now "Ted Nelson," began a new life in Washington. For Louise, it was a breath of fresh air where her father couldn't oppress and her mother couldn't depress. But for Bundy, it was nothing less than the loss of his parents at just three years old.

Louise and Bundy began attending First Methodist Church, where he went to Sunday school (he would continue to attend this church throughout high school[417]). He didn't specifically dislike the religious instruction, but he retained almost nothing of what he learned about God as a child; his memories centered more on being socially odd and introverted at church. While Louise went to work as a secretary for the Council of Churches, she frequently attended church functions and social events. At one of these events she met a man named Johnnie Culpepper Bundy, a hospital cook she had much in common with. The two hit it off, had a short courtship, and married the following year. When Louise took the last name of Bundy for herself, it was given to little Ted also.[418] Bundy was almost five when he watched his sister walk happily down the aisle to the man she would spend the rest of her life with. Bundy would never again be placed in the care of Sam and Eleanor Cowell.

Not surprisingly, after all this change and lack of permanence in his very young life, Bundy withdrew into himself, as many children in this situation do. His best friend quickly became the radio as he started to live a kid's social life vicariously through personalities over broadcasts, as he would later share:

> [I]n my younger years I depended a lot on the radio.... As a kid, I would listen for hours and hours to the Lone Ranger, Big John and Sparky, and all that stuff.... I'd get under the covers and listen as long as I could every night.

Bundy went on to explain some highlights in his radio interests, including a particular talk show in which callers would interact with the hosts. Bundy was happily by himself for hours at a time, listening to people share, debate, discuss, visit, and live pieces of their lives on the air:

> And as people would be calling in to speak their minds, I would formulate questions as if they were talking to me.... And I realized, even then, that a lot of the affection I had for programs of that type came not because of their content, but because it was people talking! And I was eavesdropping on their conversations.[419]

Tacoma proved to be an area riddled with bars, lusty, adult-themed live shows, and stores that carried enough pornographic materials to suit every wandering mind amidst the lonely soldier groups passing through from Fort Lewis.[420] Although there is much circumstantial, eyewitness, and common-sense evidence that Bundy's fascination with pretty, naked women began around three or four years old with a cousin of his (Bruce) back at the greenhouse where Sam Cowell kept his stash,[421] many speculate that it wasn't until after the newlyweds and Bundy settled into their new lives as a family in Tacoma that Bundy, now approaching six, began his infamous garbage-can and trash-barrel pilfering in a feverish search for naughty magazines.[422]

With a radio as a social existence, it is not hard to make the connection that dirty pictures would fill in as a fantasy/romance existence.

Often, the argument against the idea that Bundy would have been influenced by Sam's porn at such a young age (between one and three) or magazines he found when he was closer to the age of six or seven is that he wouldn't even know what he was looking at or what the images implied. How could a three-year-old or six-year-old boy gaze upon a nude woman's body with the same reaction as a full-grown man who has needs and desires? This is a valid argument. Sure. And it's probably very true that he wouldn't have fully comprehended what his eyes were taking in, depending on when he was initially exposed. But a vast amount of research behind the concepts of toddler psychological imprinting suggests that even if he was completely unaffected by what he saw at the time in any kind of sexual way, the images would have stuck with him and provided an eroticism for him to recall and compare to as he grew. This could easily have desensitized him to the point that he would have proceeded without bashfulness when his arousal patterns matured to the point of connecting visual stimulation to the changes within his body. And, of course, when one kind of pornography is no longer exciting, a new kind must take its place for those who would feed their carnal and human nature, and it doesn't take rocket science to see that "pretty ladies in lacy underwear" can easily evolve into a craving to see more of the body in even lewder poses. When *that* no longer satisfies the hungry nature of the beast within the individual *willing to continuously feed it*, and he has seen all there is to be bared, the next step in the world of pornography is usually a craving to see images of a very aggressive, violent, dark, and disturbing nature. A boy predisposed to preferring isolation, imagination, and solitude over a social life, and who likely viewed pornography with the same casual curiosity as he might have viewed potty-training charts, is likely to arrive at a pretty extreme endgame. There is every earthly reason to believe that Eleanor Cowell and Louise Bundy were unaware when Bundy began looking at pictures with a deeper understanding and interest—and Sam probably wouldn't have cared if he had known.

Another argument that surfaces *constantly* throughout research of Bundy is that the claims (from both him and others who knew him) that he would have been looking at these darker forms of violent pornography must be false, merely because "that kind of porn did not exist back then." This is easily debunked; "that kind" of pornography did exist, and for *years* prior to Bundy's childhood and teens, in the '50s and '60s. (Although we are about to review a sinister category of the pornographic industry involving such things as binding, gagging, and torture, that does not mean these are the kind of activities Bundy partook of with his victims; as per the confirmed list of victims, little to no evidence suggests an exact parallel between what he did to those girls and the pictures he claimed he was addicted to viewing. However, because of the numbers of people who assume he would have had no access to these materials, and because of the warning that he left the world as he exited from it, this list is relevant to his case.)

The earliest form of bondage-related reading material that was considered "pornography" was called "bondage covers" and involved "damsels in distress" being kidnapped and then rescued at the last minute by some cunning detective, all shown in drawings or paintings rather than photos in magazines as early as 1910.[423] (Note that these materials didn't show much of the human body; they featured mostly women with clothing falling off their bodies in a struggle, and often their nudity was strategically obscured from view by something in the foreground. But, because the plots were thin and the women were almost always bound and gagged, with their clothing coming off—therefore creating reading material with the sole purpose of exploiting a woman's nude body in close proximity to violence—these "bondage covers" were considered one of the very first forms of hard-core pornography. Additionally, though the early forms of violent pornography pale in comparison to the graphic and explicit nature of what is accessible today, that does not necessarily mean the materials weren't powerfully effective in stirring arousal for those who were seeking this brand of psychological stimulant. Before our country was desensitized to the idea that nudity would appear in magazines, forms of early pornography—even images with certain sections of the person's body obscured from view—carried a taboo that would certainly instigate a similar physiological reaction.) These magazines would, by 1937, start to publish actual photographs of women who posed for the roles of the damsels,[424] only a few years after the development of comic books called "weird menace pulps" and "shudder pulps," which "generally featured stories in which the hero was pitted against sadistic villains, with graphic scenes of torture and brutality [against women]."[425] The increase in this category of artistic sadism, depicting women in literal torture scenarios, did eventually cause such a stir that, by 1938, other popular voices, such as those within the *American Mercury* magazine, acted against the phenomenon, saying, "This month, as every month, the 1,508,000 copies of terror magazines...will be sold throughout the nation.... They will contain enough illustrated sex perversion to give Krafft-Ebing the unholy jitters."[426] (Krafft-Ebing was an Austro-German clinical-forensics psychiatrist with specialization in deviant sexual patterns of behavior; he wrote the famous and groundbreaking study *Psychopathia Sexualis* ["Sexual Psychopathy"].)

Despite this attack from wholesome voices against perversion, in 1946, *Bizarre Magazine* brought forth artistic depictions of women wearing black leather and frequently appearing topless. These women were shown spanking and whipping other women, often tying up unwilling participants in painful-looking positions and dressing them in chains and weird, clenching metal devices as well as impossibly tight corsets. (The difference between the "shudder pulps" and "weird menace pulps" and this more forgivable kind of imagery in *Bizarre Magazine* was the condition of the torture. Blood was gone, satanic sacrifices were gone, and, for the most part, weapons were gone. But the idea of women in uncomfortable or painful bondage easily remained. Also remaining was the leftover circulation of the torture fad from the 1930s, which, like the "Tijuana bibles" of the 1920s depicting pornographic cartoons, found their way into distribution "under the table," sold to anyone with a wink, a smile, or a password.[427])

The way was easily paved for other fetish magazines (also called "detective magazines," which appear in Bundy literature often, even though "detective magazines" can also refer to innocent magazines of the true crime genre) such as *Exotique*. Both of these magazines began, early on, publishing almost-nude photographs of real women wearing disturbing costumes looking either afraid or domineering, victimized, or sadistic. It was a quick transition from that over a short period of years to the fully nude, full-color counterpart. By the mid-1950s through the '60s (despite wars waged against this kind of literature that caused some decrease in circulation, only to rebound later with a vengeance), it was not uncommon to enter an adult store where there was "that section in the back" that everyone pretended not to know about. (By the 1970s, these magazines were available by mail order.[428]) One of the earliest studies of pornography and its influence on society was written in 1967, and "concluded that such [fetish] magazines provide a catharsis for those whose sexual needs are otherwise unsatisfied: [the author of the study] identified rubberwear magazines as the most popular at the time."[429]

"Rubberwear" fetishes as early as 1967? "Torture porn" as early as the 1930s?

Anyway, you get the idea. To say Bundy could not have had access to "that kind" of pornography in his childhood and teen years is not at all accurate, but it is *continuously* assumed in discussion. Since Bundy's first documented/confirmed victim was in January of 1974, opportunities for someone to collect and keep this kind of imagery and fantasize over it prior to murder were boundless, and, as is usually the way in these tales of sadistic hunger, imagery is rarely enough when the "real thing" is obtainable by those who crave it and feed their minds with that kind of pollution. And why would any young person like Bundy feel the temptation to feed his mind with such things? Surely it had nothing to do with early exposure to a combination of pornography and violence…

(Perhaps you have heard that, at one point, Bundy *did* admit that he chose not to read detective magazines. In a conversation with Rule, he basically said he couldn't fathom why anyone would read such rubbish.[430] People often point to this conversation as proof that these materials were not a factor for him, by his own admission. But most people don't pay attention to when and why he might have said this. Because this claim of his was given prior to any of his confessions, *and during the trials* wherein he was trying to prove his innocence of crimes related to this category of imagery, is it surprising that he would claim no association with these materials? Furthermore, Bundy scarcely ever told the truth, earning himself the reputation of being an excessive liar, so it's a wonder so many people take his word for it when he exonerates himself of having anything to do with shameful magazines.)

So much for all the "bad seed" theories that point to a "normal" kid with a "normal" childhood who "for no apparent reason" grew up with violence toward women on his mind.

(Note: Many have written articles that point to Bundy's youth and include very uneducated statements about how, during his childhood, he had "some" troubles, but was overall normal and didn't have any unusual levels of instability. Perhaps the writers of these articles say this because Bundy, himself, was never physically harmed that we know of, or perhaps they say this because of some of the statements that materialized in Bundy's final interview with Dobson [more on this later]. Yet, it should be observed that regardless of whether a journalist considers living with a man who throws his daughters down the stairs, beats dogs, swings cats by their tails, perhaps beats his wife, and leaves pornographic magazines around as "normal," evidently, Bundy didn't feel that it was "basically normal" when he decided to place knives around sleeping family members and then watch them wake up in fear, at the age when many children are still in diapers and learning motor skills. Or, perhaps worse, Bundy *did* think that it was normal living arrangements, and this was how he chose to partake in that "normalcy." Either way, if this kind of atmosphere is, as some claim, normal and stable, this author is abundantly grateful that his childhood was abnormal by comparison. Most probable is that many Bundy-haters out there hold understandable anger against him for the heinousness of his crimes, and they choose to direct their anger into writing articles that exploit his bad side, spending less time trying to understand the trigger behind his later Hyde side, and therefore incorrectly reporting that his childhood was "normal." From the beginning, his early years were anything *but* that. Additionally, studies now show that Reactive Attachment Disorder can begin to affect infants immediately after birth when they are left in certain kinds of care, such as the institutional care Bundy had been placed in for the first several months of his life at the home for unwed mothers. The disorder can even be diagnosed as early as the age of one year, especially within children whose living arrangements are upsetting.[431] This "complex psychiatric illness"[432] is a "rare but serious condition in which infants and young children don't establish healthy bonds with parents or caregivers,"[433] and "is characterized by serious problems in emotional attachments to others."[434] Much of the current medical and scientific research on early infant and child development didn't exist when Bundy was a child, so his strange behaviors wouldn't have raised the red flags that our more modern and learned world would now notice. And, supposing that Bundy *had* been brought before a psychiatric professional at the time, the diagnostics and treatment in the medical field in 1950 greatly lacked effective ways to reach children as individuals, during an era when the majority of American culture perpetuated the notion that children who act out simply need firmer punishment. A true, "digging-deeper" mentality in the psychiatric practice to reach the roots of the behavior of problematic children has only increased a great deal in *recent* years. Problems can now be more acutely dealt with, as we read about in the Sean Sellers' case study, but today's medical knowledge wouldn't help a child who was born in 1946. Lastly, current medical analysis tools flag actions that might have, in 1950, seemed relatively harmless. An unusually withdrawn child who arranged knives around a sleeping relative might have been seen in the middle of the century, by both professionals and parents alike, as a quiet child who likes to play silly jokes. Today, however, overly quiet children who play psychological games with knives while grinning raise every alarm in the medical industry. There is no way of knowing what diagnosis would have come from young Bundy's trip to any kind of help center. Help was never sought.)

The Odd Bundy Out

The years passed in a blur of estranged social hindrance. Bundy wouldn't let go of the idea that, despite his sister's concerns, he had been born a Cowell, and with the Cowells was where he belonged. According to a University of Washington professor of psychiatry, Ronald E. Smith, Bundy didn't really respect Johnnie Bundy, the newly given father figure, because he "didn't have a high enough station in life."[435] As stated earlier, Bundy had been only four when his sister had married, and he quickly developed less-than-ideal opinions about a person's worth based on where the person ranked. As it would be revealed in later years, a person's status was everything. Bundy set his sights on being more like his uncle, Jack, who had become a well established and cultured professor of music at the University of Puget Sound. Professor Smith went on to say, "It was very important for him [Bundy] to be someone special, to be recognized in some way."[436] Bundy had lofty goals: Come what may, he was going to achieve a name for himself. Someday, there would be a celebration with the name "Ted Bundy" right in the middle…

The longer he nurtured those thoughts and ambitions, the more his place in the Bundy family felt odd and mismatched. Something, or someone, wasn't right.

One just learning about this portion of Bundy's life might naturally assume that his life with Johnnie and Louise Bundy had been troubled, that he would openly rebel against his sister or say things such as, "I don't have to listen to you! You're not my mother!" Oddly, though, as far as that can be researched, that doesn't appear to be the case. Quite the contrary, actually: When Louise and Johnnie expanded their family by four children (two boys and two girls) over the next several years, Bundy became the natural babysitter. By the time he was fifteen, his sister and her husband had purchased a home, and all seven of them lived together. Bundy had no social life, and was known at school for being very shy and quiet. Between his personality and always having to look after his younger siblings, he never allowed himself to have plans or date, and yet he did not complain or lash out.[437] (It is interesting to note that, although Bundy was frequently involved in daily family gatherings, it's not merely by documentation or testimony that one can tell what an odd fit he was. The photos taken around the time that his siblings were joining the family and he was heavily involved in babysitting tell a story all their own. Even when he is smiling and no one is intentionally excluding him, Bundy's expressions are surreally distant. Everyone else, including Louise, smiles for the pictures, carefree and happy, but there's always that awkward teenager who doesn't quite fit, standing slightly farther away from the rest of the family. His smile, or lack of one, always taunts the viewer with mystery and untold secrets. If pictures could speak, those taken during this period of Bundy's life would have a lot to say.)

Over time, Bundy was a silent mystery to everyone around him. He continued to draw farther and farther away from the world, family, and friends at school, engaging in only mundane conversation and attempting and then immediately dropping sports of any kind. He developed a stutter and kept every secret to himself. When he started to suspect that there was more to his origin story than his mother, father, or sister were telling him, he was far too voiceless to ask, so he made notes and kept them, also, to himself. In later years, after Bundy found his voice, he would say of this period, "It was not so much that there were significant events [in his childhood or teen years that caused this estrangement], but the *lack* of things that took place was significant. The *omission* of important developments. I felt that I had developed intellectually but not socially."[438] Many times, he received invitations to birthday parties or other events, and he desperately wanted to accept them and socialize, but he always declined, claiming to be too serious a student to attend such parties. He was his own worst enemy, always putting another brick on the wall he was building between himself and the world. At times, he was bullied, but as far as treatment from his peers, he landed somewhere between "popular" and "outcast."

Mild, meek, well-mannered, easy to get along with on the outside; confused and stunted on the inside. Before long, Bundy's secret life would incorporate more than hidden magazines. Bundy could rise above the law, and nobody would ever have to know.

Before even his sixteenth birthday, Bundy had become a proficient shoplifter, and was named as a suspect in two burglaries.[439] Smith explained this development: "Grandiose narcissism. The ability to outwit the police. The ability to, you know, flaunt authority. The ability to shoplift. All of these things helped confer on him this sort of narcissistic sense of special-ness and entitlement."[440] These actions gave Bundy a tremendous feel-ing of power, and his secret life soon escalated to involve sneaking from window to window late in the evening, peering in at young girls from his school who were undressing for the night...[441]

In high school, his popularity increased as his teen features grew more masculine. He had the attention of girls who wished he would show an interest in dating, and the attention of the guys who wished he would start dating some girl just so he would be taken "off the market" as the object of so many of the girls' fascination. But Bundy was still a few years away from connecting to anyone.

About this time, his interest in politics was ignited. In his senior year of high school, he volunteered in local political races, and discovered it was a passion. He understood law as he had never understood anything before. Because of an academic scholarship from the University of Puget Sound, where his uncle taught, he attended that college for a time,[442] but he wouldn't be there long. The enormous campus and crowds of other students only reminded him of how small, unimportant, and anonymous he was. Behaving in a way that carried on that insignificance was all he knew how to do with the familiar faces of his past all around him. He needed a change of pace—he need to emerge from behind the wall he had built.

Ashes, Ashes, the Wall Falls Down

Between 1966 and 1967, Bundy had a radical makeover.

As long as anyone had known him, he had been a shy, stuttering, lonely, strange boy who seemed happy and sad at the same time on any given day. Nobody had ever understood him, and he had never let anyone in. Determined to present a different Ted Bundy to the world around him, as status and impression were becoming what life all was about, Bundy developed a new personality and started a new life far different from the one that had been led by the cautious little boy with the hidden magazines.

An A&E documentary on Bundy's life refers to his new personality launch as just another pretense: "As part of the façade, Bundy transferred to the University of Washington [Seattle].... He also began fabricating a new personality. If the old Bundy was shy and withdrawn, the new Bundy would be witty, cool, and self-assured. His deception was about to pay off."[443]

With his new college and new faces to impress, Bundy balled up his courage and walked, with his chin up, into campus. The "quiet" thing hadn't worked out, and although it had helped him earn good grades as a serious student, his life had never been fun—and it had always been lonely. The façade of the saintly son had swallowed him whole. This *next* façade would be the one to bind to, as it would bring him success and happiness. He was sure of this.

Right away, he met the girl of his dreams. Stephanie Brooks. Brunette. Hair parted in the middle and shoulder length. Gorgeous enough to be a model, but smart, wealthy, and confident, too. She was everything he had ever wanted, and the *new* Bundy was willing to get to know someone… maybe even let her in. This girl broke the mold. Bundy fell head over heels in love with her; the very sight of her down the hallway between classes made him sigh.

He began shuffling his life to accommodate being with her. They took a skiing trip together, and he found himself staring at her in awe on the drive back home.[444] She held his hand, and his heart would skip a beat, and at their first kiss, he knew he wanted to be with her forever. As he later recalled: "It was at once sublime and overpowering…. The first touch of hands, the first kiss, the first night together."[445] Brooks was Bundy's first love and first sexual relationship.[446] He had exposed all of his vulnerabilities to be with her. Although he kept some public image up for the rest of the world to see, Brooks was different. Bundy let her in, and let himself love.

The couple dated for a full year, one that would go down in history as the biggest turning point in Bundy's life, for better…and then for worse.

Brooks had been raised in a dramatically different household than Bundy's. Her parents were from California, well-to-do, and prestigious. The example that had been set before her allowed for nothing less than having a boyfriend who was a perfect fit for that society: someone who would promise high-class success and maturity beyond his years, a hard-working and successful businessman with a plan in one hand and a fortune in the other. (It is also safe to assume, based on interviews and stories regarding her approach to the relationship, that even though she returned Bundy's love, she wasn't as obsessively serious as he was.)

Bundy, a part of another world, was paying for his schooling at the university by working in low-income jobs.[447] Unlike some who had always known what avenue their lives would go, Bundy, around the age of twenty, was unsure of his future. He had taken some classes in this interest over here, and a few classes in another subject over there. Music, Chinese, politics, psychology…so many interests, all of them conflicting. His plan wasn't solid enough to help him hold on to Brooks' affection.

Eventually, Brooks broke up with Bundy because she was convinced that he was "foundering, that he had no real plans or real prospects for the future."[448] (According to an article on Wikipedia.com, Brooks was "frustrated by what she described as Bundy's immaturity and lack of ambition."[449])

Bundy was crushed.

The first time he had allowed someone in, exposed his heart, torn off his mask, and shown her the person left standing, she had walked away casually, unimpressed by the still-adolescent child who remained underneath the handsome, young exterior. The pain the breakup caused would stick with Bundy for a very, *very* long time.

He had brought his wall down and had taken a life-altering risk, and now, he had nothing but ashes to show for it. The beast that had been in the boy was stirring.

Loving someone that way had been a bad move, and he would never do it again.

THE MONSTER WITHIN THE MAN

Lost and hurting, Bundy dropped out of college and traveled back home to visit his relatives, wandering aimlessly, meandering around, looking for distractions. Rejected, friendless, alone: It was a world that he had created. Nothing had ever seemed real in his childhood, when he had been that quiet little boy with a heart full of secrets. Something was always off kilter. And his new personality had worked on a social level, but it had been empty as well, attracting people who were looking for superficial things.

Yet, now, back with family for a short period, a nagging ache for truth that he had suppressed throughout his whole life finally rose with a vigor that could no longer be ignored. His childhood had been strange, yes, but it had been so partially for a specific reason he never wanted to face. Deep in the darkest recesses of his mind, a truth was lurking about who he really was, who he had really been on the day of his birth. Buried under layers upon layers of awkward silences, whispered conversations, sideways glances, and gaudy innuendos was a suspicion. It was a thought that Bundy had suppressed, like a choking lump in his throat that he would repeatedly swallow back down, refusing to expel it for fear that the truth would be more than he could handle.

But now, after Brooks…he had to know.

How could he have been so stupid to let someone see behind his mask when he, himself, suspected his own identity was fraudulent?

A Lifetime of Lies, and the Lie of a Lifetime

Bundy traveled to the Burlington, Vermont, city hall, received assistance in locating his birth records, and cracked open the file.

"Illegitimate."

The word was literally stamped across the front of his birth certificate.[450]

There's that word again: "Illegitimate." Invalid. Fake. Counterfeit. Inferior. Phony. Misborn.

A mistake…

At least now he knew for sure what he had been suspecting for so many years. His parents, Sam and Eleanor Cowell, were never his parents, and his sister, Louise, was never his "sister."

Of course, he had been aware of how much he and his sister had looked alike, *just like mother and son*, one might say—not to mention that he had so many times pondered the legalities behind a "sister" taking a "brother" away from his parents or his "sister" having her "brother's" name changed in the courts. Only a true mother would have been legally able to pull that off.

He couldn't remember when or how he had begun to suspect it, but somewhere deep inside, he had known for some time: Bundy's "big sister" Louise was his real mother, and Sam and Eleanor were his grandparents.

Memories of his "sister" doing her hair, making dinner, or pouring a cup of coffee would now hold new meaning as he realized he had always been observing the woman whose womb he had been nestled into for nine months. Moments when he had watched her bouncing another of her babies on her knee or holding her other offspring when they cried would ring with a different, more piercing pitch now that he knew that it was *her* maternal touch and not Eleanor's that he should have had in infancy. Having seen Louise interact with the children she had conceived with Johnnie Bundy now caused a sting and encouraged him to question how she could flaunt her motherliness and affection to the *other* offspring yet still call her firstborn son a "brother."

Why had she lied? Why had *they all* lied? Everyone had been in on the ruse! They had all agreed to go along with this fabrication as if he weren't man enough to hear the truth, or as if he were the brunt of some casual, collective, locker-room, towel-snap joke in the family. Why was that necessary? Had Louise been so ashamed of the baby in her belly so long ago that she couldn't bear to call him her own when he was born? Perhaps, as a young girl, pregnant, scared, and panicked, she would have felt it was best for him if she'd lied…but now? Was she *still* so ashamed of him that she couldn't claim him as her own?

But would Bundy really want that? Did he even *want* to look at Louise like a mother? Would he want her reaching out to touch him the way a mother would touch her son? Something about the whole thing seemed unfathomably uncomfortable and almost bordered on bizarrely incestuous. It had been Louise's belly, now he knew for sure, that he had grown in as a result of her womanly acts with another man, and it had been her womanly body that had delivered—

It was getting weirder and weirder and weirder. There was such a vast difference between a strong hunch and solid knowledge. His "sister" was his mother and his "mother" was his grandma and his father was…

Who was his father?

The world would never know for certain. Suspicions were *ugly*.

In later years, once the supposedly seducing service-veteran/sailor father's name, "Jack Worthington,"[451] had been proven to have never actually existed in the navy or marine archives, relatives of Bundy would come forward with suggestions that Bundy's biological father was the abusive Sam Cowell, Louise's natural father and Bundy's natural grandfather. Bundy's "family members would express open doubts about [Louise's] story [of the seducing sailor], directing a defense psychiatrist's attention to Louise's violent, possibly deranged, father, Samuel Cowell."[452] "However, when Ted's cousin John once asked granddad about Bundy's paternity, the response was volcanic…. [He] became enraged and apparently he acted like a madman. He was wild. He was furious."[453]

Despite how, in some settings (while he was still claiming his innocence), Bundy would act fairly nonchalant or forgiving about the deception and rumors of his own grandfather being his own biological father, those who knew him best (and those who had been brought in late in his case for psychological evaluations) understood that "this late discovery had a rather serious impact on him."[454] According to close friend Ann Rule, Bundy "was so intense and disturbed when he said he never really knew who he was, or whom he belonged to."[455]

(Interesting fact: This exact scenario happened to Jack Nicholson, the Hollywood actor so famous for portraying insane or psychotic personalities in his movies.[456] When he found out that his sister was really his mother and that his mother was really his grandmother, he was shocked, but neither of the women was still alive for him to confront. Also interesting to note was that Nicholson's acting took a dark twist about the time he discovered the truth; he went from being cast as drama or comedy leads to weirdoes, crazies, and axe murderers. But, Jack Nicholson did not kill people when he found out his sister was really his mother. He just made his living pretending to kill people.)

Bundy never told Louise that he knew.

The wall had been rebuilt, and the mask was back on.

Façade

Every day
people live their own sweet way
Like to add a coat of paint
and be what they ain't!
That's how their little game is played
livin' out the masquerade....
Who'd want to trade?
But there's one thing I know, an' I know it for sure:
This disease that they've got has got no ready cure.
An' I'm certain life is terribly hard
when yer life's a façade.
—Street people, from the song "Façade," *Jekyll & Hyde:
The Musical* [457]

Fake, masked people are lonely people. Even when they are given precisely what they want and all the power they are after, it's never enough. Those rewards do not satisfy. Not really. Not deeply. It's like giving a starving man a single leaf of lettuce for a meal. It feeds, and might even sustain life for a bit, but it still doesn't fill emptiness. Life, for those plugged into a shell-like reality that they have manipulated for themselves, is hard. It's hungry. It craves real meat. Those with masks on are not loved for who or what they truly are, because nobody knows who or what they truly are. They have done it to themselves—with their own dishonesty, yes, but it is miserable and lonely lives they lead.

The façade that Bundy adopted to inflate his presence to those around him just prior to meeting Brooks had worked better than anything he had tried before. When he had lost her, and then uncovered the bitter truth of his illegitimacy, he fed his hunger with an unparalleled determination to prove himself to a world that had birthed something hopeless, something unimpressive, something that wouldn't ever amount to anything.

To prove himself to her.

His mask meshed well with politics.

As Bundy would later relate:

Politics gave me the opportunity to be close to people.... To be socially involved with them…as a consequence of working with them. You get very close. You drink each night—and people sleep with each other. It's a sort of built-in social life. Which I never had.

In my younger years, I was, as I've said before, socially unskilled…. In politics you can move between the various strata of society. You can talk and mingle with people to whom otherwise you would have absolutely no access.[458]

With newfound focus, Bundy placed himself in the path of every opportunity for success. After returning back to Seattle after the breakup, he became a volunteer for the Seattle Crisis Hotline (where he met Ann Rule) and, as mentioned at the beginning of the chapter, saved a lot of lives, talked many troubled callers down from suicide, and soothed many weary souls. He saved a drowning toddler and was heralded a hero. He chased down a purse-snatcher and received a lot of local attention as an upstanding citizen. He enrolled once again at the University of Washington, where he became an honor student and received many recommendation letters from professors who spoke of Bundy with the highest regard. Bundy also found himself a pretty girlfriend and stayed many nights with her, acting as a father figure to her daughter, a young girl from a previous marriage. He hobnobbed, he shook hands, he saved lives, he smiled, he posed for the cameras, he volunteered for good causes, he laughed, and he lived.

Yeah… Yeah, maybe *this* could be Ted Bundy. His self-reinvention was, once again, producing results, and this time, he was proving himself.

While this was all going on, Bundy was taking classes about criminal justice, criminal psychology, deviant personalities, deviant development,[459] law, and forensics (although most of his law-related classes would come later, in Utah). Whether he had intended for this education to perpetuate his own killer instincts or to temper them, or if the schooling was an interest regardless of whom he would soon become, that much is anyone's guess. By the time he received his degree ("With Distinction"[460]) in psychology in 1973, he was fervently applying to the University of Utah so he could obtain a law degree.

Joining the re-election campaign for Washington Governor Daniel Evans, Bundy used his collegiate connections and student appearance to pose as an undergraduate and scout Evans' competition, attending the speeches of former governor, Evans' opponent, Albert Rosellini. Bundy would bring his notes back to Evans' side of the campaign for study. These sneaky acts were not at all underhanded, however. They were merely political, all part of the game, and they showed his adeptness for succeeding in the big leagues.

After Evans was re-elected, the chairman of the Washington State Republican Party, Ross Davis, brought Bundy on staff as an assistant. Through more letters of recommendation and more reputable acts associated with law, Bundy was accepted into the University of Utah, with a declared law major. His position with Davis for the Republican Party took him to several states for job-related travel.

Even though things had ended romantically between Bundy and Brooks, the two had maintained some contact. Bundy had put his heart and soul into becoming the man Brooks would have wanted, and now, his job made it necessary for him to make a stop in California, where she lived. Despite his relationship with a girl back home, he couldn't stop himself from contacting Brooks. He simply *had* to see her again, to show her his new mask. To see if she thought this one looked nicer on him.

She was *impressed*.

He was *proven*.

Bundy and Brooks began a secret relationship. Bundy continued to live his many lives for a while: a serious student to some, a smart and aggressive political ballplayer to others, a sensitive listener to Rule and the callers at the hotline, a jovial and smiling lover to his sweetheart back home, a father to his girlfriend's daughter, and a caretaker and sweet young man for his elderly couple landlords. Not a soul knew who he really was, but everyone who came into contact with him saw nothing but a man who was sincere. Whatever mask he was wearing in front of the observer was worn well, and never questioned. (Testimonies and character witnesses for *years* to come would swear that, until just before his dying day, there was no way...simply no way...that Bundy had been capable of what investigators had charged.)

To Brooks, Bundy was a man who was *going places*: He was a real stud with a plan and a future...and a wedding ring.

He proposed. Brooks accepted. Nobody knew.

Revenge at the Proving Grounds

While Bundy continued to dote on his sweetheart and her daughter in Seattle, he continued to maintain an engagement with Brooks, who was still living in California. Neither of his flattered females knew about the other.

But what he was plotting for Brooks was never really a marriage, so his big secret wouldn't have to be kept long.

Again and again, Bundy swept Brooks off of her feet, offering her dreams and fulfilling her expectations. When she had put him down years before, when she had hurt his pride, he had been listening. Every word that she had said about his immaturity, his lack of experience, or his insufficient plans was gently coming back to flaunt his success in her face. He had shown her up, proven her wrong, and now he would have his revenge.

For so long, he had plotted to have her attention and her heart so that he could reject her as painfully as a woman could be rejected—as painfully as *he* had been rejected. So, when he felt the timing was right, at the absolute height of Brooks' love for him and excitement about their future together, Bundy let her go...with as much immaturity and pettiness as he had just spent the last several years proving he didn't have. His strategy involved instantly turning all of their remaining meetings during what was to be her final trip to see him into excuses to mystify her with his sudden aloofness. When they copulated, he was cold and uninterested. When Brooks flew back to California after a strange visit with the abruptly uncaring Bundy on January 2, 1974, she was terribly hurt and confused. She went to a counselor and poured out her heart, unable to understand why Bundy had so unexpectedly changed toward her, acting as if he couldn't wait for her to leave. At her counselor's suggestion, she wrote him a letter demanding some answers. Bundy never answered the letter, and didn't return any of her phone calls.

In mid February, Brooks called Bundy's residence at the elderly couple's home and, by chance, he answered. Brooks immediately began questioning him and sharing her anger with him over being dropped from his life without warning or explanation. But before she could finish pouring out her hurt, Bundy interrupted her. He said, coldly and simply, "Stephanie, I have no idea what you mean."[461]

Brooks heard a click, and the line went dead.

She never heard from Bundy again.

Elsewhere, young girls who looked just like her started to disappear, one by one by one.

MURDERS, ARRESTS, ESCAPES, AND TRIAL

My God! What's this?
Something is happening I can't explain!
Something inside me, a breathtaking pain!
Devours and consumes me, and drives me insane!
Suddenly, uncontrolled! Something is taking hold!
Suddenly, agony! Filling me! Killing me!
Suddenly, out of breath! What is this? Is this death?
Suddenly, look at me! Can it be?
Who is this creature…that…I…see?
Free…
—Dr. Jekyll, from the transformation scene when Dr. Jekyll first becomes Mr. Hyde in *Jekyll & Hyde: The Musical*[462]

During the next four years, Bundy killed many young girls. They all looked like Stephanie Brooks, and some so much that, seen from a distance, they could have easily been her twin. As mentioned at the beginning of this case study, some were found immediately, some were found a long time after they had been murdered, and some have never been found.

Bundy sometimes chose his victims on impulse; they were simply in the wrong place at the wrong time. However, most of his kills were people he stalked, finding out where they lived, watching their movements, keeping up with their travels, memorizing their schedules, and noting when they would be home in their beds or in a dark alleyway between two tall buildings. Some of the girls were abducted only seconds between the time they had seen another person and the time they would have entered their homes or sorority houses: There one second, gone the next. Some of the girls left a crowd of people to go with Bundy, and they never came back. Bundy sometimes grabbed the girls from the shadows. Other times, he impersonated a policeman or other member of law enforcement. And, sometimes, he showed up with a smile and an arm or leg in a cast (or with crutches) pretending to need assistance with something he couldn't do alone because of his "physical ailment."

His *modus operandi* cleverly switched patterns so often that he proved difficult to track or predict. And thanks to all those classes on law, deviant minds, and the criminal justice system, he had learned a few tips on how to cover his tracks. And thanks to all those classes on psychology, he was excellent at putting on a harmless face…

Most of the time.

The Chameleon and the Famous Photo

In addition to being in many places at once and knowing far too many things about far too many women at once, Bundy continued to put on different faces all the time. Often referred to in documentaries and literature as "the chameleon," his appearance was always changing, which meant that the descriptions in eyewitness accounts and survivors' testimonies and the composite sketches would never exactly portray his likeness. Observe the many faces of Mr. Bundy:

But the transformations involved more than just a haircut and a shave; Bundy had a very odd ability to literally change the appearance of his face by using flashes of differing expressions to look like different people entirely, usually under the influence of emotional provocation.

Generally speaking, everyone saw the same smiling, savvy, suave, dedicated, and sincere-looking Bundy face when he knew the public was watching. As a basis of comparison, here is the happy, "trial" Bundy face[463]:

Photo courtesy of State
Archives of Florida

That is, Bundy kept this "happy face" on until his arrests and trials put him under pressure, and then something, or *someone*, else would surface, usually only for a split second. This phenomenon is nothing new, actually. It has been studied by myriad groups, each offering its own explanation of the phenomenon, and it is endearingly referred to in online discussions as "the psychopathic stare." (Demon possession is often one explanation that religious groups offer to explain how people, usually murderous criminals, rapidly switch in and out of expressions that make them appear not to be themselves.) Not necessarily limited to those who are eventually labeled as "psychopaths," this ability to startle someone with a flash of the eyes or scare someone deeply with a mere glance tends to pop up frequently in studies of psychopathic individuals.

This author witnessed this startling change for himself regarding Bundy. From photo to photo and from filmed interview to filmed interview (except for his last one; more about that later), he frequently seems the cool cat, and then *flash*! Something under the surface, something carnal and hostile and menacing, shows for just the briefest moment, when he looks like someone else completely. But in the blink of an eye, that persona is gone, and Bundy's back to his self-assured, you-got-the-wrong-guy act.

When researching the phenomenon of the psychopathic stare, the following picture is one of the most famous examples of an appearance that offers a truly transparent flicker of the killer within the man. (Just next to Bundy's photo in popularity are several psychopathic-stare photos of Charles Manson and the one of Susan Atkins shown in her case study.) Note that the picture of Bundy was snapped while he was waving at the press, who had come with cameras to attend the reading of his indictment. (The full picture, including the wave of his arm, can easily be found online.) The camera snapped the image one second after Bundy said, "I'll plead 'not guilty' right now." A frame-by-frame playback of the original press video (clip available on YouTube[464]) clearly shows that Bundy's overall behavior and countenance during his indictment reading are awkward and defensive, and, in some moments, are even childish or demure—but not psychotic. The Ted Bundy in the video just seems like a goofball, some relatively normal guy who might be embarrassed to hear his name falsely associated with such charges, but he doesn't appear to be capable of murder. This photo,[465] captured and made famous before computer-imagery tampering would have been a possibility, doesn't even appear as if it came from that clip, until we compare the photo to the film and look at his hairstyle, the people behind him, the angles, etc. Observe the intensity of his expression:

Photo courtesy of State
Archives of Florida

What surfaced in the second that the camera went off? Even if someone looking at this image for the first time didn't find it frightening (because by itself, it's not frightening), the viewer would have to admit that, in this frame, Bundy looks like a different guy than he was one second before and one second after the photo was taken. Did Bundy's victims see *this* Bundy face just after being swept off their feet by the other Bundy face? Might they have had some kind of warning flash?

Lucy: "For a moment I thought it was somebody else."
Mr. Hyde: "For a moment, it almost was."
—*Jekyll & Hyde: The Musical*[466]

They did—at least sometimes, based on survivors' testimonies. After Bundy's arrest, many stories emerged from other women, would-be victims who had barely escaped. They were able to describe details about Bundy that were remarkably consistent with some of his lesser-known behavioral traits that only investigators knew about. Many of the women described a moment when Bundy's eyes had told them they were goners (*always* his eyes; so, *so* often there were stories about the "Bundy eyes"). Several of these stories had taken place in casual settings as well, and never even came close to ending in murder, giving the women no reason to talk about the event…unless Bundy's eyes or his expressions were penetrating enough by itself to cause concern.

Right before the murders of the Chi Omega House sorority girls of Florida State University in Tallahassee, Bundy was at the campus disco joint, Sherrod's. A young woman there named Mary Ann Piccano, who had never seen Bundy before, reported later that he had stared at her for a while. She said she had noticed that he was handsome. Well before Bundy approached Piccano with a drink, she said she felt terrified of him because of the way "his eyes bore into her."[467] He asked her to dance, and she agreed, rationalizing away her nervousness, since she had never seen him and her fear was probably unnecessary paranoia. Sherrod's was the kind of place where students often danced with others they didn't know; it was a social norm. As Piccano walked away with Bundy, she whispered to her friend that she thought she was heading onto the dance floor with an ex-convict. Whether or not she meant it as a joke,[468] that comment would later be used against Bundy in court. During their time together on the dance floor, Bundy behaved like a perfect gentleman and gave Piccano no further reason to be suspicious of him, but when she returned to her table, she was trembling and felt grateful to be alive. —All this because of a gut feeling…"something about the eyes, the face."

Even Bundy's own relative, his great-aunt, had a similar experience. According to a book written by one of Bundy's defense attorneys, he "seemed to turn into another, unrecognizable person…[Bundy's great-aunt] suddenly, inexplicably found herself afraid of her favorite nephew as they waited together at a dusk-darkened train station. He had turned into a stranger."[469] As Leslie Rule said in her exclusive interview with our staff, "I was not afraid of Ted, but something about him felt wrong. I was only fourteen and couldn't put my finger on what it was about him that bothered me. Ted would not meet my eyes, and he ducked his head when he was introduced to us."[470]

Ann Rule had a friendly little dog that loved everyone it met; it was a pleasant animal to have around. She sometimes brought it to work with her. Rule describes Bundy during those days as a close friend who seemed empathetic and safe. Certainly, if she didn't fear Bundy, and nobody else at the time (1971) feared Bundy, the loving dog would have had no reason to dislike Bundy. But, every time Bundy bent over the desk at the crisis hotline center with Rule, the dog's hackles would rise and she would growl at him.[471] Had Bundy given Rule's dog the psychotic Bundy face? What about the dog who was mysteriously going crazy and throwing a fit when a potential victim claimed that Bundy appeared at her door pretending to be a police officer?[472] What about the fact that, when a woman was mysteriously murdered in a hotel while Bundy was visiting that city, the dog catcher's records say that a man named "Bundy" had been bitten by a dog that week?[473] Did *those* dogs get the psychotic, Bundy-face treatment or sense something *else* about Bundy that was a little left field?

Ann Rule's daughter, Leslie, seems to believe this is possible. She shared the following words of advice for our readers:

I'd like to warn women to be careful. Look alert when you are walking. My mom always says that predators look for victims who are distracted and not paying attention.

Steer clear of bushes, where someone could hide and jump out at you. Check the backseat of your car before you get in.

And if you can give a dog a good home, please do! There are tens of thousands of good dogs put to sleep, because there are not enough homes. Rescue one of these dogs, *and she [or he] just might rescue you. Predators tend to avoid homes where there are dogs.*[474]

In any case, be it demon possession, a phenomenon of psychopathology, something weird Bundy was doing with his face, or a natural intensity that some people are born with, this author makes no specific claim. These facial expressions, these "eyes," this inability to hide an internal monster, something hungry that oddly revealed itself in traces and glimmers, would not only be a psychopathic oddity for which Bundy would forever be remembered, but it would also play a role in his coming trial.

(Note again that, because of the brutality of this case, the overwhelming number of trial details and events, and the exhaustive coverage available all over the country, should the reader wish to become extensively educated on all things Bundy, we are going to speed through the following section.)

You Can't Keep a Good Man Confined

On August 16, 1975, in Granger, Utah (near the University of Utah Law School in Salt Lake City, where Bundy was now a student), Captain "Pete" Hayward, a trusted local cop, was making his rounds in a neighborhood. When a Volkswagen Bug was seen creeping around suspiciously at 2:30 in the morning, it drew concern. The VW Bug was a very common vehicle at the time, but the cop knew the area; since he knew that nobody on the street owned that car and since it was an unusual time of day, he turned on his bright lights to get the license plate numbers. The Bug instantly turned its lights out and sped off. (This same thing happened with the same kind of vehicle in the same era as the David Berkowitz case; the two events are not in any way related. Berkowitz's case was a year later in New York. Several satanic underground theorists linked many serial killers together in coincidences like these and, although some of this research has pointed to some clever potential associations, the personalities behind the production of this book believe these things to be coincidental.)

Howard tailed the mysterious vehicle as it ran through two stop signs and then pulled into an abandoned gas station. The officer eased into the lot as well, and got out of his patrol car. A young man emerged from the VW and claimed he was lost. Howard commented about the driver's willingness to ignore two stop signs, requested the driver's identification, and asked what he was doing in the area. Theodore Bundy, as the driver's license read, responded that he had seen a late-night showing of *The Towering Inferno* at the drive-in and had gotten lost on the way home. Howard had passed the drive-in earlier that evening and knew Bundy's excuse was bogus, as that movie had not been playing there.

Howard suddenly noticed something very out of the ordinary: The passenger-side seat was missing from Bundy's car. Upon further inspection, the officer uncovered a bag with some odd items: a ski mask, a second mask fashioned from pantyhose, a crowbar, handcuffs, trash bags, a coil of rope, an ice pick, gloves, a flashlight, and strange strips of cloth.

Bundy was arrested for evading an officer, and on suspicion of burglary. Investigators had made several connections regarding the make and model of the vehicle and its similarities to one that had been reported as near the sites of recent abductions. In addition, they were putting other factors together as well: Ann Rule had called the station connecting Bundy's likeness to a composite sketch of the person suspected of the recent crimes. Daughter Leslie remembers this moment:

> After two young women disappeared from Lake Sammamish State Park, there was a big spread in the newspaper about the suspect and the missing girls. Witnesses had overheard him introduce himself to one of the victims. He said his name was "Ted," but most people assumed that that was not his real name. My mother thought that the composite sketch in the paper looked like her friend, Ted. I remember that the resemblance really troubled my mom. My sister told her that [she] was crazy, and that it couldn't possibly be her friend Ted. At that time, mother already had a contract to write a book about the girls disappearing around Seattle. What are the odds that the suspect would turn out to be her friend? I have a very vivid picture of my mom standing there, the newspaper wide open as she stared at it with a wrinkled brow.[475]

Several other concerning flags were naturally raised by Bundy possessing what appeared to be burglary tools. Further, there had been a phone call from his girlfriend at the time about Bundy's worrisome behaviors.

A search of Bundy's apartment turned up some maps and pamphlets linking him to a ski resort and a school play where two girls had been reported missing, but investigators found no evidence hard enough to hold him. He was released on his own recognizance, but was placed under twenty-four-hour surveillance. This was the first time he weaseled out of containment…

His girlfriend went to the police and told them about countless other peculiar details. Bundy had been keeping items she didn't understand, such as various kinds of weapons and the same kinds of medical supplies (crutches, plasters, etc.) that would make him fit the profile of the man who had reportedly been approaching people pretending to be injured.

Bundy had threatened to break her neck when she accused him of stealing some valuables, and she could not explain where he had been on any of the nights when girls had gone missing. In the heat of the increasing suspicion, Bundy sold his car to a teenager. However, the police impounded it and searched it for evidence; the investigation turned up hairs that matched samples taken from some of the missing girls. One of the girls who had barely escaped Bundy's attack picked him immediately from a lineup, identifying him as the man impersonating a cop who had tried to kidnap and kill her a year before.

Now investigators had enough to charge Bundy with aggravated kidnapping and attempted criminal assault. He claimed innocence, and bail was set at $15,000. Bundy's parents paid the bail, and he had once again weaseled out (again under surveillance)…

On February 23, 1976, Bundy faced trial for his kidnapping charge. On March 1, he was found guilty of aggravated kidnapping and assault, and was sentenced to one to fifteen years prison. About seven months later, he was discovered creeping around in the bushes of the prison yard "carrying an 'escape kit'—road maps, airline schedules, and a social security card—and spent several weeks in solitary confinement."[476] That month, after enough evidence had been stacked against him, he was charged with murder by the state of Colorado and transferred to Aspen. Having above-average knowledge of law as a result of his schooling, he elected to represent himself in trial as his own defense attorney, maintaining his innocence, and the judge therefore gave him the special privilege of being able to wander unshackled in the law library. Standing out of the immediate view of his escorts, he jumped out of a second-story window, sprained his ankle upon landing, and hobbled down the city sidewalks to nearby woods to temporary freedom. This was the third time he was able to weasel out of facing the music…

Bundy was lost in the woods for six days, which he spent breaking into cabins and trailers to steal food, clothing, and a rifle. He was unable to put much distance behind him, however; all he accomplished was to keep turning furious circles and limping around on an increasingly painful ankle out in the middle of the confounded trees. He stole a car and started driving, but began falling asleep at the wheel. Two officers who observed his erratic driving and pulled him over recognized him immediately and recaptured him. He was just a couple of blocks away from where he had escaped.

Back in prison, Bundy obtained a hacksaw (he never said from whom) and whittled away at a crawlspace in the ceiling of his cell for months, until an opening finally gave way. When it did, having lost a lot of weight for his escape plan, Bundy slinked up into the space and started inching through the ceilings, taking months to discover which path led where in the facility. Finally, when the prison operations had been reduced to a skeletal staff for Christmas weekend in 1977, Bundy again slipped into the ceilings. This time, he made his way out of the crawlspace, dropping down into the apartment of the chief jailor (who was out on a Christmas date with his wife), and exiting into the street. He stole a car, and, after the car broke down, he hitched a ride to town, where he took a bus to Denver…where he took a flight to Chicago…where he took a train to Michigan…where he stole another car and drove to Atlanta…where he took a bus to Tallahassee, Florida. (No chance of travel like that ever happening again, with today's security measures…) This would be the last time he weaseled. After his next arrest, Bundy would never see freedom again. But he would continue to claim he was innocent.

Once in Tallassee, Bundy stayed put. He adopted an alias: Chris Hagen. With this new identity and the ability to look like different people, his plan, initially, was to clean up his act and refrain from further criminal activity. He kept a low profile at his new location from January 8 to January 15 of 1978—just one week. Then he slipped into the Chi Omega Sorority House and, as silent as a shadow, snuck up on and bludgeoned four coeds in less than fifteen minutes, easily within earshot of more than thirty people who said they never heard a thing. Then Bundy immediately traveled eight blocks away, where he broke into another house and bludgeoned another young girl. Of his five victims that night, two died (Margaret Bowman and Lisa Levy) and three survived with terrible injuries. The next victim Bundy abducted from a junior high school a few weeks later. This girl, Kimberly Leach, Bundy's final victim, did not survive.

Four days after murdering Leach, Bundy was spotted driving a stolen Volkswagen Bug. When an officer attempted to arrest Bundy for the auto theft, Bundy kicked the officer's legs out from under him and ran. Shots were fired by the officer, nobody was hit, and Bundy was eventually wrestled into submission.

The officer was unaware that he had just arrested the murderer of dozens of young girls. He took Bundy into custody for the stolen vehicle charge and, as he was driving back to the station, he heard Bundy say that he'd wished the officer would have just killed him.

Don't Miss Tonight's Showing of *You Got the Wrong Guy!*

Ted Bundy was a lot of things, but just as much as anything else, he was a player to a fault when the cameras were pointed at him. He did more than just defend himself (until the very end, he acted as his own defense, despite the on-again, off-again, on-again game he forced public defense attorneys to play while he took first chair, then second chair, then first chair again, claiming one day to like a guy and the next day complaining about his incompetence, on and on and on). He liked to *play* lawyer. It was partly about convincing juries that he wasn't guilty of the mounting charges that slowly attached themselves to his case, certainly. But it was also about getting to be the big man on campus, give the suave, wink-and-gun treatment to the naïve Bundy fans who paraded their pretty faces and long hair (parted in the middle) into the courtroom every day. (This group of young women was made up of witnesses, court reporters, deputies, detectives, and even survivors of the attacks [who were not awake to see their attacker]! But surely, this guy couldn't be guilty, so they had to giggle and whisper like, well, *girls*, every time he flashed them the "trial" Bundy face. Most of them looked just like many of the girls who had gone missing.)

We can see that Bundy was not the innocent, charming, sophisticated knight in legal armor he was pretending to be. But he was far worse than just "guilty" in the courts. In the face of murder charges and nightmar-

ish allegations of crimes that he knew *very well* he had committed, he
made a mockery of his victims' deaths by playing like he was some jovial
celebrity, with the whole world his stage. He pretended to be enraged
by the injustice of the accusations against him, and often threatened to
stomp out of the courtroom rather than sit down, shut up, and calmly
maintain his innocence. If "innocence" was how he was going to play
his cards, the least he could have done in his deception was show some
respect to those who remained alive but were heartbroken by the hurt he
had caused. Instead of taking the trial of the deaths of young, violated
girls seriously, he continued to flatter the giggling female "audience" just
behind him with—*zing!*—a smile here and—*pow!*—a chuckle there. He
was like some flamboyant entertainer who had been cast as the role of
a serious defendant who decided to turn the production into a comedy
and roll with it to see how it turned out. It wasn't just his trial, it was his
performance. And by choosing to handle himself that way, he did a great
disservice to those girls he killed, and to their families.

Shame on him.

The worst part of his performance was his disturbing, cross-examination tap dance with Ray Crew, a Florida State University police officer
who had been one of the first responders to the Chi Omega House crime
scene. Law enforcement had been called in because of a panicked and
garbled phone call from the dorm's house mother, and the officers had
believed they were heading to the site to see what damage had been done
between two girls fighting about a boyfriend or something.[477] However,
when the officers arrived at the scene to find two girls injured and two
others dead, they were tragically affected by what they saw.

In the courtroom, Bundy set out to make Crew look like an inexperienced fool who had inadvertently tampered with the evidence. Bundy
(who was still claiming that he had nothing to do with any of the murders, and who had never left a fingerprint at the scene of any crimes) was
concocting an oh-so-brilliant scheme. In his cross-examination of Crew,
Bundy planned to take the jury step by step through Crew's discovery
of the bodies, questioning the officer about every diminutive element,

every movement he made, and everything he saw, in the hopes of exposing a moment when Crew had corrupted the crime scene. But a couple of events happened that caused Bundy's plan to backfire.

To begin with, the miniscule scrutiny and itemization of the bloody mess Bundy had left behind at the Chi Omega House—and that he was forcing Crew to recount—caused the jury to hear of the brutality on such a detailed level that they were all terribly disturbed. In addition to distressing jury members with the graphic description of the frightening scene itself, Bundy compelled Crew to relive an event so personally unsettling that his emotional delivery of the testimony greatly bothered everyone present.

Yet, that wasn't it…not by itself, anyway. There was a pivotal moment in Bundy's interview of Crew that many sources have had a hard time explaining. Movies made about the famous murderer have portrayed a scene wherein an otherwise cocky Bundy suddenly starts to stare at Crew with an unusual expression and encourages the officer to speak of every detail, while the Bundy character responds to the details with a visible, sick gratification. It's as if to suggest that the jury saw a flash of the real Bundy as he psychologically devoured the scene as a pleasant memory.

Did the inner monster flash an inappropriate Bundy face in the real-life trial? Did he drop his mask for a split second to reveal the face of the psychopath?

According to later interviews with Crew, something was indeed very twisted and bizarre about Bundy during that cross-examination. In an article by WCTV:

> He says he felt Bundy was reliving the crime as he testified. The former FSU Police Officer says it was unnerving.
> "I got the feeling I was feeding his obsession with the whole thing," says Crew.[478]

The minute Bundy had no further questions for Crew, everyone in the courtroom was aware that change was on the wind. At least for the time being, Bundy's flirting, peanut-gallery group didn't even look at him.[479]

Bundy's public defenders would never again allow him to cross-examine
during his trial; they knew that this little charade had been "a mistake."[480]

Another source relates it this way:

> On the day that the prosecution saturated the jurors with the blood
> and gore of the crimes, Bundy cross-examined Officer Ray Crew.
> Slowly and always eliciting detail, Ted led Crew back through the
> awful night, searing the crimes' bloody aftermath into the jurors'
> minds. Ted made sure everyone had an enduring impression of
> the brutal handiwork.
>
> These appearances as his own attorney grew less frequent as
> the trial wore on. Ted continued to join each bench conference
> with Judge Cowart and he did not lose his zest for courtroom
> spectacle. But he was beginning to buckle.[481]

Bundy attempted to show his innocence during trial with his casual
exterior, probably assuming that a guilty man would be solemn or scared
and an innocent man would act slapdash and far removed from the crimes
he was being accused of. And perhaps that strategy was working, up to a
point. But there's no doubt about it: When Bundy interrogated Crew that
day, the real Bundy eclipsed the cavalier, counterfeit Bundy, and the jury
found him guilty.

There had never been enough evidence to officially charge Bundy
with any of his earlier murders. In the end, he was only ever formally
charged and tried for the murders at the Chi Omega Sorority House and
for the murder of Kimberly Leach weeks later. Despite Bundy's impec-
cable ability to cover his tracks, an eyewitness had seen him leaving the
sorority house. That report, along with forensic odontologist Dr. Richard
Souviron's testimony about Bundy's dental identification in the question
of a bite mark found on a victim's body, eventually placed Bundy at the
scene of the Chi Omega crime. That murder conviction, along with eyewitness testimonies and clothing fiber analysis evidence, eventually rendered a guilty verdict in the trial of Kimberly Leach.

Although he was a strong suspect in many other murders, these three murders (Bowman, Levy, and Leach) would be the only murders the courts would ever convict Ted Bundy of.

Louise Bundy attended the sentencing, and "tearfully pleaded for her son's life."[482] Her pleas were not enough to save him.

He was sentenced to die by electric chair.

THE LAST WORD

The concluding near-decade of Bundy's life on death row is remembered as his final, constant struggle to prove everyone wrong. Bundy continued to perform his "I didn't do it" song and dance until his very last appeals and attempted stays of execution were rejected for the last time.

Then, suddenly and without warning, the world saw the newest, and last, Bundy.

Confessions of a Psychopath

Bundy had played his last card. With no tricks up his sleeve and no way to reverse the sentence, within just days and hours just before his execution, he opened his mouth and excreted the blackest, vilest accounts of murder, giving investigators exactly what they had sought for more than ten years. Then Bundy continued to fill them in on elements of his case—with details beyond anything they had ever expected to hear. Bundy was an even darker character than they had imagined. (Note that, although he had hinted at confessions, making suggestions about "how a killer might do something" and the like well before this time, this was his first official confession.)

It has been documented in several books, at least two of which this author has read and cited from in this case study, that Bundy lived out his final days without almost a wink of sleep. Some of his confession recordings, in Rule's opinion (she knew his voice and mannerisms), were a stream of words uttered in unbelievable exhaustion by a very weary man at the end of his rope, finally willing to let the families of his victims know that the girls who had come up missing were never coming home. This author has listened to the tapes. Bundy frequently says that certain details are too hard for him to talk about when he is asked for specifics. Oddly, some details he does share are incredibly unsettling, while others, the subjects he feels he can't talk about, are tame by comparison.

As he tells of the murders, at one point, the question is raised as to why he is now talking. According to Bundy, if his words are understood correctly, he wanted to fully exonerate his family from having anything to do with any of it. This close to the scheduled end of his life, with very little sleep and the reality of his situation weighing on him greatly, there are sometimes moments when his fear is evident. His stutter, a habit that he had kicked in his youth, found its way back into his dialogue on the tapes here and there. Sometimes he sounds like he's managing alright, with his intelligence intact, telling his story as if he were just a very tired person at the end of a long day talking about a clothing special at the nearest department store. Other times, sporadically, Bundy's voice drops into a darkness, a weariness, a tormented place, and it sounds as if he's struggling to get his demented memories out into the open air.

There are a few chilling moments when Bundy is afraid that some of the officers nearby will hear what he has to say, so he leans in to speak discreetly to his interviewer. These moments catch the listener off guard, because his voice jerks suddenly from being a reasonable volume at a reasonable distance away to a slow, harsh whisper only inches away from the recorder, as he reveals additional, graphic, blood-curdling details of his barbaric crimes. It's surreal, like a voice from beyond the grave rapidly flying to just behind your ear to whisper the angrier and more assaulting threats to humankind's mortal fragility.

In hindsight, it's obvious from every angle that Bundy made an enormous mistake by claiming to be innocent for as long as he did. Psychoanalysis today is much more sophisticated than it was in Bundy's day, and his state of mind is still undergoing constant review in the psychiatric field. There's no telling whether our tools of medicine will ever allow a definite diagnosis of his mental illnesses or personality disorders, especially now that he's no longer alive to analyze in person. Had he admitted what he had done and been honest at any point in his case, a Pandora's box of possibilities would have been opened, resulting in…who knows what could have been the outcome back then? Insanity plea bargains? Commutation? Successful appeals? Not to mention the advances that science might have made if allowed unrestricted access to analyze Bundy's psychological processing. But Bundy refused to allow anyone to think that any part of him was broken.

We do know that, according to the facts compiled then, and according to the sciences we had then and up to now, Bundy was an official psychopath: a man who knew the rules, was sane enough to know that it was wrong to break them, and had zero empathy for those he killed. (See the Jeffrey Dahmer case study following for insight on brainwave activity associated to empathy.) Based on what we know about psychopaths in regards to secular medicines and sciences, psychopaths are not, *and cannot be*, redeemable creatures, because they are not capable of being sorry or feeling guilty. And if someone is not capable of being sorry, if he is not remorseful, then he cannot be truly capable of repentance. Repentance is a necessary element in the process of redemption. Right? (First of all, that's a very crude assimilation, and not all psych science points to that breakdown. But many times, people take the opinions of professionals in the field to mean that precisely.)

So, when Bundy came forward at the end of his life with both confessions of murder and claims of Christ on his lips, the world scoffed. People claimed that he was only confessing his crimes in an effort to manipulate the legal system into giving him a stay of execution—and there is probably some truth to the idea that he would start to confess to gain more time before his execution. (Note, however, that even after the Supreme Court denied his final appeal only hours before his death, and even after the prison staff had shaved his head and prepared his body for execution just before collecting him to walk the hall a final time—and with therefore assumedly no ulterior motive but to confess his sin in a situation where there is no earthly reversal of his death only minutes away—he gave his last confession. Make of that what you will.)

But as far as whether Bundy was capable of sincerity upon his approach to the Lord Jesus Christ, well, that question has simply come up too many times for this book—a book focused on the subject of redemption potentially extending to the otherwise unredeemable—to skirt. Certainly, we don't know for sure if Bundy, specifically, was sincere, as we have said repeatedly throughout this work that *we are not making any solid statements about another person's sincere commitment to Christ*, and we are not about to change that now. But the question of whether he or any other diagnosed psychopath was or is *capable* of sincerity is something this book must now briefly address.

To begin, let us point to the fact that over a decade before his date with death, Bundy had begun telling his close acquaintances that he had been reading the Bible, and the words in it had comforted him and brought him peace. Sometimes those moments resulted in something poetic. As he shared with Rule:

Sleep comes on slowly
Read the words of the wholly [*sic*]
The scriptures bring peace
They talk of release
They bring us to God
In here that seems odd
But His gift is so clear
I find that He's near
Mercy and redemption
Without an exception
He puts me at ease
Jailer, do what you please
No harm can befall me
When the Savior does call me.[483]

Many who heard that Bundy had given his life to the Lord just before he died would not know that in the place called prison, that suffocating and redundant place, the place both physically and psychologically suppressing, he had been reading the Bible and talking about a personal relationship with Christ for some time before the end. But for many, none of this would matter or be taken seriously as long as the debate raged on.

The fact is that a diagnosis, though incredibly beneficial in helping one understand a person, is given by another finite human being. The science is not always exact, and in many cases (*including* Bundy), the diagnosis begins as one analysis, morphs into another, and lands at a completely different conclusion entirely, sometimes continuing to adjust to modern medicine years after the person has passed on and his or her condition is studied with more insight into the depths of the human brain. Bundy had a reputation for having confused professionals in the field from the first analysis and forward,[484] and he was even originally diagnosed with Multiple Personality Disorder/Dissociative Identity Disorder. At another time, he was diagnosed as bipolar[485]—and he is *still* the subject of much study. To believe without question the diagnosis of a psychiatric professional is to overlook the obvious contributing factor of human error. This is especially true in cases where the diagnoses jump all over the place, pointing to one human mind that is more of a mystery even to professionals than anything a label can be placed upon. And with this practice ever evolving, what we know about the human mind today greatly trumps what we thought of the mind a hundred years ago; what we will know a century from now will evermore dilute our strongest diagnoses today. (Imagine how much differently Sean Sellers' life might have turned out today, when so much more is known about his disorder than in the late '80s and early '90s.) And lastly, to believe wholeheartedly in science or psychiatric practice of any kind is to limit God...no?

The Legendary Dobson Interview

With only days left to live, Bundy turned down hundreds of requests for media interviews, refusing to see anyone except for those he would trust to handle his taped confessions and Dr. James Dobson.

The media had a heyday with the interview Dobson conducted with

Bundy. Rumors instantaneously generated headlines, many of them reporting lies as if they were fact.

Many believe, and incorrectly so, that Dobson was looking to profit from Bundy's situation. Articles with headlines like "Minister Cashes in on Bundy"[486] were shameless in broadcasting their uninformed claims. Others believed, again incorrectly so, that Dobson was jumping up and down outside Bundy's cell, begging for the chance to be the elect, final interviewer.

In fact, Bundy had reached out to Dobson through his ministry back in December of 1986, more than two years before the interview was filmed. Bundy, without directly admitting to any crimes or implicating himself in any way, had told Dobson that there would come a day when he would have things to confess, and that when that day came, he would also have statements to make about pornography and its effect on his life. Concerned that any other press or media interviewer would misrepresent his confession and warning or edit his interview to mean something other than what it meant, he told Dobson that he had nobody else he could trust. When he asked if Dobson would be willing to come to Florida, Dobson agreed, and between that day and the day of the interview, Dobson corresponded with Bundy by mail, discussing the harm of pornography with him while he waited for the interview invitation Bundy had told him to expect.[487] This shows two things: 1) Bundy had been thinking about his confessions for a long time before he finally talked, despite claims that he decided to come forward at the last minute and confess solely for the purpose of trying to stay his execution; and 2) Bundy had been thinking far in advance about a warning he wanted to leave with the world about pornography, despite claims that pornography was just the next impulsively chosen spectacle card he wanted to play for attention.

In addition, Dobson and Bundy signed a legal agreement stipulating that any money made from the sale of the video through Dobson's ministry would go first to the reimbursement of costs for the video to be recorded and produced, and then to the fight against violent pornography.[488] So, despite Dobson asking for twenty-five-dollar donations for each video, he never had a plan for "cashing in" on anything; nor was there ever a plan stating that Bundy would be paid for an interview.

Watching Dobson's interview of Bundy is like night and day compared with watching Bundy in court. The *trial* Bundy face had been cool, collected, confident, flirtatious. The *final interview* Bundy face was, after several minutes, erratic, stumbling, jumpy, and restless. It was as if all of Bundy's masks had been used up, and his very last one was cracking. It's clear on the video that Bundy is trying to hold himself together, but it's also obvious that he's scared out of his mind. He pauses a lot. Sometimes, his eyes dart around, and at other times they are completely and unusually closed—even while he's talking. He says "uh" constantly, and his overall presence is comparatively irregular. (A person talking to either Bundy for the first time might not notice anything specifically unusual. But a person evaluating the difference between the man in this final interview and the man from prior footage would easily pick up on the idea that he or she is watching a frightened grown man in the Dobson tape.)

When one knows the back story of the circumstances leading up to the interview, it is a lot easier to hold the opinion that there was nothing fake about it.

Bundy *was* scared.

When, after the interview, Dobson was asked, "So you feel [that] it was, *in fact*, the last honest statements of a condemned man?" Dobson said: "*Listen* to the man's voice. *Look* into his *eyes*, and draw your own conclusions. I think it's obvious."[489]

The interview started with Dr. Dobson reiterating that, within only a few hours, Ted Bundy would be executed. What, Dr. Dobson wanted to know, was on Bundy's mind?

Go Tell My Story

Bundy's answer was that he sometimes felt at peace about the execution and at other times he felt no peace at all.

Dobson asked Bundy to state for the record, with cameras rolling, that he was, in fact, guilty of killing many young women. Bundy confirmed that it was true. Dobson then asked for Bundy to go back to the beginning and share with the viewers how it all had gone wrong. It was about this point in the interview that Bundy didn't quite seem like his old, poised self as he shared that professionals, as well as he, himself, had been trying to answer that question, and that it remained a question.

Dobson asked Bundy to confirm that he had been raised in a good home, a *Christian* home, without any abuse, and Bundy did so. (Note that Bundy, himself, may not have ever been directly abused in any physical way, but a phenomenal amount of psychological and emotional abuse in his early developmental years has been confirmed repeatedly in his case, both by psychiatric analysis and evaluation, and also by testimonies of his then-living relatives. To many, Bundy only absolved his family, his sister-mother, and even violent Sam Cowell from having any responsibility for his developing into a bad person. When compared to the alternative answer of blaming them for his problems, this was certainly the more prudent and appreciated answer; however, this answer often leads people to think he came from a "normal" home—which is not at all true, as already discussed.) From there, he told what he could remember of his story.

At twelve, Bundy had begun acquiring soft-core pornography from the local grocery stores and other local businesses (remember, he was a master shoplifter, so he didn't have to be of age to "buy" anything), and, while exploring his neighborhood, he had discovered that he could get hold of additional pornography while digging through others' trash. These discarded publications, as he would find out, contained pictures of a much harder and more graphic nature.[490]

Dobson asked Bundy to explain how these materials had caused Bundy to become corrupted. At this moment in the interview, Bundy abruptly and firmly stopped the discussion to make a significant proclamation:

> Okay, before we go any further, I think, uh, it's important to me that people believe what I'm saying, to tell you that I'm not *blaming* pornography. I'm not saying that it *caused* me to go out and do certain things. I take *full* responsibility for…all the things that I've done. That's not the question here. The question, and, and, or,

the *issue* here, is how this kind of literature *contributed* and helped *mold* and, and *shape* [these] kinds of violent behavior.[491]

Continuing his story, after making sure that Dobson understood that he was not looking for a scapegoat for his crimes, Bundy began to explain that as he was putting these images into his mind (it wasn't the soft-core, but the violent pornography now), it slowly and gradually became an addiction. And, like with any addiction, he grew hungrier and hungrier for the next, "more potent, more explicit, more graphic"[492] materials—just like a drug.

For the next couple of minutes, Bundy struggled to explain how the addiction grew into an appetite for more than just pictures and film. Seeing that he was having difficulty, Dobson cut in and asked Bundy if he remembered what precisely it was that "pushed" him "over that edge." Bundy once again stopped the interview to reiterate his earlier proclamation: "Again, when you say 'pushed,' I—I know what you're saying, but I don't wanna confer…that I was some kind of, of helpless kind of victim,"[493] and he then went over the point that it was an influential kind of material that he was messing with. (This video is sarcastically referred to all over the Internet as Bundy's "porn made me do it" interview. This author wonders if the people who refer to it as that have even listened to what he said when he, on more than one occasion, loudly and clearly stated the opposite.)

Dobson said that he understood, and Bundy continued.

The destructive energy that built up while he was simultaneously looking at the images and drowning his moral inhibitions in alcohol, he said, eventually corroded his mind until he had given himself over to the hunger completely. He openly acknowledged that there are plenty of people who would testify that they have given in to the temptation to view pornography, and yet they didn't go out and hurt anybody. He stated that he knew that this was true, and offered that he did not know why porn had impacted him more than others.

Dobson asked what Bundy had felt, emotionally, after his first murder. With great difficulty, and after reminding Dobson that even years later it was still so very hard to talk about, he explained that it was like emerging from a horrific trance, like a kind of animalistic possession had taken over. He said he had awakened the next day with the terrible memory of it all, which was sickening, initially. Then, as time passed (not as slowly as one might think) after the first murder, life returned to some kind of regular pattern wherein his daily thoughts were not compulsively owned by the memory of what he had done. There was a dark, secret "segment" of his life that he disconcertingly compartmentalized as he continued to go on living and killing.

Finally, after much more disturbing conversation between Dobson and Bundy, the death row inmate was given his opportunity to bring home the warning for which he had begged Dobson to provide a platform: This man, Bundy, was not alone in his perversion, and from behind bars, he had a chance to see that for himself. He said of these people:

> We are your sons, and we are your husbands.... Pornography can reach out and snatch a kid out of any house today.... There is no protection against the kinds of influences that are loose in a society that tolerates—[at this moment he choked up and stopped talking until Dobson helped bring the focus back]... I've met a lot of men who were motivated to commit violence just like me, and *without exception, every one of them* was *deeply* involved in pornography, without question, without exception, *deeply* influenced and *consumed* by an addiction to pornography. There's no question about it. The FBI's own study on serial homicide shows that the most common interest among serial killers is pornography.[494]

Dobson asked Bundy what his life might have been like if he had never become entangled with pornography. Bundy answered that it would have been a different life, void of the kind of crime he had committed; of this he was certain. There was a sadness to him, a look as if to say, "What a waste." Then, the question that was on everyone's mind, the question that everyone wanted to hear Dobson ask, was finally uttered: Was Ted Bundy sorry? Did he carry remorse for his crimes?

With God's assistance, "Yes. Absolutely."[495]

Bundy, only just maintaining his composure, explained that even if those he had harmed could not believe his repentance, he hoped they at least believed him when he said that there were people just like him out there feeding their minds with the dirt and filth that society and the media allow in magazines and television.[496]

Bundy said he knew he would likely never be forgiven by those he had caused so much grief, and that he did not deserve their forgiveness. Dobson asked if Bundy believed he *did* deserve execution.

BUNDY: That's a good question and I'll answer it very honestly. I don't want to die.… I deserve certainly the most extreme punishment society has…and I believe society deserves to be protected from me.…

DOBSON: You told me last night…that you have accepted the forgiveness of Jesus Christ and [you] are a follower and a believer in Him. Do you draw strength from that as you approach these final hours?

BUNDY: Uh, I do. I can't say that being in the Valley of the Shadow of Death is something that I've become all that accustomed to and that I'm strong and that nothing's bothering me.… It gets kinda lonely. And yet, I have to remind myself that every one of us will go through this someday.… This is just an experience that we all share. Here I am.[497]

Later, Dobson would say that the experience led him to believe that Bundy was a "frightened, broken man" who was "deeply remorseful."[498]

Life Is But a Vapor

Whereas ye know not what shall be on the morrow. For what is your life? It is even a vapour, that appeareth for a little time, and then vanisheth away. (James 4:14)

At around three o'clock in the afternoon, Monday, January 23, 1989, Dobson bid Bundy farewell. Within the next couple of hours, Bundy wrote his last will, requesting that his body be cremated and scattered over the Washington Cascade Mountains.[499]

A little while before midnight, Bundy took communion with crackers and a Coke alongside another man who had become a spiritual advisor, his prison minister friend, Jack Tanner.[500] Just after this, Bundy was contacted by his defense team and told that the Supreme Court had rejected his final appeal. Bundy was shaken by the news.

At 2:12 in the morning on Tuesday, January 24, 1989, Bundy spoke to his mother over the phone for the very last time. Louise's final words to Bundy were, "You will always be my precious son."[501]

At 4:47, Bundy refused his last meal, drinking only water.[502]

Between 5:00 and 6:00 that morning, he appeared subdued during the preparations. His head was shaved, his body was showered, and a conducting gel was placed on his scalp.[503]

Between 6:00 and 6:57, Bundy recorded his final victim confession.[504]

At 7:00, Bundy had to be physically pulled into the execution chamber, as he dug his feet into the floor of the outer room in resistance. He continued to fight against the guards as they dragged him, trembling and shaking his head in fear, the whole way from the door to the electric chair.[505]

Ted Bundy's last words, while he was being strapped into Old Sparky, were, "I'd like you to give my love to my family and friends."[506]

At 7:06, the executioner received the signal to activate the chair, and did so immediately. Volts of electricity passed through Bundy's body for one minute. When the execution was over, Bundy was still. Smoke rose from his body,[507] and his spirit rose with it. Gone in a puff of smoke...

In a vapor.

He left without peace. He left without forgiveness from those he had hurt. He left without closure. He left this world as a hated man.

Ted Bundy, serial killer of young women, perpetrator of children's nightmares, was gone.

When the prison staff gave the signal to the thousands of people gathered outside the prison fence, an uproarious celebration ensued, involving chanting and cheers, voices singing about electric death, fireworks shooting up into the sky and bursting into an array of bright colors, news anchors shouting above the honking horns, and cameras flashing and filming all over the place.

It was an ironic and historic moment in memory of the man who had always wanted to be celebrated.

Ted Bundy left behind one of the most chilling legacies of evil this world has ever seen. He left behind one of the most famous stories of conversion to Christianity this world has ever seen. The contrast of those two extremes in one man would perpetuate the study of his psychological profile for decades and probably longer, using that profile as a famous basis of comparison for so many lessons this world still has, and may always have, to learn about his mind.

And the world has continued to ask, ever so skeptically: Was Ted Bundy capable of being redeemed? Was God big enough to save him?

If so, it was never because *Bundy* was amazing. It was because God is.

JEFFREY DAHMER
(THE MILWAUKEE MONSTER; THE MILWAUKEE CANNIBAL)[508]

The metal-against-metal sound of the handcuffs clanked out in the still air like a menacing alarm, competing only with the sound of Tracy Edwards' heavy breaths as he ran about the unforgivably hot city. The thirty-two-year-old African-American man didn't usually consider the police to be his friends, but on this night, July 22, 1991, around 11:30 p.m., amidst the stink of the garbage on the streets made more rank than usual by the baking summer humidity, the police were exactly whom Edwards was looking for. The search was increasingly desperate until he finally spotted the familiar red-and-blue-lighted vehicle.

As the officers sat in their car, likely tossing little more than the typical doughnut-and-coffee-shift banter between them, they saw the man running toward them. Clamped on one wrist, handcuffs dangled wildly as Edwards flailed his arms to get their attention. Assuming he was an escaped potential arrestee who had outsmarted another policeman, they jumped into action, readying themselves to recapture the man and question him. Abruptly, however, they realized that their questioning was not needed. Edwards was not evading them. He was *scared*. He was *seeking their help*.

Within moments, Edwards had launched into a suspiciously bizarre story. Perhaps their initial instinct had been correct, and this man was dangerous, or crazy, or both, considering the troubling report he had begun to tell of some freak at the apartment complex who had cuffed him and promised him imminent death. The other details of the tale he was spinning couldn't possibly be true, not even a little bit. People as bad as the man he was claiming to have escaped didn't exist outside the movies.

But then, what was with the handcuffs?

The police escorted Edwards back to the Oxford Apartments at 924 North 25th Street, Milwaukee, Wisconsin, and kept a sharp eye on him as they approached the door with the numbers "213" posted on the front. The officers knocked. The door opened. A polite young man stood there, glanced at Edwards with recognition, and cooperatively invited the trio inside, where Edwards' story now evolved to include a knife threat that had been presented to him earlier in the bedroom. As the police began to question Jeffrey Dahmer as to the whereabouts of the key to the handcuffs he had reportedly placed around Edwards' wrist, Dahmer, whose "mind was in a haze,"[509] motioned to a back room. The policeman entered the bedroom and found a knife under the bed. Taking liberties to continue the search, as the scene was growing more ominous, he pilfered around for a minute, and finally found himself opening the drawer of a nearby nightstand. The horrifying contents within sparked immediate action.

In a panic, the officer shouted, "Cuff him!" and a scuffle ensued in the front room.[510] From the hallway, a neighbor woman who knew Dahmer heard him "howl[ing] like an animal that [she'd] never heard before…a loud, screeching, un-human" sound.[511]

Once he was pinned to the floor and resistance proved futile, Dahmer made eye contact with one of the officers and said something that wouldn't quickly be forgotten: "For what I did I should be dead."[512]

Hours later…

At the police department downtown, Pat Kennedy, a rookie homicide cop, sat across from Dahmer in the interrogation room. Dahmer was drunk, but calm and responsive.

Kennedy had seen something back at the apartment that had caused him to be aware that this would be no ordinary, "things got out of hand" confession from the typical drunkard of Milwaukee's seedier alleyways. But, despite the evidence he had already seen, nothing would prepare him for how big this case *really* was. Once he and Dahmer were set up with a cup of coffee and a cigarette each, he began.

"My name is Pat Kennedy…and I'm the one who's gonna be talkin' to you about the [things we found at your apartment].…"

"I really don't think that it's in my best interest to talk to you about this."[513]

Dahmer's response was unusual. It wasn't a roughened, tough-guy "no," the kind of answer that Kennedy had heard so many times. Nor was it the instant, defeated response from one who would be easy to crack. This thirty-one-year-old white guy in the nerdy glasses had many secrets, and he protected them as politely as the surroundings of an interrogation room would allow. How odd.

Kennedy offered to speak of something unrelated. Gain the perpetrator's trust. Bring the defenses down a little. Calm the waters. Set the mood. Approach the subject from a friendlier angle. For several hours, the two men spoke of many things: Dahmer's job at the chocolate factory, religion, alcoholism…

Ah, alcoholism. *That* was the ticket. The handwriting was on the wall.

The more they spoke of alcohol, the closer they were getting to a break, and Kennedy knew it. He had struggled with alcohol abuse in his own past. The moment of bonding between cop and criminal had arrived, and Kennedy knew he had to seize it.

"If in fact you are an alcoholic, alcoholism is a disease.…" Kennedy continued on.

"Well, for what I've done, there's no excuse,"[514] Dahmer replied.

"I'm not here to judge you."[515]

After a little over three hours of questioning, Kennedy believed he was almost there. He had discovered the crack. Dahmer was now informed that the police were back at his apartment, searching for his darkest secrets, secrets that by nature could never remain hidden. The boogeyman had been captured, Milwaukee would have its monster, the people would have their public enemy number one.

This Kennedy personality was proving easy to talk to.

Finally, Dahmer spoke.

"When I tell you what I'm gonna tell you, you're gonna be famous."[516]

VICTIMS OF THE LONE BOOGEYMAN

Jeffrey Dahmer. The very name carries an evil insinuation on the air, a floating threat, an eternal, hazy fog of dread that creeps into the human psyche, inciting a vulnerability that we just can't put a finger on. When hearing mention of his name, people stop to listen to what is being said with nervous anticipation, as if even from beyond the grave, Dahmer still has the influence to terrorize. Even though he is no longer a part of this earthly world, and therefore not a possible threat to us ever again, his crimes were so ghastly and unthinkable that his legacy of horror continues to tap into a universal, shared consciousness encouraging us to look over our shoulders when the subject is brought up. It's as if he was so powerfully and inhumanly "boogeyman," and yet so completely human all at the same time, that he represents a malevolence lying dormant within humanity that could strike at any moment from somewhere or someone else. These people *do* exist outside the movies, and Dahmer was proof.

Whereas *all* "have sinned and come short of the glory of God" (Romans 3:23), and whereas there are many who would argue that the Bible says all sins are equal (see endnote; that is not necessarily the opinion of this author[517]), some sins (or crimes) are less fathomable to our human minds. Some crimes are such that our natural reaction is to wonder if *those* sins are less forgivable than others, or if *that* criminal is farther away from God than the rest of us, even after his or her story of conversion to Christianity is revealed. If there were ever a name that would thrust this topic into a raging debate wherein psychiatrists, ministers, and laymen alike all find their usually firm opinions wavering, it would be the case of Jeffrey Dahmer. Those usually representing the forgiveness argument have blogged about their struggles with this particularly vile case to the point that some have changed their opinion. Those on the condemnation side of any other debate have watched interviews with Dahmer or read about his conversion, and, *because* of the vileness of the case and the contrast of who he appeared to be after the intervention, have found his story to be the most powerful argument of forgiveness to date. Yet, not surprisingly, in many cases of online public discussion, those casting the biggest votes for or against him often reveal somewhere along the thread that they were largely unaware of *who he even was as an individual*: his childhood, his mental and personality disorders, his long-developing need for a deeper association with humankind, his potential motives for murder, etc. It's as if an invisible slingshot with the name "Dahmer" in the launcher is pulled so tight that it's quivering, and the second someone says the name, it's launched into instant debate, soaring straight past who he was as a person and directly into the accounts of his psychotic murders and Christian conversion.

Jeffrey Dahmer took the lives of seventeen men, all of whose souls were precious to the Lord, and all of whose lives were precious to their loved ones. That we know of, none of his victims were ever given the opportunity to make their final peace with their Maker before they were forced by Dahmer's hand to face eternal judgment. The victims' families were never given the chance to say goodbye before they were whisked away to participate in a murder trial that uncovered truths so disturbing that it would haunt them for the rest of their lives and force them to mourn the loss of their sons and brothers with mental imagery that is unimaginably horrific. It's understandable that people wonder if God really would allow a man like this to enter heaven through the pearly gates and share an amazing eternity with all the holy saints walking the streets of gold.

Dahmer, like Ted Bundy, definitely had a beast within. His "Hyde" remained even better hidden than Bundy's. There are many similarities between the two men, not limited to, but including:

- Both had psychopathic and sociopathic personality abnormalities leading to a lack of empathy.
- Both viewed people as pawns in their own selfish games of compulsion.
- Both had hordes of people who mistakenly assumed (without doing any research) that the men's childhoods had been simply "normal."

Like with Bundy's case study, it would do this book a great discredit to pretend that Dahmer was not a very bad and corrupt individual who carried out very bad and corrupt crimes against humanity. He was the stuff that nightmares are made of—an absolutely and wholly unbelievable anomaly of the human race, *so* mystifying that, after his death, researchers preserved his brain for further study in an attempt to discover what had made him tick.

Despite the similarities between the lives of Ted Bundy and Jeffrey Dahmer, a study of Dahmer's case reveals early on some great contrasts between these two personalities as well. Unlike Bundy, who lied about the murders until only days before his death and who shamelessly wowed those at his murder trial and on television interviews like he was a celebrity victim of the justice system, Dahmer confessed to his crimes immediately. Yes, he did so only after he was caught, when the evidence against him was obvious enough to incriminate him anyway, but he confessed of *everything* he had done, including things the world would never have known about. Further, he did so after waiving his rights to have an attorney present during his confession to Pat Kennedy. That showed that Dahmer had no interest in protecting his own hide, in saving face, or, more interestingly, in ever reentering society as a free man. Unlike Bundy, who withheld his apology to those he had hurt until his final hour, Dahmer expressed guilt, shame, and remorse for his crimes right after his capture and in the presence of the victims' family members at his trial. (Whether one chooses to believe his apologetic words, he spoke to the families with his head down in shame, took responsibility for what he had done, didn't try to blame anyone else or offer excuses for his actions, and told them he was sorry.)

So, how does a meek and mild-mannered young man, as he is repeatedly described, unconcerned with his own societal freedom, apologetic to the world (around the same time he committed the crimes), and willing to publicly confess his crimes come to be the mysterious anomaly of immorality that he was?

In Dahmer's case, this has to some degree always remained a mystery, even to Dahmer, himself. But alongside the mysteries of how or why his acts became as *extreme* as they did in his case comes an obvious contributor, about which many reliable Dahmer media and literature resources agree: He was severely and chronically lonely.

The Science of Solitude

According to Dr. John T. Cacioppo—widely considered the be-all and end-all expert in loneliness research—social depth and human interaction are far more important to mental and physical health than most people know. (See endnote for more details of Cacioppo's credentials.[518]) In a lecture called "The Lethality of Loneliness," Cacioppo builds a strong argument supported by science that spells out how and why loneliness is needed for basic human survival and normal association with the rest of the world, and that, without a balance in this area, we can *expect* a dangerous result. When these basic needs aren't fulfilled, not only do we become a very vulnerable creation, but those around us become more vulnerable to our actions (or wicked deeds) as a result of our dissociation with the world around us.

Cacioppo states:

We're born into the most prolonged period of dependency, but in our transition to adulthood, we achieve autonomy, independence. We become kings of the mountain. Captains of our Universe…. When we look out into the social world, other individuals certainly *look* distinct. Independent, selfish entities with no forces binding them together. No wonder that we forget that we are members of a social species.[519]

Humans, he argues, are in many ways not the superior earthly species when compared to nature's incredible wonders. In comparison to dogs, cats, and other creations on the planet, we are slow in movement, our instinct about other individuals or animals (and, in some people's line of thinking, spirits or other dimensions) is greatly impaired, we cannot see in the dark, we cannot "sniff" out diseases, and so on. The superiority that humans *do* have as a species is the ability to "communicate, plan, reason, and work together"[520] with an intelligence far above the rest of nature. "Our *survival* depends on our collective abilities, not on individual might [or will]."[521]

Our connection to others and need to draw from others, as well as our need to give ourselves, our talents, and abilities to others, are, as Cacioppo relates, a powerful and invisible force similar to gravity. When one thinks about this comparison, it makes perfect sense. No matter how many times you throw something into the air, assuming you have not ventured into space, the rules of gravity always apply: That item will invariably come down, submitting to a force stronger than itself. If humans venture away from meeting a powerful and instinctive social need by throwing themselves against the pull that they feel towards others (trying to escape the need to connect with others because they have been hurt before, or never fit in), they will invariably come back around to addressing that need (trying to reconnect with people), because that need is a force stronger than themselves. It was built into them as something in their wiring, in their design, that cannot be ignored. And, similar to the laws of gravity, the harder they have thrown themselves against the law of connection to others, the harder they will come crashing down. These previously hurt or estranged people are socially fragile, like glass, and when they are met with the harsh-hitting reality of their social ineptitude, they break. Sometimes they shatter. Glass can only be glued back together so many times before it's broken for good.

Without trust, communication, and interaction within a community, we would lack everything that a community provides: school systems, churches, commerce, or jobs, etc. Without trust, communication, and interaction as a nation, we would have no government, law, homeland security, international protection or peace, or funding for certain avenues of world-changing research, etc. *Our very procreation and therefore continual existence* depends on two people coming together to share a unique form of love-communication to bring new life. Our world and its superior and governing species depend completely on healthy social and interactive feeding. And *yes*, as Cacioppo explains, this need that the whole human race would become extinct without *absolutely does, and must, start with the individual*:

> Across our biological heritage, our brain and biology has been sculpted to incline us toward certain ways of feeling, thinking, and behaving. For instance, we have a number of biological machineries that capitalize on aversive signals to motivate us to act in ways that are essential for our survival. Hunger, for instance, is triggered by low blood sugar and motivates you to eat....
>
> Thirst is an aversive signal that motivates us to search for drinkable water prior to falling victim to dehydration. And pain is an aversive system that notifies us of potential tissue damage and motivates us to take care of our physical body. You might think that the biological warning machinery stops there. But there's more....
>
> The pain and aversiveness of loneliness, of feeling isolated from those around you, is also part of a biological early warning machinery to alert you to threats and damage to your *social* body, which you also need to survive... Loneliness [has] been characterized as a "gnawing, chronic disease, without redeeming features."[522]

Overweight or obese people are often heard saying, "I am fat." When approached quite literally, however, they are not fat. They *have* fat. They also *have* fingernails, but they are not fingernails. A person is not defined by a condition, not literally. However, if individuals become so obsessed with their weight that every moment of their lives and all of their relationships surround that thread of thought, their condition becomes defining, merely because that is the only way they exist within themselves and to the people around them. This is the difference between *symptoms* (a person who has put on a few pounds) and a chronic, severe *condition* (a morbidly obese person). Similarly, although almost all of us have lonely days now and then, there are those who have crossed over into a chronic, severe loneliness condition. These people might be written off by secure, happy people as just moody or brooding, when in fact they are tormented by an actual disease that the average Joe couldn't possibly understand. And there are those still who have ventured so far into loneliness that their condition defines them completely. That is how they are known within themselves and by the universe around them. Also, continuing this comparison, an obese man can be aware that he is overweight while simultaneously being oblivious that he has aquired diabetes until a medical professional makes him aware that his first condition (obesity) has caused secondary condition (diabetes). Similarly, severely lonely people may be aware that they are lonely, but are unaware that the loneliness is causing other mental dysfunctions (such as extreme obsessions, quirks, paranoia, depression, etc.) until a psychiatric professional tells them. In a same way that the obese man doesn't go straight to the doctor for treatment of his diabetes, because he doesn't yet know he has that condition, severely lonely people often don't talk about or seek help for their loneliness because they don't understand the full effects their condition is having on them.

As Cacioppo relates, "You don't hear people talking about feeling lonely.... [It is] the psychological equivalent to being a loser in life for a weak person, and this is *truly* unfortunate, because it means we are more likely to deny feeling lonely, which makes no more sense than denying we feel hunger, thirst, or [physical] pain."[523] He then goes on to reveal some of the more recent research that has proven that whereas polluted air, obesity, and heavy alcohol use increases early death by 5, 20, and 30 percent, respectively, loneliness tops the chart with a whopping *45 percent* increased chance of early death. That is quite a remarkable morbidity/mortality ratio related to a state of mind, as opposed to the other contributors, which are blatant attacks on the physical body condition.[524]

Being severely lonely is not just tragic; it is dangerous. This is not just one man's opinion. Neuroscientific brainwave analysis reveals that the brain of a lonely person shows more visual cortical activity than the brains of others when exposed to images of "social threats" within an environment of human interaction as an adverse side effect of self-preservation.[525] Yes, that's a mouthful. Put far more simply, a lonely participant of this brainwave test views a picture of a "social threat" (for instance, a picture of two people arguing or of an abandoned homeless man on a bench) with more brainwave intensity than a nonlonely person. As a result, the lonely person can react (or overreact) with more intensity to what he or she feels socially threatened by, as a direct result of the brain's self-preservation (self-protecting) mechanism. The body and brain have *physiological connections* to social health. The physiological "fight or flight" response that occurs when one perceives a threat can therefore be triggered to cause a person to act against a social threat (violence, arguments, abandonment, etc.) earlier and with more intensity and impulsiveness in a lonely person than in a nonlonely person.

Within the same brainwave study, the temporal parietal junction (the part of the brain responsible for empathy or sensitivity to another's perspective) showed *less* activity in the lonely person than in the nonlonely person.[526] This means that a lonely person will have far less concern for another's feelings. In part, this is because he or she lacks the understanding of caring for others that a nonlonely person feels after having experienced social normalcy and human connection; and in part, this is because the lonely person is *physiologically* driven and/or influenced by the brain's automatic self-preservation mechanism as opposed to a learned consideration for others. (Remember, we are referring to severe, chronic loneliness: not just a person who is left alone on a weekend, but a person who is left alone for a lifetime.)

And whereas we would never suggest that a person is not responsible for his or her own actions, Cacioppo makes an astounding observation related to modern neuroscience—a field that was not as sharp in Dahmer's day. "These…roots, tilting our brain and biology toward self-preservation also suggest that much of what's triggered by social isolation is *non-conscious*."[527]

A lonely person can lash out at another person "non-consciously"?

Cacioppo uses an example: A lonely individual has only the want or need to be plugged into and active with the people around him or her, and this is all the lonely person can literally feel. A need. A want. These people have desire for the fulfillment of something that everyone around them seems to have and enjoy. They are completely "non-conscious" of the fact that they have physiologically entered a state of natural defense response to the point of what is known as a *hyper-vigilance* for social threats. An individual in this state might see a social threat where there isn't one. Think back to all those corny movies or television shows where some guy sits at a campfire telling fellow campers spooky stories about a crazy axe murderer. When everyone goes to their sleeping bags for the night, a rustling in the bushes caused by a harmless rabbit is suddenly, to the camper in a hyper-vigilant state of self-preservation, the terrifying sound of the footsteps of an axe murderer outside the tent. The first few times this occurs, the camper might be scared, but he is at the same time aware on a literal level that there is not an axe murderer in the bushes. After a thousand times, he might be chronically and severely plagued with true belief in the threat. A severely lonely person might be simply saying goodbye to a friend he or she had over for coffee, but when the friend leaves, a lonely person who has evolved to a chronic, hyper-vigilant state of self-preservation for social threats might truly believe that the friend's exit is real abandonment.

Finally, all of these stresses listed above lead to a sharp increase in the body's release of morning cortisol (a very strong stress hormone), which therefore increases one's impulsive reactionary behaviors. This renders both the lonely person and whomever he or she interacts with more vulnerable to some form of intensified exchange (such as an attack, verbal or otherwise). For instance: In the same way that this camper would hold onto a baseball bat all night, after years of chronic fear in association with the axe murderer he is now truly convinced is just outside, the lonely person also does not let go of his defensive tools, meaning that there is no break from feeling threatened. The camper swinging at his friend who is coming back from relieving himself in the bushes at night is not doing so because he wants to hurt his friend; he is driven by a physiological and instinctual fight-or-flight response that "triggers" an impulsive reaction to his paranoid state. Was the camper responsible for his actions? Absolutely, yes! Not only should he have calmed down for a minute and assessed whether the person entering the tent was a real threat, he should have received psychological counseling early on for his fear of the axe murderer, preventing his problems from escalating to the point of endangering others. Was the camper conscious of a decision to hit his friend? Not according to Cacioppo, because he was swinging at the *perceived threat:* the axe murderer. The camper saw a threat where there wasn't one. Severely lonely people can lash out when they perceive a social threat, and though they are absolutely responsible for their reaction (and treatment of their condition early on), if their condition is far enough advanced, the question of their consciousness at the moment of an impulse is a different matter.

"But hold on," one might say, "There is a huge difference between someone protecting himself from an axe murderer, real or otherwise, versus someone protecting himself from a 'social' threat!" True. This is why the condition of loneliness is so often overlooked as a danger. But, according to Cacioppo (and other research), neuroscience recognizes that the *physiological* triggers within the human brain relating to *hyper-vigilance and self-preservation* are the same.

Chronic and severe loneliness is now considered to be a *disease*. This view is not solely that of Cacioppo, but also of many psychiatric professionals who have contributed research studies to the US National Library of Medicine within the archives of the National Institutes of Health.[528] (This is only to name the most easily accessible resources; these studies are widespread online and in science journals.)

Each case study in this book (Susan Atkins, Charles Watson, Sean Sellers, David Berkowitz, Karla Faye Tucker, and Ted Bundy), based on the symptoms of loneliness discussed by Cacioppo, might be a contender for being diagnosed with this brand of deep isolation—to the point of disease. However, one individual *so plagued* by this condition that he has been referred to in psychology as "pathologically lonesome"[529] (the root word "pathology" refers to "the study of diseases and of the changes that they cause: changes in a person, an animal, or a plant that are caused by disease"[530]) was boogeyman Jeffrey Dahmer: murderer, necrophile, and cannibal. (*Because of the graphic nature of Dahmer's crimes, that short list of crimes will be nearly the only time the details of his murders are mentioned. The responsibility of further exploration into exactly what he did and to whom must fall upon the readers, although they should be warned that the details are unsettling, and discretion is advised—especially online, where pictures and other content are posted carelessly and haphazardly. It is safe to summarize that, although Dahmer is most well known for more perverse killing in his later days of freedom, most of his earlier victims met their end by bludgeoning and/or strangulation.*)

His victims[531] were:

- Steven Hicks (aged approximately 19)
- Steven Toumi (aged 24)
- James Doxtator (aged 15)
- Richard Guerrero (aged approximately 25)
- Ronald Douglas Flowers Jr. (age unspecified in court)
  - **Survived**; drugged, escorted by Dahmer to bus station, then woke up in hospital
- S. S. (The name of this victim was omitted in court for privacy; age unspecified in court)
  - **Survived**; drugged, fled Dahmer's residence, then treated in hospital
- Anthony Sears (aged approximately 25)
- Raymond Smith (aged approximately 31)
- L. P. (The name of this victim was omitted in court for privacy; age given in court was "approximately 16")
  - **Survived**; struck with a rubber mallet, fled Dahmer's residence, returned to Dahmer to ask for taxi money, then took taxi home
- Edward Smith (aged approximately 33)
- Ernest Miller (aged 22)
- David Thomas (aged 23)
- Curtis Straughter (aged approximately 18)

- Errol Lindsey (aged 19)
- Tony Hughes (aged 31)
- Konerak Sinthasomphone (aged 14)
- Matt Turner (aged 20)
- Jeremiah Weinberger (aged 23)
- Oliver Lacy (aged 23)
- Joseph Bradehoft (aged 25)
- Tracy Edwards (aged 32 at the time)
  - **Survived**; drugged, handcuffed, threatened with a knife, fled Dahmer's residence, and then flagged down nearby police; took the officers to Dahmer's apartment where Dahmer was then finally apprehended

Just after Dahmer's arrest, media buzzed relentlessly outside the Oxford Apartment complex, with camcorders rolling and cameras flashing as police officials moved in and out of apartment 213 with boxes of evidence in tow. Reporters, bystanders, and lawmen shook their heads in disbelief at the horrifying details of the scene now being whispered in hush-tone waves through the traumatized crowds. Residents of the apartment were crying, calling loved ones, staring in shock, covering their mouths. Nobody dared sleep in his or her own apartment that night, choosing instead to rely on each other's company in a sleeping-bag campout on the floors outside the elevators.[532] People from the community surrounded the building, pressing their faces against the glass of the foyer like tourists in line for a theme park's haunted house attraction.

For some, the terror would never end.

There has never been, nor will there ever be, an excuse for Dahmer's horrifyingly sadistic misdeeds. Hands down, he is known as one of the most prolific and haunting serial killers of all time.

Lionel Dahmer, Jeffrey Dahmer's father, upon his son's incarceration, documented his story in a book, *A Father's Story*, to show the side of Jeffrey that was less known to the world than the killer he became. The author's tone throughout the book is surprisingly nondefensive, as he describes both the glorious memories of an all-American family as well as the unflattering recollections of a troubled home with secrets. Unlike what one might expect—a biographical memoir by the father of a serial killer written to exonerate himself of any responsibility in raising a killer—Lionel Dahmer's book is more or less an apology letter to the world written by a man who recognizes and admits his failures in having prevented the early development of a killer.

And the development did start early. Dahmer was born as innocent as anyone else…but complications, for *him*, began in the womb.

IT IS NOT GOOD FOR MAN TO BE ALONE (GENESIS 2:18A)

Joyce Dahmer announced her pregnancy to Lionel Dahmer in 1959. The happy couple had only been married a few months before they had to begin planning their lives to include a little one. They cherished the thought of raising a child together in the quaint towns of Ohio, but quickly, Lionel could see that Joyce was not carrying the baby comfortably. Almost all books, articles, documentaries, and case documentation of this period in their lives together reflect a repeating occurrence that could never truly be explained, and one that would initially only manifest during pregnancy, and later return with fervor, continuing for years into the lives of their offspring. In addition to having more serious and long-lasting nausea than most women, Joyce fell into mysterious physical fits, likened by some Dahmer literature to epileptic seizures and referred to by others as simply "strange seizures." Those who knew Joyce Dahmer described spells in which her whole body locked up; she was unable to move or speak, and spittle collected at the mouth ("frothing" at the mouth, as some sources refer to it[533]). Her eyes, witnesses said, would bulge, her jaw would jerk to one side, and, off and on, extreme muscle spasms would wrench her body about. Pulling her out of these episodes proved challenging and required much patience; many times, Lionel needed help. As time went on, when others' assistance proved less and less effective in slowing or stopping these incidents, Joyce's doctor began administering injections of barbiturates and morphine. The longer the treatment went on, the less physical evidence the doctor could find of any physical condition. Eventually, he suggested that the attacks were wholly stemming from a mental condition and had nothing to do with her physical state. It is unclear whether the doctor's suggestion that she seek psychiatric care was discussed at length or dismissed immediately, but it became clear that Joyce refused to undergo psychiatric treatment. As a result, the doctor increased the drug treatment, adding phenobarbital to the list.[534] Eventually, Joyce was taking as many as twenty-six pills a day.[535]

This gestational drug administration has been the subject of great attention in Jeffrey Dahmer's case, with questions raised regarding the effects the drugs would have had on Jeffrey's brain before birth. (Note: "Phenobarbital can cause fetal damage when administered to a pregnant woman. Retrospective case-controlled studies have suggested a connection between the maternal consumption of Phenobarbital and higher than expected incidence of fetal abnormalities. Following oral administration, Phenobarbital readily crosses the placental barrier and is distributed throughout fetal tissues *with highest concentrations found in the placenta, fetal liver, and brain.*... If this drug is used during pregnancy, or if the patient becomes pregnant while taking this drug, the patient should be apprised of the potential hazard to the fetus."[536]) What might have been an undiagnosed mental disorder within Joyce could have, if psychological evaluation had been sought early on, shown possible connections to Dahmer's predisposition to psychological and psychotic statuses later on.[537]

But through all the troubles came a speedy and smooth delivery, and at around 4:45 in the afternoon on May 21, 1960, Lionel and Joyce became parents to baby Jeffrey Dahmer.

From birth to age three, Dahmer was a bright-eyed joy. He was curious, intelligent, and observant, picking up communication and motor skills from an early age. (His later IQ test, conducted at Ohio State University when he was eighteen, resulted in a score of 145,[538] characterizing him as a "genius," according to a number of score charts,[539] and placing him in a category of intelligence that only 0.2 percent of the human population would ever achieve or exceed.[540]) But, for all the wonderful benefits that can come from a child being advanced in absorbing the colorful world around him as he experiences infant and toddler sensory development, there is another side to atmospheric absorption—one that was dominant in the Dahmer house.

The tension between Lionel and Joyce that had been born and nurtured during her pregnancy only increased. The couple had a beautiful little boy, but their marriage would prove to never be the same. Joyce withdrew into herself, preferring to stay in bed and refusing to come to dinner, often with little Dahmer in a bassinet near Joyce's bed. She had known no stability during her own childhood; her father had been a chronic, raging drunk described as "wildly explosive."[541] Lionel, who felt lost in his attempts to reach out to or bond with his wife, usually decided to give her just what she wanted: solitude. As the days passed, the two avoided each other for longer periods of time, while Lionel, a natural chemist, retreated to his chemistry lab and slaved away toward his graduate goals. The estrangement was almost permanent, but when it eased, as it sometimes did, the couple was filled with hope again for their relationship—until the next pitfall. This cycle kept them together, but their marriage was increasingly dysfunctional. The prospect of happiness was perpetually flaunting, never fully attainable.

Lionel found himself more and more often at his lab, many times staying overnight. The all-but-abandoned Joyce retaliated with more bite until the fighting escalated to take on a threatening, physical nature, and she was no stranger to emerging from the kitchen with a knife to "make jabbing motions" toward him; after those episodes, Lionel would leave the house again.[542] The deterioration of the Dahmers' emotional and romantic health, along with Joyce's past experiences of having an alcoholic father, caused the young wife and mother to have nightmares. Joyce began screaming in her sleep.[543]

Dahmer remained a bubbly little boy, in spite of the fact that he was hearing Mommy scream at night, hearing Daddy shout at Mommy, seeing Mommy threaten to stab Daddy with a knife, and watching Daddy leave again. He knew no other reality than the one they had painted, and despite everything, he seemed well adjusted, happy, *normal*. His physical *health*, however, wasn't always ideal. Suffering from recurring ear and throat infections, he stayed awake at night in tears when the infections peaked, was taken frequently to the doctor, and received shots in the buttocks for treatment. This continual stress led to his developing anxiety about the doctors and nurses, and involved incidents of Dahmer lashing out at medical staff. Yet, besides the constant trips to the scary-shots place, he was a well-adjusted child who liked to play in the sandbox, ride his tricycle, and run to his daddy's arms every time he came home.

In one memory Lionel recalls of this time, Lionel had placed his son on the chrome handlebars of his bicycle and went for a casual ride. (A clip on YouTube shows Dahmer's home video footage of this and of other precious father-son interactions during this period. See endnotes.[544]) Something in Dahmer's sight sparked extreme interest, and he told his dad to immediately stop the bike. Upon closer inspection, Lionel realized that his son had spotted a baby nighthawk that had fallen from its nest. They took the fledgling home and, for the next several weeks, carefully nursed it to maturation. When they released it back into its habitat, the moment the bird flew away, up and out of Lionel's hands and back into the soaring, carefree life it was meant to have, Dahmer's expression was one of such delight that Lionel wrote of it: "It may have been the single, happiest moment of his life."[545]

It was also quite possibly the last moment in his life when his wide-eyed curiosity about an animal would originate from a healthy place.

Sharp Things, Fiddlesticks, and Roadkill

> The person who tries to live alone will not succeed as a human being. His heart withers if it does not answer another heart. His mind shrinks away if he hears only the echoes of his own thoughts and finds no other inspiration.—Pearl S. Buck[546]

In 1964, when Dahmer was almost four, something changed the course of his thoughts. It began when he started to feel a small pain begin to grow in his groin. Rapidly, the spot became more painful and tender, and then an alarming lump appeared. Lionel and Joyce took him to the doctor immediately. There, among the scary people who stuck sharp things into his buttocks, he was diagnosed with a double hernia and informed that surgery, the event in which the scary people would cut him open in his most sensitive and private area, was the only option for treatment.

The double hernia had been a *birth defect.*[547]

For a week, Dahmer awaited the frightening surgery. When he was finally brought in to the clinic/hospital and sedated, he awoke in the recovery room to what Lionel observed to be an incredible amount of pain. "So much pain…" Lionel recalls, "that he had asked Joyce if the doctors had cut off his [boy parts]."[548]

Dahmer lost his happy glow then and there, and it never again fully returned.

Coming home after several days at the hospital, amongst the doctors and nurses and sharp objects, Dahmer moved around the house "like an old man."[549] His boyish bounce had been replaced with quietness, his smiles replaced with expressions of pondering, his joy replaced with a loss of innocence. Nobody in that operating room had gone outside the bounds of standard surgical practice, none of the hospital staff had done anything inappropriate, but Dahmer internalized the memory of the incident intensely, with his imagination blemished by images of blood and his—

But he would work it out. Lionel was sure of that. Joyce was depressed and unhappy, and there were simply too many things to do at the lab for him to think much about that now. His boy would be fine.

In the following autumn, strange animals called civet cats (very odorous cousin to the skunk) heavily populated the woods around the Dahmer home. The creatures had taken to various rodent-hunting and discovered that the crevices of earth under the house were where they liked to loiter and devour their prey. The bones of these rodents attracted even more civet cats, which caused a terrible stink. Lionel set out into various crawl spaces to extract the attractive buffet of rodent remains and drive away other potential civet cats.

As he dragged large piles of bones out from under the house and placed them in a bucket, Joyce emerged to talk to him. Dahmer, standing nearby, showed an instant and strange fascination with the bones. He began to pick them up and drop them again, listening to the clickety-clack as they fell against each other. Lionel approached and began to clean up the scattered bones, but Dahmer simply continued to toy around with them, picking them up, dropping them, examining them, dropping them again, listening to the crackle…over and over. As Lionel began to dispose of them, Dahmer, in a little world of his own, showing interest in something for the first time without parental introduction (such as toys or bicycles), said quietly, "Like fiddlesticks."[550]

Lionel had no reason to think this sudden intrigue with dead animals was anything of consequence. Boys will be boys. And besides, Lionel had had a deep and concentrated obsession with fire as a child; that obsession had grown into a chemistry hobby, which had led to a chemistry college major, which had paved the way for an eventual PhD in chemistry, which had laid the foundation for lifelong work that provided for his family. Dahmer was four. It likely meant absolutely nothing to see him treat a pile of rodent bones like they were toys. But, even if this fascination did turn out to have meaning in his son's life later, it could be something fantastic, like a future in anatomical research, medicine, or one of those artistic but dirty jobs nobody likes to do, such as taxidermy. Only wonderful things could be ahead for such a bright child. And, for bright children with bright futures, curiosity was a priceless tool! Besides, the boy had been acting sad or lonely or something lately, so whatever brought interest back into his eyes might as well be let alone.

Shortly thereafter, when Dahmer asked what would happen if someone cut out his belly button, his father wrote it off as silly talk. When Dahmer broke out the windows of a nearby building, Lionel called it kid stuff. When Lionel and his son took a fishing trip and Dahmer once again got that "fiddlesticks" expression on his face while staring at the exposed innards of a fish they had caught and gutted, well, what child wouldn't react with fascination?[551] When Dahmer chose to entertain himself by hiding in the bushes and watching people, once again, his father thought it was no big deal.[552] And when the boy became more introverted, saying very little, staring off into space, wearing blank expressions as he sat in the middle of a room or stretched across his bed to stare at the ceiling, his dad just considered him a kid with a big imagination and lots to think about.[553]

Actually, Dahmer *was* a kid with a big imagination. Sadly, while living in his own little world in a dysfunctional and tense home, he was feeling himself winding tighter and tighter, and he had no outlet for expressing the terror that was budding in his thoughts.

These were only some of oh-so-many red flags that would be missed or misinterpreted—by a father who saw only inquisitiveness in his offspring—as a result of his working far too much at the lab to pay close enough attention. (Looking back, in his writings of 1992, Lionel admits that although he should have seen these signs and intervened, this was his first child, and even he, himself, had turned his own obsessive, boyish curiosity into a lucrative career. Based on interviews and the fatherly love and concern he conveys in his book, there seems no reason to believe that he ever intended anything but the best for his son. This author believes that Lionel tried his best, and that only within recent years in this country's cultural evolution has the fatherly figure been expected to be as involved a child's life as the motherly figure; so, though he was disappearing to his workplace all the time, Lionel was bringing home the bread. It's all just a strange tragedy of bizarre circumstance, and in so many ways, Lionel can be considered one of the victims—as well as part of the cause—of Dahmer's troubles, and he has spent every moment of his life since 1991 with unfathomable regret.)

Physically, Dahmer grew up fast. Mentally, Dahmer's development was stunted. He had no friends, his father was always at the lab or involved in his studies, and, by the fall of 1966, Joyce was pregnant again—which meant she was depressed again, having seizures again, taking crazy meds again, and again driving the angst between her and Lionel even farther into the suffocating and antisocial atmosphere that left little room for any young boy to process the violence in his head. And, when children have nothing to connect to but themselves—in their own bedrooms, in their own heads, with their own dark thoughts—that's the connection they embrace and hold steadfastly to. (Sound familiar? There seems to be a pattern among people who grow up to hurt people, doesn't there?)

Dahmer became a sort of mechanical child. His responses to interaction were often short, only offering the minimal requirement of words to satisfy a question, and never offering up his own thoughts or ponderings—especially as they grew increasingly abnormal. The images constantly developing in his mind were terrifying, so he kept them secret. When he was hungry, he ate; when he was thirsty, he drank; when Lionel and Joyce were fighting, he retreated to his room to escape the tension. But, beyond addressing the only needs he identified as necessary, he merely existed. Why would anyone consider warm, human interaction a basic need?

Dahmer's fear of even speaking to another person was so intense that when he began the first grade, he finally made an impression on his parents. Lionel recalls:

> On the morning of his first scheduled school day, I remember the terror that swept into his face. He appeared nearly speechless, his features frozen. The little boy who'd once seemed so happy and self-assured had disappeared. He had been replaced by someone else, a different person, now deeply shy, distant, nearly uncommunicative.[554]

The boy's first-grade teacher mirrored these observations, and met with Lionel expressing her feelings about this "inordinately shy and reclusive boy" who gave her the "impression of profound unhappiness."[555] (Note that in one interview, Dahmer stated that he didn't think he was as withdrawn as others claim. However, the majority of sources, including this teacher's reflection, point to an intense isolation. Also, keep in mind that, as mentioned earlier, a person suffering from chronic and severe loneliness is often too close to the problem to see the degree of his or her condition.) When the teacher continued to tell Lionel of how his son completely avoided all communication with children his own age and spent recess wandering around by himself, Lionel was concerned, but convinced that this was a side effect of having just moved to a new home. Oh sure, there were kids around, and sometimes Dahmer even visited with them. As long as he could fade into the background and only rarely utter barely audible responses to his "buddies," he had lots of friends.

He would adjust...

And then, it seemed like he did.

Six-year-old Dahmer's brother, David, was born into the family now, and as an infant, he provided no deep company for his older brother—but at least he was another presence in the home that did not directly engage in the ceaseless fighting. The baby was someone for Dahmer to develop somewhat of an attachment to, someone unthreatening and safe, but there is little evidence that the brothers were ever really close—at least not any more than Dahmer was to his pet, Frisky. (After the murders, David Dahmer legally changed his name and disassociated from the family.) Frisky was a close companion to Dahmer through the years, and it was certainly better than nothing, but having a dog as a sole companion isn't what modern psychiatric medicine considers healthy. Lionel, feeling that some time together with the boy would be good, and wishing to encourage his son's odd string of interests in something productive, took him to the chemistry lab one day and showed him various chemical reactions. Dahmer wasn't particularly interested, so Lionel concluded that his son would find another way to channel his hobbies.[556]

It was now 1967. Lee, a new neighbor boy, befriended Dahmer, and for a time the two boys enjoyed what was probably one of only a few normal relationships that Dahmer would ever have. In the afternoons, they played like typical kids, limiting their experimentation of their curiosity to sticks, rocks, and other equally innocent tools. The following October they went trick-or-treating together, and it was that night when one of the more well known pictures of Dahmer was taken; he was smiling next to his friend before their night of candy-collecting began. Before long, although they remained in contact sometimes, the friends' relationship fizzled (the exact reason for this is uncertain).

Dahmer returned to his isolation, mentally and emotionally pitching himself in the opposite direction of any connection to people. Then, when he was in the third grade, he felt that familiar gravitational pull, the basic need for human contact, and decided to give friendship another try.

His teacher's assistant was very nice to him, and he found her presence slightly less menacing than the rest of the "scary" human species. Excited about his new acquaintance, and wanting to please her, he decided he would give her a gift to seal their friendship. It was a huge risk, but one he was willing to take, because the pulling force of connecting with another person was a force stronger than himself. Having never developed any rational understanding of an appropriate gift from one friend to another, he took a bowl out to the creek, filled it with tadpoles, and affectionately and proudly presented it to her upon their next meeting.

He was falling now, into that warm connection that promised happiness, enjoying the descent into blissful camaraderie, accepting another's familiarity as an alliance against seclusion.

His landing, however, broke him like glass.

When he found out that his teacher had nonchalantly given the precious gift to his neighbor, Lee, Dahmer took his first step toward some semblance of violence. His trusting plunge into a people connection had betrayed him. She couldn't possibly have cared about his gift if her intention had been to shove it into the hands of the next kid who came along, like a burden, an encumbrance upon her life, a cramp in her style. Dahmer's heartfelt present was nothing more than taxing.

When heads were turned, he slipped into Lee's garage and dumped motor oil into the bowl. The tadpoles suffocated and died.

It was fascinating.

As time passed, Dahmer fell into patterns of incomparable introversion. Slowly, he shared less and less contact with the world around him, and, as he approached puberty and his body began to change, his fantasies plummeted into perversion. As his father would later discover, Dahmer started to entertain the fleeting notion that a person lying still and not saying anything would be easier to talk to and bond with than someone who demanded a certain behavior or dialogue from him. But it would be years still before Dahmer ever acted upon this urge. For now, he continued to live in a torment that his parents couldn't recognize and no one else could do anything about. Dahmer's isolation became so profound that it began to manifest itself physically. Slowly, he began to walk with a peculiar gait, a rigidity, like a toy soldier. His arms were always at his side and his hands were pressed against his clothing, knees only barely bending and shoes almost scraping the ground.[557] (High-school acquaintances would later remember his walking form, describing it as a strange thing to observe.[558] After watching hours of interview and documentary footage, one can see that, as a child, Dahmer was loose-limbed and unassuming in his movement, but in rare clips and some photos, his posture and movement do appear to be slightly robotic later on, always standing at attention, and almost like an awkward attempt at something funny that never arrives at a punch line. Then, interestingly, from his first appearance in court and until his dying day, his body language was completely normal. It seems to suggest that the minute his secrets were blown wide open and he no longer had anything to hide, his mind and body let the tension dissipate.)

Moths and insects are irritating. People kill them all the time. Nobody would think Dahmer was weird for killing them. Dissecting them wasn't a big deal for a chemist's son, either—if you weren't a total girl. Still, nobody was ever around, so nobody would need to know.

All the while, the fiery, festering pit of anguish was ever brewing in his mind. As a way of channeling his thoughts and satisfying his irregular curiosities, Dahmer began walking and riding his bike around his neighborhood in search of roadkill or dead animals in the woods.

It was then that he began retrieving the lifeless animals and carrying them to a secluded area for his own scientific visceral study. Not yet even out of elementary school, Dahmer was toying with a chemistry all his own: Evidently, he was interested in chemical reactions when they involved something no longer breathing. The "hut,"[559] as Dahmer referred to it once or twice when he chose to speak out loud, was an outbuilding behind his house. It was where his father stored spare chemicals and jars, and it was fascinating what the roadkill would do in formaldehyde. On one occasion, when some acquaintances were cutting through his yard as a shortcut, they happened upon Dahmer carrying cat remains. They reacted with repulsion, and asked him what he was planning to do with it. Feeling cornered, and challenged by their judgmental gazes, Dahmer told them the truth: He was planning to dissolve the carcass in acid. Naturally, the other kids thought he was teasing, so he opened the door of the hut, pointed at a jar of "murky liquid,"[560] and told them it was a raccoon. Further challenged by their scoffing disbelief, and suddenly angered, Dahmer lifted the raccoon jar from its shelf and smashed it on the ground, revealing that his claim had been true. The boys ran from the hut, vomiting from the sight and smell and calling Dahmer a freak.[561] (Lionel noted that he was not aware of this incident, nor similar incidents, until the trial.[562])

When Dahmer met his friend Greg, he was once again intrigued by the concept that he could spend time with someone, and maybe even talk to that person sometimes. This friendship would be the closest one he ever had during those dark days. It lasted longer than any other, and even though Dahmer was still slipping into a void of black, creeping always closer to an edge from where he would eventually trip and die on the inside, this one, normal relationship in his life held him to reality like a string.

The bond between Dahmer and Greg is not one that this author can write about—not because it involved anything inappropriate or shocking, but because, by this time, Dahmer never talked about anything with those who would go on to speak out about who he was and what his friends did. Dahmer never came home from a movie with Greg to tell his family about his favorite scenes. He never participated in contact sports at all, or touched anyone, ever, so he never had any bruises to laugh about "that time when Greg kicked the ball too hard." He never went to group events and "chilled" with the guys on skateboards, returning to his house to ask his dad for money for some new wheels. Because he never talked about this relationship, and because nobody else ever saw Dahmer—due to the fact that he was an enigmatic shadow who lurked around when required and disappeared off to the far corners of isolation when his presence wasn't obligated to mandatory people-mingles such as school—the only fact we have is that Dahmer considered this Greg fellow to be his best friend.

For a while, until Dahmer was around the age of fourteen, his behaviors seemed only marginally sinister. He floated for some time in the limbo between the will of his own species' people-connection laws and his own will to crawl in a hole of perversion and think thoughts that nobody,

nobody, could ever know about. If the people around him had any idea, *any idea at all*, what compulsive deliberations went on in the foul recesses of his mind... But it was no matter, because he would never let that happen. He would just avoid people while he dissolved his dearly departed animals in jars. Those were his friends now.

Except for Greg. He never avoided Greg.

Then Greg wanted to have other friends.

So the two drifted apart, and Greg was the last friend Dahmer had prior to his final days.

"DOING A DAHMER"

A "graphic novel," for those who don't already know, is a book the same size and approximate page count as a standard trade novel. It is called "graphic" not for anything unsettling (although those are also available), but because it tells its story with graphics (illustrations) instead of text. It's just like a comic book, except smaller in width and height, much thicker, and bound like a regular paperback.

John Backderf, who went to high school with Dahmer, learned that he was a talented cartoonist and graphic illustrator. Calling himself "Derf Backderf" after graduation, he went on to struggle through a few odd drawing jobs here and there, but didn't get his lucky break as a high-profile illustrator until after he self-published what was initially a short comic book called *My Friend Dahmer*. The title of his comic book was a transparent statement of irony, because the story unfolded to show precisely that Dahmer had absolutely no friends in high school. Not one. Not ever. When the comic gained so much attention, Backderf went on to express his art more prolifically as doors of opportunity opened. Eventually, he came back to the Dahmer comic book, now with the professional abilities and prospect to see it done correctly, and he rereleased it as a full-length graphic novel. The finished product is hard to describe. It's a surreally intimate glance at an awkward high school student who, through the drawings of someone who knew him, appears desperate, floating, grasping... He seems fake, but not fake as in immaturely superficial or phony, but fake as in putting up a front for people to see. He seems like a cardboard man trying so hard to disappear into the background that his effort ends up being counterproductive: a kid so tragically painted with bully targets that blending in really meant popping out. He seems like a person who is dead, but physically animated. Even during the scenes that depict Dahmer bursting explosively out of his shell, causing a spectacle (more on this later), Backderf managed to capture something in the lines and shading of Dahmer that bleeds off the page and into your mind for days after reading it, haunting you with the imagery of a teenager's expression that is so counterfeit, so covering of something underneath, and so hopelessly deserted. (Some of the scenes from this graphic novel will be referred to in this study, because, even though Backderf used sketches rather than text to inform his readers, the information in the book was well-documented and follows truth, as seen in the book's endnotes. Backderf's perspective is also unique because the scenes reflect eyewitness accounts of fellow schoolmates and events that took place in public, rather than news reports, which results in a personal touch: Backderf is able to convey who Dahmer was to those around him instead of just listing his name on another crime report. Note: To anyone considering reading this graphic novel, be warned that some of the content is unsuitable for young readers. Most of the dark events portrayed in the book are insinuated or suggested rather than blatantly drawn, and Backderf has tried to tell the story as cleanly as possible, but Dahmer, by default, is a case that should be approached with caution.)

We don't know exactly what year Dahmer started getting ruthlessly bullied, because that information would have depended upon Dahmer actually talking to someone long enough to report it, which, as readers can already guess, never happened. But from the start of the *My Friend Dahmer* graphic novel, we can see that the bullying was already well established shortly into high school, so it likely began years prior. Known by some only as the demeaning nickname "Dumber," while minding his own business, Dahmer would be grabbed by passing students, who shoved him into the walls or lockers.[563] For mandatory physical education class, it was always an extreme humiliation to "get stuck with" Dahmer.[564]

Exiting the school bus inspired schoolmates to randomly punch him in the back of the head and knock him to the ground, shouting for him to get out of their way.[565] Sometimes the bullying escalated to extreme acts, not limited to one incident in which Dahmer, walking home at night, was assaulted by two seniors who snuck up behind him and clubbed him in the back of the neck with a billy club.[566] The bullying was constant, and the result was a further plunge into solitude. As Backderf remembers, "For most kids, [high school] was an opportunity to make new friends by the bushel. Several of the guys I met during this time would be lifelong pals. Dahmer didn't make new friends. As far as I could tell, he didn't have any friends, period. He was the loneliest kid I'd ever met."[567]

Backderf continued: "But what struck me most about Dahmer was that stony mask of a face, devoid of any emotion."[568]

It was no surprise that Dahmer turned his attention to the sweetly numbing effects of alcohol, becoming a full-fledged alcoholic years well before he was legally allowed to drink. Coffee vending machines were scattered throughout the high school; Dahmer would wander the hallways holding an inconspicuous Styrofoam coffee cup loaded with scotch. School leadership just thought he was, like the other students, addicted to caffeine. As one classmate recalls: "I remember sitting next to him in first period, I believe history class, and he had a Styrofoam cup of scotch…and I remember saying, 'Jeff, what is that?'…and he said, 'It's my medicine.' But, clearly, he was getting drunk at eight o'clock in the morning."[569]

When he wasn't at school stealing fetal pigs from the science class cabinet, getting his head shoved into walls, or walking like a consciously controlled mannequin out of a 1970s department store window, Dahmer was at home in what was now an unbearably dreadful place to be.

His mother, Joyce, had suffered from her unexplainable medical or psychiatric issues in the past, especially while pregnant, but the past suffering was nothing compared to what she experienced during Dahmer's high school years. Her pill dosages were increased, and new medications were added to her daily regimen. Still, her body would "lock up" and only allow her to make long, strange, barbaric sounds as she frothed at the mouth and convulsed uncontrollably—more often now than ever before. She underwent test after test for physical conditions, never receiving any report but the professional opinion that her ailments were more mental than physical. Eventually agreeing to treatment, Joyce attended a few sessions with a psychiatrist, but it didn't help. Then she was admitted for a short time to the psychiatric ward of a hospital, but she left a few days later, insisting she was normal. The next time she was admitted to a facility, she was hospitalized for psychiatric assistance for a month. After later spotting a UFO and chasing it in her vehicle, among other hobbies like macramé (this author views the transition between these activities as odd), she recruited the help of a hypnotist. Her marriage with Lionel had reached a dip from where there was no return.[570] Talk of divorce began.

The constant, incessant, ceaseless, perpetual, unrelenting fighting—fighting—fighting—fighting—*fighting*, verbal and physical, that took place beyond the threshold of the Dahmer kingdom was inescapable. Angry words, hysterical shouting, walls too thin, bedcovers too thin… not enough objects in the whole house to put over one's head to drown out the noise. More dead-animal chemistry experiments would have to happen when Dahmer wasn't frightening the neighbors by angrily beating sticks against the trees in the nearby woods.[571]

Dahmer was now convinced that he was a homosexual. Relationships between men and women, based on the example his parents had set, along with his own experiences and thoughts, had led him to this conclusion. Alongside that was a developing obsession with a nearby male jogger whom Dahmer observed every day outside his home and while riding the school bus. The world had its own opinions about the natural and expected union between two people, and it was this all-American standard that would once again silence Dahmer from ever sharing his taboo passions with anyone else. But Dahmer always had and always would live in a little world of his own. The more he drove down into himself as his own singular companion, the more his attraction to this jogger became an undeniable reality.

On one occasion, when Dahmer was around the hormonally charged age of fifteen and feeling overwhelmed by his ever-present yearning to feel the physical warmth of another person—yet growing each day more intrigued by the idea of that person lying still and nonjudgmental—he obtained a baseball bat and crouched in the bushes in the woods at the edge of the highway. Waiting for the man to appear huffing and puffing over the hill, Dahmer's anticipation of his plan to knock the jogger unconscious and lie next to him for a while grew intense. The jogger ran every day. But, for whatever reason, on this one day, the jogger didn't come by. Dahmer went home and never attempted to wait for the jogger again.[572] The memory of his plan and intentions, however, remained with him from that day on, giving him a grisly boost of courage toward the unthinkable future event that would end one man's life and change Dahmer's forever.

The Fascinated Boy Becomes the Fascinating Sideshow

> It was 1975, my sophomore year at Revere High School. My friends and I, a small group of band nerds and advanced-placement brains, became fascinated by this strange guy who threw fake epileptic fits and mimicked the slurred speech and spastic tics of someone with cerebral palsy.
> —John "Derf" Backderf, *My Friend Dahmer*[573]

Similar to Ted Bundy, when reservation and normal interaction didn't bring anything fulfilling to Dahmer's life, he donned a new mask. In this case, it was that of the class clown. Prior to this moment in *My Friend Dahmer*, Dahmer is not generally noticed by anyone, save for those who wanted to inflate their social status by finding a punching bag. But at some point early in his high school years, alcohol emboldened him to interject an explosive outburst of nonsense once in a while, and then immediately return to his usual, cardboard self. After inspiring a few laughs, however, he adopted this behavior more often, inducing a fit of laughs around him as he would click in and out of this alternate personality. (In later interviews, on more than one occasion, Dahmer openly admitted that he didn't think he had a literal alternate personality, but that he sometimes *felt* like there was another personality within him.)

Dahmer's classmate during this time, Mike Kukral, gives an example of this behavior in his interview with the A&E Network's Biography Channel: "All of a sudden you'd be walking down the hall and you'd hear someone yelling and hollering and running through the hallway, and it's Jeff Dahmer in the middle of the day, running, flapping his arms, yelling, 'Hurricane drill! Hurricane drill! Everybody hide!'"[574] But the thing he was most remembered for by Backderf and *his* crowd of friends was when Dahmer would pull his hand up to his chest in a crippled position, tilt his head stiffly to the side, and loudly shout, "BAAAAAHHHHHH!" or "THMAAA!" as if suddenly overtaken by an uncontrollable attack. Such events usually drew snickers from students and attention from teachers who would race over just in time to find the typical, introverted Dahmer minding his own business calmly while everyone around him was exchanging amused glances, in awe of his paroxysmal gallantry.

Nobody at school knew how close to home his outbursts were. None of them had any clue that by mimicking his mother's "interior decorator" (whom she actually hired, and who did have a condition), Dahmer was actually copying his mother's mysterious spasms and seizures.

He kept this up for the rest of high school, learning that by making a complete donkey of himself, he could connect in a bizarre fashion to those around him. Quickly, a phrase was born: "doing a Dahmer." It could be heard whenever his blasts entered the scene, catching people off-guard. The initial "What is that kid *doing*?" reactions became, overnight, "Oh, check it out! He's 'doing a Dahmer'!" and the phrase eventually extended to other peoples' silly moments as well. The high fives around Revere High reflected that anytime something moronic or clownish occurred, that person was "doing a Dahmer." It was a catchphrase to explain away awkward or foolhardy head-turners and assign the inspiration of that idiotic moment to the buffoon of a Dahmer-mascot sprouting mock-paraplegic wings and jerking about the hallways.

Dahmer was finally the center of attention, and it appeared that even though he would never carry his shtick across the line from being the mascot of the nerd group into any actual friendship, it was the start of something new for him, a side of his personality he didn't know he had. As long as he continued to suck down his "coffee" all day, he would be drunk enough to explode at any second and jazzed enough to put energy behind it, assuming he was also always willing to secretly exploit his mother's weaknesses for a few laughs.

And, as Dahmer basked in his sunshine, he seemed oblivious to the fact that this "niche" connection to people he had at long last dug up from the hellish mud of isolation was, sadly, only solidifying his social status as the village idiot—the one nobody, even those who held affectionate endearment for his humor (like Backderf's circle), could ever possibly know how to connect with for real.

But one incident reveals more than any other the moment when Dahmer crossed over from oddball to permanent reject. One schoolmate approached Dahmer and offered him thirty-five dollars to be the star of a "show" the following Saturday: Dahmer, the willing participant of his own celebrity-turned-spectacle presentation, guzzled a six-pack of beer to set the mood and then rode with Backderf and some other boys to the local shopping mall. Upon entrance, students waited, grinning, with bated breath, to see what he would do. Following him at a distance great enough that none of the mallgoers would suspect they were associated with Dahmer, the classmates watched in wonder as Dahmer made one public disruption after another: He was shouting, pretending to be mentally deranged, calling loudly for a "MISTER BURLMAN!!" and wandering up to the edge of restaurants, where he would clink patrons' wine glasses together and shout "BAHHHH!"[575] Both as remembered in Backderf's graphic novel and as per Mike Kukral's recollection of one part of the event: "A woman was handing out sunflower seeds, and Jeff is taking one, and then another, and another, and being very polite like he always was, and then just spits them out, all over the place, and starts yelling at the top of his lungs, 'I'm allergic!'"[576]

At school, this behavior, though certainly not adored by all, offered some pleasant relief for the students in an atmosphere of rules, grades, and adherence to authority. At the mall, the behavior caused even more excitement, because there, off campus, Dahmer and his fan club had no fear of visiting a principal's office. Even so, the stunts quickly became a regrettable show when the concentrated saturation of one outburst after another suddenly wasn't as funny as it used to be. The group tired of Dahmer's one-trick wonder, only able to only take so many "BAAAAAAAHHH" sounds before the hilarity lost its edge. The jokes had gotten old by that afternoon, and the students concluded the game with a shrug. As it turned out, Dahmer was just some kind of an awkward fool. Instead of a buildup to one big, amazing finale that *really* knocked 'em dead and thereby allowed the show to end strong and whet the palates of a student body that would pay even more the *next* time, the belly laughs diminished to half-hearted chuckles until the show completely fizzled out, ending with a one-name credit sequence that wouldn't inspire a sequel. Dahmer was the circus act, the freak, the bearded lady, the dog-faced man. He had even accepted payment for his fellow man to—step right up, step right up—and view his defects like a sideshow. A man with all the attention in the world, but one who, when the show ends and all the dignified people go home to their normal families, is left to spend the night alone behind the bars of his cage until the curtains are raised for the next people in line to exploit his deformity.

But there wouldn't be another show. The circus was pulling the stakes, collapsing the tents, and leaving town, and Dahmer wasn't the ring leader he hoped he would be. He was the clown, and like all other failed clowns of history, when he was finished "doing a Dahmer," he had the choice between fading into the background or letting his makeup run.

When all his "friends" had lost interest in the event, they broke into groups and dispersed to their typical Saturday-afternoon hang-out sessions. Not one of those who had come to point and laugh "with" Dahmer invited him to go along.

"As we walked back to the car, Kent and I made plans for later that evening. Dahmer, following silently, was not invited. In truth, I couldn't ditch the guy fast enough. And when we dropped off Dahmer at his house, that marked the end of the Dahmer fan club. From here on, we excluded Dahmer from our group."[577]

Shucks. It was okay, though. He understood. He probably couldn't have made it anyway. He had some…you know…stuff he had to do. He was a pretty busy guy, that Dahmer! Heh…

More dead animals were melted, and a dog's head was found impaled on a stick outside of town. Dahmer, the fool, was never a suspect.

A Social Threat Trigger

Dahmer told me that one fantasy that he had was that he would encounter a hitchhiker, and he would have a narrow waist, broad shoulders, a bare chest, he would not have his shirt on, [and] he would have very little hair on his body. He would pick up this hitchhiker and they would have a great time together… [Then, one day,] he was driving down the road, and he *saw* his fantasy hitchhiker.—Robert Ressler, former FBI behavioral analyst[578]

That night in Ohio, that one impulsive night. Nothing's been normal since then. It taints your whole life. After it happened I thought that I'd just try to live as normally as possible and bury it, but things like that don't stay buried. I didn't think it would, but it does, it taints your whole life…. I wish I hadn't done it…. If I'd been thinking rationally I would have stopped.
—Jeffrey Dahmer[579]

Dahmer had for so long been left to his own social devices that he had developed the kind of loneliness we discussed at the beginning of this case study. He was so severely and chronically lonely, based on his symptoms, interviews, psychiatric evaluations, and eyewitness accounts, that the day he saw his free-spirited, fantasy hitchhiker and invited him to his house for beer and companionship, he was willing to do almost anything to get the man to stay.

Following his fifteen minutes of fame as a glorified circus freak, Dahmer had once again returned home and face-planted it into the array of his parents' marital squabbles.

Joyce, still having bizarre breakdowns and addicted to every weird pill on the prescriptions list, could no longer be left alone. Trips to the psych wards weren't helping her, and no matter what she set her idle hands to do, she was either being pushed farther into the depths of craziness or she had to abandon her motherly and wifely duties to apply herself somewhere unrelated. Lionel, still intimidated by his wife's continual brooding and peaks-and-valleys emotional patterns, with no doctor so far able to provide help, continued to flee to his lab with its sweet, welcoming, chemical chaos that followed predictable patterns of scientific law.

Finally, after almost two decades of marriage, Lionel and Joyce agreed to divorce.

Dahmer attended his homecoming dance with a freshman girl. It was an awkward date, so he left the dance early, deserting her while he went to chow down at McDonald's. At the conclusion of his senior year, while everyone else was partying and attending socials, Dahmer returned home one day to learn that his parents' divorce was final. Lionel moved out of the house and into a local motel, leaving Joyce and her two sons behind.

Just when Dahmer thought he couldn't take any more solitude, the social threat of seeing the back of his father's head as he walked out the front door for an indefinite period put him in a spin unlike the others he had felt in past rejections. Lionel had wanted to leave, so he did. *Simple as that.*

Dahmer internalized the pain of the split as he had internalized the pain of every other loss and tragedy in his life. As he was lying on his bed and dreaming about dead things or going outside to beat trees with sticks, Lionel was escaping the tension. Dahmer couldn't. He had no choice but to breathe, living alone now with the crazy lady he called "Mom." But this was only the beginning. Dahmer, now graduated from high school, had almost no follow-up phone calls from students who had greeted him with fake-seizure hellos in the hallways between classes. His childhood acquaintances were far removed from his life. His best friend now was the bottle, and he had no sober moment—a fact that was still a secret from his family. He wasn't close to his brother, his mom was impossible to deal with, and his thoughts were haunted by so many taboo subjects you could fill a watering hole and bathe a whole community of people in it, and they would still think it was just his next gag. He couldn't talk to anybody now, or ever. Even if he could have before, now, he was just the clown nobody would take seriously. Besides, psychiatric help hadn't done anything for his mother, and he lacked confidence in any intervention program.

But then came the news that would seal the deal for his postgraduate, broken-homed, open-scheduled, pointless existence.

Joyce, wasting no time, informed him of one last blow to his coping machinery. She used to live in Wisconsin, and she was going back there.

She was taking his brother David, but Jeffrey would be fine by himself.

After all that messy custody battle nonsense, dragging the kids in and out of their final drama, curtains down, Joyce winning custody of both children (Dahmer was seventeen at the time[580]), *Jeffrey would be fine by himself.*

Like everyone he had ever known, and just like Lionel, his mother wanted to leave, so she did. *Simple as that.* The back of her head while she walked out the door was a mockery of his last and final thread of humanity.

The house was now without a single sound. He could look out the windows. That was basically all there was to do. Numbness and profound depression overtook his every waking moment, adding fuel to the fire that was his tormented mind.

But one day, while driving home from getting something to eat, Dahmer spotted a man at the edge of the highway with his thumb out. Dahmer's heart skipped a beat as he slowed down and took in the vision. The man was someone Dahmer had met so many times in his fantasies.

Dahmer invited him over for beer.

The hitchhiker, Steven Hicks, agreed.

The two men drank and visited for hours. Dahmer was mesmerized. The man was so very kind to him. And then the man wanted to leave. *Simple as that.*

But he didn't.

On June 18, 1978, Jeffrey Dahmer murdered Steven Hicks. Seeing the back of Hicks' head as he attempted to walk out the door was a mockery of the humanity that, by now, was only a memory of the old Jeffrey, so Dahmer hit Hicks' head with a barbell. Twice.

Kennedy recalled that part of Dahmer's confession:

When the guy wanted to leave, Jeff did not want him to leave. He wanted him to stay because he was lonely.… When he tried to stop the guy from leaving, a little bit of a wrestling match broke out, and as they were wrestling around, that's when Jeff grabbed the hand barbell and [hit him in the back of the head]. Now, he said [that] when he hit him, he wasn't thinking "I'm gonna kill this guy," [he was thinking] "I just wanna *keep* him here."[581]

It was an impulsive act. Dahmer's socially threatened environment and too many people having deserted him too many times in a row (and likely throwing him into a state of hyper-vigilance for self-preservation) produced a dramatic result. He would have done anything to connect with this man. He would have done anything to keep the man there. Then he did. But this time, "doing a Dahmer," had been fatal.

Speed Read Past the Ghastly

As mentioned earlier, due to the graphic and unthinkable nature of Dahmer's crimes, we will skip over most of his life between the moment of this, his first murder, and the moment of capture. Dahmer's mental state has been well described up until this point, and there is certainly a plethora of continued study that we could delve into in order to learn about how he continued his downward spiral into a mental hell, if this book were simply a true crime report. But, because the mission statement behind this work does not require forcing the readers to put disturbing details or imagery into their minds, we will respect that, as well as the victims and their families, and proceed with this portion of Dahmer's life with a more hasty reflection.

(As people are likely already aware, Dahmer disposed of his victims' remains in terrible ways. Knowing of his familiarity with the dissection of roadkill, his above-average experience in the world of chemical dissolving, and the fact that he was known as "The Milwaukee Cannibal," readers can put the pieces together without another word on that. [Note that, although he was known as a cannibal, he did not make this disgusting rite a part of his ghastly habits until his final string of victims. Hicks was not included in this category of Dahmer's crimes.])

Within just weeks after Dahmer reached his snapping point, his father returned to the home, not having heard a word from anyone for some time. He was shocked to find that not only had Joyce and David long since moved out without leaving him a forwarding address, but the house was a wreck. He found Dahmer in a state like one he had never seen his son in before. Dahmer was likely drunk off his rocker at that moment, but Lionel didn't specifically say that. Lionel's retelling describes a young man who was void to the world, unable to connect to anything as he stared out windows almost catatonically. Teenagers were roaming around the house in an inebriated state that first day, loafing with the personalities of those who would have taken Dahmer up on the invite to crash his place. It's not surprising that Dahmer would have opened his home to anyone at that point, since he was still in shock and disgusted with himself over what he had done, and now, more than ever, didn't want to be alone. On one of the house's tables, Lionel saw that a séance had been conducted: A pentagram was drawn on the table with chalk. Dahmer had been trying to contact the dead.[582]

Lionel had a new love interest with him, Shari, who would become his new wife in the near future (this time, "'til death do us part" would be upheld). She entered the home and helped calm the troubled waters with a firmly sane and maternal approach to Dahmer, whom she described as "a lost little boy."[583] Dahmer and Shari got along fairly well the longer they were around each other in the coming days, weeks, and eventually years, and Dahmer came to accept her as a kind stepmother when Lionel and Shari moved back into the home.

Seeing that Dahmer was all but spent as a human being and would not, under any stretch of the imagination, put his almost-genius level brain to good use without proper direction, Lionel and Shari tag-teamed to push Dahmer into registering to attend Ohio State University in Columbus. He attended for a semester, but his education ended because of his addiction to alcohol. Lionel and Shari tried again, this time getting Dahmer to agree to enlist in the US Army, but his stint there ended quickly for the same reason.

If Lionel couldn't "fix" Dahmer, he decided he would ship the boy off to his grandmother in West Allis, Wisconsin, to see if she could fare better. The initial plan had only been for Dahmer to visit Lionel's mother for a lengthy stay, but Dahmer moved in with his grandmother in 1981, and for a while, things went smoothly between them. But eventually, between landing a couple of charges of indecent exposure (during the summers of 1982 and 1986), sometimes bringing strange men to the house, the discovery of a male mannequin that Dahmer had stolen from a store and hidden in his closet (in early 1985), and the strange behavioral patterns he was showing, she also understandably gave up on him and asked him to leave.

(Note: During this time with his grandmother, Dahmer claimed several more victims, but his second victim, Steven Toumi, killed *nine years* after Hicks [in November of 1987], was a weird mystery. Dahmer had not killed in just under a full decade, having kept his murderous impulses under control, and later claimed that he was always so shocked about the first murder that his second kill was not, under any circumstances, intended. The two men had met at a bar and agreed to spend the night together at a hotel. The story that Dahmer had stuck to, without deviation, amidst a score of other murders wherein every detail was remembered and confessed without reservation, was this: Dahmer gave Toumi a cocktail of sleeping pills, the signature move he would use in subsequent murders, to render Toumi unconscious. Being around people in that state was, for Dahmer, a comfort. When he awoke the next morning, he found Toumi dead on the bed, surrounded by evidence that he had been beaten to death. Dahmer was, once again, shocked at his own capabilities, but in this particular case, has no recollection of the altercation. He was convicted of this murder later simply because he had already shown that he was willing and able to murder, there was no evidence that Dahmer could remember of anyone else having been the culprit, and because Dahmer, himself, admitted that despite his memories, he figured he must have done it. Dahmer found this kill to be alarming, and it was the single event that thrust him into committing further murders. In dealing with the acceptance of that first murder, which never left his thoughts, and now a second one, which he couldn't remember committing, he had tossed out any self control, and the madness of his devilish compulsions were in full swing.)

After agreeing to leave his grandmother's house in May of 1990, Dahmer landed at a small apartment for a time; while living there, he incurred a sexual assault charge and was sentenced to five years of probation, required to register as a sex offender (he spent his first year of the sentence in a correction facility with a work release and was discharged a couple of months early). He then moved back in with his grandmother for a few weeks, then finally relocated to another low-income apartment: the infamous apartment 213 at 924 North 25th Street in Milwaukee, Wisconsin. He held a job as a chocolate mixer at a chocolate factory for a while, secretly killing on the side.

One of his victims, Konerak Sinthasomphone, escaped from Dahmer, and this case has gone down as one of the most unbelievable screw-ups in local law enforcement this world has ever seen. Dahmer had lured his victim with the promise of giving him money for allowing Dahmer to take some photos, and Sinthasomphone agreed. After getting the young man to his apartment, taking a few pictures, and drugging him (as well as other things), Dahmer left his apartment to go buy some beer, not thinking that Sinthasomphone would wake up. Dahmer arrived back at his apartment to find his victim staggering outside, speaking in Laotian to three women. These three women had placed an emergency call to 9-1-1, and a dispatcher sent police to the corner near Dahmer's apartment. They found a boy there, who appeared to be much older than he really was, completely unable to communicate (the language barrier and the drugging had played a part in that), and without any clothing. As the women pointed to various evidence that the boy was in danger, they were told to stay out of it, as it was a domestic dispute. Then, escorting Dahmer and the towel-draped Sinthasomphone back to Dahmer's apartment, the police viewed the photos Dahmer had taken of the boy and considered them enough evidence to believe Dahmer's story that they were in a relationship and simply having a quarrel. One officer opened the door to the bedroom and took a quick glance, oblivious to the fact that a longer look would have revealed a body of one of Dahmer's previous victims. As the officers left, they told Dahmer to "take good care" of Sinthasomphone. Dahmer politely shut the door behind them, and then proceeded with Sinthasomphone's murder.[584]

Dahmer's last victim, whom he intended to murder, was Tracy Edwards, the man described at the beginning of this case study who managed to slip out of the apartment and flag down local policemen. This brings us back to where we started, at the capture of the Milwaukee Monster.

As mentioned prior, Dahmer confessed to all his crimes only a little more than three hours after he was arrested. If one were to watch all the related interviews and read all the quoted material from him, one could see that collectively, Dahmer never enjoyed killing. Shocking questions from interviewers produced shocking answers in so many other areas that many believe he is telling the truth when he does share something about his feelings even during the events. There was, of course, an element of sick and temporal pleasure that he garnered from having someone around, and he would have done anything, including murder, to *keep* them around. But as Dahmer, himself, explained in an interview with Stone Phillips from NBC News, ending lives never gave him a thrill:

PHILLIPS: Was it the killing that excited you? Or was it what happened after the killing?

DAHMER: No. The killing was just a means to an end.… I didn't enjoy doing that.[585]

And in an interview with Robert Ressler, Dahmer stated that he even held some level of care for the people he forced so violently to stay: "Dahmer did state that…there was not a victim of his crimes that he did not personally love and would like to have stayed with on a permanent level. It all boiled down to the same routine. When they were going to leave, that's when they died."[586]

The studies available for what makes someone with a deviant mind become a cannibal also reflect, in so many cases, a relation to severe loneliness: a "becoming one" with someone, so even after they have "left" the world through death, the connection can remain. "[A]nd in perhaps the ultimate effort to keep his victims with him, [Dahmer became a cannibal]... '[Dahmer speaks] It made me feel like they were a permanent part of me.'"[587]

It was no mystery whether Dahmer was guilty or not. The trial that commenced was short and precise, questioning only the mental state of Dahmer as a candidate for the insanity plea. There was much debate, both sides of the argument holding convincing evidence that he was, or was not, within his right mind at the time of the murders. The jury eventually came to a decision: the majority ruled against an insanity plea. The state of Wisconsin did not have the death penalty, so between Wisconsin and Ohio, Dahmer was sentenced to sixteen terms of life imprisonment and nine hundred and fifty-seven years in prison.

DARK JOURNEY, DEEP GRACE

But what Dahmer would destroy his own life and the lives of so many others to eventually discover is that there was one Friend who would come in when invited, who would always be there, who would never set aside His feelings to deal with spousal drama, who would never escape to the lab, who would love him despite the darkest workings of his mind, and who would never show him the back of His head as He walked out the door. *Simple as that.*

Salvation for Dahmer? Absurd!...

After I agreed to baptize him, he heaved a deep sigh of relief, because he was afraid that I would say, "I can't baptize you, because

your sins are too grievous, your sins are too bad, your sins are unforgiveable." Well, that violates everything I have ever believed and I would never say that. Jesus Christ came to save sinners. Jeffrey Dahmer was a sinner. It's as *simple as that.*
—Wisconsin prison minister and Church of Christ minister Roy Ratcliff[588]

When Roy Ratcliff was contacted to baptize and minister to a local prisoner in early 1994, he was told to sit down before the caller revealed the name of the inmate. Ratcliff found the request shocking, as anyone would, and for obvious reasons. The Milwaukee Monster/Cannibal wanted to be baptized! However, despite Ratcliff's surprise, from the very beginning, he had no doubt that if Dahmer truly wanted to be saved and baptized and have a relationship with Jesus Christ, he would see to it. Ratcliff's faith in God's saving grace was so strong that even the name "Dahmer" didn't rattle him.

Soon after Dahmer's incarceration, when the news headlines were first blasting the country with blood-chilling facts about a gentle and polite young man who had been arrested for gruesome murder and was being questioned for links to as many as seventeen homicides, Curtis Booth, a prison minister in Oklahoma, was the first to send Dahmer a Bible correspondence course. That was followed shortly by another Bible course from Mary Mott, a concerned Christian woman from Virginia.[589] Dahmer, who tossed out almost all his "junk" mail, kept these materials for some reflection. He had looked everywhere else, and now, away from access to the streets, where he was consumed by the craving to act upon his compulsive thoughts, he had time to fill his mind with a subject he had never taken seriously before: Jesus Christ.

He had done everything, including kill, to try to connect with someone who wouldn't leave him, and now, this Bible professed of One who would never leave. Dahmer was more alone at this point in his life than he had ever been. If there was ever one moment that all others had boiled down to, one last chance to befriend someone who would love him—not because he was lovable, as he had already thrown that characteristic away years ago, but because he was in need of a love and acceptance that would transcend the depravity that he had become and that he had wrought— now was the time. But to toss all the complications of this need into one Man's hands couldn't possibly be fair—not fair, that is, for anyone other than the one Man who was capable of overcoming those complications. At least that's what the Bible seemed to say. This Jesus, this Messiah, had come to the world for exactly that purpose: not only to care for and love those who had sinned against Him and His heavenly Father, but to completely recreate them. He could make them new creatures, no matter how dark they had become.

> In the twelve-step programs made famous by Alcoholics Anonymous, a key principle is that a person must hit rock bottom before being motivated enough to make genuine life changes. The Bible tells of the Prodigal Son, who left his home and family to live a dissolute life. After much wickedness, he ends up in a pigpen feeding the pigs, so hungry, "he longed to fill his stomach with the pods that the pigs were eating, but no one gave him anything" (Luke 15:16).
>
> Only when the Prodigal falls so low that he has no way out does he decide to go back, to go home. Such is the rock-bottom reality that convinces a person to change.[590]

Dahmer had reached rock bottom.

There were two men on the cross beside Jesus on the day that humans had beaten, bloodied, betrayed, and crucified Him, leaving Him to bleed to death in a public humiliation sacrament. One man, a criminal, asked for Jesus' forgiveness, and Jesus responded by saying that the man would live with Him in paradise. Jesus did not respond with, "Well, hang on. That depends. What are you up here for?" He promised the man paradise simply because of his remorse, confession, and belief. And since that was written, people—an uncountable number of souls—have not only accepted Jesus' promise to that man, but they have *celebrated* it. And, just before Jesus died, He cried out to His Father to forgive even those who had strung Him up on the cross in a graphic and barbaric display of the most violent murder imaginable, uttering that they could not possibly fathom what it was their violence had done (Luke 23:34). There was forgiveness available for the crucifiers? Jesus Christ, Himself, was a victim of terrible murder, and those were His last words? Jesus Christ, Himself, was the One Christians believed to be the final word on everything, and His final words before He gave up His spirit were to forgive those who had ended His earthly life?

But no, Jesus Christ was not the "victim." He had been violently killed, yes. Yet, in the grandness of what the Almighty had planned for His children and their access to eternity with Him, He was the victor.

Paradise.

Was that a promise that could possibly extend also to the likes of the Milwaukee Monster?

> Jeff confessed to me his great remorse for his crimes. He wished he could do something for the families of his victims to make it right, but there was nothing he could do. He turned to God because there was no one else to turn to, but he showed great courage in his daring to ask the question, "Is heaven for me, too?" I think many people are resentful of him for asking that question. But he dared to ask, and he dared to believe the answer.
>
> —Roy Ratcliff, at the Jeffrey Dahmer memorial service,
>   December 2, 1994[591]

How arrogant and pompous could one man be, to assume God's grace extends to him after the laundry list of people murdered by Dahmer... And yet, as Ratcliff pointed out at Dahmer's memorial service, how *brave*. But we don't normally think of it that way, do we?

At the end of his trial, Dahmer made clear his thoughts on what our *earthly* justice should be for him: "Your Honor...I know my time in prison will be terrible, but I deserve whatever I get because of what I have done. Thank you, Your Honor. I am prepared for your sentence, which I know will be the maximum. I ask for no consideration."[592]

Our heavenly justice system operates differently than our government's justice system operates, and it is for that reason that Dahmer had the courage to step forward with his faith and ask to be baptized.

Christ was the *propitiation* for his sins (Romans 3:25; 1 John 2:2; 1 John 4:10).

The Baptism and Death of Jeffrey Dahmer

When he was ready, I placed my hands on his head and one shoulder. I said, "Jeff, upon your confession of faith in Jesus as the Christ, the Son of God, I now baptize you in the name of the Father and of the Son and of the Holy Spirit for the forgiveness of your sins."

I pushed him under the water until he was completely immersed. When his head broke the surface, I said something I always say when I baptize someone. "Welcome to the Family of God!" —From *Dark Journey Deep Grace* by Roy Ratcliff[593]

Salvation does not wash away our crimes against people on earth. It washes away our sins against God.

The physical immersion of Dahmer's human body into a prison whirlpool did not mean a thing. The position of his heart towards God, a position that only he and God would know, and the symbolism of giving himself over fully to be washed in the forgiveness of Jesus Christ and thereby becoming a new creature in Christ was the matter of life and death, eternally.

People often wonder about the position of Jeffrey Dahmer's heart. There are those who celebrate his conversion to Christ and subsequent baptism, as well as those who doubt its validity. Of the number of those who believed Dahmer was sincere and is therefore with God right now is Ratcliff, Dahmer's spiritual advisor and mentor.

"Over the years," Ratcliff said, "people have questioned me about Jeff's sincerity of faith. If they could have looked into his eyes and spoken to his heart, as I did for months, they would understand his great desire to make things right."[594]

On May 10, 1994, at two o'clock in the afternoon, Ratcliff baptized Dahmer in the name of the Father, the Son, and the Holy Spirit. After the event at the whirlpool, Dahmer found comfort in his ongoing visits with Ratcliff for Bible study. Ratcliff felt the need to be sure that Dahmer was not abandoned during his early days of Christian growth, so their meetings remained a weekly event. Dahmer always had many questions, and Ratcliff was patient enough to address each one with as much balance and thought as possible. Ratcliff shared the love of Christ. The two men studied together, they prayed together, and they cared about each other. There was no perversion. There was no death. Their friendship, one Dahmer could not have fathomed possible in years past, was solid, because Christ had influenced yet another man's ability of seeing past the sin and into the man. Not only was Jesus Christ a Friend for anyone, forever, but He had sent another to care for Dahmer in a way that only a Christ-filled person could. The world, and the sinners within it, needed Christ. Dahmer had never been more convinced of this fact.

And it showed in his behavior. The once completely silent introvert who almost never uttered a sound besides the nonsensical blasts of clownisms in high school now had no trouble opening his mouth and showing the true intelligence he had always held behind the demons of his mind. No longer did he walk like a toy soldier or hang his head; he now walked with a smile and a "bounce in his step."[595] He no longer feared interaction with the human race, but embraced it. As Lionel noted of his son's mannerisms after his conversion to Christ: "He was *so* interactive, and *so* concerned about our welfare. You know, he was reaching out. He was— he was *re-humanizing*."[596]

On July 3, 1994, an attempt was made on Dahmer's life, but he escaped with merely a scratch because the weapon, forged by a fellow inmate with a razor blade, a toothbrush, and a length of tape, gave out and broke in the process.

Dahmer prayed his first public prayer at one of his follow-up meetings with Ratcliff: "Father in heaven, thank you for sending Roy into my life, and having him help me to better understand your words and your ways.... And please bless my dad and his wife, and my mom, too.... Help me to be a better person. Amen."[597]

The next November, after maintaining their companionship and growing closer each time, Ratcliff received a Thanksgiving card from Dahmer. It said, "Dear Roy, Thank you for your friendship, and for taking the time and effort to help me understand God's word. God bless you and your family! Sincerely, Jeff Dahmer."

Dahmer had a friend. His life had just begun.

Within days after Ratcliff received Dahmer's Thanksgiving card, Dahmer was murdered.

A fellow inmate, who called himself "Christ,"[598] bludgeoned Dahmer and another prisoner to death. There was no apparent motive. Dahmer was murdered with a barbell: the same instrument of death he had used against Steven Hicks, his first murder victim.

At Dahmer's memorial service, Ratcliff gave a few reflecting words:

> Every life is important. Some would mock us for gathering here to remember a life that has caused so much hurt. But we come to focus not on the crimes he committed, but on the faith that changed his life. I know Jeff believed in God and trusted Christ to save him. I baptized him, studied with him, and got to know his heart. He was truly sorry for the things he had done.
>
> Many people were shocked and scandalized by his baptism... but I think their shock is really anger. They cannot conceive that anyone who committed Jeff's terrible crimes could come to Christ. If he did, indeed, come to Christ, they would rather Christ turn his face away and reject him. But they did not understand why Jesus came to earth. He came to save sinners. Jeff was a sinner.[599]

Attending his memorial were two of his victims' family members. Unbelievably, one approached Ratcliff after the service and said, "I believe

God has forgiven him."[600] (The identity of these two women is concealed in this work to protect their privacy.)

Dahmer's last words are a mystery, as they were not recorded before his unplanned death. However, some of his last words to the public and the media just before he died were recorded during an interview with NBC's Stone Phillips:

> If a person doesn't think that there is a God to be accountable to, then, then what's the point of trying to modify your behavior to keep it within acceptable ranges? That's how I thought, anyway. I have since come to believe that the Lord Jesus Christ is truly God, the Father, the Son, and the Holy Spirit.[601]
>
> I always believed the lie that evolution is truth, the theory of evolution is truth, that we all just came from the slime, and uh, when we died, that was it. There was nothing. So, the whole [evolution] theory cheapens life... I've since come to believe that the Lord Jesus Christ is the true Creator of the heavens and the Earth.... I've accepted Him as my Lord and Savior, and I believe that I, as well as everyone else, will be accountable to Him.[602]

INTERVIEW with Roy Ratcliff

In order to gain further insight on Dahmer's case, we reached out to Roy Ratcliff, telling him about our book. He agreed to an exclusive interview and informed us that he would consider our project prayerfully. After his consent, we sent him a list of questions, asked by several people in our publishing group as well as by Donna Howell.

BETWEEN DONNA HOWELL, DEFENDER PUBLISHING GROUP AND ROY RATCLIFF, PRISON MINISTER FOR JEFFREY DAHMER EMAILS BETWEEN JUNE 17–28, 2014

Many people believe that psychopaths are "born." Psychopaths by definition lack empathy, and therefore inherently lack remorse. Remorse is essential to a true repentance. Some would therefore say that psychopaths cannot be saved. What are your thoughts on this?

I believe everyone can be saved. I don't know that Jeff would be, by this definition, a psychopath. He expressed remorse to me for what he had done, and I believe he was truly repentant. I don't think anyone can say of anyone else that they cannot be saved. Certainly remorse and repentance would be critical in salvation. I believe everyone is capable of remorse and repentance. I don't think people lack empathy. I think even the most hardened criminals still have that capacity. I know, from my experience with prisoners since Jeff, that the worst scenario you can have for entering prison is to be known as a child sexual abuser. The other prisoners will despise you and will try to punish you for that. If they were psychopaths by the standard psychiatric evaluation, they wouldn't care. But from what I understand, all the prisoners care about child sexual abusers, psychopaths included.

We at Defender Publishing appreciate your antilegalistic approach to ministering to Jeff before he died. We believe that many other prisoners would have found belief in God much less of a strain if this approach had been available to them. If you could say something to other prisoners reading this book, what would it be?

I would tell them to let Jeff's story encourage them. Few of them would be guilty of the kind of crimes Jeff committed. But every one of them would feel as bad about themselves as Jeff felt about himself. The point of Jeff's story is that, no matter how bad you feel about yourself, no matter how low of a self-esteem you have, God is able to pull you out of the deepest hole you can put yourself in. You just have to be willing to turn to God and ask for His help.

We know you have received the question of Jeff's sincerity more times than anyone can count. We also know this question bothers you because, by nature, questioning someone else's sincerity in his or her faith is in a way inappropriate. As you stated on page 161 of your book, turning to Christ creates a new creation of that person. But because this is a book that perpetuates the belief in the Lord's forgiveness toward those who have committed the unthinkable, we also understand why many continue to ask about this. Some reading this book will likely be inspired by the sincerity of others and their stories of coming to the Lord. What would you say to someone in the balance? What would you say to those who may feel they have a better chance at redemption for themselves based on the inspiring testimony of the sincerity of someone like Jeff?

The question about sincerity is an effort on the part of the one asking the question to say, "Well, his turning to Christ doesn't mean anything at all, because he was insincere." It is inappropriate because no one knows the heart of another well enough to judge. That's our problem. We like judging one another. But God is the only true Judge. If you are sincere, God will know it. If you are not sincere, eventually we will figure that out for ourselves, but God will know that, too. I don't know that redemption is based on chance. I believe that if you turn to God for help, He is there to help you, no matter what you've done or how bad you've been. God is not scandalized by our sins. His forgiveness is available to all who seek it.

In your book, you mention that you and your wife installed a clock in your home as a memorial of Jeff. Do you still have "Jeff's clock" in your living room? Do you still think of Jeff when you see it? What memory of him sticks out the most?

Yes we still have the "Jeff" clock in our living room, and yes, I often think of Jeff when I see it. The point about the clock has to do with Jeff's sudden and unexpected death. The words of Ephesians 5:15–16 come to mind, "Be very careful then, how you live—not as unwise but as wise, making the most of every opportunity, because the days are evil." The memory that sticks out the most is our last meeting, when he gave me a Thanksgiving Day card and was grateful that I was in his life. I can't think of a better "good-bye" than that.

One reading your book will see that your reaction to the invitation to baptize such a high-profile criminal was as anyone could have expected it to be: surprise, shock, curiosity, and the wanting to be sure that it was something Jeff completely understood before he followed through with it. You went on to meet him in person and discuss the meaning and symbolism behind that step of faith, and found that Jeff was actually quite educated in the meaning behind baptism and the washing away of sins. Once you decided then and there that this was something you would carry out for Jeff, what were the effects that it had on your family, friends, and congregation, especially after the unexpected media invasion upon your life?

My family and friends were pleased that I had this opportunity. The congregation was also pleased. After the media invasion, they were concerned and sympathetic towards me. They were a little fearful how the media would deal with the subject of baptism. There is much debate about it, and some were afraid that the media would present it in a bad way.

After baptizing Jeff, you continued to visit him and mentor him at his prison. Have you baptized others in their own prison environments similar to this? If so, did you give the same continual mentorship attention to them all equally? Or was there something special about Jeff?

Jeff was my first prison experience. I have had others request baptism, but when I visited with them learned that they had already been baptized and therefore wanted a repeated baptismal for other reasons. One particular instance involved a prisoner who had written me, explaining that he had been baptized before, and wanted to be re-baptized as his previous experience did not bring about the results he had expected. He was guilty of sexually abusing his niece and nephew, and thought that baptism would "fix" him so that he wouldn't do it again. But after his baptism, he still abused them, so he thought something with his baptism had gone wrong. As of yet, I have not baptized others in prison beyond Jeff. I have baptized people in hospital bath tubs. Regarding mentorship, I made the request for this with Jeff out of instinct. I have used the experience with Jeff to connect with other inmates. I have what I call a "commitment statement." That is, I tell them that I am committed to them and that I will visit them and pray for them and do what I can to bring blessing into their life. I will not leave them unless they ask me to go away. I've done that with every inmate since Jeff; it was a lesson I learned. I believe we all need to hear a commitment statement from someone; we all need to know someone is there for us and is willing to stay with us, no matter what. Jeff was special only in the sense that he was the first one.

Just after handing you the Thanksgiving card, Jeff was murdered unexpectedly, and the two of you were not given a proper goodbye. If you had been given an opportunity to speak with him one last time, what would you have said?

His death *was* unexpected. I had no idea this was my last meeting with him. Had I known, or had any kind of idea, I would have told him to keep his faith in God. My favorite passage of Scripture is Proverbs 3:5–6, and I would have shared that with him: "Trust in the LORD with all your heart and lean not on your own understand; in all your ways acknowledge him, and he will make your paths straight." I would have said to keep God first, no matter what happens. Even if you die, if you die with faith in God, you are better off than if you threw God out of your life.

You are likely one of the only few who can attest to Jeff's final days as a Christian. Your book documented this period very well. (Note to our readers: Roy Ratcliff's book does not include any graphic details of Jeff's crimes. One interested in hearing Jeff's story on a more personal and intimate level than this book you are holding can divulge will find **Dark Journey Deep Grace: Jeffrey Dahmer's Story of Faith** *a clean, safe read that focuses entirely on God's grace toward humanity.) We also know that he was only within his new faith for a short time before he was killed. That you know of, did Jeff reach out to anyone or help anyone else come to the Lord within prison walls before he died?*

Yes, Jeff wanted me to send him pamphlets and brochures about his faith that he could give to other prisoners. I never got those materials to him, because prisons are very sensitive about how literature is given to prisoners. I know he wanted others to know about Jesus. I don't know if he ever helped anyone else to come to faith.

Since your book was written, has anyone contacted you with positive feedback regarding the impact that Jeff's conversion to Christianity has had on others after his death? How has Jeff's story helped others?

Yes, many people have contacted me about how the book has changed their lives and changed their perception not only of Jeff, but others around them. Many who have given up on themselves have told me that Jeff's story helped them. The idea that someone as bad as Jeff could come to Christ has inspired others to believe they certainly could. Most people consider themselves not as lost as Jeff was. I have received testimonials from other prisoners who have heard of Jeff's story and how it helped them. One prison minister who worked with a serial killer in Kansas had me write encouraging words to the inmate based on my experience with Jeff. Generally, Jeff's story gives them hope; it builds faith.

After your encounter with Jeff, you went on to become a prison minister in several Wisconsin prison facilities. Please tell us about this ministry.

After Jeff was murdered, I had no prison ministry. I went a year without visiting anyone in prison. Then, on the one year anniversary of Jeff's death, I was interviewed by a local television anchor about Jeff and went over his story again on television. I then received a letter from an inmate who had seen the interview, and who knew Jeff; he asked me to come see him. That's where my prison ministry really started. One led to another, which led to another, and on and on it went. My experience with Jeff was often an introduction into an inmate's life. Some knew of my experience with Jeff and reasoned that if I could go see Jeff, I could come see them also. Others emerged because they heard that I would come speak with troubled inmates. My commitment statement [mentioned above] began to get around, and before long, the numbers of those who wanted someone who would stick with them and stay committed began to increase. I had learned how important and vital a commitment statement was with Jeff, so what started with one man flourished into many.

Is there anything else you would like to share with a reading audience while you have the platform to do so?

I have often used Jeff's story to tell people that, although they haven't done the terrible things Jeff did, still, I know they often feel as bad about themselves as Jeff did. I call this a "personal commentary." They may have made it up about themselves, or they may be quoting someone else. It is usually that they think of themselves as worthless, a failure, a person who has wasted their life, never should have been born, a curse on everyone they've met, etc. And my message is that no matter how deep a hole you've put yourself in, no matter how low you feel about yourself, Jeff's story shows that God can reach you even there. Once God reaches you, a "divine commentary" replaces the personal commentary. If you come to God with the message, as the Prodigal Son did, that "I don't deserve to be your son, make me a hired hand," God will respond by saying, "But you *are* my son, and I'm glad you're home!" The way to God is always open and it's always there. You have only to reach out and he will grasp your hand.

———

Roy Ratcliff has ministered with churches in Wisconsin for more than twenty-five years. He is a graduate of Oklahoma Christian University. Since his unexpected encounter with Jeffrey Dahmer in 1994, he has ministered to prisoners in several Wisconsin prison facilities.

WHO ARE THE KILLERS?

Dear Readers,

My name is Donna Howell. I am the coauthor of this book. I have not yet spoken personally on this subject. However, what I went through to help create this manuscript, and what I realized along the journey to its completion, is relevant to this book, so I will share it now.

When Thomas Horn first approached me and asked me to assist with this project for Defender Publishing, I willingly agreed. Historically I have had an informal interest in documentaries and books on the subject of true crime, and I am not squeamish. I also believe that people are a bigger mystery than the seven wonders of the ancient world, so tales of reformation were not outside my realm of thinking. An enormous perk of the project was when Tom mentioned that our mission would be to get the gospel into as many prisoner's hands across the nation as we could. The decision, then, was really a no-brainer. My agreeing to help with the work was more or less a casual move, with an anticipation that I had a full assignment that might help change someone's heart.

I had no idea what I was agreeing to; I had no idea this book would change me.

First, there was the gut-wrenching reality of reinventing my expectations about research in this area. How naïve I was to assume that I could delve so deeply into the study of crimes like these without putting unforgettably disturbing images into my mind, from whence there is no regurgitation as long as the studies continued. The moment I completed one case study and embraced the expunging of all that horror from my mind, I had to begin another; slowly, my waking thoughts throughout the day were taken over by a haunting canvas of unparalleled revulsion. At night I dreamed of things so horrible that I can't write of them here. Afraid that someone might think me incapable of completing the book, I spoke very little of this side of the experience. My closest family and friends observed a small change in my behavior, which had become slightly more introverted, but they related it to the long work hours and constant demand for further focus on my research. Some days weren't as bad, and I could make it through a lunch break with my mind on something else. Other days were just surreal. I remember that, one specific night during my study on David Berkowitz, I was afraid to walk from a friend's social I had just attended to my car parked on the street. There were so many fresh, Berkowitz-style shootings in my thoughts that I couldn't shake, and too many shadows between where I was standing and my car down the road, ominously lit by the deep, flickering yellow of the streetlamp. It was like I was a child all over again, afraid of something I knew wasn't really a threat, but frozen in place by an overactive imagination: one that, as a writer, I've always had. I stood outside that house for several minutes before deciding I simply wasn't brave enough to walk to my car alone. I called a friend to stay on the cell phone with me until I had fully checked in and around my vehicle and turned the key in the ignition. You, readers, don't know me, so you will have to take my word for it when I say that this was an extremely unusual moment for me. During the entire drive home that night, I was laughing and shaking my head, thinking that, just the night before, I had been sitting on the edge of my four-year-old son's bed, telling him there was nothing in the closet. And now, "Mommy" was afraid of the dark.

The book was consuming me. I had begun the project every day by praying at my desk that the Lord would protect my mind. My prayers eventually expanded to ask for Him to cover me throughout the day and night as well. Having been troubled in my past with terrifying nightmares, I was concerned that those days would come back full throttle. But the Lord was faithful. I had many anxious days, but nothing was larger than what I could handle. I believe He knows what cloth I've been cut from and just how far I can be pushed. This, a biblical promise, kept me strong.

And then something else started to occur. In public places, I started seeing Charles Watsons and Ted Bundys everywhere. Not literally, of course, but similarities were popping up in my line of sight and sound all around me. When I saw a young kid on a street corner with a skateboard, wearing gothic clothing that openly glorified Satan, I immediately thought of Sean Sellers. Before this book, I would have simply kept driving. This time, I smiled and nodded a greeting as I turned the corner in my car. The boy surprised me when he waved back, with a look on his face that could have been translated to say, "Do I know that lady? Why is she smiling at me?" In my conservative area of the country, it was likely the only smile he received that day from anyone he didn't already know.

A few days later, on Easter Sunday, I was in the foyer of my church getting some coffee, and I spotted a woman who looked a little out of place. Amidst crowds of women in pastel skirts and cardigans, with every hair in the right place for the Lord's Resurrection Day, chatting it up with their buddies, this one woman stood still and quiet, clutching her Bible against her ripped jeans and threadbare, plaid, long-sleeved, button-up shirt. With her curly mane, she could have passed for an older, blond Karla Faye Tucker. I dropped my kids off at their Sunday school classes and took my usual seat with my husband in the auditorium. After the sermon, the pastor announced that there was a small presentation to follow, and that we should remain sitting. A song started to play, and people began to file onto the stage from a side door, each person carrying a handwritten cardboard sign. On one side was a statement about the person's past ("I was addicted to porn"; "I was dying of cancer"; "I miscarried three times" as examples), and on the other was a testimony of divine intervention

("Now freed from addiction"; "Doctors find no trace of cancer"; "Now a mother of three" as examples). Each time the participants held up a sign and then slowly turned it to reveal the words on the back, everyone would clap and praise the Lord for the glorious update. Our Karla Faye walked on stage toward the end. As she lifted her sign, I choked up. Even from my seat in the large room, her likeness of Karla Faye Tucker was striking, but it was her sign that got me. On one side, she had drawn prison bars, behind that colored the words, "I was a prisoner." When she flipped it, the other side said, "Found freedom in Christ." Obviously, there is no way of knowing what she had been incarcerated for without approaching her with nosy questions, but, by her own admission, she had been headed down a destructive path until something divine had happened for her. I have prayed for her several times since, whenever that memory hits me.

Years back, when I was a chubby fifteen year old with red hair reaching to my lower back, I worked in landscaping and maintenance at a Christian retreat center. A volunteer staff member who helped around the grounds sometimes put odd feelings in the pit of my stomach. He was in his mid to late fifties, painfully shy, and a little overweight. He walked with a terrible limp and, as an awkward way of retreating from conversation, frequently laughed about being the "black sheep" of a family who had disowned him. (To me, most of the time, his one-liner about being a black sheep didn't make sense, but he would follow his statement with a wave, turn his body away, and appear relieved that he didn't have to talk. Generally, everyone left him alone at this point because they didn't know how to respond.) This man had a way about him that was a little off-kilter, and he was always smirking with a strange little tilt to his mouth, as if he was amused about something nobody else could see. One day, I was on tabernacle cleaning duty, sweeping the floors and spraying freshener on the wooden pews, as it was the first time that season the building was getting use. The building was very dark and dusty, and the power hadn't been turned on yet. I was singing really loud (a favorite pastime of mine), working alone like I always did, sweeping away and appreciating the citrus scent of the freshening solution, when I became suddenly aware that I was being watched. To this day, I don't know how I knew, as I hadn't heard one sound around me anywhere, and I was lost in my own little world on the chorus of "How Great Thou Art," but, somehow, I knew I wasn't alone. In addition to that "watched" feeling, a sense of dread crept over me, as if something bad was about to happen. I stopped singing, stopped working, and halted. The tabernacle building was huge, and there were shadowy rafters in the back, above the pews near the sound booth. My eyes must have swept over that area ten times as I stood there, looking all around, listening for even the faintest creak of movement in the building. After a moment, when nothing came of it, I decided it was a random bout of paranoia, and went back to my duties. The feeling never left, though, and I eventually decided I would come back to it later, when someone had brought power to the lights in the main room. Right as I was bending over to pick up my things, something caught my eye. I jerked my head up to the rafters again, and I saw him standing there, perfectly still. The light pouring in from a window made the faded orange of his shirt contrast sharply against the drab grays of the building around him, but other than that one sliver of color from his shirt, he blended into the shadows perfectly. When I think about it, I can still see him there watching me, completely still. I shouted a "hello" up at him, and he didn't respond for several seconds. Finally, when he did, his words sent a wave of fearful flutters down my spine as he said slowly, "I like your singing." Thoughts flew through my head as I noted the exits at the back of the room. He was closer to them, but because of his limp, I knew I was faster. I shouted out some nonsense about having to check in with the management about chemicals or something and booked it to the rear doors underneath him. I didn't stop running until I was in the manager's office. My manager was a jolly, white-haired, slightly oblivious fellow from Bermuda who was always handing me another list of things to do and then returning to his desk with a happy little song whistling from his lips. This time was no different, and I didn't say a word as I took his checklist and busied myself in the bathrooms just outside his door until quitting time. It never happened again, but I saw the odd volunteer around the grounds many times after that, and he was always staring. Always smirking. Always standing halfway behind something and watching. Shortly after that event, he fell from a ladder and died from his injuries. I have never forgotten him, and I continue to wonder if he was simply a social anomaly (which I have no reason to think otherwise, barring a gut feeling), or if I had a valid reason to be spooked that day. But not one person I have seen since has displayed that same, amused expression, that lingering little Mona Lisa smirk that held so much suggestion…until I viewed old news footage of David Berkowitz on the day of his arrest. Observing his peculiar appearance as he was being ushered into the squad car, looking more entertained than concerned, I was suddenly reminded of that volunteer that day in the tabernacle. The similarity of those hinting faces is uncanny.

Who are the killers?

According to the Federal Bureau of Investigation, "14,827 people were murdered last year in the United States… But the 2012 murder rate…was significantly higher than in most other wealthy nations."[603] It's possible that you, yourself, have encountered one without even knowing it. It's also possible that you, yourself, have encountered a will-be murderer (or violent criminal) who, at the time of your encounter, was naught but a struggling individual looking to connect with another human or get help for an internal festering of painful and socially debilitating thoughts. One that he or she may take, and apply, personally. As these case studies that you have just read have illustrated, no matter *what* people have done or will do, once upon a time, they were just people. Not monsters. And whether we hate them, love them, begrudge them, forgive them, disregard them, fear them…whatever feelings people have toward them, they were once baby girls or boys brought into this world just as innocently as the rest of us, probably bright-eyed and curious and joyful. He or she has always been and will always be a soul that the Lord "commandeth [or extends] his love toward" and sent His Son to die for even "while [he/she] was yet [a sinner]" (Romans 5:8). *Their reformation and conversion to Christ does not constitute release, nor does it guarantee any safe reintegration into society. Our American justice system does not concern itself with the Lord's judgment of souls, and vice-versa.* But, in the light of eternity, the Lord loves the victims, and the Lord loves the criminals.

That's hard to fathom for the rest of us, sometimes. Perhaps it is within our human nature to assume that the Lord has forgotten or rejected those who have caused humanity so much grief. This book has highlighted a small group of individuals whose conversions drew both controversy and celebration, and whose depth of sincerity only the Lord irrefutably knows. But when individual sincerity is set aside for the Judge to handle, the rest of us can know with certainty that "there is joy in the presence of the angels of God over one sinner that repenteth" (Luke 15:10), and that God is "not willing that any should perish" (2 Peter 3:9).

The Bible, the Final Word, has much to say on the subject of sin, forgiveness, pain, heartache, loss, longsuffering…and, believe it or not, *who* the killers are. Jesus Christ, Himself, made an interesting and reflective comment during one of His teachings. Let us quickly visit some golden insight left behind in 1898 by Dwight L. Moody, one of the preachers of the Great Awakenings, who has formally trail-blazed a more fascinating rationale than any I could attempt to pen:

There is that other kind of murder that is increasing at an appalling rate among us… I want to speak of other classes of murderers that are very numerous in this country, although they are not classified as murderers. The man who is the cause of the death of another through criminal carelessness is guilty. The man who sells diseased meat; the saloon-keeper whose drink has maddened the brain of a criminal; those who adulterate food; the employer who jeopardizes the lives of employees and others by unsafe surroundings and conditions in harmful occupations,—they are all guilty of blood where life is lost as a consequence. When I was in England in 1892, I met a gentleman who claimed that they were ahead of us in the respect they had for the law. "We hang our murderers," he said, "but there isn't one out of twenty in your country that is hung."

I said, "You are greatly mistaken, for they walk about these two countries unhung."

"What do you mean?"

"I will tell you what I mean," I said; "the man that comes into my house and runs a dagger into my heart for my money is a prince compared with a son that takes five years to kill me and the wife of my bosom. A young man who comes home night after night drunk, and when his mother remonstrates, curses her grey hairs and kills her by inches, is the blackest kind of a murderer." ...

One young man at college, an only son, whose mother wrote to him remonstrating against his gambling and drinking habits, took the letters out of the post-office, and when he found that they were from her, he tore them up without reading them. She said, "I thought I would die when I found I had lost my hold on that son."

If a boy kills his mother by his conduct, you can't call it anything else than *murder*, and he is as truly guilty of breaking this sixth commandment as if he drove a dagger to her heart. If all young men in this country who are killing their parents and their wives by inches, should be hung this next week, there would be a great many funerals.[604]

But surely, this comparison is sensational and unfair: How can those who belong to the general population and whose sins are only marginal in comparison to causing bloodshed be synced with murderers? Could it be that the actions of one who fits into the more respectable circles of sin have anything in common with the actions of these vile people? Moody went on to say:

Let us look once again at the Sermon on the Mount, that men think so much of, and see what Christ had to say: "Ye have heard that it has been said by them of old time, Thou shalt not kill; and whosoever shall kill shall be in danger of the judgment: but I say unto you, that whosoever is angry with his brother without a cause shall be in danger of the judgment: and whosoever shall say to his brother, Raca, (an expression of contempt), shall be in danger of the council: but whosoever shall say, Thou fool, (an expression of condemnation), shall be in danger of hell fire [Matthew 5:21–22]."

"Three degrees of murderous guilt," as has been said, "all of which can be manifested without a blow being struck; secret anger—the spiteful jeer—the open, unrestrained outburst of violent abusive speech."

Again, what does John say? "Whosoever hateth his brother is a murderer: and ye know that no murderer hath eternal life abiding in him [1 John 3:15]."[605]

Who are the killers? You will know them by more than a defining crime scene. You will recognize them by more than a bloody weapon. They are identifiable for sins that gain far less attention than a serial killer in court. For whoever breaks one commandment, breaks them all (James 2:10). If we go by what has been said above by the Bible and by Preacher Moody, we may find our concepts changing.

There is no one sinless except Him, and I have it on good authority that He would want us—you and me, the sinners—to support our fellow sinners in the never-ending search for human connection that may have an enormous impact on their spiritual connection with God and the path they choose on this planet from that moment forward.

Certainly, there is a time to run to the back of the tabernacle to escape potential harm. If we study those whose names are on the survivors' lists, of even just Bundy and Dahmer, we see that those who fled, kicked, screamed, and fought back were the lucky ones who continued to draw breath, and eventually aided in the criminals' capture.

But, I beseech you: There is also a time to smile, say a kind word, pray for someone you don't know, reach out, be there, and *connect*.

The next time you see a young, pimple-faced, giggling girl following the crowd, before you scoff, know that you might be looking at the next Susan Atkins. When you next see that trophy jock leading the crowds of swooning girls appearing to those around him that he knows exactly who he is, before you roll your eyes, remember that you might be observing the behaviors of a potential Charles "Tex" Watson. When a child in your Sunday school class presents you with a strange gift you don't know how to accept, before you toss it out or pass it on, remember that you might be missing a chance to pull that little Dahmer boy out of his silent torment and into the light of Christ. And, when nothing else is appropriate—and there *will* be those times—run from the tabernacle and pray from a distance.

This book focuses specifically on those whose intervention came too late, but there are others out and about, free in society now, whose moment of intervention might be closer to you than you think.

Care. Pray. Love.

That is all.

Sincerely,

Donna Howell

NOTES

1. David Berkowitz, *Son of Hope: The Prison Journals of David Berkowitz*, volume 1 (Morning Star Communications: New York, NY, 2006), 108 (sidebar).
2. Produced by Lloyd Bryan Adams, et al., directed by Mike Dorsey, hosted by Scott Michaels, *The Six Degrees of Helter Skelter* (Tenacity Entertainment; Echo Bridge Home Entertainment: 2009), 0:21–0:51.
3. Unless otherwise noted, or in the case of a specific quote, all information given in this case study has been a collection of well known, easy-access facts, repeated transparently through light research of the Manson Family. Most of these facts are covered in further detail and with further referencing online here: "Charles Manson," *Wikipedia, The Free Encyclopedia*, last modified December 9, 2013, http://en.wikipedia.org/wiki/Charles_manson, and, when referring to a personal memory of Susan Atkins, here: Susan Atkins and Bob Slosser, *Child of Satan, Child of God* (Menelorelin Dorenay's Publishing, 1978; Kindle Edition 2005). Any information specific to a certain book, website, or other material will be cited individually.
4. Vincent Bugliosi and Curt Gentry, *Helter Skelter: The True Story of the Manson Murders* (W.W. Norton & Company, 2001, 25th Anniversary Edition), 26.
5. "People v. Anderson," *Wikipedia, The Free Encyclopedia*, last modified March 14, 2013, http://en.wikipedia.org/wiki/California_v._Anderson.
6. "California Proposition 17 (1972)," *Wikipedia, The Free Encyclopedia*, last modified February 24, 2013, http://en.wikipedia.org/wiki/California_Proposition_17_(1972).
7. See: Heidi Cuda, "Charles Manson May Have Committed More Murders," *MyFoxLA*, posted February 4, 2013, last modified April 5, 2013, http://www.myfoxla.com/story/20962297/audio-tapes-charles-manson; and Lara Kirkner, "Back to the Barker Ranch," February 15, 2013, *The Sheet*, http://thesheetnews.com/2013/02/15/back-to-the-barker-ranch/.
8. "Jane Doe, Los Angeles 1969," *True Crime Diary*, May 30, 2012, http://www.truecrimediary.com/index.cfm?page=cases&id=179.
9. "Helter Skelter (Manson Scenario)," *Wikipedia, The Free Encyclopedia*, last modified December 10, 2013, http://en.wikipedia.org/wiki/Helter_Skelter_(Manson_scenario).
10. Ibid.
11. "Charles Manson," *Wikipedia*, http://en.wikipedia.org/wiki/Charles_manson.
12. "CPI Inflation Calculator," *United States Department of Labor: Bureau of Labor Statistics*, last accessed February 26, 2012: http://www.bls.gov/data/inflation_calculator.htm.
13. Bugliosi and Gentry, *Helter Skelter*, 127.

14. Catherine "Gypsy" Share, as quoted on: Forensic Psychiatrist Dr. Michael Stone, "Cult Leaders," *Most Evil*, season 2, episode 11, 35:11–35:26 and 36:27–36:44, aired January 31, 2008 (on The Discovery Channel: Investigation Discovery, 2010), DVD.

15. Susan Atkins and Bob Slosser, *Child of Satan, Child of God* (Menelorelin Dorenay's Publishing, 1978; Kindle Edition 2005) Kindle Locations 586–587.

16. Ibid., 1488–1503.

17. Ibid., 1711–1713.

18. Ibid., 1873–1893.

19. Ibid., 1915–1917.

20. "Diane Sawyer Meets Manson, Krenwinkle, and Van Houten—Part 2," YouTube video, 1:12–1:56, posted by The Tate LaBianca Videos, uploaded on June 17, 2010, last accessed December 27, 2013, http://www.youtube.com/watch?v=Zn2zULFwB_w.

21. Atkins and Slosser, *Child of Satan, Child of God*, 3194–3204.

22. Ibid., 2417–2422.

23. "Susan Atkins Sexy Sadie Mae Glutz Speaks about Life on Spahn Ranch," YouTube video, 3:00–7:32, posted by MichaelsBackporch, uploaded January 28, 2012, last accessed December 27, 2013, http://www.youtube.com/watch?v=fXUqxxubjT0.

24. Catherine "Gypsy" Share, as quoted on: Forensic Psychiatrist Dr. Michael Stone, "Cult Leaders," *Most Evil*, season 2, episode 10, 31:17–31:51, aired October 14, 2007 (on The Discovery Channel: Investigation Discovery, 2010), DVD.

25. Atkins and Slosser, *Child of Satan, Child of God*, 2504–2518.

26. Ibid., 2559–2565.

27. Ibid., 2808–2810.

28. Ibid., 3219–3221.

29. Ibid., 3262–3279.

30. Ibid., 3474–3485, emphasis added.

31. Mick Brown, "Manson: The Life and Times of Charles Manson, by Jeff Guinn, Review," *The Telegraph*, August 3, 2013, http://www.telegraph.co.uk/culture/books/10218984/Manson-the-Life-and-Times-ofCharles-Manson-by-Jeff-Guinn-review.html.

32. Atkins and Slosser, *Child of Satan, Child of God*, 4053–4057.

33. Ibid., 4231.

34. Ibid., 5321–5333.

35. "Susan Atkins Interview (1976)–Part 2," YouTube video, 1:01–2:18, posted by Rachel Wicca, uploaded January 29, 2010, last accessed December 30, 2013, http://www.youtube.com/watch?v=fmdRJW_9Dg8.

36. Atkins and Slosser, *Child of Satan, Child of God*, 6588–6594.

37. To read about the works she did, visit the site still operated and maintained by James Whitehouse here: "Accomplishments," *SusanAtkins.org*, last accessed December 30, 2013, http://www.susanatkins.org/02-Accomplishments.html.

38. "Charles Manson Family Member Susan Atkins' 23rd Psalm 'Death Bed Last Words' ABC News GMA," YouTube video, posted by MichaelsBackporch, uploaded September 13, 2011, last accessed December 31, 2013, http://www.youtube.com/watch?v=85sf0EFkbEA.

39. "Susan Atkins," *Wikipedia, The Free Encyclopedia*, last modified December 25, 2013, http://en.wikipedia.org/wiki/Susan_Atkins.

40. Unless otherwise noted, or in the case of a specific quote, all information given in this case study has been a collection of well known, easy-access facts, repeated transparently through light research of the Manson Family. Most of these facts are covered in further detail and with further referencing online here: "Charles Manson," *Wikipedia, The Free Encyclopedia*, last modified December 9, 2013, http://en.wikipedia.org/wiki/Charles_manson, and, when referring to a personal memory of Charles "Tex" Watson, here: Charles "Tex" Watson and Chaplain Ray Hoekstra, *Will You Die for Me?: The Man Who Killed for Charles Manson Tells His Own Story* (Fleming H. Revell Company, 1978). Any information specific to a certain book, website, or other material will be cited individually.

41. Information given in the second LaBianca homicide report. Also see: "Thoughts on the LaBiancas and the Motive on August 10th," *The Manson Family Blog*, September 5, 2012, http://www.mansonblog.com/2012_09_05_archive.html; and, "Manson and Haight-Ashbury: Just Another Hippie," *Man from Spahn/The Family Guy*, February 24, 2013, http://manfromspahn.tumblr.com/page/5.

42. Bugliosi and Gentry, *Helter Skelter,*, 50.

43. Ibid., 50–52.

44. "Manson Family Creepy Crawl," Vimeo video, uploaded by Propagandery, 2010, last accessed January 19, 2014, http://vimeo.com/4441059.

45. Bugliosi and Gentry, *Helter Skelter*, 214.

46. Alice LaBianca, *No More Tomorrows* (M. C. M. Entertainment, 1991), 409.

47. Ibid.

48. Ibid., 410.

49. "Rock and Roll's Most Infamous Tour Manager," YouTube video, 4:52–4:55, posted by VICE, uploaded December 5, 2012, last accessed January 24, 2014, http://www.youtube.com/watch?v=2a2b3rBrHM4.

50. Ed Sanders, *The Family* (Thunder Mouth's Press, an imprint of Avalon Publishing Group Inc., 2002), 29.

51. "Rock and Roll's Most Infamous Tour Manager," 5:05–5:16, http://www.youtube.com/watch?v=2a2b3rBrHM4.

52. See: Jeff Obiga, "Today is the 42nd Anniversary of Charles Manson's Debut Album," *Vice Noisey Blog*, March 6, 2012, http://noisey.vice.com/blog/today-is-the-42-nd-anniversary-of-charles-manson-s-debut-album.

53. See more information under the "Recordings" heading at: "Charles Manson," *Wikipedia, The Free Encyclopedia*, last modified January 23, 2014, last accessed January 24, 2014, http://en.wikipedia.org/wiki/Charles_manson.

54. For example, see: "Harold True's House Waverly Drive," *CharlieManson.com*, last accessed January 20, 2014, http://www.charliemanson.com/true-1.htm.

55. See and hear one recorded interview between Judy Hansen and Harold True at the following link: *The Tate-LaBianca Homicide Research Blog*, uploaded September 8, 2012, last accessed January 24, 2014, http://www.lsb3.com/2012/09/labergewatson-hello-everyone-it-seems.html. Also see: Phil Kaufman and Colin White, *Road Mangler's Deluxe* (Colin White & Laurie Boucke, 3rd ed., 2005).

56. See: David López, "Entrevista Exclusiva con Charles Manson ["Exclusive Interview with Charles Manson"]," *Vanity Fair Spain*, last accessed January 24, 2014, http://www.revistavanityfair.es/articulos/exclusiva-charles-manson-habla-para-vanity-fair-espana/12496.

57. "Full Transcription of Interview between David López and Charles Manson," uploaded March 23, 2011, last accessed January 24, 2014, http://www.mansondirect.com/spain%20interview.html.

58. See: "Phil Kaufman," *CharlieManson.com*, last accessed January 24, 2014, http://www.charliemanson.com/kaufman-1.htm.

59. Almost all reports of the Tate/LaBianca murders point to the claim that these victims were ultimately dealt the life-ending blow by Watson. Although this author does not recommend further research to those who may find the details of these evenings disturbing, the chronological order of the murders and number of stab wounds and by whom and when can be found in: Bugliosi and Gentry, *Helter Skelter*. Summarily, Wikipedia has covered the order of events here: "Charles Manson," *Wikipedia*,, last modified December 9, 2013, http://en.wikipedia.org/wiki/Charles_manson, and *Wikipedia* has most often quoted from Bugliosi's book.

60. Paul McGinty (actor), Marc Caso (actor), Melanie Van Betten (actress), Mark Wangerin (composer), Michael Gonzales (director), Tom Nash (producer), *Forgiven: The Charles "Tex" Watson Story*, Cutting Edge Film International, 1993, videocassette (VHS), 30 min. Also viewable online here: "Forgiven—The Charles 'Tex' Watson Story (1993) (Full)," YouTube video, 3:14–3:27 posted by Wicked Leakz, uploaded on November 10, 2013, last accessed February 5, 2014, http://www.youtube.com/watch?v=251fD8wPWVo.

61. Charles "Tex" Watson and Chaplain Ray Hoekstra, *Will You Die for Me?* (Fleming H. Revell Company, 1978), 33.

62. Ibid., 34.

63. Ibid.

64. Ibid., 37.

65. Ibid., 39.

66. Ibid., 50.

67. Ibid.

68. Ibid., 12, emphasis in original.

69. Ibid., 71.

70. Bugliosi and Gentry, *Helter Skelter*, 238.

71. These listed odds are not to be taken as literal. However, the similarities in the Beach Boys' song to the one Manson previously recorded, *during a friendship between these acquaintances*, are far too close to be coincidence. To hear both songs in succession, see: "Charles Manson 'Lie' Cease to Exist 1970," YouTube video, posted by 9711886, uploaded April 8, 2011, last accessed February 3, 2014, http://www.youtube.com/watch?v=UbtaYTLBhy4; "The Beach Boys—Never Learn Not to Love (RARE 45" mono Single Version)," YouTube video, posted by JayandCompany95, uploaded October 23, 2012, last accessed February 3, 2014, http://www.youtube.com/watch?v=xwI-6_WMX8Q.

72. Watson and Hoekstra, *Will You Die for Me?*, 82.

73. Ibid., 91.
74. "Charles 'Tex' Watson," *Wikipedia, The Free Encyclopedia*, last modified February 8, 2014, last accessed same day, http://en.wikipedia.org/wiki/Charles_Tex_Watson.
75. This author does not suggest that all citation leads be followed. However, information regarding the buck-knife, practice-killing sessions following the Tate/LaBianca murders is available in Watson and Hoekstra, *Will You Die for Me?*, 26–27.
76. Atkins and Slosser, *Child of Satan, Child of God*, 336.
77. Watson and Hoekstra, *Will You Die for Me?*, 26–27.
78. Ibid., 12.
79. Ibid., 29.
80. Ibid., 153.
81. The "sold for a pitcher of beer" story is one that circulates through much Manson literature. It appears to be one that he likes to tell, as it pops up often in his own speech. See: Marilyn Bardsley, *Charles Manson and the Manson Family*, true crime biography report, "Sold for a Pitcher of Beer" page, *CrimeLibrary.com*, last accessed July 29, 2014, http://www.crimelibrary.com/serial_killers/notorious/manson/14.html.
82. Bugliosi and Gentry, *Helter Skelter*, 597.
83. Watson and Hoekstra, *Will You Die for Me?*, 182.
84. Ibid., 171, ellipses in original.
85. Ibid., 172.
86. Ibid., 185.
87. Forensic psychiatrist Dr. Michael Stone, "Cult Followers," *Most Evil*, season 2, episode 5, 17:44–18:22, aired September 9, 2007 (on The Discovery Channel: Investigation Discovery, 2010), DVD.
88. Watson and Hoekstra, *Will You Die for Me?*, 187.
89. Alisa Statman and Brie Tate, *Restless Souls (Enhanced Edition): The Sharon Tate Family's Account of Stardom, the Manson Murders, and a Crusade for Justice* (Kindle Edition: Harper Collins, 2012), Kindle Locations 3297–3301.
90. "About Charles—Past," *Abounding Love Ministries*, last accessed February 8, 2014, http://www.aboundinglove.org/about.php.
91. Ibid.
92. "Tex Watson and Susan LaBerge Vs. Doris Tate," YouTube video, 0:24–0:28, posted by bretg78, uploaded November 16, 2006, last accessed February 8, 2014, http://www.youtube.com/watch?v=g2hosmU4l80.
93. Ibid.
94. "Tex Watson 700 Club Interview.avi," YouTube video, 7:34–7:46, posted by Gladys Knight, uploaded January 15, 2012, last accessed February 8, 2014, http://www.youtube.com/watch?v=815A84JZz-4.
95. Ibid.
96. Statman and Tate, *Restless Souls*, 3305.
97. "About Charles—Past," http://www.aboundinglove.org/about.php.
98. "Monthly View," *Abounding Love Ministries*, last accessed February 8, 2014, http://www.aboundinglove.org/mv/index.php.
99. Charles "Tex" Watson, *Manson's Right-Hand Man Speaks Out* (Kindle

Edition, Abounding Love Publishers, May 24, 2013). Available here: http://www.amazon.com/Mansons-Right-Hand-Man-Speaks-Out-ebook/dp/B00D0CXKQQ/ref=sr_1_1?s=digital-text&ie=UTF8&qid=1391917344&sr=1-1&keywords=charles+tex+watson.

100. Charles "Tex" Watson, *Our Identity in God's Family*, a.k.a., *Our Identity: Spirit, Soul, and Body* (Kindle Edition, Abounding Love Publishers, June 18, 2013). Available here: http://www.amazon.com/Identity-Gods-Family-Charles-Watson-ebook/dp/B00DH7XBTA/ref=sr_1_3?s=digital-text&ie=UTF8&qid=1391917619&sr=1-3&keywords=charles+tex+watson.

101. Charles "Tex" Watson, *Christianity for Fools* (Kindle Edition, Abounding Love Publishers, July 26, 2013). Available here: http://www.amazon.com/Christianity-Fools-Charles-Tex-Watson-ebook/dp/B00E6TCYZK/ref=sr_1_2?s=digital-text&ie=UTF8&qid=1391917619&sr=1-2&keywords=charles+tex+watson.

102. "Charles 'Tex' Watson," under the heading, "Conviction," http://en.wikipedia.org/wiki/Charles_Tex_Watson.

103. Unless otherwise noted, or in the case of a specific quote, all information given in this case study has been come from: 1) research information put forth by Amnesty International USA regarding psychological evaluations and childhood living circumstances in hopes to stay his execution; 2) archived press releases and news updates through papers and periodicals local to Sellers at the time, primarily from *The Daily Oklahoman* and *Tulsa World*; 3) Amy Goodman, Sean Sellers, and Dr. Dorothy Lewis, "An Interview with Death Row Inmate Sean Sellers/Interview with Dr. Dorothy Lewis," *Democracy Now! Radio*, Monday, February 1, 1999; and 4) public case records. When referring to a personal memory or claim of Sean Sellers, information was found in his personal writings originally at SeanSellers.com, and then in redirected archives through: 1) the website of Steve Presson, Sellers' defense attorney; 2) Indiana Clark County prosecutor's website; 3) research information put forth by Amnesty International USA; 5) Sean Sellers, Dr. Fletcher Brothers, *Escaping Satan's Web*, documentary/filmed interview available for purchase from Freedom Village USA (http://www.freedomvillageusa.com/1.4.html) (also viewable on YouTube, see endnotes specific to this interview); and 4) Sean Sellers, *Web of Darkness* (Victory House Inc.: Tulsa, OK, 1990). Any information specific to a certain book, website, or other material will be cited individually. Permission has been granted by Amnesty International and by the Clark County Prosecutor website to quote unlimitedly. PLEASE NOTE that the following book was not used in any way as a reference, as it fell under extreme scrutiny for falsified information, and the front matter of the book expressly admits that sections were fictionalized for dramatic effect: Vickie L. Dawkins and Nina Downey Higgins, *Devil Child: A Terrifying True Story of Satanism and Murder* (St. Martin's Press, NY: 1989).

104. This beginning narrative was based on a truthful compilation of testimonies by Sellers; nothing in this opening sequence was assumed. All thoughts, feelings, and actions described in this case study introduction were thoughts, feelings, and actions as related by Sellers, himself, in the interviews and reading materials cited within this case study.

105. The term "lies for Christ" is one that frequently appears cynically in secular media

referring to the unfortunate occurrence of ministers stretching the truth in service to God. Often their intention is to make the listener take them more seriously by raising more sensational or alarming details in their message, causing a threat to appear more imminent, and thus, the listener is likely encouraged to take action against the threat immediately. The threat could essentially be anything the speaker wanted it to be, all the way from the dangers of the street to the dangers of the afterlife. A "lie for Christ" could be told both by a sincere minister who believes that raising the bar of his message is the only way to get someone's attention, and also by an insincere minister looking to gain power by fear-mongering. However, regardless of the varying levels of sincerity that may be at play at any given moment, thankfully, this trend has appeared to have taken a significant dip after the Satanic Panic era, especially since it is the opinion of these authors that God does not need the assistance of a lie to further His kingdom in the first place.

106. Fox News Insider, "Woman Admits to Craiglist Killing, Claims She Murdered at Least 22 Others," *Fox News*, February 16, 2014, http://foxnewsinsider. com/2014/02/16/pa-woman-miranda-barbour-admits-craigslist-killing-claims-she-murdered-least-22-others.

107. Juan A. Lozano, "Official: Deal with Devil Prompted Girl's Killing," *ABC News*, February 11, 2014, http://abcnews.go.com/US/wireStory/charged-slaying-15-year-houston-girl-22463967.

108. "DOCUMENT–USA: Killing Hope—The Imminent Execution of Sean Sellers," December 1998, *Amnesty International*, last accessed February 25, 2014, http://www.amnesty.org/en/library/asset/AMR51/108/1998/en/bc370239-e759-11dd-b8d3-c95de5982fed/amr511081998en.html.

109. Journal of Sean Richard Sellers, "Sixty Days Before I Die," entry: Friday, December 25, 1998. Viewable here: "The Sean Sellers Case: His Journal, 'Sixty Days Before I Die,'" *Jackson/Presson Case Files*, last accessed February 25, 2014, http://www.jacksonpresson.com/Sellers.html.

110. "Sean Sellers—Escaping Satan's Web," YouTube video, 14:08–14:15, posted by Dust House, uploaded June 10, 2013, last accessed February 25, 2014, http://www.youtube.com/watch?v=N3SXyrexi3w. Note that for a donation, this documentary can be purchased on DVD from Dr. Fletcher Brothers' ministry directly: Freedom Village USA (http://www.freedomvillageusa.com/1.4.html).

111. "Sixty Days Before I Die," entry: Wednesday, December 23, 1998, http://www.jacksonpresson.com/Sellers.html.

112. "An Interview with Death Row Inmate Sean Sellers/Interview with Dr. Dorothy Lewis," *Democracy Now! Radio*, Monday, February 1, 1999, 42:00–58:00; and: Sean Sellers, "The Confession of My Crimes," August 24, 1998, originally appearing on SeanSellers.com, and now as viewable here: "Sean Richard Sellers: Executed February 4, 1999 by Lethal Injection in Oklahoma," *ClarkProsecutor.org*, last accessed February 25, 2014, http://www.clarkprosecutor.org/html/death/US/sellers512.htm.

113. Amy Goodman and Dr. Dorothy Lewis, "Interview with Dr. Dorothy Lewis," *Democracy Now! Radio*, 51:36, Monday, February 1, 1999.

114. Sellers, "Sixty Days Before I Die," entry: Tuesday, February 2, 1999, http://www.jacksonpresson.com/Sellers.html.

115. "Escaping Satan's Web," 8:25–8:33, http://www.youtube.com/ watch?v=N3SXyrexi3w.

116. Sellers, "The Confession of My Crimes," http://www.clarkprosecutor.org/html/ death/US/sellers512.htm.

117. Ibid.

118. "DOCUMENT–USA: Killing Hope," http://www.amnesty.org/en/library/ asset/AMR51/108/1998/en/bc370239-e759-11dd-b8d3-c95de5982fed/ amr511081998en.html.

119. "Escaping Satan's Web," 14:24–14:56, http://www.youtube.com/ watch?v=N3SXyrexi3w.

120. Sellers, "Sixty Days Before I Die," entry: Saturday, January 23, 1999, http://www. jacksonpresson.com/Sellers.html.

121. "DOCUMENT–USA: Killing Hope," http://www.amnesty.org/en/library/ asset/AMR51/108/1998/en/bc370239-e759-11dd-b8d3-c95de5982fed/ amr511081998en.html.

122. Sellers, "Sixty Days Before I Die," entries: Saturday [was supposed to be Sunday], January 3, 1999; Monday, January 4, 1999, http://www.jacksonpresson.com/Sellers. html.

123. "DOCUMENT–USA: Killing Hope," http://www.amnesty.org/en/library/ asset/AMR51/108/1998/en/bc370239-e759-11dd-b8d3-c95de5982fed/ amr511081998en.html.

124. Sellers, "Sixty Days Before I Die," entry: Thursday, January 28, 1999, http://www. jacksonpresson.com/Sellers.html.

125. "The Dungeons and Dragons Experience Documentary PT 1," YouTube video, 0:23–1:02, ellipses represent dramatic pauses as voiced in the original, posted by Triffid, uploaded October 12, 2009, last accessed February 26, 2014, http://www. youtube.com/watch?v=RWCh7hoK0_Q.

126. Sean Sellers, *Web of Darkness* (Victory House Inc.: Tulsa, OK, 1990), 80.

127. "CPI Inflation Calculator," http://www.bls.gov/data/inflation_calculator.htm.

128. "Vin Diesel on Dungeons and Dragons," YouTube video, 0:16–1:53, emphasis placed where emphasis was spoken verbally in the original, posted by sandokanw73, uploaded March 15, 2010, last accessed February 26, 2014, http://www.youtube. com/watch?v=36_-DauQi0s.

129. "Vin Diesel," *Wikipedia: The Free Encyclopedia*, last modified February 22, 2014, http://en.wikipedia.org/wiki/Vin_diesel.

130. Ibid.

131. National Coalition on Television Violence, "Press Release from Washington," May 12, 1987. This research has been quoted in many books and articles. Here are a few: Sean Sellers, *Web of Darkness*, 85; Scott Poland, *Suicide Intervention in the Schools* (The Guilford Press: New York, NY, 1989); "Deliver Us from the Evil One," *Orthodox America*, under the heading "The Games People Play," last accessed February 26, 2014, http://www.roca.org/OA/73/73e.htm.

132. "Escaping Satan's Web," emphasis placed where emphasis was spoken verbally in the original, 17:40–22:34, http://www.youtube.com/watch?v=N3SXyrexi3w.

133. Ibid.
134. William Schnoebelen, "Should a Christian Play Dungeons & Dragons?" *Chick Publications, Inc.*, reproduced with permission in 2004, last accessed February 26, 2014, http://www.chick.com/articles/frpg.asp.
135. Sellers, *Web of Darkness*, 86.
136. Sellers, "The Confession of My Crimes," http://www.clarkprosecutor.org/html/death/US/sellers512.htm.
137. Ibid.
138. "Escaping Satan's Web," 12:05–12:21, http://www.youtube.com/watch?v=N3SXyrexi3w.
139. Sellers, *Web of Darkness*, 24.
140. Sellers, "The Confession of My Crimes," http://www.clarkprosecutor.org/html/death/US/sellers512.htm.
141. Ibid.
142. Ibid.
143. Sellers, *Web of Darkness*, 28.
144. This section is merely a rewrite of his testimony. This is the story he has repeated multiple times, and no liberties have been taken to deviate from it. As far as citing the materials that this series of events have come from, one could essentially copy/paste almost every source that Sean Sellers has ever written or spoken in or from.
145. "DOCUMENT–USA: Killing Hope," http://www.amnesty.org/en/library/asset/AMR51/108/1998/en/bc370239-e759-11dd-b8d3-c95de5982fed/amr511081998en.html.
146. "Escaping Satan's Web," 32:54–33:50, http://www.youtube.com/watch?v=N3SXyrexi3w.
147. Ibid., 33:55–36:36.
148. "The Confession of My Crimes," http://www.clarkprosecutor.org/html/death/US/sellers512.htm.
149. Sellers, "Sixty Days Before I Die," entry: Wednesday, February 3, 1999, http://www.jacksonpresson.com/Sellers.html.
150. "Escaping Satan's Web," 36:00–36:35, http://www.youtube.com/watch?v=N3SXyrexi3w.
151. Sellers, "The Confession of My Crimes," http://www.clarkprosecutor.org/html/death/US/sellers512.htm.
152. Sellers, *Web of Darkness*, 28.
153. Ibid., 28–29.
154. "Geraldo Rivera—Exposing Satan's Underground FULL," YouTube video, 33:39–40:02, posted by kahnblows, uploaded September 5, 2013, last accessed March 3, 2014, http://www.youtube.com/watch?v=EcWbuBPNtPw.
155. Anton LaVey, originally from *The Satanic Bible*, here as quoted by: "On the Choice of a Human Sacrifice," *Dancing with Nazis*, last accessed March 3, 2014, http://raumfahrer.wordpress.com/manson/levay-on-sacrifice/.
156. Sellers, "The Confession of My Crimes," http://www.clarkprosecutor.org/html/death/US/sellers512.htm.

157. Sean Sellers, one of his writings originally appearing on SeanSellers.com, and now as viewable here: "Who is Sean Sellers," *Exposing Satanism*, last accessed March 3, 2014, http://www.exposingsatanism.org/satanism/seansellers.htm.

158. Ibid.

159. Ibid.

160. Ibid.

161. Sellers, *Web of Darkness*, 32.

162. "Escaping Satan's Web," 50:10–50:19, http://www.youtube.com/watch?v=N3SXyrexi3w.

163. "Sean Sellers—Executed February 4, 1999," originally appearing on the Death Penalty Institute of Oklahoma website, and now as viewable here: "Sean Richard Sellers: Executed February 4, 1999 by Lethal Injection in Oklahoma," *ClarkProsecutor.org*, last accessed February 25, 2014, http://www.clarkprosecutor.org/html/death/US/sellers512.htm.

164. "Mental Health Center: Dissociative Identity Disorder (Multiple Personality Disorder)," *WebMD*, last accessed March 3, 2014, http://www.webmd.com/mental-health/dissociative-identity-disorder-multiple-personality-disorder.

165. "DOCUMENT–USA: Killing Hope," http://www.amnesty.org/en/library/asset/AMR51/108/1998/en/bc370239-e759-11dd-b8d3-c95de5982fed/amr511081998en.html.

166. Goodman and Lewis, "Interview with Dr. Dorothy Lewis," emphasis placed where emphasis was spoken verbally in the original, 49:00–52:48.

167. Ibid., 54:09–54:15.

168. Ibid., 55:23–55:27.

169. Nolan Clay and Anthony Thornton, "Sellers Executed for 3 Murders," *NewsOK*, February 4, 1999, last accessed March 3, 2014, http://newsok.com/sellers-executed-for-3-murders/article/2641662.

170. Goodman and Lewis, "Interview with Dr. Dorothy Lewis," 55:51–55:52.

171. Kenneth L. Smith, "Bob Larson: Selling Out Sean Sellers," *Satanic Media Watch and News Exchange*, last accessed February 29, 2014, http://www.smwane.dk/content/view/156/.

172. Sean Sellers, "Who I Am," originally appearing on SeanSellers.com, and now as viewable here: "Sean Richard Sellers: Executed February 4, 1999 by Lethal Injection in Oklahoma," *ClarkProsecutor.org*, last accessed February 25, 2014, http://www.clarkprosecutor.org/html/death/US/sellers512.htm.

173. Vickie L. Dawkins and Nina Downey Higgins, *Devil Child: A Terrifying True Story of Satanism and Murder* (St. Martin's Press, NY: 1989), "Note to the reader" in front matter of book.

174. As shared in a personal phone conversation between author Donna Howell and a former warden of death row, February 12, 2014.

175. Sellers, "Sixty Days Before I Die," http://www.jacksonpresson.com/Sellers.html.

176. References to these masses of letters are mentioned frequently in the documents compiled by Amnesty International, defense attorney Steve Presson, as well as Sellers' own references to them in his writings (all cited herein) and from concerned activist groups and individuals online.

177. "DOCUMENT–USA: Killing Hope," http://www.amnesty.org/en/library/asset/AMR51/108/1998/en/bc370239-e759-11dd-b8d3-c95de5982fed/amr511081998en.html.

178. "CARMAN LIVE! THE SEAN SELLERS STORY—11th Hour Pt 1," YouTube video, 1:29–1:32, posted by floridamusik, uploaded on March 25, 2007, last accessed March 3, 2014, http://www.youtube.com/watch?v=bH1swVz1ybM.

179. Ibid., 3:22–3:32.

180. *Dead Kid Walking*, Australian Broadcasting Corporation documentary by FOUR CORNERS, BBC Correspondant Special program, aired August 16, 1999. Transcript of documentary viewable here: *Dead Kid Walking*, transcript, last accessed March 3, 2014, http://www.abc.net.au/4corners/stories/s50027.htm.

181. Ibid.

182. "Sean Sellers," *Wikipedia: The Free Encyclopedia*, last modified January 11, 2014, last accessed March 4, 2014, http://en.wikipedia.org/wiki/Sean_Sellers.

183. *Dead Kid Walking*, transcript, http://www.abc.net.au/4corners/stories/s50027.htm.

184. Ibid., emphasis added.

185. Unless otherwise noted, or in the case of a specific quote, all information given in this case study has been a collection of well known, easy-access facts, repeated transparently through light research of David Berkowitz. Most of these facts are covered in further detail and with further referencing online at the following links: 1) "David Berkowitz," *Wikiepedia: The Free Encyclopedia*, last modified February 27, 2014, last accessed March 7, 2014, http://en.wikipedia.org/wiki/David_Berkowitz; 2) Marilyn Bardsley, *David Berkowitz: The Son of Sam*, True Crime biography report, *CrimeLibrary.com*, http://www.crimelibrary.com/serial_killers/notorious/berkowitz/letter_1.html; and 3) Lawrence D. Klausner, *Son of Sam: Based on the Authorized Transcription of the Tapes, Official Documents and Diaries of David Berkowitz* (McGraw-Hill Book Company, New York, NY: 1981). When referring to a personal memory: 1) "David Berkowitz: Son of Sam," *A&E Television Networks: Biography*, A&E Home Video Studio, DVD, 1997; and 2) David Berkowitz, *Son of Hope: The Prison Journals of David Berkowitz*, volume 1 (Morning Star Communications: New York, NY, 2006). Some specific case details regarding the possibility that Berkowitz did not act alone were drawn from: 1) "Inside Evil: Serial Killers Jeffrey Dahmer & Son of Sam," *NBC News* special report, reported by Stone Phillips, NBC Universal Inc., DVD, 2006; 2) Maury Terry, *The Ultimate Evil: An Investigation into America's Most Dangerous Satanic Cult* (Doubleday Publishers: New York, NY, 1987); and 3) Maury Terry, *The Ultimate Evil: The Truth about the Cult Murders: Son of Sam & Beyond* (Barnes & Noble Books: New York, NY, 1999). Any information specific to a certain book, website, or other material will be cited individually.

186. "David Berkowitz: Son of Sam," *A&E Television Networks: Biography*, A&E Home Video Studio, DVD, 1997, 32:30–34:21.

187. "Abortions in America," *Operation Rescue*, last accessed March 12, 2014, http://www.operationrescue.org/about-abortion/abortions-in-america/.

188. "Roe v. Wade," *Wikipedia: The Free Encyclopedia*, last modified February 16, 2014, http://en.wikipedia.org/wiki/Roe_v._Wade.

189. "Planned Parenthood v. Casey," *Wikipedia: The Free Encyclopedia*, last modified February 24, 2014, http://en.wikipedia.org/wiki/Planned_Parenthood_v._Casey.

190. Microsoft Word embedded program thesaurus, 2007 Windows version.

191. "bastard," synonyms, *Thesaurus.com*, last accessed March 12, 2014, http://thesaurus.com/browse/bastard.

192. In a personal interview between Borison the cab driver and author Donna Howell, March, 2014.

193. David Berkowitz, *Son of Hope: The Prison Journals of David Berkowitz*, volume 1, (Morning Star Communications: New York, NY, 2006), 86–87.

194. "David Berkowitz: Son of Sam," *A&E Television Networks*, 3:51–4:05.

195. Berkowitz, *Son of Hope: The Prison Journals of David Berkowitz*, 1.

196. Ibid., 3.

197. "David Berkowitz: Son of Sam," *A&E Television Networks*, 5:01–5:14.

198. Berkowitz's mother's parakeet has been repeatedly reported as poisoned to death by Berkowitz because: 1) he expressly claimed this, and 2) it lines up with the "inflicting pain or torture on animals" research that often associates itself to serial killers in psychopathology studies. However, Berkowitz has shared with us personally—and has notified us of letters between him and his father regarding the issue—that the bird died from beak rot. Obviously, since the letters from his father confirming this truth are in Berkowitz's personal correspondence collection, we are not able to cite the witness account of Mr. Nathan Berkowitz, but he and his wife would have been the only witnesses to this story besides Berkowitz, himself.

199. Berkowitz, *Son of Hope: The Prison Journals of David Berkowitz*, 2.

200. "David Berkowitz: Son of Sam," *A&E Television Networks*, 7:40–7:48.

201. Ibid., 7:40–7:48.

202. Ibid., 8:04–8:13.

203. Berkowitz, *Son of Hope: The Prison Journals of David Berkowitz*, 74–75.

204. "David Berkowitz: Son of Sam," *A&E Television Networks*, 9:12–9:29.

205. Berkowitz, *Son of Hope: The Prison Journals of David Berkowitz*, 87–88.

206. Edited by Tim McLoughlin and Thomas Adcock, *Brooklyn Noir 3: Nothing But the Truth* (Akashic Books: New York, NY, 2008), Kindle Locations 2366–2367.

207. Berkowitz, *Son of Hope: The Prison Journals of David Berkowitz*, 216.

208. "David Berkowitz; The Son of Sam (Documentary)," YouTube video, 13:49–14:00, posted by Esoteric Nation, uploaded June 18, 2013, last accessed March 13, 2014, http://www.youtube.com/watch?v=Q98oVN_xjng.

209. "David Berkowitz: Son of Sam," *A&E Television Networks*, 10:00–10:18.

210. Ibid., 11:33–11:44.

211. Ibid., 12:31–12:48.

212. Ibid., 15:19–15:34. Please note that in a personal letter from Berkowitz to Tom Horn dated August 19, 2014, he says, "I barely recall journalist Jack Jones…. I do not recall mocking my mother's speech. If I did comment about her voice and speech, I may have shared it in a humorous way in that I found she had the typical Jewish/Brooklyn accent that many people from Brooklyn have."

213. In a personal letter from David Berkowitz to Thomas Horn, dated August 19, 2014.

214. "David Berkowitz; The Son of Sam (Documentary)," 16:06–16:41, http://www. youtube.com/watch?v=Q98oVN_xjng.

215. Marilyn Bardsley, *David Berkowitz: The Son of Sam*, true crime biography report, "Cry for Help" page, *CrimeLibrary.com*, last accessed March 13, 2014, http://www. crimelibrary.com/serial_killers/notorious/berkowitz/20.html.

216. In a personal letter from David Berkowitz to Thomas Horn, dated August 19, 2014.

217. Berkowitz, *Son of Hope*, 3.

218. "David Berkowitz: Son of Sam," *A&E Television Networks*, 19:50–19:55.

219. Lawrence D. Klausner, *Son of Sam: Based on the Authorized Transcription of the Tapes, Official Documents and Diaries of David Berkowitz* (McGraw-Hill Book Company, New York, NY: 1981), 240; spelling, punctuation, and capitalization as in original.

220. Berkowitz, *Son of Hope: The Prison Journals of David Berkowitz*, 35.

221. "David Berkowitz: Son of Sam," *A&E Television Networks*, 19:55–20:14.

222. Maury Terry, *The Ultimate Evil: The Truth about the Cult Murders: Son of Sam & Beyond* (Barnes & Noble Books: New York, NY, 1999), 23–24.

223. "David Berkowitz: Son of Sam," *A&E Television Networks*, 22:53–23:16.

224. "One of the Two Girls Shot Is in Serious Condition," *The New York Times*, archives, only accessible with paid archival subscription, last accessed March, 15, 2014, http:// select.nytimes.com/gst/abstract.html?res=FA081FFF355C107B93CAAB178AD9 5F428785F9. See also: "David Berkowitz," *Wikiepedia: The Free Encyclopedia*, last modified February 27, 2014, last accessed March 7, 2014, http://en.wikipedia.org/ wiki/David_Berkowitz.

225. "David Berkowitz: Son of Sam," *A&E Television Networks*, 23:16–23:28.

226. "Woman Dies in Mystery Shooting," *The New York Times*, archives, only accessible with paid archival subscription, last accessed March, 15, 2014, http://select.nytimes. com/gst/abstract.html?res=FA0C11F83E5D167493C3AA178AD85F438785F9. See also: Terry, *The Ultimate Evil*, 32.

227. Ibid.

228. Terry, *The Ultimate Evil*, 36–37.

229. Klausner, *Son of Sam*, 121.

230. Terry, *The Ultimate Evil*, 36–37.

231. Ibid.

232. "David Berkowitz: Son of Sam," *A&E Television Networks*, 25:31–26:13.

233. Klausner, *Son of Sam*, 5.

234. This letter seems to be viewable everywhere one might look regarding the Son of Sam murder cases. However, for a quick and easy reference that anyone would have access to, see here: "David Berkowitz," *Wikipedia*, http://en.wikipedia.org/wiki/ David_Berkowitz; spelling, punctuation, and capitalization as in original.

235. Terry, *The Ultimate Evil*, 47.

236. "David Berkowitz: Son of Sam," *A&E Television Networks*. Please note that the portion of this letter that is included in this case study here is not a quotation of verbalized content put forth on the DVD biography. Rather, it is a retyping of the letter as it appears on screen during the biography within six seconds at the time signature: 28:25–28:31.

237. "David Berkowitz: Son of Sam," *A&E Television Networks*, 28:30–28:34.

238. This letter seems to be viewable everywhere one might look regarding the Son of Sam murder cases. However, for a quick and easy reference that anyone would have access to, see here: "David Berkowitz," *Wikipedia*, http://en.wikipedia.org/wiki/David_Berkowitz; spelling, punctuation, and capitalization as in original.

239. Terry, *The Ultimate Evil*, 53.

240. Ibid., 68.

241. Ibid., 70.

242. Ibid.

243. Ibid., 70–72.

244. Ibid., 70–72; 79.

245. Ibid., 91.

246. Ibid.

247. John Hockenberry, "Did 'Son of Sam' Really Act Alone?: Some Original Detectives Wonder if There's Something or Someone They Missed," *ABC News DATELINE*, July 2, 2004, last accessed March 7, 2014, http://www.nbcnews.com/id/5351509#.UyR1w_mwJcQ.

248. "David Berkowitz; The Son of Sam (Documentary)," 28:18–28:20, http://www.youtube.com/watch?v=Q98oVN_xjng.

249. Terry, *The Ultimate Evil*, 67–68.

250. Ibid., 81.

251. Ibid., 96–99.

252. Hockenberry, "Did 'Son of Sam' Really Act Alone?" 28:55–29:21, http://www.nbcnews.com/id/5351509#.UyR1w_mwJcQ. See also: "David Berkowitz: Son of Sam," *A&E Television Networks*, 32:13–32:23.

253. Klausner, *Son of Sam*, 32; emphasis added.

254. Hockenberry, "Did 'Son of Sam' Really Act Alone?" 28:55–29:21, http://www.nbcnews.com/id/5351509#.UyR1w_mwJcQ. See also: "David Berkowitz: Son of Sam," *A&E Television Networks*, 32:13–32:23.

255. "Inside Evil: Serial Killers Jeffrey Dahmer & Son of Sam," *NBC News* special report, reported by Stone Phillips, NBC Universal Inc., DVD, 2006, 9:06–9:17.

256. Ibid., 12:12–12:18.

257. Ibid., 18:48–19:03.

258. See: "Inside Edition—David Berkowitz," http://www.dailymotion.com/video/xmr0xg_inside-edition-david-berkowitz_shortfilms.

259. "Inside Evil: Serial Killers Jeffrey Dahmer & Son of Sam," 17:24–17:36.

260. Ibid., 19:26–20:00.

261. "Inside Edition—David Berkowitz," 41:50–41:56, http://www.dailymotion.com/video/xmr0xg_inside-edition-david-berkowitz_shortfilms.

262. Hugo Harmatz, J.D., LL. M., *Dear David: Letters to Inmate #78-A-1976 (David Berkowitz)* (Benra Publishing Corp: Colts Neck, NJ, 2005), 6.

263. Ibid.

264. To see a comparison of the Carr brothers to the other composite sketches, see: "Inside Evil: Serial Killers Jeffrey Dahmer & Son of Sam," 21:00–23:32.

265. "Inside Evil: Serial Killers Jeffrey Dahmer & Son of Sam," 24:37–24:58.

266. Ibid., 26:06–27:14.

267. Ibid., 34:13–34:24.

268. "Inside Edition—David Berkowitz," 11:10–13:42; 42:35–42:50, http://www.dailymotion.com/video/xmr0xg_inside-edition-david-berkowitz_shortfilms.

269. Ibid., 11:10–13:42.

270. Ibid., 17:32–17:49.

271. Ibid., 30:43–31:05.

272. Ibid., 38:54–39:43.

273. This quote is repetitiously cited throughout biographical sources on Berkowitz, and is very easy to find. Following are a couple places one can locate this information: Robert K. Martin and Eric Savoy, *American Gothic: New Interventions in a National Narrative* (University of Iowa Press: Iowa City, IA, 1998), 220; Elliot Leyton, *Hunting Humans: The Rise of the Modern Multiple Murderer* (Carroll & Graf: New York, NY, 2001), 203;

274. "David Berkowitz: Son of Sam," *A&E Television Networks*, 38:51–39:18.

275. Noah Hutchings, in the collaborative work *God's Ghostbusters: Vampires? Ghosts? Aliens? Werewolves? Creatures of the Night Beware!* (Defender Publishing: Crane, MO, 2011), Kindle Locations 5955–5957.

276. "Irish mythology in popular culture," *Wikipedia: The Free Encyclopedia*, under the heading "Samhain," last modified February 18, 2014, http://en.wikipedia.org/wiki/Irish_mythology_in_popular_culture#Samhain.

277. In a personal letter from David Berkowitz to Thomas Horn, dated August 19, 2014.

278. Ibid.

279. In a personal email between Noah Hutchings and Tom Horn, dated March 15, 2014; emphasis added.

280. "David Berkowitz: Son of Sam," *A&E Television Networks*, 37:48–38:18.

281. Harmatz, J.D., LL. M., *Dear David*, 19.

282. "Inside Edition—David Berkowitz," 55:00–55:43, http://www.dailymotion.com/video/xmr0xg_inside-edition-david-berkowitz_shortfilms.

283. "David Berkowitz: Son of Sam," *A&E Television Networks*, 36:45–37:02; emphasis added.

284. This part of the narrative was taken from two sources, both written by David Berkowitz; emphasis added: 1) "Behind the Wall: Early Testimony," *Forgiven for Life*, written early after Berkowitz's initial salvation, last accessed March 21, 2014, http://www.lettersfromdavid.com/behindthewall/id10.html; 2) "David Berkowitz's (Former Son of Sam) Testimony & Translations," *Arise and Shine: The Official Website of David Berkowitz* (this site has replaced "Forgiven for Life" as the official website of David Berkowitz), last accessed March 21, 2014, http://www.ariseandshine.org/Testimony-&-Translations.html.

285. Ibid.

286. Ibid.

287. "A Conversation with David Berkowitz Part 6 of 6," YouTube video, 4:24–6:04, posted by Daniel Lefkowitz, uploaded February 2, 2009, last accessed March 21, 2014, https://www.youtube.com/watch?v=U9dY7wD_5PE.

288. In a personal letter from David Berkowitz to Thomas Horn, dated August 19, 2014.

289. Transcript of a portion of the interview between David Berkowitz and Scott Ross of *The 700 Club*; viewable here: Scott Ross, "INTERVIEW: Son of Sam Becomes Son of Hope," *Christian Broadcasting Network*, last accessed March 21, 2014, http://www.cbn.com/700club/scottross/interviews/sonofsam.aspx.

290. In a personal letter from David Berkowitz to Thomas Horn, dated August 19, 2014.

291. "Son of Sam/Son of Hope Part 1," YouTube video, posted by miketelz, uploaded May 18, 2007, last accessed March 23, 2014, https://www.youtube.com/watch?v=8rZfEyHeM-w; "Son of Sam/Son of Hope Part 2," YouTube video, posted by miketelz, uploaded May 18, 2007, last accessed March 23, 2014, https://www.youtube.com/watch?v=QA9LUEgKNRg; "Son of Sam/Son of Hope Part 3," YouTube video, posted by miketelz, uploaded May 18, 2007, last accessed March 23, 2014, https://www.youtube.com/watch?v=L3scm2sY7OM; DVD purchasable here: Son of Sam, Son of Hope (DVD), *AskDrBrownStore*, currently $15.00, http://askdrbrown.myshopify.com/products/son-of-sam-son-of-hope-dvd.

292. Transcript of the encore airing available here: "TRANSCRIPTS—CNN Larry King Live Weekend—Encore Presentation: Interview with David Berkowitz," *CNN*, last accessed March 21, 2014, http://transcripts.cnn.com/TRANSCRIPTS/0210/26/lklw.00.html.

293. See the listing of this film at the Internet Movie Database here: *The Choice Is Yours*, 2000, last accessed March 22, 2014, http://www.imdb.com/title/tt1967613/.

294. "'Son of Sam' Says He Does Not Want Parole," *UPI News*, August 6, 2006, last accessed March 22, 2014, http://www.upi.com/Top_News/2006/08/06/Son-of-Sam-says-he-does-not-want-parole/UPI-40451154877295/.

295. Louise Boyle, "Son of Sam Serial Killer Skips Parole Hearing Because He Believes 'Jesus Has Forgiven Him and Set Him Free,'" May 13, 2014, *DailyMail UK*, http://www.dailymail.co.uk/news/article-2627100/Son-Sam-killer-skips-parole-hearing-believes-Jesus-forgiven-him.html.

296. In a personal letter from David Berkowitz to Thomas Horn, dated July 7, 2014.

297. David Berkowitz, "Misinformation: Nancy Grace Program," *LettersFromDavid.com*, last accessed March 22, 2014, http://www.lettersfromdavid.com/id73.html.

298. David Berkowitz, "Letter to Crime Victim's Board," *LettersFromDavid.com*, last accessed March 22, 2014, http://www.lettersfromdavid.com/id27.html.

299. Elizabeth Cronin, director of New York State OVS, "Annual Report Fiscal Year 2012–2013," *Office of Victim Services*, last accessed March 22, 2014, http://www.ovs.ny.gov/files/annual_reports/2012-2013_Annual_Report.pdf; emphasis added.

300. "David Berkowitz: Son of Sam," *A&E Television Networks*, 36:16–36:23.

301. "Inside Edition—David Berkowitz," 44:58–45:11, http://www.dailymotion.com/video/xmr0xg_inside-edition-david-berkowitz_shortfilms.

302. Berkowitz, *Son of Hope: The Prison Journals of David Berkowitz*, 167; 241–252.

303. Andrea Peyser, "A Mom Dies—Forgiving Son of Sam," September 28, 2006, *New York Post*, last accessed March 22, 2014, http://nypost.com/2006/09/28/a-mom-dies-forgiving-son-of-sam/.

304. David Berkowitz., "A Ticket," *LettersFromDavid.com*, last accessed March 22, 2014, http://www.lettersfromdavid.com/id30.html.

305. Berkowitz, *Son of Hope: The Prison Journals of David Berkowitz*, 98.

306. Ibid., 36.

307. Unless otherwise noted, or in the case of a specific quote, all information given
     in this case study has been a collection of well known, easy-access facts, repeated
     transparently through light research of Karla Faye Tucker. Most of the materials used
     for the compilation of this study covered all aspects of Tucker's life needed herein:
     her early life, the murders, her trial, and her conversion to Christ. Karla Faye shared
     her personal past openly with anyone who asked without reservation in her final
     days, and most tell the same facts, so anyone wishing to look into this case study
     further will not have a hard time finding them should a specific detail not be readily
     cited. Other than the court transcripts which were ordered from Texas public record
     departments, a brief list of the most-used research materials follows: Beverly Lowry,
     Crossed Over: A Murder, A Memoir, updated edition with 2002 foreword (Vintage
     Books: New York, NY, 2002); Linda Strom, *Karla Faye Tucker SET FREE: Life and
     Faith on Death Row* (Waterbrook Press, a division of Random House: Colorado
     Springs, CO, 2006); Willem van Schaaijk et al, Evangelische Omroep International,
     Gateway Films, Vision Video, *The Power of Forgiveness: The Story of Karla Faye
     Tucker*, 1999; among other sources including interview transcripts, which are cited
     individually throughout.

308. Most prisons will not allow inmates to carry sharp objects of any kind for security
     purposes, so prisoners are often barred from wearing crosses, as they may be used as
     a weapon. However, wearing a cross around one's neck is considered a religious right
     within most prisons. This is why some facilities issue their own plastic renditions of
     religious "jewelry."

309. Beverly Lowry, *Crossed Over: A Murder, A Memoir*, updated edition with 2002
     foreword (Vintage Books: New York, NY, 2002), Kindle Location 1698.

310. Ibid., 1700–1701.

311. Ibid.

312. Ibid., 3310–3312.

313. "Aileen Wuornos," *Wikipedia: The Free Encyclopedia*, last modified March 24, 2014,
     http://en.wikipedia.org/wiki/Aileen_Wuornos.

314. Ibid.

315. Ibid.

316. See: "Aileen Wuornos Coming Clean," YouTube video, posted by AileenWuornos
     (the name of the channel, not the individual), uploaded January 13, 2007, last
     accessed April 3, 2014, http://www.youtube.com/watch?v=3yi2dbaQ3mM.

317. See: "Was the Movie 'Monster' Factual?" YouTube video, posted by spybug51,
     uploaded January 27, 2013, last accessed April 3, 2014, http://www.youtube.com/
     watch?v=NmfmUtxwtlY.

318. "Aileen Wuornos Coming Clean," 4:57–5:04, emphasis placed where emphasis was
     spoken verbally in the original, http://www.youtube.com/watch?v=3yi2dbaQ3mM.

319. Joseph Geringer, *Karla Faye Tucker: Texas' Controversial Murderess*, true crime
     biography report, "Early Days, Dark Days" page, *CrimeLibrary.com*, last accessed
     April 8, 2014, http://www.crimelibrary.com/notorious_murders/women/tucker/2.
     html.

320. Lowry, *Crossed Over*, 2049.

321. Ibid.,2133.
322. Geringer, *Karla Faye Tucker*, "Early Days, Dark Days" page, http://www.crimelibrary. com/notorious_murders/women/tucker/2.html.
323. Lowry, *Crossed Over*, 2180–2182.
324. Geringer, *Karla Faye Tucker*, "Early Days, Dark Days" page, http://www.crimelibrary. com/notorious_murders/women/tucker/2.html.
325. Lowry, *Crossed Over*, 2215–2216.
326. Ibid., 2152–2158.
327. Geringer, *Karla Faye Tucker*, "Early Days, Dark Days" page, http://www.crimelibrary. com/notorious_murders/women/tucker/2.html.
328. Lowry, *Crossed Over*, 2254–2265.
329. Ibid., 2251–2253.
330. Ibid., 2275–2276.
331. Ibid., 2217–2220.
332. Ibid., 2373–2379.
333. Ibid., 2453–2497.
334. Ibid., 2402–2405.
335. Ibid., 773–775.
336. Ibid., 2233–2241.
337. Ibid., 2430–2434.
338. "A Letter Written to Gov. George Bush: Ms. Tucker Asking for a 30-Day Stay of Execution," posted January 30, 2000, retrieved through Internet archives from the following two links, accessed April 8, 2014: http://web.archive.org/web/20050406114222/http://www.geocities.com/RainForest/Canopy/2525/karla2bush.html; and https://groups.google.com/forum/#!topic/alt.christnet/IWdXL01B734.
339. Lowry, *Crossed Over*, 2412–2419.
340. Ibid., 1859.
341. Ibid., 2533–2538.
342. Ibid., 2541–2551.
343. Linda Strom, *Karla Faye Tucker SET FREE: Life and Faith on Death Row* (Waterbrook Press, a division of Random House: Colorado Springs, CO, 2006), Kindle Locations 725–727.
344. Lowry, *Crossed Over*, 731.
345. Ibid., 751–755.
346. Barri R. Flowers, (2013-05-31). *The Pickaxe Killers: Karla Faye Tucker & Daniel Garrett (A True Crime Short)* (Ebook; Copyright Barri R. Flowers, 2013), Kindle Locations 146–150.
347. In an episode of *Deadly Women* called *An Eye for an Eye* on The Discovery Channel: Investigation Discovery, aired August 10, 2010, season 4, episode 1. Viewable here: "Deadly Women: An Eye for an Eye," YouTube video, posted by kerry wilks, uploaded March 2, 2014, last accessed April 12, 2014, http://www.youtube.com/watch?v=R8YuouMr32s, 7:06–7:30.
348. Lowry, *Crossed Over*, 266.

349. Tucker's version of the story is reported by many; the most authoritative *outside* official court transcripts would be the one told in: Lowry *Crossed Over*, 997–1215.

350. "Deadly Women," 10:09–10:19, http://www.youtube.com/watch?v=R8YuouMr32s.

351. Willem van Schaaijk et al, Evangelische Omroep International, Gateway Films, Vision Video, *The Power of Forgiveness: The Story of Karla Faye Tucker*, 1999, 7:00–7:27.

352. Gateway Films, *The Power of Forgiveness*, 7:30–7:54.

353. Ibid.

354. Ibid.

355. Strom, *Karla Faye Tucker SET FREE*, 584–594.

356. Ibid.

357. Lowry, *Crossed Over*, 3133–3134).

358. Ibid., 3140–3141.

359. Ibid.

360. Ibid., 3307–3309.

361. Strom, *Karla Faye Tucker SET FREE*, 264.

362. Ibid., 546–547.

363. "777 (number)," *Wikipedia: The Free Encyclopedia*, last modified April 2, 2014, last accessed April 14, 2014, http://en.wikipedia.org/wiki/777_(number).

364. Strom, *Karla Faye Tucker SET FREE*, 1546–1547; brackets in original.

365. Strom, *Karla Faye Tucker SET FREE*, 542.

366. "Karla Faye TUCKER," *Murderpedia*, last accessed April 12, 2014, http://murderpedia.org/female.T/t/tucker-karla.htm.

367. Strom, *Karla Faye Tucker SET FREE*, 1977–1979.

368. Gateway Films, *The Power of Forgiveness*, 16:41–17:00.

369. Ibid., 15:11–16:30.

370. Ibid., 29:18–29:35.

371. Strom, *Karla Faye Tucker SET FREE*, 717–722.

372. Ibid., 727–733.

373. Ibid., 734–776.

374. Ibid., 805–809.

375. Ibid., 686–694.

376. Ibid., 2055–2057.

377. Ibid., 1549–1550.

378. Ibid., 947–948.

379. Ibid., 864.

380. Lowry, *Crossed Over*, 107–108.

381. Ibid.

382. Strom, *Karla Faye Tucker SET FREE*, 1867.

383. Gateway Films, *The Power of Forgiveness*; the entire documentary shows blips in and out of this interview, so there is no appropriate time signature to be placed on this summary.

384. Ibid., 24:52–25:09.

385. Strom, *Karla Faye Tucker SET FREE*, 1699–1700.

386. Ibid., 1719–1724.

387. "Karla Faye Tucker," *Wikipedia: The Free Encyclopedia*, last modified April 4, 2014, last accessed April 14, 2104, http://en.wikipedia.org/wiki/Karla_Faye_Tucker.

388. Ibid.

389. Strom, *Karla Faye Tucker SET FREE*, 1886–1887.

390. Ibid., 2498–2499.

391. Ibid., 2518–2524.

392. Unless otherwise noted, or in the case of a specific quote, all information given in this case study has been a collection of well known, easy-access facts, repeated transparently through light research of Ted Bundy. Most of these facts are touched upon with further referencing online here: "Ted Bundy," *Wikipedia, The Free Encyclopedia*, last modified April 30, 2013, http://en.wikipedia.org/wiki/Ted_bundy. A few of the central resources used on this case study are as follows: Ann Rule, *The Stranger Beside Me* (Planet Ann Rule e-book Kindle edition: Seattle, WA, 2012; originally published by W. W. Norton & Company, 1980); "Ted Bundy," *A&E Television Networks: Biography*, A&E Home Video Studio, DVD, 2002; Stephen G. Michaud and Hugh Aynesworth, *The Only Living Witness: The True Story of Serial Sex Killer Ted Bundy* (Authorlink.com e-book Kindle edition, 2012; New American Library, a division of Penguin Putnam USA Inc./Signet Books, 1989); and Stephen G. Michaud and Hugh Aynesworth, *Ted Bundy: Conversations with a Killer: The Death Row Interviews* (Authorlink.com e-book Kindle edition, 2000; originally published by New American Library, a division of Penguin Putnam USA Inc./Signet, 1990). The recorded interview between Ted Bundy and Dr. James Dobson can be purchased on VHS online, but this author chose to quote from the YouTube version of the interview for the reader's convenience. That is available here: "Fatal Addiction: Ted Bundy's Final Interview with Dr. James Dobson [1989]," YouTube video, posted by theodorerobertcowellnelsonbundy, uploaded January 8, 2014, last accessed May 5, 2014, https://www.youtube.com/watch?v=fcuU17TOgAQ. Any information specific to a certain book, website, or other material will be cited individually.

393. Ann Rule, *The Stranger Beside Me* (Planet Ann Rule e-book Kindle edition: Seattle, WA, 2012; originally published by W. W. Norton & Company, 1980), Kindle Locations 921–922.

394. Ibid., 922–924.

395. Ibid., 870–872; 1225–1226.

396. Ibid., 913–914.

397. Please note that the relationship between Ann Rule and Ted Bundy was always purely platonic. Romantic feelings were never shared between either of them, despite many rumors suggesting otherwise. This is stated repeatedly throughout Rule's book, and is ignored repeatedly throughout historical media and literature.

398. Rule, *The Stranger Beside Me*, 2243.

399. Ibid., 2244–2245.

400. Spoken by the character of Dr. Jekyll, *Jekyll & Hyde: The Musical*, music by Frank Wildhorn, book and lyrics by Leslie Bricusse and Steve Cuden, premiered at the Alley Theater in Houston Texas in May of 1990; based on the book *Strange Case of Dr.*

Jekyll and Mr. Hyde. This quote was taken from the 1994 pre-Broadway audio CD recording: *The Complete Work: Jekyll & Hyde: The Gothic Musical Thriller*, featuring Anthony Warlow as Jekyll/Hyde, Linda Eder as Lucy, and Carolee Carmello as Lisa, track 03, "Prologue," 0:09–0:33.

401. "Adaptations of *Strange Case of Dr. Jekyll and Mr. Hyde*," *Wikipedia: The Free Encyclopedia*, last modified March 25, 2014, last accessed April 24, 2014, http://en.wikipedia.org/wiki/Adaptations_of_Strange_Case_of_Dr._Jekyll_and_Mr._Hyde.

402. "Seven deadly sins," *Wikipedia: The Free Encyclopedia*, last modified April 22, 2014, last accessed April 24, 2014, http://en.wikipedia.org/wiki/Seven_deadly_sins.

403. Karen Edmisten, *Deathbed Conversions: Finding Faith at the Finish Line* (Our Sunday Visitor Publishing Division, Our Sunday Visitor Inc.: Huntington, IN, 2013), Kindle pages 11–12.

404. Leslie Rule, in an exclusive interview with Donna Howell on August 10, 2014.

405. Rule, *The Stranger Beside Me*, 8870.

406. "Ted Bundy," *A&E Television Networks: Biography*, A&E Home Video Studio, DVD, 2002, 10:01–10:18.

407. Stephen G. Michaud and Hugh Aynesworth, *The Only Living Witness: The True Story of Serial Sex Killer Ted Bundy* (Authorlink.com e-book Kindle edition, 2012; New American Library, a division of Penguin Putnam USA Inc./Signet Books, 1989) Kindle Locations 6047–6048.

408. "Ted Bundy," *Wikipedia, The Free Encyclopedia*, last modified April 30, 2013, http://en.wikipedia.org/wiki/Ted_bundy.

409. Michaud and Aynesworth, *The Only Living Witness*, 6067.

410. "Ted Bundy," *A&E Television Networks: Biography*, 9:50–10:00.

411. Rule, *The Stranger Beside Me*, 8857–8858.

412. "Ted Bundy," *A&E Television Networks: Biography*, 10:19–10:30.

413. Ibid., 10:25–10:45; Rule, *The Stranger Beside Me*, 8881–8886.

414. Michaud and Aynesworth, *The Only Living Witness*, 6034.

415. Rule, *The Stranger Beside Me*, 711–713.

416. "Ted Bundy," *A&E Television Networks: Biography*, 10:57–11:04.

417. Stephen G. Michaud and Hugh Aynesworth, *Ted Bundy: Conversations with a Killer: The Death Row Interviews* (Authorlink.com e-book Kindle edition, 2000; originally published by New American Library, a division of Penguin Putnam USA Inc./Signet Books, 1990), Kindle page 6.

418. "Ted Bundy," *A&E Television Networks: Biography*, 11:05–11:26.

419. Michaud and Aynesworth, *Conversations with a Killer*, 7–8.

420. Rule, *The Stranger Beside Me*, 718–719.

421. Michaud and Aynesworth, *The Only Living Witness*, 6048–6049.

422. Michaud and Aynesworth, *Conversations with a Killer*, 8.

423. "Bondage cover," *Wikipedia: The Free Encyclopedia*, last modified April 26, 2014, last accessed May 1, 2014, http://en.wikipedia.org/wiki/Bondage_cover.

424. Ibid.

425. "Weird menace," *Wikipedia: The Free Encyclopedia*, last modified March 12, 2014, last accessed May 1, 2014, http://en.wikipedia.org/wiki/Weird_menace.

426. Bruce Henry, *The American Mercury*, April 1938; as quoted in Robert Kenneth Jones, *The Shudder Pulps: A History of the Weird Menace Magazines of the 1930s* (New American Library, 1978), 138–139.

427. "Tijuana bibles," *Wikipedia: The Free Encyclopedia*, last modified April 27, 2014, last accessed May 1, 2014, http://en.wikipedia.org/wiki/Tijuana_bibles.

428. "Bondage cover," *Wikipedia*, http://en.wikipedia.org/wiki/Bondage_cover.

429. "Fetish magazine," *Wikipedia: The Free Encyclopedia*, last modified April 24, 2014, last accessed May 1, 2014, http://en.wikipedia.org/wiki/Fetish_magazine.

430. Rule, *The Stranger Beside Me*, 9414–9422.

431. "Reactive Attachment Disorder," *American Academy of Child & Adolescent Psychiatry*, No. 85, March 2011, last accessed April 30, 2014, http://www.aacap.org/aacap/Families_and_Youth/Facts_for_Families/Facts_for_Families_Pages/Reactive_Attachment_Disorder_85.aspx.

432. Ibid.

433. "Diseases and Conditions: 'Reactive Attachment Disorder' Definition," *Mayo Clinic*, July 6, 2011, last accessed May 1, 2014, http://www.mayoclinic.org/diseases-conditions/reactive-attachment-disorder/basics/definition/con-20032126.

434. "Reactive Attachment Disorder," *American Academy of Child & Adolescent Psychiatry*, http://www.aacap.org/aacap/Families_and_Youth/Facts_for_Families/Facts_for_Families_Pages/Reactive_Attachment_Disorder_85.aspx.

435. "Ted Bundy," *A&E Television Networks: Biography*, 11:30–11:39.

436. Ibid., 11:56–12:02.

437. Rule, *The Stranger Beside Me*, 725–727.

438. G. Michaud and Aynesworth, *Conversations with a Killer*, 9; emphasis in original.

439. "Ted Bundy," *A&E Television Networks: Biography*, 12:45–13:02.

440. Ibid., 13:00–13:22.

441. Ibid., 13:23–13:33.

442. Rule, *The Stranger Beside Me*, 761–762.

443. "Ted Bundy," *A&E Television Networks: Biography*, 15:45–16:12.

444. Rule, *The Stranger Beside Me*, 782–783.

445. Ibid., 785–786.

446. "Ted Bundy," *A&E Television Networks: Biography*, 16:40–16:48.

447. Rule, *The Stranger Beside Me*, 790–791.

448. Ibid., 819–820.

449. "Ted Bundy," *Wikipedia*, http://en.wikipedia.org/wiki/Ted_bundy.

450. Rule, *The Stranger Beside Me*, 846.

451. Also note that the birth certificate actually said the father was a "Lloyd Marshall" of the Air Force, but Louise stuck to her story about the seducing sailor named "Jack Worthington." It's likely that nobody will ever know without any doubt who this man truly was.

452. Michaud and Aynesworth, *The Only Living Witness*, 943–944.

453. Ibid., 6055–6056.

454. Rachael Bell, *Ted Bundy*, true crime biography report, *CrimeLibrary.com*, "A Time of Change" page, http://www.crimelibrary.com/serial_killers/notorious/bundy/3.html.

455. Rule, *The Stranger Beside Me*, 8880–8881.

456. "You Don't Know, Jack," *Snopes*, last updated June 9, 2013, last accessed May 2, 2014, http://www.snopes.com/movies/actors/nicholson.asp.

457. Sung by the extra characters on the streets of London, *Jekyll & Hyde: The Musical*, Wildhorn, Bricusse, and Cuden. This quote was taken from the 1994 pre-Broadway audio CD recording: *The Complete Work: Jekyll & Hyde: The Gothic Musical Thriller*, Warlow, Eder, and Carmello, track 03, "Façade," 0:41– 1:24.

458. Michaud and Aynesworth, *Conversations with a Killer*, 11–12.

459. Rule, *The Stranger Beside Me*, 880–883.

460. Ibid., 1170–1171.

461. Ibid., 1307–1308.

462. Sung by the character of Dr. Jekyll, *Jekyll & Hyde: The Musical*, Wildhorn, Bricusse, and Cuden. This quote was taken from the 1994 pre-Broadway audio CD recording: *The Complete Work: Jekyll & Hyde: The Gothic Musical Thriller*, Warlow, Eder, and Carmello, track 14, "Transformation," 2:53–4:12.

463. In accordance with the provisions of Section 257.35(6), Florida Statutes, "Any use or reproduction of material deposited with the Florida Photographic Collection shall be allowed pursuant to the provisions of paragraph (1)(b) and subsection (4), ***provided that appropriate credit for its use is given***." Photo courtesy of State Archives of Florida.

464. "Ted Bundy Evil Look at Reporters," YouTube video, 0:42–0:46, posted by Theo Bundy, uploaded March 25, 2013, last accessed May 3, 2014, https://www.youtube.com/watch?v=sR8SZ93h-Wc.

465. In accordance with the provisions of Section 257.35(6), Florida Statutes, "Any use or reproduction of material deposited with the Florida Photographic Collection shall be allowed pursuant to the provisions of paragraph (1)(b) and subsection (4), ***provided that appropriate credit for its use is given***." Photo courtesy of State Archives of Florida.

466. An exchange between the characters of Lucy and Mr. Hyde, *Jekyll & Hyde: The Musical*, Wildhorn, Bricusse, and Cuden. This quote was taken from the 2001 live-audience DVD recording: *Jekyll & Hyde: The Musical*, directed by Don Roy King, featuring David Hasselhoff as Jekyll/Hyde, Coleen Sexton as Lucy, and Andrea Rivette as Emma, DVD title 2, chapter 16, 1:36:52–1:37:00.

467. Rule, *The Stranger Beside Me*, 5207.

468. Ibid., 7210–7213.

469. Polly Nelson, *Defending the Devil: My Story as Ted Bundy's Last Lawyer* (William Morrow: New York, NY, 1994), 154.

470. Leslie Rule, in an exclusive interview with Donna Howell on August 10, 2014.

471. Rule, *The Stranger Beside Me*, 506–509.

472. Ibid., 293–305.

473. Ibid., 7914–7915.

474. Leslie Rule, in an exclusive interview with Donna Howell on August 10, 2014; emphasis added.

475. Ibid.

476. "Ted Bundy," *Wikipedia*, http://en.wikipedia.org/wiki/Ted_bundy.

477. Rule, *The Stranger Beside Me*, 5254–5255.

478. Art Myers, "The Ted Bundy Murders," January 28, 2011, *WCTV*, last accessed May 4, 2014, http://www.wctv.tv/news/headlines/108154829.html.

479. Rule, *The Stranger Beside Me*, 6881.

480. Ibid., 7072–7074.

481. Michaud and Aynesworth, *The Only Living Witness*, 5139–5143.

482. Bell, *Ted Bundy*, "The First Trial" page, http://www.crimelibrary.com/serial_killers/notorious/bundy/14.html.

483. Rule, *The Stranger Beside Me*, 3167–3173.

484. Ibid., 182.

485. Ibid., 184–185.

486. "Fatal Addiction: Ted Bundy's Final Interview with Dr. James Dobson [1989]," YouTube video, 7:05–7:12, posted by theodorerobertcowellnelsonbundy, uploaded January 8, 2014, last accessed May 5, 2014, https://www.youtube.com/watch?v=fcuU17TOgAQ.

487. Ibid., 8:15–9:03.

488. Ibid., 7:18–8:00.

489. Ibid., 11:41–11:57; emphasis placed where emphasis was spoken verbally in the original.

490. Ibid., 15:28–16:19.

491. Ibid., 17:04–17:37; emphasis placed where emphasis was spoken verbally in the original.

492. Ibid., 18:53–18:56.

493. Ibid., 20:37–21:04.

494. Ibid., 28:16–30:39; emphasis placed where emphasis was spoken verbally in the original.

495. Ibid., 32:25–32:29.

496. Ibid., 33:06–33:52.

497. Ibid., 38:10–41:23.

498. Ibid., 10:30–10:43.

499. Michaud and Aynesworth, *The Only Living Witness*, 6266–6269.

500. Ibid., 6274–6275.

501. Louise Boyle, "Ted Bundy's Mother Dies Aged 88 Following Long Illness After a Lifetime Spent Defending Her Serial Killer Son," January 9, 2013, *DailyMail UK*, last accessed May 6, 2014, http://www.dailymail.co.uk/news/article-2259961/Ted-Bundys-mother-dies-age-88-following-long-illness.html.

502. Michaud and Aynesworth, *The Only Living Witness*, 6288–6289.

503. Ibid., 6292–6293.

504. Ibid., 6297–6299.

505. Rule, *The Stranger Beside Me*, 425–427.

506. Charles Montaldo, "Any Last Words?: The Last Words Spoken by Ted Bundy Before Being Executed," *About.com*, last accessed May 6, 2014, http://crime.about.com/od/history/qt/lastwords_bundy.htm.

507. Rule, *The Stranger Beside Me*, 447–448.

508. Unless otherwise noted, or in the case of a specific quote, all information given in this case study has been a collection of well known, easy-access facts, repeated

transparently through light research of Jeffery Dahmer. Most of these facts are covered in further detail and with further referencing online here: "Jeffrey Dahmer," *Wikipedia, The Free Encyclopedia*, last modified June 16, 2014, http://en.wikipedia. org/wiki/Jeffrey_Dahmer. Most details of his murders and his trials were only lightly addressed in this work because of the graphic nature of his crimes. When referring to a personal memory of Lionel Dahmer regarding his son's childhood: Lionel Dahmer, *A Father's Story* (William Morrow and Company Inc., New York, NY: 1994); and when referring to his baptismal and story of conversion: Roy Ratcliff, *Dark Journey Deep Grace: Jeffrey Dahmer's Story of Faith* (Leafwood Publishers: Abilene, TX, 2006). Any information specific to a certain book, website, or other material will be cited individually.

509. "Jeffrey Dahmer 2 of 2 Inside Edition Interview," YouTube video, 6:06–6:40, posted by dahmervideos, uploaded November 12, 2011, last accessed June 6, 2014, https://www.youtube.com/watch?v=COKYJdoUV2w.

510. Ibid. Please also note that the shouting of "Cuff him!" was as per Dahmer's personal memories. Pamela Bass, Dahmer's direct neighbor in the complex, remembers the officer shouting, "Get the [expletive] cuffs!" (See next endnote.) There are still others who remember a slightly different phrase being called out, but the end result is always some form of command from one officer to another to retrieve the cuffs and place Dahmer under arrest.

511. Testimony by Pamela Bass, neighbor of Jeffrey Dahmer at 12:07–12:22 in the following: *Jeff* (also known as *The Jeffrey Dahmer Files*), a docudrama written and directed by Chris James Thompson, produced by Chris Smith *et al.*, starring Andrew Swant as Jeffrey Dahmer (IFC Films, March 10, 2012); currently available for streaming on Netflix and Amazon Instant Video.

512. Brian Masters, *The Shrine of Jeffrey Dahmer* (Hodder and Stoughton: London, 1993), 4.

513. Testimony of Patrick Kennedy, *Jeff* (*The Jeffrey Dahmer Files*), 22:39–22:55.

514. Ibid., 26:59–29:25.

515. Ibid., 34:04–35:18.

516. "Jeffrey Dahmer: The Monster Within," *A&E Television Networks: Bio. True Story, Bio Channel*, A&E Home Video Studio, DVD, 1996, 34:13–34:19.

517. People, and most often Christians, can derive this opinion as a result of: James 2:10: "For whosoever shall keep the whole law, and yet offend in one [point], he is guilty of all"; 1 Corinthians 6:9–10: "Know ye not that the unrighteous shall not inherit the kingdom of God? Be not deceived: neither fornicators, nor idolaters, nor adulterers, nor effeminate, nor abusers of themselves with mankind, Nor thieves, nor covetous, nor drunkards, nor revilers, nor extortioners, shall inherit the kingdom of God"; Matthew 12:31: "Wherefore I say unto you, All manner of sin and blasphemy shall be forgiven unto men: but the blasphemy [against] the [Holy] Ghost shall not be forgiven unto men"; and others. It is not necessarily the opinion of this author that all sins are the same in the eyes of the Lord as Paul stated in Romans 2 that man will be "judged according to his works," which implies that what we did and did not do during our time on earth will play into our ultimate judgment. But finally, 2 Corinthians 5:17 says, "Therefore if any man be in Christ, he is a new creature:

old things are passed away; behold, all things are become new." So whether all sins are equal or not, when a person comes to Christ, "all things" are new and fresh, and the "old things" are dead, which implies that we will be "judged according to [the] works" we have done from the day of "new creature" and forward.

518. Information about John Cacioppo, as taken from *Wikipedia*: "Tiffany and Margaret Blake Distinguished Service Professor at the University of Chicago…founded and is Director of the University of Chicago Center for Cognitive and Social Neuroscience and the Director of the Arete Initiative of the Office of the Vice President for Research and National Laboratories at the University of Chicago.… a member of the Department of Psychology, Department of Psychiatry, and the College, and one of the founders of the field of social neuroscience." See: "John Cacioppo," *Wikipedia: The Free Encyclopedia*, last modified May 13, 2014, last accessed June 10, 2014, http://en.wikipedia.org/wiki/John_Cacioppo.

519. "The Lethality of Loneliness: John Cacioppo at TEDxDesMoines," a YouTube video, 2:37–3:00, posted by TEDx Talks, uploaded September 9, 2013, last accessed June 10, 2014, https://www.youtube.com/watch?v=_0hxl03JoA0; emphasis placed where emphasis was spoken verbally in the original.

520. Ibid., 3:44–3:49.

521. Ibid., 3:49–3:55.

522. Ibid., 5:36–7:32; emphasis placed where emphasis was spoken verbally in the original.

523. Ibid., 8:59–9:22.

524. Ibid., 9:32–10:05.

525. Ibid., 10:46–12:34.

526. Ibid.

527. Ibid., 13:05–13:18; emphasis added.

528. Sarvada Chandra Tiwari, "Loneliness: A Disease?" *Indian Journal of Psychiatry* (viewable within the *US National Library of Medicine by the National Institutes of Health*), October–December 2013, issue 55, last accessed June 11, 2014, http://www.ncbi.nlm.nih.gov/pmc/articles/PMC3890922/.

529. "Jeffrey Dahmer: The Monster Within," *A&E Television Networks*, 29:45–29:48.

530. "pathology," *Merriam-Webster Dictionary Online*, last accessed June 11, 2014, http://www.merriam-webster.com/dictionary/pathology.

531. Note that many books, articles, encyclopedia entries, media, and other documentation report different ages of Dahmer's victims. This list included here was taken directly from the trial transcripts and should therefore be the most accurate attainable for those with a definitive age. For those victims marked with an approximate age, this is because either the age was not consistently referenced in trial, or that the trial transcripts did not specify (or only specified as "approximate"), and we had to choose an approximation based on a collective report from other resources.

532. *Jeff* (*The Jeffrey Dahmer Files*), 46:53–47:40.

533. Lionel Dahmer, *A Father's Story* (William Morrow and Company Inc., New York, NY: 1994) 34.

534. Ibid.

535. Ibid., 36.

536. "Phenobarbital," *RxList, The Internet Drug Index*, last accessed June 12, 2014, http://www.rxlist.com/phenobarbital-drug/warnings-precautions.htm; emphasis added.

537. It should be noted that Joyce, in a later interview with Stone Phillips from NBC News, denied these seizures ever occurred in pregnancy or afterward, and likewise denied that she had ever been treated for them with the drugs that have been associated to Jeffrey's odd development. Her side of the interview was defensive, nervous, and tentative. When pressed, she appeared offended and didn't seem to know how to respond, often relying completely on a friend she had brought with her to answer on her behalf. (This friend was a coauthor of a book Joyce Dahmer was writing at the time. The book was never released.) Those who knew her, including Jeffrey and Lionel, have expressed that she not only suffered from strange seizures, but that she did so for years. After Jeffrey's death, Joyce insisted that Jeffrey's brain be kept for study, despite his specific request to be cremated, and many view this to have been one last attempt for her to give public proclamation that Jeffrey's development had nothing to do with any drugs she had taken, thereby offering up her son's brain as "proof." This assumption of her intent is merely conjecture by the public, and not a hard fact, but one merely needs to compare the claims of those who knew her against her own claims, alongside her defensive personality, to see why the public would come to this opinion. In any case, this book reports this part of the story for two reasons: 1) Joyce's mental and physical state is constantly drawn into the layout of "what went wrong" during Jeffrey's early development, and 2) chemistry/science has for years confirmed that dangerous drug administration during pregnancy can have massive implication on a fetus, and can lead to both mental and physical abnormalities later on.

538. "32 Serial Killers with High IQs," *Examiner.com*, November 6, 2013, last accessed June 12, 2014, http://www.examiner.com/article/22-serial-killers-with-high-iqs.

539. "IQ scale," *IQ Test for Free*, last accessed June 12, 2014, http://www.iqtestforfree.net/iq-scale.html.

540. Kendra Cherry, "How are Scores on IQ Tests Calculated?" *Psychology.About.com*, last accessed June 12, 2014, http://psychology.about.com/od/psychologicaltesting/f/IQ-test-scores.htm.

541. Lionel Dahmer, *A Father's Story*, 40.

542. Ibid., 45.

543. Ibid.

544. "Jeffrey Dahmer Childhood Home Videos and Pictures," YouTube video, posted by dahmervideos, uploaded November 11, 2011, last accessed June 12, 2014, https://www.youtube.com/watch?v=Q4axZoP-q68.

545. Lionel Dahmer, *A Father's Story*, 47.

546. Pearl S. Buck, quote viewable at *BrainyQuote*, last accessed June 18, 2014: http://www.brainyquote.com/quotes/quotes/p/pearlsbuc121440.html.

547. Lionel Dahmer, *A Father's Story*, 58.

548. Ibid., 59.

549. Ibid.

550. Ibid., 53.

551. All three of these memories: Ibid., 54.

552. Ibid., 57.

553. Ibid., 59–60; 76–77.

554. Ibid., 62.

555. Ibid., 63.

556. Ibid., 56.

557. Ibid., 76.

558. Written and Illustrated by John "Derf" Backderf, *My Friend Dahmer: A Graphic Novel by Derf Backderf* (Abrams ComicArts, and imprint of ABRAMS: New York, NY, 2012), Kindle Location 54.

559. Robert D. Keppel, *Signature Killers: Interpreting the Calling Cards of the Serial Murderer* (Pocket Books: New York, NY, 1997), 302.

560. Ibid.

561. Ibid. Also: Backderf, *My Friend Dahmer*, 21–31.

562. Lionel Dahmer, *A Father's Story*, 80.

563. Backderf, *My Friend Dahmer*, 35.

564. Ibid., 54.

565. Ibid., 123–125.

566. "Jeffrey Dahmer—Serial Killer—Twisted," 5:02–5:18, https://www.youtube.com/watch?v=sqBPcvCoNMM.

567. Backderf, *My Friend Dahmer*, 37.

568. Ibid., 54.

569. "Jeffrey Dahmer: The Monster Within," *A&E Television Networks*, 9:11–9:21.

570. Lionel Dahmer, *A Father's Story*, 87–88.

571. "Jeffrey Dahmer: The Monster Within," *A&E Television Networks*, 8:36–8:58.

572. Ibid., 8:00–8:22.

573. Backderf, *My Friend Dahmer*, 51.

574. "Jeffrey Dahmer: The Monster Within," *A&E Television Networks*, 9:49–10:02.

575. Backderf, *My Friend Dahmer*, 140–141.

576. "Jeffrey Dahmer: The Monster Within," *A&E Television Networks*, 10:07–10:25; John "Derf" Backderf, *My Friend Dahmer*, Kindle Locations 131–143.

577. Backderf, *My Friend Dahmer*, 144–145.

578. "Jeffrey Dahmer—Serial Killer," 8:07–8:39, https://www.youtube.com/watch?v=sqBPcvCoNMM.

579. "Jeffrey Lionel DAHMER," *Murderpedia*, under the heading "Selected Quotes from Jeffrey Dahmer," last accessed June 16, 2014, http://murderpedia.org/male.D/d/dahmer-jeffrey.htm.

580. Lionel Dahmer, *A Father's Story*, 90.

581. "Jeffrey Dahmer—Serial Killer," 9:04–9:28, https://www.youtube.com/watch?v=sqBPcvCoNMM; emphasis placed where emphasis was spoken verbally in the original.

582. Lionel Dahmer, *A Father's Story*, 95.

583. Ibid., 94.

584. Brian Masters, *The Shrine of Jeffrey Dahmer*, 179–180.

585. "Jeffrey Dahmer Stone Phillips Interview. www.Dore1.com," YouTube video, 14:58–15:12, posted by an anonymous user who calls themselves "Jeffrey dahmer,"

uploaded on July 8, 2012, last accessed June 16, 2014, https://www.youtube.com/watch?v=vPMBfX7D4WU.

586. "Jeffrey Dahmer—Serial Killer," 34:23–34:43, https://www.youtube.com/watch?v=sqBPcvCoNMM.

587. "Jeffrey Dahmer: The Monster Within," *A&E Television Networks*, 30:37–30:55.

588. "Jeffrey Dahmer—Serial Killer," 38:36–39:00, https://www.youtube.com/watch?v=sqBPcvCoNMM; emphasis added.

589. Roy Ratcliff, *Dark Journey, Deep Grace: Jeffrey Dahmer's Story of Faith* (Leafwood Publishers: Abilene, TX, 2006), 21.

590. Ibid., 57.

591. Ibid., 9.

592. Ibid., 23.

593. Ibid., 71.

594. Ibid., 99.

595. Ibid., 71.

596. "Jeffrey Dahmer: The Monster Within," *A&E Television Networks*, 41:19–41:48.

597. Ratcliff, *Dark Journey, Deep Grace*, 127.

598. "Jeffrey Dahmer—Murdered in Prison—News Clip," YouTube video, 3:03–3:09, posted by dahmervideos, uploaded November 11, 2011, last accessed June 16, 2014, https://www.youtube.com/watch?v=aeHVQra1Wzw.

599. Ratcliff, *Dark Journey, Deep Grace*, 147.

600. Ibid., 148–149.

601. "Jeffrey Dahmer—Serial Killer," 31:23–31:51, https://www.youtube.com/watch?v=sqBPcvCoNMM.

602. Ibid., 28:55–29:58.

603. Agence France-Presse, "U.S. Murder Rate Higher than Nearly All Other Developed Countries: FBI Data," *The Raw Story*, September 16, 2013, last accessed June 30, 2014, http://www.rawstory.com/rs/2013/09/16/u-s-murder-rate-higher-than-nearly-all-other-developed-countries-fbi-data/.

604. Dwight L. Moody, *Weighed and Wanting (Addresses on the Ten Commandments)* (The Bible Institute Colpertage Association, 1898), 75–77; as quoted in *The Researchers Library of Ancient Texts: Volume 5: Preachers of the Great Awakenings* (Defender Publishing: Crane, MO, 2014), 912–913.

605. Ibid., 913.